CORVETTE

AMERICA'S STAR-SPANGLED SPORTS CAR
THE COMPLETE HISTORY

AN AUTOMOBILE QUARTERLY LIBRARY SERIES BOOK

CORV

AMERICA'S STAR-SPA
THE COMPLETE HIST

PUBLISHED BY AUTOMOBIL

ETTE

NGLED SPORTS CAR

ORY by Karl Ludvigsen

QUARTERLY PUBLICATIONS

dedicated to the
Corvette enthusiast

The author and publishers acknowledge with thanks the permission of the following to reproduce copyright materials:
G. P. Putnam's Sons for excerpts from *Adventure on Wheels* by John Fitch with William F. Nolan, copyright © 1953, 1955, 1956, and 1959 by John Fitch and William F. Nolan. *Road & Track* for excerpts from "Corvette vs. Cobra: the Battle for Supremacy," copyright © 1963. Enthusiasts' Publications, Inc. Bernard Cahier for excerpts from "Corvette Grand Sport and Scarab-Corvette" in *Sports Car Graphic*. copyright © 1964, Petersen Publishing Co. *Car and Driver* for excerpts from the column of Steve Smith, copyright © 1967, Ziff-Davis Publishing Co. *Motor* for excerpts from the Paul Frère article, "Beat this!", copyright © 1967, IPC Transport Press Ltd. *Corvette News* for appendices tables II, III, VI, VII, VIII, copyright © 1972 Chevrolet Motor Division, General Motors Corporation. Corvette illustrations by Ken Rush, pages 265-275, copyright © 1969, 1975, 1977, Automobile Quartlery Inc.
Typesetting by Kutztown Publishing Company, Kutztown, Pa.
Printing and binding by South China Printing Co., Hong Kong

SECOND EDITION—FIFTH PRINTING

Library of Congress Catalog Number: 72-85847

SBN-0-915038-06-4: Automobile Quarterly, Inc.

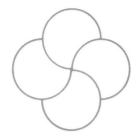

AUTOMOBILE QUARTERLY PUBLICATIONS

STAFF FOR THIS BOOK

Publisher and President: L. Scott Bailey

Editorial Director: Beverly Rae Kimes

Art Director: Theodore R. F. Hall

Book Designer: Kenneth N. Drasser

Production Editors: Courtlandt van Rooten and Ian C. Bowers

Editorial Assistants: Judy Faulkner, Kathy Sammis

Contributing Artists: Ken Rush, Yoshihiro Inomoto

In the early nineteen-sixties, when I was working with him on a story about the Corvette SS, Zora Arkus-Duntov took some extra time to cover some of the details with me and to elaborate on the chronology of Chevy's involvement with road racing. "After all," he said, "someday you may have the job of writing the history of what happened in those days." Like so many of Zora's intuitive predictions this too came true, as a result of Scott Bailey's suggestion that I tell the story of the Corvette's evolution from a feckless fiberglass roadster to one of the premier sports cars of the world.

Zora Duntov ranks first among the many to whom I owe thanks for help in the compilation of this history. He and I first met in 1959; since then he's always been generous with his time and knowledge in explaining to me each year's changes as well as the experimental cars that played such an important role offstage. Zora also kindly consented to read the galley proofs of the book, which nevertheless lifts no blame for errors of commission or omission from the shoulders of the author.

I am also indebted to L. Scott Bailey, publisher and president of AUTOMOBILE *Quarterly, for many acts of kindness and encouragement, among them the invitation to write this book, and to his outstanding staff for continuing support, most notably Don Vorderman, Beverly Rae Kimes, and Ted Hall.*

Present and past GM stylists have also gone out of their way to lend a hand with this story. I owe to Bill Mitchell the opportunity to rejoin General Motors in 1961 which allowed me to see some key Corvette history first-hand. Clare MacKichan recently reviewed with me the early developments of Corvette styling. And when I first worked for GM Styling in 1956 my boss was Bob McLean, co-creator of the original Corvette and still one of the most brilliant automotive architects as an executive of the John Z. DeLorean Corporation. McLean provided me with the clue that led to a meeting with Earl Ebers and Bert McNomee, creator and promoter respectively of the fiberglass "Alembic I" sports car that had been so influential in winning support at GM for both the sports car concept and the use of fiberglass as a body material. Both are still with U.S. Rubber, now Uniroyal, and luckily preserved both memories and mementoes of events two decades ago.

PREFACE

I am grateful to two men for constant prompting to learn more about Corvette, past, present, and future.
One is Chevrolet's Joe Pike, Corvette salesman extraordinary and editor of the excellent
Corvette News. The other is Eric Dahlquist of Motor Trend, whose curiosity about "The Corvette that never
made it" is insatiable. Pike and Dahlquist backed many of my stories into unexplored Corvette territory.

For advice, information, help, photos, and criticism I am thankful to many others.
These are some of them: Harry Bradley, Bob Clift, John Cutter, Tony DeLorenzo, Bob D'Olivo, John Fitch,
the late Warren Fitzgerald, Gib Hufstader, Harold Jackson, the late Warren Jollymore, Omer LaRue,
Jim Lunn, Walt Mackenzie, Larry Nies, Bob Rosenthal, Myron Scott, Larry Shinoda, Judy Stropus,
Dick Thompson, Jerry Thompson, Edgar Thorne, Ed Wayne, Jim Williams, George Wintersteen, and Walter Zetye.
Henry Haga, Charles Jordan, Clare MacKichan, David McLellan, Jerry Palmer, Ben Pope and
Otto Soeding are among those who deserve thanks for the additional information in this Revised Edition.

All these people have been eager to share with me their impressions of the Corvette
because they love it so much. It is still the only car made in America that inspires that kind of
affection. Because they love it so, Chevy's engineers and designers can't stop dreaming up
spectacular new Corvette prototypes like those in Chapter 18 and the Wankel-powered cars in
Chapter 19. These are magnificent machines that I am certain will deeply influence
the design of production Corvettes yet to come.

In 1977 the Corvette, the car that so narrowly missed being a monumental embarrassment to the
Chevrolet Motor Division, entered its twenty-fifth model year. It did so with its sales and
its reputation at all-time highs. The Corvette has shrugged off all competition, all the
Pantera and Bricklin pretenders. It still sits securely on its throne as the only American
production sports car. I have just the sneakiest suspicion that Chevrolet would like to
assure it a long and prosperous reign.

Karl E. Ludvigsen

CON

NTS

Chapter 1

AMERICA REDISCOVERS SPORTS CARS

Even as late as 1952 there was no evidence — not of the hard, irrefutable character that Detroit demands — that there was any reason to take sports cars seriously in the United States. That year 11,199 new sports cars were registered in America. This was an anything-but-staggering 0.27 percent of the total car registrations of 4,158,394. It hardly seemed worth getting excited about. But some American makers were not only excited about it; they were actually doing something about it.

There wasn't much they could do about the most popular sports car, the M.G. TD, of which 7,449 were registered in 1952. The M.G. was selling well because it was a neat-looking and well-made sports roadster offered at a reasonable price. But it was too small in engine size and overall dimensions to be duplicated, or even comprehended, by American makers. Only Crosley, whose cars were miniscule to begin with, gave it a try. And at $861 FOB Marion, Indiana, the original Hotshot was a creditable effort. Few Americans took any Crosleys seriously, however, and even less so the company's sports cars.

Much more impressive than Jaguar's registrations of 3,349 cars in the United States in 1952 was America's universal acceptance of the fact that the XK120 was one hell of an automobile. Unlike the M.G. or any other imported sports car of significance it had sizzling performance that commanded respect from the owners of America's hottest production cars, offered at a price that was within reach. It looked terrific and backed up its svelte lines with acceleration that needed no apology. But at less than 1/1000th of the American market, was the XK120 worth worrying about?

According to one Distant Early Warning system of the industry, the popular press, sports cars *were* worth more than a passing thought. In 1949 Ken Purdy highlighted the XK120, the Hotshot, and Frank Kurtis's Kurtis-Kraft roadster in a *True* feature titled "The Two-Seater Comes Back." In stories like this one Purdy, together with Ralph Stein and Tom McCahill, told Americans they could expect more from their automobiles than mere transportation. Wrote Purdy, "Comes now a cloud on the

horizon bigger than a man's hand which may portend a revival on this side of the water of the sports car — an automobile built for the sole purpose of going like a bat out of hell and never mind whether the girl friend likes it or not."

This was an emotional reaction, which was the only kind possible in the late Forties. "Considering the statistics, the American public does not want a sports car at all," engineer Zora Arkus-Duntov told the Society of Automotive Engineers in 1953, adding, "but do the statistics give a true picture? As far as the American market is concerned, it is still an unknown quantity since an American sports car catering to American tastes, roads, way of living and national character has not yet been on the market."

In saying "not yet" he was, of course, referring to the post-World War II years. But frankly there wasn't much in the earlier decades of which Americans could be overly boastful. It's polite to refer to some Cords, Auburns, and Duesenbergs as sports cars, but in fact few of them were. Only the Stutz and Dupont cars that raced at Le Mans truly deserved that designation during all the years between the wars. Before that, the Stutz, Mercer, Lozier, Simplex, and Chadwick had been highest among those that had been able to speed on the highways and compete on the tracks with equal ease — the infallible hallmark of the true sports car.

These were all big cars with big engines — inspired by the sheer size of a big country. Thinking small has never been the American way with automobiles. Miller and Duesenberg built some superb small-displacement racing cars and engines, but unlike their European counterparts — Maserati and Bugatti — they didn't also produce and sell them in sports-racing versions. The few road-going Millers that were made only hint at what marvelous machines might have been created then if sports cars had been in style in America.

After World War II, increasing familiarity on the part of American enthusiasts with the new sports cars from Europe bred a level of contempt that helped generate the confidence needed to

Crosley Hotshot, above, could readily be stripped for racing. Frank Kurtis shows off his Kurtis-Kraft, below left, basis of later Muntz Jet, at right.

encourage the rebirth of home-grown sports machines. Ralph Stein, reviewing the sports car situation in *Argosy* in 1950, expressed a view that was becoming widespread: "There is no good reason why America should not be able to produce a good sports car. We have engineers and designers with enough on the ball to create a crackerjack car, but, from observations, it looks very much as if they don't know what it takes. With a fast-growing band of sports-car fans, however," Stein concluded, "the demand will gradually make itself felt."

One designer who *did* get the job done — but, as was often the case, far ahead of his time — was Frank Kurtis. In 1949 he showed an impressive two-seater sports machine using Ford front suspension components. It was typically Kurtis in being novel and boldly good-looking, but Frank lacked the resources needed to make more than a few cars at his Glendale, California, plant. The Kurtis became the four-seater Muntz Jet, which was not really a sports car but was still an eye-opening performer with its Lincoln V-8 engine.

On the East Coast others were putting Yankee ingenuity to work to create home-bred sports cars. Contributing to several such ventures were the rugged cars built in Warwick, England, by Donald Healey. One of Healey's cycle-fendered Silverstone models was imported by Briggs Cunningham, the Connecticut collector and sportsman who raced two Cadillacs at Le Mans in 1950. Cunningham and his crew replaced the Healey's Riley engine with a Cadillac V-8.

There was nothing very unusual about the installation of one of the new overhead-valve Cadillac engines in a sports car at that time; the Cad-Allard was already a well-known hyphenation. Cunningham's Healey, however, became a test bed for experimentation with wheels, brakes, and suspension that contributed to the final design of the 1951 Cunningham sports car, the first serious effort since the war to produce an all-American sports machine that could be both raced and toured successfully. The Chrysler-powered C-2 Cunninghams and the much improved C-4R models of 1952 became the cars to beat in American sports car racing and competed honorably abroad. They were like the sports cars from the United States of earlier decades in being big cars, with big engines. Some generic traits are irrepressible.

The Healey chassis contributed to American sports car history in another important way. It became the basis of the Nash-Healey, the first postwar sports car marketed by a U.S. auto company. The courtship that led to the marriage between Healey and Nash began in December, 1949, on the westbound *Queen Elizabeth* when George Mason, head of Nash, met by chance

Cunningham C-2's swept the board in 1951 Grand Prix at Watkins Glen.

Nash-Healeys from top: 1952 Le Mans, 1953 production, 1953 Le Mans.

Donald Healey, who was on his way to the New World to look for U.S.-made engines for export models of his sports cars. He got more than he'd hoped for, ending up with a complete Nash drive train for a new Nash-Healey model and a complete network of American dealers to sell and service it.

The seven-main-bearing Nash six acquired an aluminum head and twin S.U. carburetors for its debut in the Healey chassis. This was made unofficially with a provisional body at Le Mans in 1950, where the first Nash-Healey placed fourth overall — not a bad start. Handsomely shaped in a sheer-sided style, bench-seated to seat three abreast, the production model made its bow in Paris in October and was launched in the United States in February, 1951, at the $4,000 level.

This Nash-Healey and the Pininfarina-bodied version announced in 1952 at a price more than $1,000 higher had some features that were offputting to many American drivers. The original dash was anything but attractive and lacked a tach. The accelerator pedal was between the brake and the clutch, and the "horn ring" operated the overdrive kickdown. Later models eliminated this but replaced sliding windows with side curtains. Nash's original plan was to sell 500 of these cars a year, but the program never shifted into high gear. When production stopped for good in August, 1954, only 506 cars had been made.

As one of the "independents" of the U.S. auto industry, Nash wasn't able to set a style with its sports cars, but they did create an atmosphere of activity and acceptance in and around Detroit. Another independent that was attracted to the sports car world was Kaiser-Frazer. Its announcement of the small Henry J late in 1950 waved the starting flag for many designers who felt this car's one hundred-inch-wheelbase chassis could be the basis of an American sports car. Californian Sterling Edwards, for example, built and raced several sports cars founded on the Henry J.

Milwaukee industrial designer Brooks Stevens displayed the American flag proudly on his Excalibur J, a handsome cycle-fendered sports car that he hoped Kaiser-Frazer would tool for a production run of 2,000 cars. Using the Henry J chassis and a modified Willys six engine, the first Excalibur J made its racing debut in July, 1952. Though Kaiser never took the step toward production, Stevens continued to campaign the three Excalibur J's he built, and showed thereby that stock American chassis components, suitably tuned and modified, could get the job done in sports car competition.

Kaiser did indulge in the production of a sports car, but it wasn't Stevens's design. While Stevens had been building the Excalibur J in the first half of 1952, independent stylist Howard "Dutch" Darrin had been fabricating a sports car in California with sweeping, distinctive lines, also on the Henry J chassis. Named the DKF-161 after its 161-cubic-inch Willys F-head engine, it attracted widespread attention with its unique sliding doors and rakish profile. First shown publicly late in 1952, Darrin's design was a thoroughly professional effort that implied the imminence of some kind of breakthrough in sports car production in America. After the manufacture of sixty-two prototypes, production of the Kaiser-Darrin started in December, 1953, under official Kaiser auspices. No more than 435 were made.

Both the Edwards and Darrin efforts on the Henry J chassis had a significant feature in common: bodies made of plastic reinforced with glass fiber. Also known as glass-reinforced plastic, or GRP, this was a material that became more attractive to the automotive industry in 1951 when the escalation of the war in Korea led the Federal government to cut back on civilian uses of some metals, among them nickel, zinc, and tin. Steel wasn't immediately threatened, but it was obviously a good time to give some thought to the potential of alternate materials. On the other side of the coin, the preoccupation of the big car makers with defense production meant that exotic new ideas like sports cars were given the lowest priority rating from the war's beginning in mid-1950 until the truce was signed at Panmunjom on July 26, 1953. Nevertheless these were the years of gestation of the Chevrolet Corvette.

The technology of GRP had been accelerated by the more severe material shortage during World War II, and also by some special applications to which GRP was uniquely suited. One of these was as a protective cover for radar antennae that wouldn't interfere with their transmission and reception. During World War II naval minesweeper hulls were also made from this new material, a combination of polyester resins with strength-giving woven fibers of fine glass. One of the pioneers in the production of the necessary glass material, initially as insulation, was Owens-Corning under the Fiberglas trade name. This was eventually to become confused with the completed structural GRP material, which was popularly given the generic name of "fiberglass."

As early as 1944 Owens-Corning was cooperating with Henry Kaiser in the experimental development of GRP bodies for automobiles. At the Kaiser labs in Emeryville, California, known as "Henry's Hobby Lobby," several prototype bodies were produced. Howard Darrin, who was to style the postwar Kaiser-Frazer cars, built his first GRP car, a pontoon-fendered convertible, in 1946. That same year saw Owens-Corning assisting engineer William Stout in the design and construction of a com-

Kaiser-Frazer's compact Henry J chassis was inspiration for production Kaiser Darrin, at left, and Excalibur J of Milwaukee designer Brooks Stevens.

plete GRP body for one of his rear-engined Scarab prototypes. None of these creations, however, was convincing enough to get the auto industry thinking seriously about this material at a time when they had their hands full satisfying the pent-up demand for new cars by stamping them out of steel the old-fashioned way.

It was left to the amateurs to experiment further with plastic bodies for cars, and they met this responsibility very well. Southern California, with a generous supply of space and sun for the curing of bodies and boat hulls, became the natural center of this activity. In Costa Mesa, Eric Irwin built a shapely body he dubbed the Lancer. In Pasadena, Jack Wills worked with body designer Ralph Roberts to create the stubby Skorpion for the Crosley chassis. And in Montecito, Bill Tritt turned from boat-building, which he had begun in 1949, to an experimental plastic car. All three showed their first efforts in the Los Angeles Motorama at the Pan-Pacific Auditorium, November 7-11, 1951. Bill Tritt's car, which was shown in the *Motor Trend* booth, was destined to become the most significant of these early efforts, a milestone along the road to the creation of the first Corvette.

Tritt built his first GRP boat because a friend wanted one made of this light and maintenance-free new material. He formed the Green Dolphin Boat Works in Montecito to produce replicas and other boats of different sizes. Capable partners joined Tritt: Otto Baeyer, in charge of production; salesman Jerry Niger; financial man Louis Solomon. In 1950 these men established the Glasspar Company to expand in the building of boats and boat

hulls, learning a lot about GRP in the process.

Tritt got a different kind of commission in 1950 from an Air Force officer, Major Kenneth B. Brooks. The major had presented his wife with a Jeep, for her personal use, but she didn't enjoy being seen in this angular vehicle. To pacify her, Brooks asked Bill Tritt to design and build a fiberglass body for the Jeep chassis. Tritt set to work, modeling a shape in plaster and taking a mold from it, just as he'd done with so many boat designs. His flair for fine lines showed in the design he developed for Brooks, marrying the sweeping fenders of an XK120 with a broad, distinctive grille and front end.

By the spring of 1951 the Glasspar crew had completed the conversion of Mrs. Brooks's Jeep to an exceptionally good-looking, light green sports car. A more-than-ordinarily-interested observer was Bud Crawford, the West Coast sales engineer for the Naugatuck Chemical Division of the U.S. Rubber Company. He'd been keeping in close touch with Glasspar, which was becoming an important customer for Naugatuck's Vibrin polyester plastic as an element in its GRP boat hulls. He'd also been asked by his management for tips on any promising developments in the use of GRP for auto bodies. Crawford sent word to that U.S. Rubber Division in Naugatuck. Connecticut, that something rather special had just been born at Glasspar.

The news from California was welcomed by Dr. Earl S. Ebers, who was in charge of selling Naugatuck's Vibrin plastics. He'd already knocked on lots of doors in Detroit without getting the

Stevens continued to modify Excalibur J shape as cars were raced. Example at speed at Watkins Glen in 1955 had supercharged Jaguar XK-120 powerplant.

slightest favorable response toward the idea of fiberglass bodies for cars. "There's only one way to convince people out here," U.S. Rubber's Detroit man told Ebers. "You have to drive right up with something that's already built and running, that shows it really can be done. They won't believe you otherwise."

Ebers hastened West in June, 1951, to see the Brooks Boxer, as the rebodied Jeep had been nicknamed. Impressed by its design and by the ability of the Glasspar crew, Ebers huddled with them to find out how Naugatuck could help them take the big step from this one-off prototype to series production of GRP car bodies. Negotiations with a Studebaker distributor for the production of complete cars seemed promising, but fell through, and there were no other potential automotive customers for Tritt's sports car body.*

Finally Tritt and Ebers reached an agreement: If Naugatuck would write an order to buy the first four production bodies, Glasspar would make the necessary female mold from a new plaster model and set up to manufacture the bodies.

---

*Some months after the events described here a would-be car builder did emerge in the person of a West Coast Willys dealer, Woody Woodill, under whose auspices a small series of Woodill Wildfire cars was produced with Willys chassis and a retouched version of the original Tritt body design. The Wildfire is chiefly notable for its starring role in the film *Johnny Dark*, starring Tony Curtis and Piper Laurie.

Naugatuck general manager John P. Coe signed the order — in effect a guarantee which was never exercised — and Glasspar embarked on what proved to be a very successful enterprise. On February 21, 1952, Glasspar and Naugatuck announced jointly that the bodies would be built and sold for $650 to suit a one hundred-inch-wheelbase chassis.

In managing this announcement, U.S. Rubber public relations man Bert McNomee achieved the dream of a P.R. pro: He had a substantial spread on this new kind of car body in the February 25, 1952, issue of *Life*. Headed "Plastic Bodies for Autos," it added that "Rustproof, dentproof plastic shells go on market in California," and devoted several pages to details of the Glasspar body-building process and the bodys' high resistance to damage and easy repairability.

This article, recall Ebers and McNomee, marked a watershed in the acceptance of fiberglass body panels for cars. After it appeared in *Life* they were inundated with inquiries about the bodies and the material. One of the first to call was a Chevrolet production engineer who contacted the U.S. Rubber plant at Mishawaka, Indiana, where some radomes and fuel cells of GRP had been produced during World War II. Technicians from Mishawaka came straight to Detroit and showed the Chevy men how to take a mold from a fender and make an identical part out of fiberglass. This marked the official introduction of GRP to GM, early in 1952. "We didn't have to show them how to do it again," Earl Ebers recalls. "Once was enough."

From Brooks Boxer to Alembic I: Bill Tritt and Glasspar inspire GM.

GM Styling and Chevrolet Engineering jointly explored the potential of this new material. They saw in it a far easier way to make experimental bodies and new styling studies than the traditional plaster and hand-hammered steel. During 1952 they made a complete Chevrolet convertible body out of GRP, to see how it would work. "A collision test was conveniently provided by the accidental rolling over" of this car, Maurice Olley of Chevrolet later reported. He said that it "survived the accident with remarkable freedom from damage. It rolled over three times. The driver got out with a cut finger. The doors, hood cover, and trunk lid all operated normally.

"The physical properties of fiberglass," Olley observed on the basis of Chevy's early tests, "vary considerably with the percentage of glass in the mixture, the texture of the glass, and the hardness of the resin. Too hard a material containing too high a percentage of glass is likely to suffer from flex-cracking or stone bruises in fenders and body panels. An acceptable material will have physical properties which are remarkably similar to those of the woods used in older body construction.

"What we get from all this," the British-born engineer summed up, "is a very usable body, somewhat expensive, costing a little less than a dollar a pound, but of light weight, able to stand up to abuse, which will not rust, will not crumple in collision, will take a paint finish, and is relatively free from drumming noise. A fiberglass panel of body quality three times as thick as steel will weigh half as much and will have approximately equal stiffness."

GM's technicians rapidly came to grips with the qualities of GRP and put it to use for advanced styling studies and experimental cars. Fiberglass was used for the body, seat, and other key elements of the turbine-powered Firebird, built in 1953. All this came about when it did because *Life* gave so much space to Tritt's good-looking sports car. But this wasn't the only contribution to the Corvette made by Mrs. Brooks's Glasspar-bodied Jeep.

To publicize its new car body concept, Naugatuck Chemical decided to put it on display at the National Plastics Exposition in Philadelphia in mid-March, 1952. The original light-green car was acquired by Naugatuck and renamed the Alembic I, after the technical term for the hexagonal benzene ring that was the Division's symbol. Concerned about the possible effects of road vibration on the GRP body, Earl Ebers decided to drive the car east to the show, which opened March 11. The seven-day journey did produce some paint crazing around the cowl, indicating that a more flexible surface coating for the fiberglass was called for.

At the show in Philadelphia's Convention Hall half a dozen engineers from Chevrolet descended on the Alembic I to uncover the mysteries of its construction. Immediately after the Exposition Ebers took it on the road again, to Detroit. There it was shown and demonstrated to all the car makers. First on the list was the biggest, General Motors. The light-green car with its wide white-walls was put on the elevator of the GM Research building, across the street from Chevrolet headquarters, and taken to the eleventh floor. There it was rolled to the high-ceilinged auditorium built especially for GM Styling Staff, and prepared for an informal showing.

This was the first time Harley Earl had seen Alembic I in the flesh, and he was impressed. The veteran head of car styling for GM had been at Watkins Glen for the sports car races the previous September. He'd brought along his just-completed Le Sabre, an elaborate two-seater dream car that was good-humoredly ridiculed by enthusiasts like Briggs Cunningham, who chided Earl for not making a proper sports car that could be raced. He saw plenty of sports cars that weekend, from M.G.'s to Allards and Ferraris and the very impressive Cunninghams. And now Earl was looking at an American-built sports car in his own auditorium, one that was every bit as attractive as anything that was then on the market.

Earl had also been intrigued by the rakish simplicity of another sporty American car of the 1940's, the Willys Jeepster. This had been mutated from the Jeep Station Wagon of 1946 by Brooks Stevens, who trimmed off its top and gave it a sloping screen and a continental spare. The spartan Jeepster went on sale in 1948, was priced at only $1,614 in 1949, and remained on the market through 1951. Earl liked the fun and the affordability of the jaunty Jeepster: "He'd talk sometimes about the Jeep market," a GM designer remembers, "and other times about the Jaguar, the English cars."

Another GM man with his fingers on the pulse of the sports car market was Edward N. Cole. As an engineer at Cadillac, the inquisitive, enthusiastic Cole had responded readily to the queries of the Cunningham men about the preparation of their 1950 Le Mans entries. Intrigued by Bill Frick's Fordillac conversions, Cole put one of them through its paces on Cadillac's chassis dynamometer in the fall of 1950. Ed Cole was, in short, well aware of some of the realities of the world of sports cars when he was promoted to the chief engineer's post at Chevrolet in May, 1952. Cole brought chassis expert Maurice Olley to Chevy, to head a new research and development department that would help implement some of Cole's ambitious future plans for the division.

Korean War production had depressed Chevrolet's output of cars and trucks in 1952 to the lowest level since 1948 — 1,210,100 units. It had peaked in 1950 at just over two million units and Cole and Chevy general manager Thomas H. Keating were eager to see it up at that level again. They would reach that goal in 1955 — with very little help from a sports car they would add to their line, a fiberglass-bodied roadster that would, in 1955, be little more than an expensive headache to GM's biggest division.

Harley Earl's 1951 LeSabre was the king of the dream cars, powered by a supercharged V-8. It was the springboard for his creation of the first Corvette.

Chapter 2

STYLED BY HARLEY EARL

He was a big man, six feet four and slope-shouldered, slow and imprecise in elocution but lightning-fast in intuition. He impressed a visitor, Lawrence Fisher, the head of Cadillac, with his knack for automotive style and line when that executive was on a trip to California in 1925. Early the following year Fisher brought this promising coachbuilder — thirty-two-year-old Harley J. Earl — to Detroit to work on the design of a companion car to Cadillac, a project that became the LaSalle.

The meeting in Los Angeles at the Earl Carriage Works was an important one, Alfred P. Sloan wrote later, "for Mr. Fisher's interest in this young man's talent was to result in actively influencing the appearance of more than fifty million automobiles from the late 1920's to 1960." Earl, Fisher, and Sloan together created the concept of a center for car styling within an automobile company. Though Earl headed the GM Styling Staff until his retirement in December, 1958, he obviously didn't personally design the thousands of models of cars for which he was responsible. But some were pet projects, cars that embodied Harley Earl's own ideas and enthusiasms. One of these was the first Corvette.

During 1950 and early 1951 Earl and Charles Chayne, head of GM Engineering Staff, had contributed to the engineering and styling of those two experimental two-seaters that were so ambitious and advanced at that time, the Le Sabre and its sister, the Buick XP-300. The Le Sabre was first seen and briefly driven by the press at GM Proving Grounds on July 17, then publicly displayed at the Detroit Fairgrounds in August. In September it made its appearance at Watkins Glen, where Earl was so openly exposed to the sights and sounds of authentic racing sports cars and the points of view of the men who built and drove them.

As an antidote to post-Le Sabre creative depression, Harley Earl began thinking seriously about a low-priced, sporty car during the late fall of 1951. He'd do this in his office on the eleventh floor of the anonymous-looking brick structure on the south side of Milwaukee Avenue, opposite the imposing GM Building. Then he'd wander down past the tenth floor, where the divisional styling studios were located, to the ninth floor. There, in a small enclosure adjacent to the main Body Development Studio, Earl could work privately with a personal crew on projects — like this one — that he wanted to shield from premature exposure. Earl was well aware of the perishable quality of a new idea.

Among Earl's closest associates on this job were Vincent Kaptur, Sr., who headed the body engineering effort at Styling, and Carl Peebles, the draftsman through whom many of Earl's ideas became reality. Others involved were stylists Bill Bloch and clay modeler Tony Balthasar. Their sketches and models were, at first, most like an amalgam of the classic British sports cars and the Jeepster, for Earl had in mind a very simple car, one that could be priced at only $1,850 — about as much as a Ford, Chevy, or Studebaker sedan in 1952. A price this moderate meant that the design had to be based on a more or less stock chassis, and that's the way the first tentative studies went.

No convincing direction had been established before Harley Earl saw the fiberglass Alembic I, on show in the Styling auditorium just down the hall from his office. Gaining new enthusiasm from the sight of this car, Earl accelerated the work in the small ninth-floor studio. Among the additional men he put on the job was Robert F. McLean, a Cal Tech graduate with degrees in both engineering and industrial design who also happened to be a real sports car enthusiast.

McLean's assignment was to do, from scratch, a general basic layout for the car. Traditional Detroit practice was to begin such a layout from the dash line, actually the firewall, and work fore and aft to locate the wheels, engine, and passengers. Working full-scale on a large, flat drafting table, McLean began instead with the rear axle centerline and started constructing the car from the back to the front. The horrified Styling veterans assured him that the method was "impossible," that you just couldn't lay out a car like that. The blond, crew-cut designer went ahead and did it anyway.

Earl the master designer, above left, shows off LeSabre's rain-sensitive top. Below Ed Cole, left, and Tom Keating admire first Corvette at Motorama.

Placing the rear axle, McLean brought the seats as close as he conveniently could to the rear wheel houses. Then he drew in the occupants, seated low with legs outstretched in classic sports car style. Locating the dash line, he brought the rear of the six-cylinder Chevy engine as near to it as possible — another revolutionary idea. Finally arriving at the front wheel centers, McLean established the Corvette's 102-inch wheelbase and a classic sports car profile. From McLean's drawings Bill Bloch prepared full-size white-on-black illustrations that allowed the outline to be viewed from the side in a natural manner, the so-called "blackboard" drawings that can make or break a new design.

Earl kept an open mind when he looked at McLean's unusual layout, unusually arrived at. He saw the startling engine placement, three inches lower and seven inches more rearward than the stock Chevy. "Is that how the Jaguar and M.G. are?" Earl asked. "Yes, sir," Bob McLean replied. "Well, that's how we'll do it." the pioneer stylist decided. McLean's layout and Earl's acceptance of it were pivotal in the story of the Corvette, for they determined two things:

1. That the car's basic proportioning gave it the potential to be a real sports car, with a low center of gravity (eighteen inches from the ground) and good weight distribution (53/47 front/rear).

2. That it could never be cheap, for it would surely need a special frame and other chassis components that would only be made in limited numbers and so would be more expensive than stock Chevrolet hardware.

Earl still hoped that the car's cost could be kept from going sky-high, visualizing wide acceptance for the GM two-seater among college people if the specifications were kept simple and the price kept right. He envisioned new popularity for sports car racing throughout America with these cars readily available, saying expansively that people would soon forget about those English cars as soon as these sporty Chevys were on the market.

An exposed spare tire at the rear had been a feature of the early Jeepster-style designs, and this was retained as the stylists developed a lower, more rounded profile for the embryo sports car. In one incarnation the spare was placed more nearly flat atop a rear deck that was recessed to suit it and rounded at the back to match its shape in plan view. When the idea of an outside spare was finally dropped, the rounded contour of the car's rear end was retained. A conventional trunk was adopted and the spare was neatly hidden beneath its flat floor. The fuel tank was placed high, just above the axle, ahead of the trunk and

Motorama show Corvette compared to 1953 Chevrolet, at top: under the hood at center, and below in montage made for Chevrolet Janesville plant.

to the rear of the passenger compartment; it was filled through a concealed cap in the leading edge of the left rear fender.

Harley Earl was chiefly responsible for the concept of the basic shape of the first Corvette. He gave it the wraparound windshield that had been introduced on Le Sabre, and originally favored transparent plastic covers for the headlights recessed into the rounded front fenders. The traditionalists at GM Styling were uncomfortable with the car's exceptionally wide and flat appearance from the front, occasioned by its wide track — 57/59 inches front/rear — and low overall height. Bob McLean produced a chart of ratios of track to wheelbase that showed that they did indeed have a wider track than the XK120 Jaguar but were still well short of the extra-wide proportions of the Porsche sports cars.

Earl chose carefully the time and the viewer for the unveiling of his newest brainchild. From the full-size clay model, developed rapidly in April, 1952, a plaster model was made and prepared for showing. Not long after his promotion to the top engineering job at Chevy, Edward N. Cole became one of the first men from that division to see the car. "He literally jumped up and down," remembers an eyewitness to the scene. The delighted Cole promised Earl all the support he could provide.

In the further refinement of the car's shape other stylists assisted. Joe Schemansky was responsible for the interior, with its separate bucket seats and symmetrical cowls — as well as the low-placed row of central instruments that both road-testers and owners were later to find so hard to read. Though he wasn't part of the special studio group, Chevy stylist Clare MacKichan was able to help refine the car's lines before its basic features were frozen for a final review under the searching gaze of the top management of GM. The plaster and wood mockup was trimmed and painted inside and out to look as realistic as possible for its all-important debut.

Harlow "Red" Curtice was then president of General Motors, perhaps the last man to approach single-handed rule of that vast company. It was under ace-salesman Curtice that GM developed its system of Motorama shows, starting with a January kickoff in the grand ballroom of New York's Waldorf-Astoria Hotel and then touring major cities from Boston to the West Coast. Curtice was more than amenable to the idea of spicing these shows with modified production models and later with cars that were purely experimental. Earl gave him a private preview of the white Chevy roadster as a candidate for the 1953 Motorama. A little pre-selling, Earl well knew, never hurt.

For the formal unveiling in the styling auditorium, Curtice and

Cole were joined by Thomas H. Keating, Chevrolet's white-haired general manager. With appropriate drama a curtain opened to reveal the mockup on a stage, with Carl Peebles behind the wheel, helmeted and goggled in racing style. Peebles vanished as the curtains were closed and then opened to allow the executives, led by Earl, to inspect the "car." They all agreed they liked what they saw sufficiently to build it for the next Motorama and also to engineer the chassis to the point where at least provisional plans for production could be made. It was the decision that marked the genesis of the Chevrolet Corvette.

Technically Maurice Olley's R&D department had full responsibility for the design of the new car's chassis. As Olley told the Society of Automotive Engineers a year and a half later, "On June 2, 1952, Chevrolet engineers were shown a plaster model of a proposed car of 102-inch wheelbase, for which a chassis was required. The need was to produce a sports car, using components of known reliability, with adequate performance, a comfortable ride, and stable handling qualities, in something less than seven months before showing, and twelve months before production. There was not much time," noted Olley, with characteristic lack of exaggeration.

Though it was Olley's project, Ed Cole was really in charge — as he's always been whenever an unusual new car was taking shape somewhere within his reach. "Cole was there in the shop in his shirtsleeves," recalled one Chevy man, "every night, after his other day's work was done." Sailing under an "Opel" code name, reasonable enough because Chevy often did design work for GM's German subsidiary, a chassis concept for the car rapidly took shape. An Olley sketch dated only ten days after he was handed the assignment shows the frame and suspension in virtually final form.

That the Chevy engineers were able to fit all the machinery inside the skin they were shown, without the almost inevitable hood bulge, is a tribute both to Olley's firm grasp of the needs of sports car engineering and also to the excellent preliminary layout work done at Styling by McLean. Though it started with the standard Chevrolet front suspension, the frame design was entirely special for the new car. It was given boxed side members and a central X-member to assure high rigidity; often stiffness is sacrificed by piercing the center of such an X-member to allow the drive shaft to pass through, but the drive line of the "Opel" was high enough for it to travel above the central crossmembers. The complete frame weighed 213 pounds.

While stock Chevys still had torque-tube rear axles in those days, Maurice Olley realized at once that the Corvette-to-be would have to give that up for a conventional Hotchkiss drive, relying on the rear leaf springs to locate the axle. The latter was adapted from the stock Chevy axle and carried by four-leaf springs which were fifty-one inches long and two inches wide. Excessive joint angularity in the very short (thirty-six inches) propeller shaft was prevented by the addition of straps to the rear axle to limit its rebound travel.

Inherited from the production Chevrolet, the front suspension had been completely redesigned for the 1949 model and was of normal parallel-wishbone layout, with the wishbone centerlines trailing toward the rear as seen in plain view. The one-inch Delco tubular shock absorbers were mounted inside the coil springs. A front anti-roll bar was retained, located higher on the front crossmember than it was on the sedans. The wheel rates of the suspension were 110 pounds per inch in the front and 115 in the rear, about the same as a stock Ford or Mercury of that era.

The rear springs sloped upward toward the rear, where they were held by tension shackles, to give about fifteen percent understeer effect when the car rolled. "This may appear excessive," Olley observed (and the decision was later to be questioned), "but some of the handling qualities of a car depend on the amount it is allowed to roll on turns. When a car is designed to roll very much less than normal, and with a low center of gravity, so that the overturning couple on the tires is reduced, it may become necessary to put a strong understeering tendency into the rear axle control, [for] an adequate tail for the arrow."

Aiming for the arrow was achieved by an adaptation of the stock Chevy steering system. A new Saginaw worm and sector steering box was made with a faster ratio of 16.0 to one. The steering linkage had a two-part track rod divided at the center, where it was actuated by a trailing idler arm. This had a leftward extension which was pushed back and forth by a drag link from the Pitman arm at the steering gear. The lower engine position required a new design for the idler arm, which swung from a double-row ball bearing.

Studies showed that the car's weight distribution would be 53/47 front/rear in running trim with two passengers, approaching 50/50 with a reasonable load in the trunk. Recognizing this and the lower center of gravity, the braking proportion was changed from the normal forty-four percent at the rear to forty-seven percent. For faster braking response the master cylinder bore was also increased in diameter from seven-eighths inch to one inch. Otherwise the brakes were standard production Chevrolet with eleven-inch composite drums of iron and steel, two inches wide in front and one and three-fourths inches in the rear.

More than many observers believed at the time, Cole and Olley were clearly creating a very special chassis for this sports car. They did not do all that they might have, especially with respect to the brakes, but then there was precious little time to do it at all, and none for false starts and major changes. "This was a crash program," a Chevy engineer recalled. "They took their sketches right into the build shop and roughed up the chassis in wood and styrofoam right off the drawing boards. If it wasn't right, they tore it down and started over."

Equally remarkable, in view of the time constraints, was the transformation that Ed Cole worked on the Chevrolet engine to give it power and performance that were up to real sports car standards. He had a much-improved basic engine to work with, the new 1953 version of the large-displacement six that had been paired since 1950 with the Powerglide transmission. With its dimensions of 3 9/16 x 3 15/16 inches (235.5 cubic inches), it was in fact a passenger-car edition of a truck engine Chevy had introduced in 1941.

For 1953 the Powerglide engine was already scheduled to have aluminum pistons — for the first time in Chevy history — and a revised bottom end with full-pressure lubrication and steel-backed inserted rod bearings. With its stock 7.5 to one compression ratio this engine delivered 115 bhp at 3600 rpm — not nearly

First 1953 production Corvettes left plant with simple domed wheel discs.

enough for Ed Cole's sports car. The c.r. was put up to 8.0 to one, which called for high-test fuel, and many other changes elevated the output to a respectable 150 bhp at 4,200 rpm. Torque rose from 204 pound-feet at 2,000 rpm to 223 at 2,400.

Improved induction, timing, and exhaust made all the difference. Mechanical lifters were matched to a new camshaft which gave a lift at the valve of 0.405 inch for the intakes and 0.414 inch for the exhausts. These were at the time the highest stock valve lift figures in the industry. Timing became 19.5°/44.5° for the one-and-seven-eighths-inch intake valves, and 59°/5° for the one-and-a-half-inch exhaust valves. A steel driven gear on the camshaft replaced the fiber gear that was usually fitted. To permit revving to 5,000 rpm and more without disaster, dual springs were provided for each valve. The exhaust valve was also shortened and made of a tougher silichrome alloy steel.

On the inlet side, some form of horizontal induction was mandatory because the stock carburetor would have poked through the Corvette's hood. Cole went all the way to three horizontal Carter carburetors mounted on a special aluminum manifold. Each basically fed a single siamesed pair of inlet ports, but all three were also connected by a small-diameter surge pipe to even out the fuel/air distribution at all engine speeds.

Cast into the manifold were passages to allow it to be warmed by exhaust heat. This was not felt to be strictly necessary at first, but production Corvette sixes did make use of manifold heating. A double-acting mechanical pump supplied fuel to the single-throat carburetors. "Automatic chokes were tried," noted Maurice Olley, and in fact they were fitted to the carbs of the Motorama show Corvette, "but could not be used because of choke valve flutter and fast idling. A manual choke is therefore fitted." Large pancake-type air cleaners on the Motorama car were replaced by smaller bullet-shaped filters in production.

The radiator was so low, in relation to the cylinder head, that the cooling system needed a separate header tank. This became a cylindrical tank along the left-hand side of the Motorama car's rocker cover; in production it was changed in shape and moved to the righthand side. "A special high efficiency water pump is fitted low down at the front of the engine block," wrote Olley in describing the final design. "It is driven at 9/10ths of engine speed, giving a water circulation of 27 gallons per minute at 2000 rpm. It was originally intended to shroud the fan, which is some distance behind the bottom of the steeply inclined radiator. But cooling tests showed this was unnecessary, as the cooling is far above normal passenger car standards." The lower water pump position, which was originally urged by the stylists, became a standard feature of the production Chevrolet six.

Buyer appeal of first production Corvettes was limited by leaky cockpit with side curtains, hard-to-read gauges and lack of a manual gearbox.

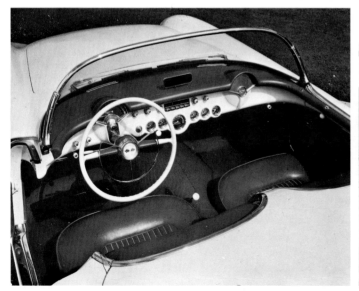
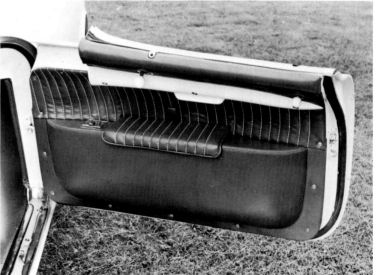

The engineers did have time to experiment with several different exhaust manifold layouts in search of added power. They tried twin exhaust pipes fed by a single central outlet from the manifold, but this wasn't too successful. Better results were given by a split manifold, much like those favored by early-Fifties hot-rodders, giving separate passages and outlets in a single casting for the gases from the front and rear sets of three cylinders. The manifold passages were shaped, Olley said, "to keep the exhaust gases in the throat of each of the two downpipes always whirling in one direction. This was found essential and picked up some 8 or 10 pound-feet of torque in the mid-speed range." Individual pipes and mufflers led back to the dual outlets in the rear of the body.

Both on the Motorama car and the early production Corvettes a rocker cover was used which differed from the stock model only in having its oil filler cap more toward the rear, to make it easier to reach since the car's hood was hinged at the front — unlike the standard Chevrolet hood. In later production both the Corvette and stock Chevys had a newer, trimmer-looking rocker cover with the oil filler at the front.

Electrical systems were six-volt in those days; the battery was at the engine's right. For positive ignition at and above 5,000 rpm the breaker cam was modified to give a longer dwell, and a special coil and condenser were specified. An ordinary AC 44-5 spark plug was all right for normal driving. "For continuous high-speed operation," however, Chevy suggested that the colder AC 43-5 COM plug be used. Because the car's GRP body provided no shielding, the complete ignition wiring loom was enclosed by sheet steel shrouding to prevent interference not only with the car's radio but also with radio and TV sets by the roadside. The antenna for the car's radio was a wire mesh, molded into its rear deck lid — a technique that other firms adopted decades later.

Apparent logic at various levels impelled the Chevy engineers toward one of the most controversial decisions made on the original Corvette: to offer it only with the Powerglide automatic transmission. The basic engine was the Powerglide unit, so it was easiest to build it for use with that transmission. It was also simple to equip it with a floor-mounted shift range control, which was indispensable because the extra shaft needed by a column shift would have interfered with the rearmost of the three carburetors.

Modifications to the Powerglide included higher hydraulic line pressure to help it handle the engine's ten percent higher torque, and alteration of the tailshaft extension to suit the open drive shaft instead of the stock model's torque tube. The shifter valve

Ed Cole and his Chevy engineers worked wonders to turn staid overhead-valve six into a very capable sports car engine. Yet cost of the extensive changes helped raise the Corvette's price tag.

was reset to give an automatic upshift from the 1.82 to one low gear at 4,500 rpm on full throttle, equivalent to fifty-five to fifty-seven miles an hour. An automatic downshift from high to low was possible at any road speed up to forty-seven; some override of these speeds with the hand shift control was also built in. After evaluation of higher axle ratios, 3.08 and 3.37 to one, the ratio chosen for production was 3.55 to one. This gave 108 mph at 4,800 rpm on the 6.70 x 15 tires.

"The use of an automatic transmission has been criticized," Maurice Olley admitted, "by those who believe that sports car enthusiasts want nothing but a four-speed crash shift. The answer is that the typical sports car enthusiast, like the 'average man,' or the square root of minus one, is an imaginary quantity. Also, as the sports car appeals to a wider and wider section of the public, the center of gravity of this theoretical individual is shifting from the austerity of the pioneer towards the luxury of modern ideas." This shift did in fact take place, but about twenty years too late to be of help to the original Powerglide Corvette.

Equally precedent-setting was the Corvette's GRP body. GM Styling had seized quickly on this new construction technique as being ideal for display and experimental cars. Most of its special cars at the 1953 Motorama made extensive use of fiberglass. But

Corvette chassis was completely special design, using some standard Chevy suspension and drive components. Ignition shielding is shown partially removed to reveal plugs and wires, below coolant header tank.

that was all that GM had in mind for the material at the time. "The body on the show model was made of reinforced plastic purely as an expedient to get the job built quickly," reported Chevy's top body engineer, Ellis J. Premo, to the SAE. "At the time of the Waldorf Show, we were actually concentrating on a steel body utilizing Kirksite tooling for the projected production of 10,000 units during the 1954 model year."

Plaster molds taken from the clay styling model of the roadster were used to make the body of the Motorama car. The thickness of its hand-laid GRP skin was two-tenths of an inch, about twice that later used in production. "The combination of glass cloth and mat had a rigid resin of one half of one percent elongation at the rupture point," Premo recorded. "This resin was not sufficiently flexible to utilize the strength of the fiber glass, which had an elongation of approximately three percent at rupture, and it was necessary to refinish the model several times during the various displays across the country because of crazing of the resin which showed through the paint."

Other body shells were made from the same provisional molds, roughly trimmed shells that were used to get chassis development work started. They used a resin that permitted greater elongation: five and a half percent. A test car with one of these bodies

was already sliding around the icy roads of GM's Milford Proving Grounds in January, 1953, when its beautiful sister, the show Corvette, was surrounded by throngs of admirers at the Waldorf in New York. At that time the public was told that the car had a 160 bhp engine. "An experimental sports car in its present form," an official Chevy statement read, "the Corvette is reportedly six months to a year away from production. It is named after the trim, fleet naval vessel that performed heroic escort and patrol duties in World War II."

On that first car at the Waldorf the Corvette name appeared in subtle script across the nose, just above the grille, and over the enclosed rear license plate. The choice had been a last-minute one ("Corvair" was one of the other candidates), so nothing more elaborate had been possible. This was rectified when the final styling refinements were made, after the Waldorf showing, by the Chevrolet production studio, located on the tenth floor of GM's research building. They didn't make many changes, because so little time was left that few were possible.

A short chrome dart along each front fender grew into a full-length rub-rail, more directly aligned with the wrapped-around front and rear bumpers. A small "fin" was now above the strip instead of below it, adjacent to "Chevrolet" in script. The Corvette name became part of the circular medallion at the front of the car. The two tiny scoops disappeared from the sides of the cowl. (On the show car these had been painted red inside, and the exposed portions of the wheel rims were also red.) Production men confirmed the simple mesh design of the headlight covers, which had evolved from a more elaborate egg-crate concept after the idea of Plexiglas had been given up.

Exterior door locks vanished. For entry when the top was up, one had to reach in through the quarter-window in the side curtain and operate an interior knob. One of the oddest changes was on the wheel discs. While the show car's imitation knock-off cap had the Chevrolet bow-tie emblem at right angles to the cap's ears, it was decided to align the emblem with the ears for the production cars. Where pictures of the original show car were retouched for catalogue use, this change was made too, but many of the photos released to the press of the "production" car were clearly taken with the earlier wheel discs in place.

Some early Corvettes, in fact, left the line with a simple domed wheel disc, supplied until the final revised design was ready. Clearly it had taken longer to tool up for mass production of this simple metal wheel disc than it had for Chevrolet — working under the most intense pressure — to start making the rest of the Corvette. How they achieved that is a story in itself.

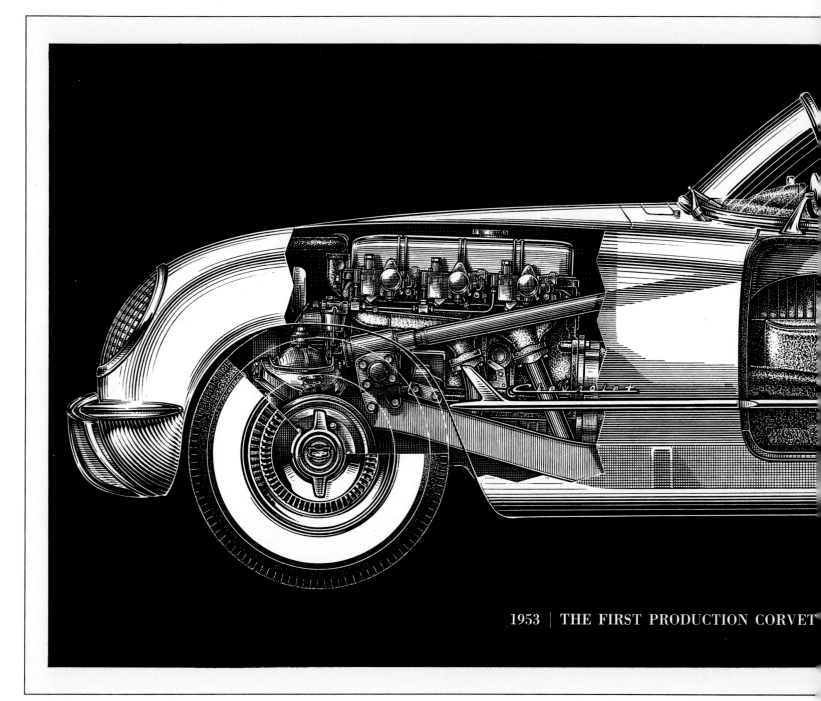

drawing by Yoshihiro Inomoto

Chapter 3

BLUE FLAME CORVETTE

It *did* look like a million dollars on its revolving turntable before a mural of the Manhattan skyline at the Motorama. It hadn't cost quite that much; one Chevrolet executive estimated that the actual construction time invested in that first car was worth "in the neighborhood of $55,000 or $60,000." The people who saw it in New York and its subsequent showings, including a lengthy spell in the lobby of the GM Building in Detroit, liked its looks very much indeed. It didn't cost anything to express interest, so many did tell Chevrolet and its dealers that they would seriously consider buying one of those cute little cars, and the sooner the better.

"There was no denying the demand which existed for an American-built sports car," recalled "Jim" Premo. "People just would not wait until 1954 — they wanted delivery right now, and so our management decided to build 300 Corvettes with plastic bodies during 1953, starting in June. This meant that we had five months to complete a suitable plastic body design and tool it for production, an undertaking which was not unreasonable using the hand lay or bag method."

This last remark was technical talk, indicating that body man Premo and his associates had been doing some boning up on plastics. They took a cram course, in fact, visiting plants using three different systems for making GRP products. One laid up the parts by hand, the same way the first part of the Corvette body program was carried out by the GM Engineering Parts Fabrication Department. Two others used pressure from an air-inflated bag to help form and cure large GRP parts. Still another used mating molds made of iron castings or high-carbon plate steel to form the parts. Known as the "matched-metal die method," this offered by far the fastest cycle time for making a single part. "We were quite impressed by this process," Premo noted, "and the possibility of production of over 20,000 parts per year from one set of tools, operating an eight-hour day."

These field trips weren't taken just for fun. Hot on the heels of the initial decision to make 300 cars in fiberglass, Keating and Cole began to reconsider their plan to use dies of Kirksite, a special metal easily processed but short in lifespan, to produce 10,000 bodies in steel. It would take quite a while, they knew, to get even that temporary tooling ready. And there was another factor, as Jim Premo reported. "People seemed to be captivated by the idea of the fiberglass plastic body. Furthermore, information being given to us by the reinforced plastic industry seemed to indicate the practicability of fabricating plastic body parts for automobiles on a large scale."

Undoubtedly the makers of glass-fiber and polyester resins, grasping the import of GM's potential role as a customer for their products, were doing all they could to encourage Chevrolet to take a long step in their direction. And that's what the Division finally did. Very early in 1953 they let it be known that they would accept bids on the building of 12,300 sets of Corvette body parts of GRP, the first 300 to be available in 1953 and the rest to be delivered at the rate of 1,000 sets per month in 1954. That's what they felt they'd need to satisfy the pent-up demand on the part of the eager enthusiasts who couldn't wait to get their hands on America's first (postwar) production sports car.

This was a big job that required a major commitment from any would-be manufacturer. GM's own Fisher Body Division submitted a bid, backed by U.S. Rubber's Naugatuck Chemical Division, which had done so much with its work with Glasspar and the Alembic I to get GM thinking about both sports cars and fiberglass. They calculated their bid in terms of bodies which would come out of the molds with smooth outer surfaces, almost ready for painting, requiring a minimal amount of subsequent hand finishing.

Another bid came from the Molded Fiber Glass Company of Ashtabula, Ohio. A native of Ashtabula, Robert S. Morrison had been operating a Ford dealership there for two decades when, in 1948, he took over the plant of a bankrupt pulp-molder whom he had encouraged to locate in that northern Ohio city. Morrison gradually converted the plant to the molding of GRP products at

Behind the production of these simple reinforced plastic parts and their assembly into a completed Corvette was an awesome saga of hectic improvisation.

Panels began in Ashtabula with spraying of glass fiber on preforming mold.

Underbody was foundation to which other panels were added in body assembly.

Mahogany die models were made for all panels. Underbody was the largest.

a time when the technology for doing this was still in its infancy. It was his use of the advanced and rapid matched-metal die method that had so impressed the Chevy men during their exploratory field trip.

After a series of meetings in Detroit, the contestants for this prize retired to await the outcome. At 1:30 a.m. in Ashtabula Morrison's home phone rang with a call from Elmer Gormsen, Chevrolet purchasing agent, who was wasting no time in passing the word on a project that had the highest possible priority: Morrison's firm had won the assignment, an order worth some four million dollars. Now all he had to do was build the plant to fill it.

In April, 1953, Bob Morrison founded the Molded Fiber Glass Body Company and began planning and building a plant of 30,000 square feet to produce the parts that Chevrolet needed. He fitted it with fifteen large presses for molding the pieces between matched-metal dies. Fed by hydraulic pressure of 2,000 p.s.i., their capacities ranged from 250 to 500 tons. The largest presses had beds measuring seven by twelve feet, these being needed to form the one-piece underbody that served as a foundation for the rest of the Corvette body. There were also ten smaller presses, rotary suction tables for preforming the glass-fiber mats, curing ovens and a department for trimming and checking the finished pieces.

The original Corvette body was composed of a relatively large number of separate GRP pieces, because the Chevy engineers

Corvette manufacture in St. Louis Chevy plant began in December, 1953.

Mating of body with chassis was done in Flint plant for first 500 cars.

Distance from body drop to end of line was short in Flint assembly operation.

laid it out to be suited to production by the matched-metal die process. Each body was composed of thirty parts considered major and some thirty-two other minor fiberglass pieces. "The total weight of the Corvette reinforced plastic body parts is 340 pounds," summarized Jim Premo, "the basic materials making up this total being 136 pounds of fiber glass, 153 pounds of polyester resin, and 51 pounds of inert filler." The completely assembled body, ready to be mated to the chassis at eleven points, weighed 411 pounds.

Metal dies were needed in Ashtabula to make these parts, however, and while they needed to be neither so numerous nor so exact as those for steel bodies, it still took time to machine and finish them by the conventional Kellering process from the wood die models that Chevrolet had made. Morrison knew that he'd have to use some other method to get the parts flowing to Chevrolet until his new plant and molds were ready. At about that time he was contacted by Jim Lunn of Long Island, New York, whose Lunn Laminates was making GRP parts, mainly for the government, by the bag method. His was the process that Morrison needed.

These were the most hectic months of all in the gestation of the Chevrolet Corvette. In the spring and summer of 1953 the pressure was on full blast to get that car into production, the best way possible, and the hell with what it cost. A man who was close to the intense effort remembered: "I was awfully impressed with

Here's the car you hear so much about!

The Chevrolet Corvette

The Corvette features a 2-passenger cockpit with individual form-fitting bucket seats. Fabric top folds into concealed compartment.

The special Corvette engine has dual exhausts and also triple carburetors which are horizontally mounted to permit a lower hood.

Everywhere you go you hear talk about the new Chevrolet Corvette. And small wonder, for here is something distinctly new and different in automobiles. Here is a car that combines all the grace and sparkling performance of a true sports car with all the comfort and convenience today's motorists desire.

But, more than that, the Corvette embodies important new concepts of automobile design and construction. The body, for example, is of glass-fiber reinforced plastic. Height from road to door top is only 33 inches. A special 150-h.p. version of the famed Chevrolet "Blue-Flame" engine provides spirited acceleration and instant response to the slightest command.

The Corvette is not a drawing board "dream car," but a fully tested reality—the first all-American sports car to reach production. Chevrolet, builder of America's first-choice car, is proud to be first in bringing you this "years ahead" automobile. ... Chevrolet Division of General Motors, Detroit 2, Michigan.

CHEVROLET

The first attempts by Chevrolet and their advertising agency, Campbell-Ewald, to tell the world that the Corvette was waiting were notable for their restraint.

the GM organization. Anybody who says that a big company can't move fast just doesn't know what they're talking about. Cole and Premo were down there all the time, and they put a buyer on the job who had total authority to get whatever parts and equipment were needed. He was smart; he had good judgment, and he was always backed up one hundred percent by his management. And like all the other GM people who came to Ashtabula he didn't hesitate to work all day and all night for days in a row if there was an emergency, if something was needed in a hurry."

As a subcontractor to Morrison, Lunn set up a plant in rented quarters in Ashtabula to make parts by the vacuum-bag method. From the wooden die models and plaster casts, as needed, the phenolic plastic molds were produced for this purpose. Because this was a much slower process — curing in the mold could take a full hour — more than one mold was often needed for each part, as production was accelerated early in 1954.

Almost all the parts were made by the vacuum-bag process at first. As soon as Morrison had the necessary tooling to make a part in his matched-metal dies, that part would be switched over from Lunn to the MFG Body Company. The larger the part, the longer it took to make the tooling, the result being that Lunn was still making major Corvette parts well into 1954. The last one was the largest, the underbody measuring ten by six by two feet. At one time Lunn had five separate molds all making this same part, at a cost of $14,000 each, and was working three eight-hour shifts

Sports car fans liked the Corvette but had to wait in line to buy one.

per day six days a week to keep up with the schedule. By the end of July, 1954, the matched metal underbody dies were in place and running at MFG and complete conversion to this production method had been achieved.

Directly related to the production of panels but entirely separate from it was the question of how and where they were to be assembled into a complete and finished body. The first 300 were built close to the home of Chevrolet on one floor of the Division's Plant Number 35 near Flint, Michigan. In the center of the floor the bodies were glued together and hand-finished. Along one side were the paint booths and along the other side of the floor was the body drop and final assembly area, no longer than it needed to be to produce three cars a day — all that was required of it. The Flint operation served as a pilot line to help Chevrolet learn the assembly methods that it installed, on a much larger scale, at the Corvette's permanent home at the Division's plant in St. Louis, Missouri.

Job Number One had rolled off the Flint line on June 30, 1953, the first official production Corvette after several pre-production cars had been assembled by Chevrolet Engineering. By one of these first cars the builders were given an unpleasant surprise: When they bolted it all together they flicked the switches to operate important items like the lights, the horn, the radio — and nothing worked! Soon it dawned on them that it wasn't enough to attach these units to the body and expect it to provide the

Harbor Freeway was scene of March, 1954 Corvette driveaway in Los Angeles.

grounded side of the electrical circuit, as they had done for so many years with steel bodies. When separate grounding wires were added, the electrical system suddenly came to life!

By the time they reached St. Louis any such teething troubles had long since been eradicated. There the bodies were assembled in an area measuring 200 by 500 feet, subassemblies coming together to a central line where the body was built up, starting with the underbody, into which some 180 holes had been drilled at the outset. While the first 300 cars had all been Polo White, a blue exterior color was added in St. Louis. Fourteen cars, officially 1954 models, were turned out in St. Louis in December, 1953, as the line was just getting started.

The first Corvette assembly line in St. Louis departed from standard Detroit practice in more than a few ways. Along the body-trim line, the radiator, steering column, and wiring harness were put in along with the seats, upholstery, and folding fabric tops. Arriving from Flint, the "Blue Flame" engines were equipped with carburetion, ignition, and transmission and then tuned and tested for thirty minutes on three dynamometer stands. Built-in equipment on the chassis assembly line spun and balanced the road wheels in position. After completion, each Corvette was driven off the line and taken for a brief run around the plant grounds.

These were some of the refinements that made it, to quote Maurice Olley, "possible for a great mass-production organization to step out of its normal role of producing over 500 vehicles an hour, to make 500 specialized vehicles in, say, two weeks. This is an interesting fact even outside the United States, where it is generally considered that American manufacturing methods are too inflexible to meet modern conditions. This was well disproved within our own knowledge by the wartime performances of the automobile industry. It is proved to the whole world by such a specialized vehicle as the Corvette."

There was, of course, a saving in tooling cost as a result of the decision to make the Corvette body in fiberglass. Ed Cole said at the time that dies for a steel body would have cost $4,500,000, compared with only $400,000 for the GRP production molds. This didn't include, of course, the tremendous extra expense incurred in accelerating the early production with additional shifts and the many provisional molds needed for the temporary vacuum bag installation in Ashtabula.

These and many other considerations, both tangible and intangible, were factored into the Corvette's initial advertised price, including handling and excise tax, of $3,490. Standard equipment items included the Powerglide automatic, windshield washers,

Child of the magnificent ghosts

Years ago this land knew cars that were fabricated out of sheer excitement. Magnificent cars that uttered flame and rolling thunder from exhaust pipes as big around as your forearm, and came towering down through the summer dust of American roads like the Day of Judgment.

They were the sports cars in a day when all motoring was an adventure, and no man who ever saw one can forget the flare of sun on brass, the brave colors and the whirlwind of their passage.

They have been ghosts for forty years, but their magic has never died. And so, today, they have an inheritor — for the Chevrolet Corvette reflects, in modern guise, the splendor of their breed.

It is what *they* were: a vehicle designed for the pure pleasure of road travel. It handles with a precision that cannot be duplicated by larger cars — and it whistles through curves as though it were running on rails.

You can watch a Corvette in action and imagine some of

the elation it offers. But you have to put your own hands on that husky steering wheel to taste the full pleasure of really *controlling* a car.

Who can tell you about the cyclone sound of that 195-horsepower V8 engine, or the fantastic surge of acceleration that answers an ounce of throttle pressure? Who can describe the wonderful feeling of confidence and relaxation that stems from true sports car roadability, or the genuine astonishment that comes when you first tap those rock-solid brakes?

Who can make you feel what it is like to drive a car that always has more on hand — in road-holding, acceleration, stopping power — than you'll virtually ever use? You'll have to try it for yourself. And when you drop in at your Chevrolet dealer's, he'll take particular pride in showing you the car that is a true child of those magnificent ghosts — the V8 Corvette! . . . Chevrolet Division of General Motors, Detroit 2, Michigan.

CHEVROLET CORVETTE

Admen were beginning to wax more poetic in 1955, showing Corvette as spiritual successor to the Mercer Raceabout. And the optional V-8 engine gave them more to talk about.

Urge for more power in 1954 six was satisfied by Paxton supercharger.

whitewall tires, a clock, a cigarette lighter, an outside rear-view mirror, and a feature that was novel at that time: a bright red warning light that came on when the parking brake was applied.

Chevrolet did not officially launch the Corvette to the press until September 29, when it brought eight cars to Milford to allow each of more than fifty newsmen to drive one car for seven miles. Chevy's nine-page news release of that date was headed by a quote from general manager Tom Keating that deserves repetition in full because it was the closest that Chevy came to describing what it was trying to achieve with this car:

"In the Corvette we have built a sports car in the American tradition. It is not a racing car in the accepted sense that a European sports car is a race car. It is intended rather to satisfy the American public's conception of beauty, comfort and convenience, plus performance. Just as the American production sedan has become the criterion of luxury throughout the world, we have produced a superior sports car. We have not been forced to compromise with the driving and economic considerations that influence so broadly the European automotive design."

Some question as to whether the Corvette was really "a sports car in the American tradition" might justifiably have been raised by Finley R. Porter, designer of the Mercer Raceabout, who was an eighty-two-year-old resident of Long Island when the Corvette was launched. But this wouldn't have worried the 20,000 Americans who had, since the car's first showing, told Chevy's

Paxton blower, at upper right, delivered high-pressure air to carburetors.

7,600 dealers that they'd be interested in buying a car like that. "To all of these inquiries," said general sales manager William E. Fish, "we have avoided definite commitments.

"The problem of distribution," Fish continued, "is not insolvable. Many times since the war Chevrolet has been faced with far more dealer orders than we could hope to handle." With only a handful of cars to deal with in 1953, Fish decided to make them available only to outstanding high-volume dealers and, at those dealerships, only to Very Important People in the community — industrial leaders, town officials, those socially prominent, military officers, celebrities. At the end of September, fifty cars had been delivered to such "prestige owners." By the end of 1953, total sales had been 183 cars. This was short of the production that had been reached but not alarmingly so at that time, because many cars were still being used for special dealer displays, as showroom attractions to draw attention to the rest of the Chevy line. And if sales were a little slow during the winter, well, perhaps that just wasn't the time for selling sports cars.

By the spring of 1954, however, it began to dawn on those in charge of Chevrolet Motor Division that all was not running according to plan. While Cole and Premo were practically living in Ashtabula and St. Louis to get production up to speed, sales were lagging catastrophically. Not every V.I.P., Chevy found, was eager to own a Corvette. Those who did accept the invitation to buy one were not uniformly pleased with the side curtains, the

Californian George Barris gave the Kustom touch to these 1953-1955 models.

awkward access to the door latches, the low windshield, the water leaks around the doors and the top, and the way that the top, as one GM man said, "fell into your lap" when you were putting it up or down. Reporting on the difficulty of erecting the top, Don MacDonald wrote that Chevrolet's "conception of the Corvette market is that no owner will be caught in the rain without a spare Cadillac."

Writing in *Motor Trend* of June, 1954, MacDonald referred to Bill Fish's "eyedropper distribution" of the first Corvettes. "There is still a waiting list," Don reported, "but the long gap between initial publicity and availability has cooled the desires of many buyers. Chevrolet dealers (distribution is now in their hands) now find that they have to contact as many as six people on the list before they find one who will honor his original commitment."

Not until the summer of 1954 did Chevy give up the V.I.P.-first marketing policy. That spring a truck salesman at a Chevy dealership was able to buy a car by having an Air Force officer "front" for him; the salesman was Bob Rosenthal, who later became the Number One Corvette dealer in America. In Wisconsin a Chevrolet field man, Joseph P. Pike, bought a Corvette because a V.I.P. gave up his option. That Chevy man became, in 1960, the Division's national Corvette sales manager.

Extended road tests of the Corvette didn't appear in the automotive magazines until the June, 1954 issues. The absence of impartial opinion about the car had given free rein to those who tended to condemn it without a hearing. *Road & Track* commented that "the die-hards, the pro-foreign advocates have been especially loud in their derision of the new car, maintaining that the Corvette is not a genuine dual-purpose sports car, but more of an effete high-speed touring type. Some have been more specific, claiming that nothing from Detroit could possibly be any good — least of all from Chevrolet," the last rebuke being a good indication of how much Chevy needed a car like the Corvette at that time.

Yet when they did get their hands on a Corvette, the magazine writers found that it was a remarkably good car. Its acceleration from rest to sixty could be as good as 11.0 seconds and its top speed was 106 mph. Testers found the engine would rev easily to 5,000 rpm and even took it to 5,500 in low range, the equivalent of sixty-eight miles an hour. *Road & Track* said, "Frankly, we liked the Corvette very much," finding outstanding "its really good combination of riding and handling qualities." *Motor Life* judged it "a true sports car, offering the prospective buyer tops in performance," and *Motor Trend* said that "Chevrolet has pro-

One of three Corvette-based dream cars for '54 Motorama had bolt-on hardto

Ron Cadaret sketched Nomad wagon version of Corvette, for 1954 Motoram

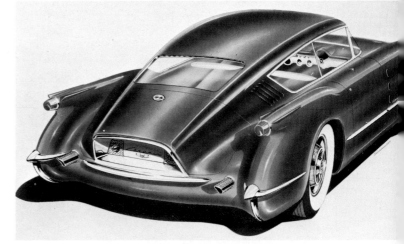

Corvair coupé made '54 Motorama bow, was drawn by stylist Joe Schemansk

Hardtop-equipped 1954 dream car had roll-down windows, exterior door locks.

Nomad, a "double cross" of the competition, was built on stock Chevy chassis.

Sleek Corvair coupé was production possibility until Corvette sales sagged.

duced a bucket-seat roadster that will hold its own with Europe's best, short of actual competition and a few imports that cost three times as much."

Considering the speed with which the Corvette had been designed and its almost negligible amount of development, these reviews could scarcely have been better. But they came too late to change the image of the Blue Flame six Corvette, which the country club set found too spartan and the sports car enthusiasts considered too decadent. At the end of June, 1954, the production line in St. Louis was finally moving at the planned rate of fifty cars per day, and the plastic panels were coming from Ashtabula in a steady stream. That lasted only a couple of days. Alarmed at its swelling inventory of Corvettes, Chevrolet management brought Bob Morrison's GRP plant to a full stop and slashed the assembly pace in St. Louis to less than a third of the peak rate, building out the remaining stock of components.

Not until late in 1954 did Chevrolet begin to place advertisements for the Corvette in the automotive magazines. They began with the tag line "First of the dream cars to come true," then switched to a more direct appeal to the enthusiast with a bolder ad style and headlines like "For experts only!" But sales only limped along. Of the 3,939 Corvettes made in 1953 and 1954, only 2,863 were sold, leaving a January 1, 1955, surplus of 1,076 unsold cars. Clearly it was time for an agonizing reappraisal of the potential of Chevrolet's sports car.

Ed Cole recalled his thoughts at the time for writer Robert O'Brien: "We really didn't know what we wanted. We had no real feeling of the market. Was Corvette for the boulevard driver, or the sports-car tiger? We weren't quite sure. But we loved that car. We weren't going to let go." Cole's last comment reflects the very heavy pressure that GM applied to Chevrolet to shut down the Corvette project, which in mid-1955 looked like a rathole of almost limitless depth, down which good money could only be poured after bad.

Though Chevrolet could have left Bob Morrison holding a very big bag, a brand-new but useless plant for making GRP body panels, it didn't do so. Instead it revived a dormant project for a new kind of pickup truck, one on which the sides of the rear bed were styled as flush extensions of the sides of the cab, in fact the first pickup of modern conception. This was Chevy's Cameo Carrier, which was offered to the market in March, 1955 — with rear side panels made of fiberglass by Bob Morrison in Ashtabula. This helped tide him over until Corvette body production could be resumed.

While the fate of the first serious (postwar) American sports car was being decided at high levels, Maurice Olley's research and development department had not been idle. In May, 1953, it acquired a new employee, Zora Arkus-Duntov, Belgian-born and Berlin-educated, an engineer with remarkably varied experience in the design, testing, and driving of sports and racing cars. He'd seen the first Corvette at its Motorama debut, and through subsequent contact with Ed Cole, eventually found his way to Chevrolet.

When he arrived at R&D, shortly before Corvette production began, Duntov found in the shops the first engineering prototype of the sports car, one that had been fitted with a wooden grille. He put it through its paces at the Proving Grounds and found that it was not very controllable when pressed to the limit. Some road testers had noted this also. As *Road & Track* put it: ". . . high speed four wheel drifts required a certain amount of dexterity . . ." Reported *Motor Life*: "When we tried to 'break it loose' at high speed on a rather severe corner the Corvette . . . showed a definite unwillingness to 'tuck back in.' "

Duntov's trials confirmed that the Corvette was oversteering at the limit. Noting that the rear-spring inclination gave a roll understeer of fifteen percent and that the front-end geometry incorporated ten percent oversteer, Duntov concluded that "we had a car in which the two ends were fighting each other. I made some changes, limiting the rear-spring travel and putting a larger stabilizer bar in front. Before long I produced a car which I could put into a drift and have it respond as the car should."

Maurice Olley also asked Duntov to address his attention to the tendencies of the Corvette exhaust system to stain the back of the body and to contaminate the passenger compartment with exhaust gases. One test report showed that this contamination was worse when the heater was working. "Why is that?" Duntov wondered. "Maybe they opened the window, I thought, or the Ventipane, and that affected the air flow. I attached many wool tufts to one Corvette and in my hand I held another tuft, on a long welding rod, to show where the gases were going. I showed this by movie film, taken from another car. Sure enough, if you opened the Ventipane, then you reversed all the air flow from the rear to the front!" Relocation of the exhaust outlets to the tips of the rear fenders cured both this and the staining problem.

The six remained the standard engine on the 700 cars that were built during 1955, its power rating slightly improved to 155 bhp and its air cleaning system changed to a manifold feeding the three carburetors, topped by two mesh-filled pancake filters. Some enthusiasts, however, sought more in the way of performance. McCulloch developed a supercharger kit for the Corvette six; Frank McGurk recommended the installation of the 261-cubic-inch Chevrolet truck block bored out to 278 cubic inches; Nicson Engineering replaced the Powerglide with a three-speed Ford manual gearbox — and Chicagoan Jim Gaylord had a Buick Century V-8 developing 240 brake horsepower complete with Dynaflow, gingerly installed in his Corvette.

Chevrolet's performance-minded engineers had been busy in

A 1954 model was reworked by Styling to show proposed changes for 1955 or '56 with rear deck from Corvair coupé, handsome new egg-crate grille design.

the meantime. A new V-8 engine had already been under development when Ed Cole arrived at Chevy, and as engineer Russ Sanders recalled, "it was a natural move to see how this engine would perform in a Corvette." Late in 1953 it was installed in the actual Motorama show car, which had by that time been returned to Engineering. Its excellent performance helped convince Chevrolet to make the 265-cubic-inch V-8 a 195 bhp option, with either Powerglide or a three-speed manual transmission, in the 1955-model Corvettes. The show car was also submitted to a 25,000-mile durability test at the Proving Grounds with its V-8 engine, then totally disassembled for examination of rates of wear. Rebuilt, the ex-Motorama star served for 5.000 miles in courtesy service before being sold. It's still on the road today.

GM's stylists had also been exploring Corvette combinations and permutations. These began to coalesce in the brainstorming sessions in which Earl's designers generated ideas for the show cars for the 1954 Motorama. They came up with three special Corvettes, all of which had one feature in common: side windows that rolled up and down. One was almost standard except for this, its exterior door locks, and its rounded, slim-pillared fiberglass hardtop. Another brought the "Corvair" name to life on a very handsome fast-back coupé. This had vertical windshield side pillars instead of the standard forward-sloping pillars, and decorative vents on the hood top and side, the rear quarters, and above the rear window. This car, seriously considered for production until the Corvette market turned sour, had

an exterior trunk opening and a cowled enclosure at the rear framing the license plate against a fine Chevrolet bow-tie pattern.

The third Motorama entry was a Corvette of a quite different kind. "We thought this would be a good double-cross," recalls Clare MacKichan. "Nobody would expect to see a wagon version of the Corvette." In one of the GM Styling special studios Carl Renner made the first sketches of the Nomad. Though this unique four-seater used some Corvette body panels at the nose and tail, it was built on the stock Chevrolet 115-inch chassis of 1953 and had doors and hardware that were more like those of a passenger car than the sports car. Its transverse roof flutes, side exhausts, vertically-ribbed rear gate, electrically-operated back window and wrap-around rear glass were novel and impressive features of the Nomad. The desired double-cross was a complete success, the Nomad one of the freshest ideas ever in automotive design. Harley Earl phoned from New York on the second day of the January, 1954 Motorama to tell MacKichan that he wanted a version of the Nomad in production as soon as possible. Carl Renner took down his blackboard drawing of the show Nomad and cut and spliced it to fit the 1955 production lower body. Presto: the 1955 Chevrolet Nomad. From that year through 1957, 22,898 Nomads were produced as well as 10,988 Safaris, the sister version marketed by Pontiac.

Other post-Motorama plans were made for a possible facelift of the Corvette for the 1955 model year. By March, 1954, a styling model had been completed — a rework of an actual car — showing the proposed changes. At the front an egg-crate grille was suggested, mirroring the looks of the standard 1955 Chevy. For V-8 equipped models a special hood was recommended with a central air scoop. Four sloping vents were incised into the side of each front fender.

Different headlight treatments, including a vertical plexiglass divider for the lamp nacelle, were explored for 1955. At the rear, the exhaust outlets — benefiting from Duntov's tests — were relocated in the tips of the fenders. The trunk lid was given a shrouded cove for the license plate, like that on the Motorama Corvair coupé, with the same bow-tie-pattern insert. A feature in common with the 1955 Corvettes equipped with the V-8 engine was a modification of the script along each side with a very dominant central letter to read "cheVrolet."

There was, however, no styling facelift for the 1955 Corvette. Not long after this proposal was presented it became clear that the sports car program was in deep trouble, trouble from which it might never be rescued. Yet against these tremendous odds a recovery was engineered, and achieved.

Suggested 1955 facelift added fender side vents. But it was not to be.

Chapter 4

V-8: SPEED SPELLED SURVIVAL

Corvette's original conception as a low-priced sportster and the enthusiasm of Ed Cole and others that led to its adoption by the Chevrolet Motor Division assured that the car would be powered by one of the least potent engines in America's automotive arsenal. Only the Plymouth flathead six might have ranked lower in power-producing potential at that time. Ed Cole and his assistant, Harry Barr, worked wonders in vitalizing this veteran engine enough to give the first Corvette such lively performance.

The Polo White roadster went well, but not well enough. Its acceleration to sixty in eleven to twelve seconds was about on a par with that achieved by some other 1953 production cars. The Oldsmobile Super 88 made it in 12.3 seconds with Hydra-Matic and even faster with a manual box. In 1953 the Olds could reach 110 mph and the Cadillac 62 could top 115. Zero-to-sixty time for the 1954 Cadillac 62 was only 11.3 seconds. So the Corvette owner was in danger of being beaten from the lights not only by the Jaguar XK120M (zero to sixty: 8.5 seconds) but also by some cars that were considerably cheaper and others that were anything but sporty.

Zora Arkus-Duntov was aware of this deficiency and had feared that it might slow the Corvette's acceptance, especially in America, where fast acceleration has always been rated highly. In most countries, Duntov knew, sports cars were capable of outperforming and outspeeding anything else on the road, in a straight line as well as around corners. He felt that the Corvette should have this ability too, and this point of view would continue to have a powerful influence on the car's development over the next two decades.

This dedicated engineer, who had learned to drive as a chauffeur's assistant in Russia, brought to Chevrolet a wide-ranging interest in automotive development and especially in engine design. During the 1930's he had worked with supercharged sports car engines, and after the war Zora and his brother Yura built the famous Ardun overhead-valve conversions for the Ford V-8. Zora went back to Europe for several years, developing and driving racing sports cars for Allard in England and consulting with Porsche and Daimler-Benz. Seeing greater opportunity in the United States, he returned there in the fall of 1952. He kept on racing after joining Chevrolet, co-driving an 1,100 cc Porsche Spyder to class wins at Le Mans in 1954 and 1955.

"I thought it wasn't a good car yet, but if they're going to do something, this looked good." That was Duntov's opinion when he saw the first Corvette at the Waldorf. The potential he saw in the car was dramatically enhanced by the new V-8 engine Chevrolet unleashed on an astonished and unbelieving world in 1955. Design of the engine had begun under Ed Cole's predecessor, E. H. Kelley. Cole and his associates, Harry Barr and Russ Sanders, modernized its combustion chambers, gave it the novel and light stamped-steel rocker arms, and brought its displacement up from 231 to 265 cubic inches before it was released for production.

The optional installation of the V-8 in the Corvette was a necessary reaction in 1955 to the introduction of Ford's very trim and practical two-seater Thunderbird. *Consumers Union* tested the 1955 automatic-transmission models of both cars side-by-side and concluded that "the Corvette buyer finds himself with a car that easily outperforms the Fordomatic Thunderbird, steers and handles better and more easily, and has a more comfortable and better laid-out cockpit. The Corvette, of the two, should please the true sports car driver more." The times to sixty miles an hour were 11.1 seconds for the Ford, 9.1 seconds for the Chevy. Other magazines timed the Powerglide V-8 to sixty in between 8.5 and 9.0 seconds. Manual-shift boxes were available, but no more than two dozen were supplied in the 700 cars made during 1955.

The arrival of the T-Bird surely played a strong role in Chevrolet's decision, which seemed to go against all corporate logic, not only to continue with the Corvette after its disastrous first year but even to improve it. Ford's two-seater "personal car" was first shown as a plastic styling model at an auto show in Detroit in February, 1954. Though production didn't begin until September, the impending presence in the market of the un-

The first hesitant steps did not make racing history: a C Production Corvette being overhauled by an Allard at Cumberland airport on May 15, 1955.

The Corvette could go racing with the V-8 engine: at center the stock 1955 V-8, at right installed in a '55 Corvette, and at left the dual-quad '56 V-8.

deniably handsome Thunderbird was enough to keep some potential sports car customers from casting their lot with the Corvette.

Ford's car was what the 1956 Corvette catalogue obliquely referred to as a "scaled down convertible." Was this the way to go, the Chevrolet men wondered? Or should they listen to the writers like Ben West who urged that Chevrolet "bring the American sportsman a truly good sports car." In *Autosport* West added, "Let's all pray that the new GM pride and joy [the 1956 Corvette] is just that and not a beast burdened under automatic window raisers and other useless chrome adornments." Finally Chevrolet decided to go *both* ways — but somewhat more in the direction Mr. West desired.

The 1956 Corvette was the last of its breed to be styled entirely on the tenth floor of the downtown building, before GM Styling's move to magnificent new quarters at the GM Technical Center north of Detroit. When the decision was made to continue, there was relatively little time to make drastic appearance changes; yet every aspect of the original body was altered and refined. At the rear the protruding taillights were shaved off and replaced by inset lamps. An original suggestion of exhaust pipes through the sides of the rear fenders — shown also on the 1954 Motorama Nomad — was replaced by combined rear outlets and fender protectors like those on the by-passed 1955 styling model.

Two powerful influences affected the changes in the 1956 styling. One was the LaSalle II roadster shown at the 1955 GM Motorama. In modern emulation of the classic sports car fender line, it had a curved inset in its side that swept back from the front wheel housings, well into the doors, painted in a contrasting color. A more subdued depression of this type, reversed in direction, had also been used on the 1955 Chevrolet Biscayne dream car. The scooped-out parabolic curves in the fenders of the 1956 Corvette combined the best features of both these experiments.

The other influence was the Mercedes-Benz 300SL, the production version of which had been shown early in 1954. It was responsible for the 1956 Corvette's forward-thrusting fender lines to more conventional headlights, and the twin bulges in its hood panel. These changes blended admirably with the Corvette's horizontal grille concept and gave the new car a very handsome "face." Wind-up windows (with *optional* automatic raisers) were added, with external door handles, optional power operation for the convertible top, and a much sportier-looking three-spoke steering wheel. The hardtop first shown in the 1954 Motorama was also available.

Though the basic shape of the new car was set by February, 1955, the flexibility allowed by bodybuilding in fiberglass permit-

Photos of the clay styling model of the '56 Corvette were taken February 1, 1955.

42

GRP model of '56 car was shown to Chevrolet management on April 16, 1955.

Final '56 production Corvette had more comfort as well as better appearance.

ted some last-minute detail changes. One was the addition of a chrome trim piece around the depressions in the flanks of the fenders. Another was the installation — at the last minute — of small scoops at the corners of the cowl like those on the original show Corvette. Ducts to make them functional had been designed, recalled stylist Clare MacKichan, but cost ruled out their use, so the scoops were fakes on an otherwise very honest car.

One other "dummy" item, the pseudo-knock-off wheel cover, was revised at the eleventh hour, so late that some early photos of the 1956 model show the older discs. The new covers were more convincing, so much so that you had to take a very close look before you could be sure they weren't real. They were also good enough to remain unchanged in production through 1962, an almost unheard-of seven-year lifespan in Detroit, where the wheel disc is practically the first thing the stylist thinks of changing.

Improvements under the Corvette's skin made it a sports car that commanded far more respect from the true believers. Zora Arkus-Duntov's trials with his V-8-equipped 1955 prototype led to some significant chassis improvements. "The target," he wrote in *Auto Age,* "was to attain such handling characteristics that the driver of some ability could get really high performance safely. The main objects of suspension changes were: increase of high-speed stability, consistency in response to the steering wheel over a wide range of lateral accelerations and speeds, and improvement of power transmission on turns (that is, reduction of unloading of inside rear wheels)."

Several chassis changes were made to reach these ends. Shims between the front crossmember and the frame increased the caster angle to two degrees. Shimming also altered the angle of the central steering idler arm so that the roll oversteer geometry was taken out of the front suspension. In concert with this, the roll understeer at the rear was reduced by changing the rear spring hangers so the slope of the springs would be less precipitous.

With these adjustments, Duntov reported, "the car goes where it is pointed, and does so without hesitation. On turns taken hard, it does not plow or skid, but gets into a drift. If the right amount of power is fed, the drift can be maintained without danger of the rear end getting presumptuous and assuming the position of the front." The brakes themselves weren't changed, but were fitted with linings that were more resistant to fade and wear.

The kind of handling that Zora described wouldn't have been possible without the extensive changes that took place under the hood of the 1956 Corvette. Weight distribution was improved to 52/48 front/rear, thanks in part to the installation of the new V-8

V-8 powered '54 car was taped for tests at GM's Phoenix Proving Grounds, above and left. Duntov is at the wheel of finned, tonneau-covered prototype.

Duntov's snow-tired car, below, starts acceleration run on Daytona sand.

engine, which weighed 531 pounds minus accessories — forty-one pounds less than the Blue Flame six! Its 3¾ x 3 inch dimensions accounted for its 265-cubic-inch displacement. Cylinder head changes squeezed the thick end of the wedge-shaped chamber closer around the spark plug, increasing the compression ratio from 8.0 to 9.25 to one for 1956. Atop the heads were special finned Corvette rocker covers die-cast of aluminum.

New cast-iron exhaust manifolds with central outlets had larger-capacity internal passages, and tougher exhaust valves of 21-4N alloy steel were specified. Ignition at higher crank speeds was improved by the use of a twin-breaker distributor, and the steel shielding for the ignition wiring was much improved over the provisional 1955 arrangement. With the single Carter four-barrel carburetor and the "power pack" cast-iron inlet manifold, peak power was 210 bhp at 5,200 rpm. This rose to 225 bhp at the same speed with twin four-barrel Carters connected by a progressive linkage on an aluminum manifold. Torque with this version was 270 pound-feet at 3,000 rpm.

The new engine was a spectacular improvement. Even more significant to most sports car enthusiasts was the adoption of a three-speed manual transmission as standard equipment. And what a three-speed! It was driven by a ten-and-a-half-inch clutch with a dozen coil springs, instead of the diaphragm-spring type used earlier. Inside the standard passenger-car three-speed transmission housing were fitted a new clutch shaft gear, new

Tests at Phoenix paid off with Daytona record-breaking successes. Seen in February, 1956, left to right: Betty Skelton, Zora Duntov and John Fitch.

countershaft gears and a new second gear to give the remarkably close ratios of 1.31 in second and 2.2 to one in low gear. Zora Arkus-Duntov had in fact argued in favor of an even higher bottom gear, 1.83 to one, but had been overruled. The floor-mounted shifter was attached to the transmission case extension, and showed as early as 1956 the smooth, fast control for which Corvette gearboxes were to become world-famous.

Axle ratios were 3.55 to one as standard and 3.27 to one an option with the manual gearbox. Other ratios were readily available because the 1956 Corvette had a new rear axle, more closely related to that of the latest passenger car, with better support for the pinion shaft and differential. This rounded out the improved specification of a transformed sports car, on which such additional new options were available as a fresh-air heater and dealer-installed seat belts. And unlike its predecessors, the 1956 model was available in Onyx Black, Venetian Red, Cascade Green, Aztec Copper and Arctic Blue as well as Polo White. Progress had been made in every possible direction.

Progress isn't achieved overnight, and the overhaul of the Corvette, making a late start from the blocks, was also tardy at the tape. It didn't bow publicly in stock production form until the Motorama at the Waldorf in January, 1956. On its turntable there it was a handsome machine, a decorative two-tone plastic sculpture, but without credentials. That changed suddenly with news from Daytona Beach of an astonishing record run, news

Bring on the hay bales!*

The new Corvette, piloted by Betty Skelton, has established a new record for American sports cars at Daytona Beach.

But that's only the start.

Corvette owners may enter other big racing tests in the months ahead — tests that may carry America's blue-and-white colors into several of the most important European competitions. We won't venture even a modest prediction of results, but for the first time in all too long, an entry designed by an American mass producer really qualifies for the hay-bale-lined road.

There's a lot of satisfaction to be had in owning a car that travels in such fast company and still offers Corvette's style, comfort and ease of maintenance. Your Chevy dealer should have one soon. See it! . . . Chevrolet Division of General Motors, Detroit 2, Michigan.

*From feature article on Corvette — *Sports Illustrated*, pg. 18, Jan. 16, '56.

NEW FEATURES

Convertible fabric top. Plastic hardtop or power-operated fabric top at extra cost. Roll-up windows.

210-h.p. V8 engine with 4-jet carburetor. 225-h.p. V8 engine with dual 4-jet carburetion, extra cost. Three-speed close-ratio "stick" shift or Powerglide automatic transmission at extra cost.

. . . And many other power, styling and convenience improvements.

CORVETTE

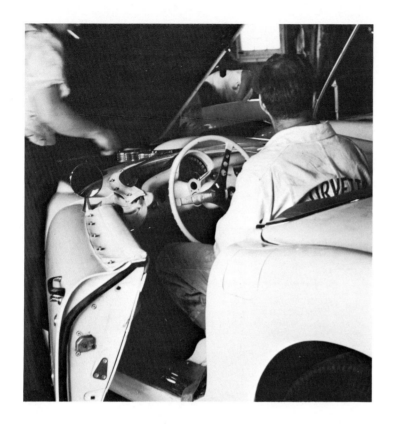

that, as Zora Duntov said, "got the word about the new Corvette to sports-car people. We told them, 'Look, now it is not a dog.'"

Ed Cole had been proud of the added performance he'd engineered into the 1956 Chevrolet V-8, and he wanted the world to know that the staid, stock Chevy sedan was no longer a dog either. He found an ally in Zora Duntov, who drove a disguised version of the new 1956 model to the top of Pikes Peak in the record time of seventeen minutes, 24.05 seconds on September 9, 1955. Duntov realized that he needed a similar dramatic achievement to let people know about the Corvette's new personality, and hit on the idea of a high-speed record run. One hundred and fifty miles per hour, he figured, should be within the new car's reach. In the happy afterglow of the fast run up the Peak's twelve and a half miles, Cole gave the green light to Duntov's scheme.

Zora used a veteran V-8-engined 1954-bodied prototype car for tests on the gently-banked circular track at GM's Phoenix Proving Grounds to find out what he'd have to do to be reasonably sure of being able to top 150 at Daytona Beach, where national attention was focused on high speed in those days. Fitting a small windscreen and a finned headrest, Duntov ran checks on the amount he'd be able to block off the grill opening to reduce drag while still retaining enough cooling to survive the standing mile and flying mile runs. He also calculated that he needed about thirty horsepower more than the V-8 was then delivering.

Drawing on his considerable experience with pushrod-and-

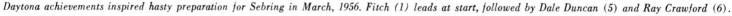

Daytona achievements inspired hasty preparation for Sebring in March, 1956. Fitch (1) leads at start, followed by Dale Duncan (5) and Ray Crawford (6).

rocker valve gear, acquired with racing engines from the Talbot-Lago to the Ardun, Duntov proposed a new camshaft design that he felt would give him the power increase he needed. Though it had less lift than the then-current factory high-performance cam, it stressed high positive acceleration and low negative acceleration to suit the characteristics of the valve gear and to provide a fuller valve opening curve. The comparison with other Chevrolet mechanical-lifter cams for the V-8 was as follows:

		Duntov Mark I	1955 Power Pack	1955 Standard
Inlet opens	BTDC	35°	22°	12°
Inlet closes	ABDC	72°	63°	54°
Exhaust opens	BBDC	76°	66°	52°
Exhaust closes	ATDC	31°	24°	20°
Inlet lift		0.393 in.	0.404 in	0.336 in.
Exhaust lift		0.399 in.	0.413 in.	0.343 in.

Arkus-Duntov's camshaft idea was not orthodox and some time elapsed before he was able to get it approved and get a sample cam to Phoenix for testing in his "mule" Corvette. When he finally got it, he found that it had the desired characteristics. The engine ran easily to 6500 rpm without valve bounce and produced enough power for the Corvette to reach 163 mph at 6,300 rpm at

ing ninth-place finish in '56 by Walt Hansgen (at wheel below) and John Fitch in number 1 provided ammunition for a classic automotive advertisement.

Phoenix with 3.27 to one rear axle gears. This, Zora felt, should be good enough for Daytona.

The "mule" with the early body metamorphosed into the first Chevrolet Engineering prototype of the 1956 model, with the latest front and rear fiberglass panels, but retaining the small screen and plastic tonneau cover used in the Phoenix tests. The Chevy entourage came to Daytona Beach late in December to run for a record speed under the watchful eye of NASCAR, which had also timed the Pikes Peak climb. This time there was waiting, the numbing nemesis of all record attempts, for the sand, water, and wind to be right.

"The sand must be a little wet," Zora said, "hard-packed, with no tongs of tidewater reaching in, for once you start you cannot deviate." The stay stretched into January before there was an acceptable combination of wind and sand. Zora climbed into the Corvette, with its side-bolstered driver's seat and dash cluttered with extra test dials, and set off down the beach. The breeze had quieted but the sand was only fair, allowing the wheels to slip as much as five percent. Yet Duntov clocked a two-way average speed of 150.583 mph — an impressive accomplishment for a stock-bodied sports car. It was far less exotically streamlined and tuned than the "stock" XK120 Jaguar that had been timed in Belgium at 172.412 mph two years earlier.

The Duntov cam, as it came to be known, was technically an option in 1956, enough so to qualify it for production-car competition, but it wasn't fitted that year to the normal catalogued Corvette engines. Dynamometer tests showed that it gave about 240 bhp at 5,800 rpm, with a very fat power curve from 5,000 to 6,000 rpm. Maximum torque was 265 pound-feet at 4,400 rpm. For the official NASCAR Speed Weeks runs at Daytona in February, 1956, the engine in the record-breaking prototype was fitted with experimental heads with a 10.3 to one compression ratio, for it was to run in a modified production sports car class. Its output was increased thereby to about 255 bhp.

Just as Chevy and Ford sedans had begun to race each other semi-officially on the nation's stock car tracks in 1955, so the sports cars of the two firms met face-to-face for the first time on the sands of Daytona in mid-February. All three of the official Corvette entries were white with paired blue racing stripes down their centerline, following a style for use of the American racing colors that had been popularized by Briggs Cunningham. Their fender cove areas were also painted blue.

Duntov himself handled the "modified" car, which had cone-shaped fairings for the headlights and a finned fairing for Zora's helmeted head. It lacked, as it always had, the pseudo-scoops at

Hard-hitting ads for Corvette successes helped bring about AMA racing ban.

ix Goldman raced in Haven Hill Climb (Michigan) in '56 in former Sebring team car.

Stock '56 Corvette was capable racer, as in Vermont's Mount Equinox Hill Climb.

Corvette raced north of the border in 1956 at Harewood Acres in Ontario, Canada.

the corners of the cowl. The two other roadsters looked standard apart from their tonneau covers and aero screens. One was driven by John Fitch, then considered America's best road-racing driver after a season with the all-conquering Mercedes-Benz factory team, and the other was assigned to Betty Skelton, justly famous for her exploits in the air as well as on the racetrack.

Detroit's first all-out assault on the Speed Weeks left Daytona and the NASCAR officials groggy. Rules were bent, stretched, warped, and shattered by racers eager to make corporate history. Among the "accidents" reported by *Motor Trend*'s Don MacDonald were "the engine block found in the trunk of John Fitch's Corvette prior to the acceleration run and possibly (but we do not say positively) the penchant of Chevrolet fanbelts to slip their moorings at speed." Don added that "the cars that eventually won were legitimate enough."

Getting good traction on the sand with snow tires, the Corvettes still weren't quick enough to match Chuck Daigh's Thunderbird in the standing-mile acceleration contests. Fitch placed third with an average of 86.872 mph against Daigh's winning 88.779 mph, another T-Bird finishing second. Duntov's was the fastest modified sports car at an 89.753 mph standing-mile average — the fastest official acceleration run of the week. Daigh's T-Bird didn't fly in the top-speed runs on February 22, which saw the Fitch Corvette the fastest production sports car at 145.543 mph. Betty Skelton was next fastest at 137.773 mph. Both were troubled by a strong wind, which also kept Duntov from equaling his previous mark with the modified car. He clocked 147.300 mph, being prevented by the tach redline from going any faster than 156 mph on his downwind leg. Only a Grand Prix Ferrari went faster, by less than one mile per hour, during the official Speed Weeks.

Speed runs, even competitive ones, were one thing. Road racing the Corvette would present quite a different challenge. Trying it was not a new idea. In 1954, in the Andrews Field races at Washington, D.C., Bob Rosenthal brought along a Corvette for Dr. Richard Thompson to evaluate during practice. Thompson, who had graduated from Porsches, was then a leading driver of production Jaguars in SCCA events.

"The Corvette was a six-cylinder Powerglide model with standard passenger car brakes and seat belts," Thompson found. "But, surprisingly, when I drove it in practice the times were comparable to our Jaguar. Then the brakes heated and faded out. But I kept punishing the Corvette and by the end of the day I had blown the rear seal out of the transmission as well. Regardless of the damage I had inflicted on the car, I was im-

Special one-off car for Sweden's Prince Bertil (photographed March 26, 1956) had Dayton wire wheels, quick-fill fuel cap and special European headlights

pressed with its possibilities. The potential was there."

In 1955 a Norwalk, Connecticut, Chevrolet dealer, Addison Austin, decided to explore that potential, newly enhanced with the optional V-8 engine. He bought such a car with the Powerglide transmission in mid-1955 and raced it with very little preparation, leaving the windshield in place and even using the stock brake linings at first. Thus equipped Austin's car was tenth overall and seventh in his class, against Jaguars and Mercedes-Benz 300SL's, in a major production car race at Watkins Glen in September. With Raybestos heavy-duty linings the car did much better at the end of the season at Thompson and Hagerstown, getting a third and first in class and beating some highly respected names among imported sports cars. Thunderbirds had been no competition at all.

While the Corvette crew was in Florida to set the 150 mph record, they'd taken a side trip to Sebring to see how the famous airport circuit there would suit the Chevy sports car. In a few test laps the Corvette, stripped for lightness and softly sprung, showed it could turn impressively quick times. This information went back into the Division's decision-making apparatus, and out came the conclusion that a full team of four Corvettes should be entered in the twelve-hour race at Sebring, to be held on March 24.

Actual preparation of cars for the race didn't begin until February 18. John Fitch was hired to boss the effort, from the readiness of the cars to the hiring of drivers and the running of

the team, which was nominally entered by Dick Doane's Raceway Enterprises of Dundee, Illinois, but which in fact was a full Chevrolet factory effort. To begin with, however, all Fitch had was the prototype with the old body that Duntov had used for his speed tests at Phoenix. "It was quite some time," recalled Fitch, "before we could finish a full lap of the course before breaking something!"

Working out of a shed on the Sebring airport, Fitch and his crew of Chevy mechanics worked literally night and day on the "mule," and then on the four actual race cars, to set them up so they would — hopefully — go fast for half a day. Major changes had to be conceived, built, tested, verified, and then catalogued by Chevrolet Engineering and Sales so the cars could qualify as production vehicles, not only for Sebring but also for other events the Corvettes might enter in 1956. This was a colossal job, with men like Fitch, Walter Mackenzie, and former Indy racer Mauri Rose at the Florida end and Chevy engineers like Andy Rosenberger, Russ Sanders, and Zora Arkus-Duntov in Michigan — except when they were running at Daytona Beach.

Engines for three of the four cars were twin-carb Duntov-cammed units, as already described. Cylinder heads supplied with the twin-carburetor manifold had porting larger by about twenty percent than that of the standard head, and the piston crowns had clearance cut-outs for valve heads, giving a greater margin for error in engine speed; up to 7,000 rpm was possible. The engine of

Another special car built by GM Styling in the summer of '56 was for GM president Harlow Curtice, a more subtle version of the racing SR-2 Corvette.

one car was enlarged to 307 cubic inches to bring it over five liters, to take it into Class B where there was little competition, by boring and stroking to dimensions of 3.81 x 3.30 inches. Since it was running as a modified car, this one had valves one-sixteenth inch larger, the 10.2 to one compression ratio, a straight-through exhaust, and a four-speed German ZF transmission.

All the cars had thirty-seven-gallon fuel tanks, Hi-Tork limited-slip differentials, Houdaille dampers at the rear, Halibrand magnesium wheels and knock-off hubs, and Firestone Super Sport 170 tires. Brakes were, of course, a big problem, as they were for all cars at Sebring. At least four different systems were tried, including Halibrand disc brakes and huge Al-Fin drums. The only combination that proved it could stay the distance was that of Bendix Cerametallix linings inside heavily finned iron drums, liberally supplied with cooling air through screened scoops. These brakes worked, and they continued to serve the Corvette well at Sebring in later years. But they were heavy, and they forced the Corvette to become heavier too. Looking back, Zora Arkus-Duntov feels their adoption during this period was a watershed decision that took the Corvette irrevocably in the direction of a larger, heavier car, barring any possible return to a lightweight design concept.

Preparation for Sebring imposed almost impossible demands. None of the drivers, not even chief tester Fitch, had any practice time to speak of in the actual cars they were to race. A Lam-

bretta scooter served to give them hundreds of laps of the track so they could memorize which way it went. Finding that the cars would run perfectly in the warm sun and poorly in the cool evening, or vice versa, but not well simultaneously with the same carburetor settings, John Fitch contacted the responsible GM expert, who responded that he was entirely familiar with the problem and could do absolutely nothing about it. He even came to Sebring to prove that he couldn't.

Chevrolet's race performance, Fitch admitted, "was less than we had hoped but more than we deserved." Two cars failed in the early going. Fitch and Walt Hansgen had a slipping clutch from the second lap in the modified car and nursed it through to a ninth-place finish, while Ray Crawford and Max Goldman had top gear only in the production model they brought home fifteenth. A stove-stock private entry placed twenty-third and next to last of the finishers. But this was the first time they'd tried, and the crowd at Sebring cheered the Corvettes that had dared to race and had finished the twelve-hour marathon.

Sebring gave Arthur B. "Barney" Clark of Campbell-Ewald, Chevrolet's advertising agency, the ammunition to create the first classic Corvette ad. Its copy was not so remarkable, though it did call the Corvette "a tough, road-gripping torpedo-on-wheels with the stamina to last through the brutal 12 hours of Sebring." What seized your attention was a front view of the grille-less modified car in the pits, in full race trim, stripped and dirty, with a simple headline in the sky: THE REAL MCCOY. That's what the Corvette had become. Without Sebring it would not have been possible to say it so forcefully and believably.

Within Chevrolet there was active discussion of a massive Le Mans campaign that year. One Chevy ad headed "Bring on the hay bales!" even said that "Corvette owners . . . may carry America's blue-and-white colors into several of the most important European competitions." Not until 1960 did this finally come to pass. Meanwhile, the know-how gained at Sebring was put to work to win the Sports Car Club of America's 1956 Championship for Class C Production cars. The driver: Dr. Richard Thompson.

Dick first raced the GM-prepared car, a hardtop, at Pebble Beach, California, in April of 1956. It was another red-letter day for the Corvette. The car led the production car event until brake problems let one 300SL past before the finish; the Corvette still won its class. Dick Thompson took that car east, running and doing well in Texas and Maryland, piling up SCCA points. Nursemaiding the machine was Frank Burrell, a veteran hot-rodder and racer as well as a Chevy engineer who, Thompson said, "observed every race and compiled a stack of technical notes a foot thick." The Corvette belonged to Thompson, who recalled, "After every race General Motors would put it on a test course and run it to destruction. Then they would rebuild it for me for the next race."

Meanwhile a second car was being prepared in California. After the Pebble Beach event, W.G. "Racer" Brown and Bob D'Olivo confronted Zora Duntov with the information that they could prepare a Corvette that would run much better than the one they'd seen there. Not long afterward they had a call from the local Chevrolet zone sales office asking, in effect, "Where do you want your 'Vette?" Bill Pollack drove the car in California Sports Car Club events, in which they were allowed to use a limited-slip differential, and Dick Thompson handled it in late-1956 West Coast SCCA races. In these they were frequently protested for the supposed use of a limited-slip unit, because the car came out of corners so convincingly, but none was ever found. The protesters were looking in the wrong place. To suit some tracks, such as Seattle's Seafair, where Thompson trounced Paul O'Shea's 300SL for the first time, the car sometimes used an illegally high low gear.

Except for such confidential matters, Racer Brown described in detail the preparation of this car in *Hot Rod* of October, 1956. He had a special word of praise for the fiberglass body: "In the course of a couple of races, our Corvette wiped out the entire side of an Austin-Healey, demolished a 300SL rear fender and scattered a few hay bales. The damage amounted to three small, easily-repaired cracks in the body, some chipped paint and some bent side trim."

The standard manual-gearbox 1956 Corvette staggered road

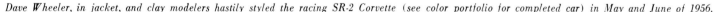

Dave Wheeler, in jacket, and clay modelers hastily styled the racing SR-2 Corvette (see color portfolio for completed car) in May and June of 1956.

testers with its acceleration, and the race-prepared cars, with the Duntov camshaft, were even more vivid performers. This will give an indication of their relative capabilities:

1956 Corvette Acceleration Tabulation			
	Standard 2x4bbl carburetion	SCCA Preparation	Sebring Preparation
Final drive ratio	3.27:1	4.10:1	3.55:1
0-60 mph	7.5 sec	6.3 sec.	6.3 sec.
0-80 mph	12.5 sec	11.2 sec.	9.6 sec.
0-100 mph	19.3 sec.	———	15.1 sec.
Standing ¼ mile	15.9 sec.	15.0 sec.	14.9 sec.
Terminal ¼ mile speed	91 mph	94 mph	99 mph
Maximum speed	120 mph	130 mph	148 mph

The very much improved 1956 Corvette scored points with the road testers and road drivers as well as the road racers. Its moderate price structure was certainly beneficial. The FOB factory base figure was $3,120. At $107.60 the power-operated top was a fascinating folly, carrying out its whole operation, including raising and lowering the solid tonneau cover, automatically. Other factory options were the twin-carb kit ($172.20), the Duntov camshaft kit ($188.30), the hardtop ($215.20) and Powerglide ($188.50).

With the 1956 Corvette at its disposal, and glorying in its fine new Technical Center facilities, GM Styling built some fresh variations on this basic theme. A hardtop was built for Prince Bertil of Sweden with wire wheels, a toothless grille, exhaust outlets in the sides of the rear fenders, and two chrome bars down the rear deck, flanking a quick-fill gas cap and foreshadowing the looks of the 1958 Corvette — which was then being styled.

For Jerry Earl, Harley's son, a special racing SR-2 model was styled atop a Sebring competition chassis. It had a low fin on the rear deck, air scoops in the side coves, twin rounded windscreens, larger front lamps under the headlights, and a grille section and nose extended substantially farther forward — all this making the car look a lot more aggressive. The fin, side scoops, extended nose, and special lights were also incorporated in a street Corvette, with handsome chromed Dayton wire wheels. This was for the use of the GM president, Harlow Curtice, and was finished in the special metallic blue used for all his family cars.

Nineteen fifty-six had brought the Corvette a long step forward. From a car that was rejected by V.I.P.'s it had been transformed into a prize package fit for princes and presidents. This was progress indeed. But it was nothing compared to what Ed Cole had in store for 1957.

 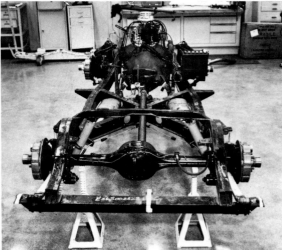

Chassis of SR-2 for Jerry Earl was built in Styling's mechanical assembly shop using Cerametallic brakes, other components developed for Sebring cars.

1956 | RACING SR-2 | *drawing by Yoshihiro Inomoto*

Chapter 5

FUEL INJECTION

In July, 1956, Edward N. Cole became a vice-president of General Motors and the general manager of its Chevrolet Division. At this late date he was already deeply involved in the introduction plans for the 1957 model, the press previews, dealer meetings and final conferences on advertising strategy. This would be the first new Chevrolet that he could call all his own, that would kick off his career as the man in charge of GM's largest division.

For Cole the 1957 Chevrolet was just not new enough. The stylists had done a major facelift with finned rear fenders and an extra-wide grille, but the basic body still dated from 1955. Against it, Ford and Plymouth were stacking all-new body designs. A new engine option was to be offered, using the three-and-seven-eighths-inch bore of the 1956 Sebring modified Corvette to bring the displacement to 283 cubic inches, but this alone wasn't likely to make engineering history. For his 1957 Chevys, and especially for the Corvette, Ed Cole wanted fuel injection. The industry had been talking about it and experimenting with it for years. GM had its own system, but in the spring and summer of 1956 it wasn't yet cleared for production. Ed Cole wanted it cleared and he wanted it for Chevrolet.

Since the early 1950's GM's Engineering Staff had been working on different types of injection systems — devices that pump carefully metered amounts of fuel directly to each cylinder of an engine instead of relying on the vagaries of carburetors and twisting manifold passages to do a precise and consistent job. In the Engineering Staff's power development section the research on injection was conducted by John Dolza. Telling the SAE about the GM system in 1957, Dolza cited some of the familiar problems of conventional carburetion, and added, "A fuel system capable of correcting even 50 percent of the average carburetor deficiencies may produce a 10 percent improvement in fuel economy that would ultimately result in substantial savings to the customer. The possibility of an exhaust free from hydrocarbons and a fuel system free from evaporation would greatly help in an important phase of reducing air pollution."

Dolza's work, spurred by the Daimler-Benz announcement of fuel injection on the production 300SL in 1954, was conducted at first on a single-cylinder test engine with an 8.0 to one compression ratio. This showed that the lowest fuel consumption rates were obtained with constant-flow injection into the inlet ports, spraying downstream, with only slightly less peak torque than timed injection. This led Dolza to focus on constant-flow systems from the outset. Then he had to decide what method to use to tell the injection nozzles how much fuel to deliver at any given time.

Among the talented men working with Dolza to solve these problems was an engineer on loan from Chevrolet: Zora Arkus-Duntov. Zora recalls: "Ed Cole, when he was chief engineer, called me one day and said, 'Listen, if I didn't have my job to do, I'd give my right arm to be working on fuel injection.' And I think that he was being truthful." By early 1955 injection was Zora's chief assignment. His drives at Pikes Peak and Daytona were extracurricular adventures. The 150 mph run at Daytona, in fact, had only marginal approval and became possible because Zora was able to charge some of its costs to his fuel-injection development budget, which was such a top-secret affair that no official accounting of its use was required.

Following the examples of successful aircraft injection systems, Dolza had been working on fuel-metering controls that were sensitive to the speed of the engine and the density of the air that was being inhaled by it, comparing these to decide how much fuel to deliver. It worked well enough but promised to be expensive. In a discussion one day, Duntov suggested that measuring directly the mass of air entering the engine might achieve their ends more easily. He mentioned a Holley carburetor used by Ford that provided full vacuum control of the distributor advance, from several pressure taps in the venturi and above the throttle plate.

"John Dolza is a splendid man," Duntov recalls with ad-

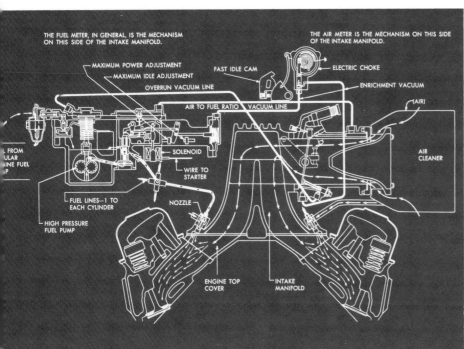

THE FUEL METER, IN GENERAL, IS THE MECHANISM ON THIS SIDE OF THE INTAKE MANIFOLD.

THE AIR METER IS THE MECHANISM ON THIS SIDE OF THE INTAKE MANIFOLD.

MAXIMUM POWER ADJUSTMENT

MAXIMUM IDLE ADJUSTMENT

OVERRUN VACUUM LINE

FAST IDLE CAM

ELECTRIC CHOKE

ENRICHMENT VACUUM

AIR TO FUEL RATIO VACUUM LINE

(AIR)

AIR CLEANER

L FROM ULAR GINE FUEL P

SOLENOID

WIRE TO STARTER

FUEL LINES—1 TO EACH CYLINDER

NOZZLE

HIGH PRESSURE FUEL PUMP

ENGINE TOP COVER

INTAKE MANIFOLD

Production Rochester-Chevrolet 1957 fuel injection, above, developed from "sturdy dog" manifold, left below and lower center, to final design at right.

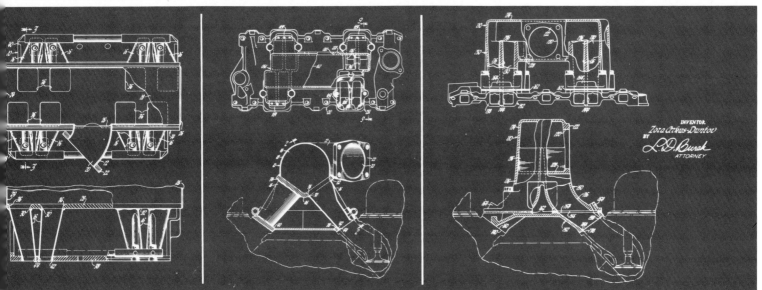

INVENTOR
Zora Arkus-Duntov
BY
L. D. Burch
ATTORNEY

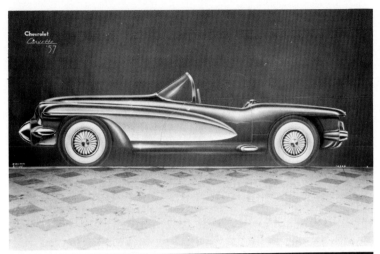

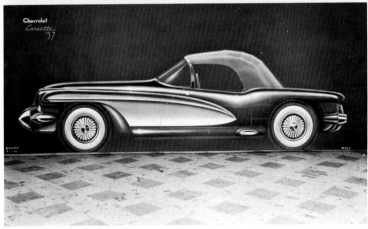

Styling ideas explored early in 1955 included Buick proposal, center.

miration, "brilliant and clear-thinking. I can spare no words to say how powerful this man is intellectually." In a matter of days Dolza came up with a totally new metering system based on a venturi through which all the incoming engine air passes, with taps that send vacuum readings to the fuel-metering unit. At first a conventional venturi was used, but this was later replaced by a radial-entry annular venturi, during development by GM's Rochester Carburetor Division, and this turned out to be simpler to make and more compact.

The first tests on complete Chevrolet engines in 1955 used normal intake manifolds fitted with injection nozzles and the inlet venturi in place of a carburetor. This allowed direct comparison with the carbureted version, and such comparisons in dynamometer tests showed there was virtually no difference between the two in power output. Though such avenues as ram-tuned intakes and higher compression ratios hadn't yet been explored, this was hardly an auspicious beginning for Chevrolet, which was planning to exploit injection to extract maximum power from its V-8 engine.

But the Dolza system had a surprise up its sleeve. Tests of injection versus carburetion were run in a 1956 Chevy, keeping all other factors as identical as possible. The injected version accelerated to speeds of sixty miles an hour and above nine percent faster than the carbureted example! "The spectacular increase in vehicle performance with otherwise identical dynamometer power," reported Duntov, "can be attributed to the ability of fuel injection to maintain the best power mixture throughout the transition. The difference in performance indicated that fuel injection brought out the work potential in an engine which otherwise existed in the test graphs only. We valued this quality since it meant more work per engine pound and dollar."

Similar results were given by an improved injection system feeding a two-carburetor manifold: similar dynamometer output but "startlingly superior" acceleration for the injection in a car. Then work began to find out what size and length of ram pipe to each cylinder would give the best results on the new larger 1957 Corvette engine with the Duntov camshaft. With this established, the ram pipes were united by a fore-and-aft plenum chamber that was fed by the metering venturi.

The first such complete injection manifold was fabricated of sheet steel, with a barrel-shaped body and tapering "legs" to the inlet ports that won it the nickname of "sturdy dog" for its pugnacious stance atop the engine. An intermediate cast aluminum manifold was made in some numbers for the first extensive vehicle tests. This was a one-piece manifold that, like the normal carburetor-fed part, also served as the V-8 valley cover. This was also a function of the final injection manifold design which, however, was made in two levels, an upper and a lower section, to slow the transmission of heat to the injection nozzles and to make the engines easier to manufacture and install. The manifold's original nickname was echoed by the one generally given the finned production design: the "doghouse."

Chevy's chances of seeing injection in its 1957 production cars received a radical setback in April, 1956, when Zora Arkus-Duntov was seriously injured in a Proving Grounds accident. Through May and early June the white-haired engineer was laid up with nothing less than a broken back. That summer Ed Cole urged Zora, back brace and all, to come to Colorado again to help them get another Pikes Peak record. Cole knew the injection wasn't perfect, especially in its refinement and low-speed behavior, but he was willing to accept it as it was for the Corvette because he needed its newness.

Harry Barr, Cole's successor as Chevrolet chief engineer, was less satisfied with the injection's development status. It wasn't yet approved for production, and the nominal date for the manufac-

ture of Job One was only days away. "If you're well enough to think of going to Colorado," Barr said to Zora, "then at least come and work on the fuel injection, maybe one hour a day, or something, because it's standing still!" So Duntov went to work again: "I wore a skirt, because I could not bend! No trousers, nothing. A skirt, and nothing under it!" Corvette buyers might have wondered why the Ramjet fuel injection was a little late to the market in 1957. If they'd seen the emigré engineer at work that summer they'd have been less surprised in that direction and more so in quite another!

Approval for production of the injection came not at the eleventh hour but the twelfth, with the first units being built under virtual laboratory conditions at Rochester. The Ramjet system was offered across the board on V-8-powered Chevrolets; it was an important element in the Division's plan to keep winning in the short-track stock car races. On the hydraulic-lifter Corvette engine with a 9.5 to one compression ratio the injection produced 250 bhp at 5,000 rpm and 305 pound-feet of torque at 3,800 rpm. With the Duntov cam and 10.5 to one compression ratio the injected gross output was 283 bhp at 6,200 and 290

Unchanged in appearance, the 1957 production model offered outstanding performance with fuel injection and four-speed gearbox, both new to the Corvette.

TOWARD AN AMERICAN CLASSIC . . . THE 1957 CORVETTE
WITH FUEL INJECTION!

It is with considerable pride that Chevrolet invites you to examine an engineering advance of great significance, available on the 1957 Corvette. It is fuel injection, and in the Corvette V8 it permits a level of efficiency hitherto unrealized in any American production car: *one horsepower for every cubic inch of displacement . . . 283 h.p.!* In addition, there is unprecedented responsiveness, even during warm-up; virtually instantaneous acceleration and significant gains in overall gas economy.

This is another major step in the creation of a proud new kind of car for America: *a genuine* sports car, as certified by its record in competition. But *a unique* sports car in its combination of moderate price, luxurious equipment and low-cost maintenance with fiery performance, polo-pony responsiveness and granite stability on curves.

It is our intention to make of the Corvette a classic car, one of those rare and happy milestones in the history of automotive design. We take pleasure in inviting you to drive the 1957 version—and see just how close we have come to the target. . . . *Chevrolet Division of General Motors, Detroit 2, Michigan.*

SPECIFICATIONS: 283-cubic-inch V8 engine with single four-barrel carburetor, 220 h.p. (four other engines* range to 283 h.p. with fuel injection). Close-ratio three-speed manual transmission standard, with special Powerglide automatic drive* available on all but maximum-performance engines. Choice of removable hard top or power-operated fabric top, Power-Lift windows.* Instruments include 6000 r.p.m. tachometer, oil pressure gauge and ammeter. *Optional at extra cost.*

CORVETTE *by Chevrolet*

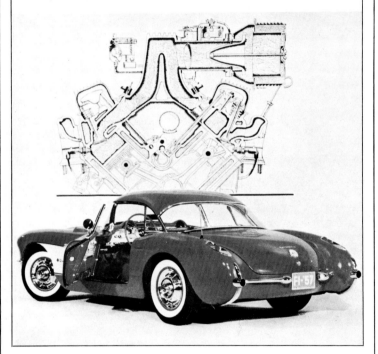

"It is our intention to make of the Corvette a classic car," said Chevy in 1957, and in fact it did just that.

Red SR-2 Corvette for Bill Mitchell was originally built in fall of 1956.

pound-feet at 4,400 — high enough for Chevrolet to say that "the senior engine in the Corvette line has attained a milestone in American automotive history — one horsepower for every cubic inch." Eyebrows rose at this and also at the price tag on the injection: $481. Only 240 of the 6,339 1957-model Corvettes made were injected.

Another last-minute surprise for the opposition was a four-speed fully-synchronized manual transmission for the Corvette. Though it was built for Chevrolet by Borg-Warner, the four-speed T-10 gearbox was a creation of Chevy engineers. They started with a rugged three-speed box, the Borg-Warner T-85, and by moving the reverse gear set into the otherwise unused tailshaft housing they made room for four speeds forward inside the main cast-iron casing. Control levers protruding from the left-side cover were linked to the shifter, which was mounted at the end of the tailshaft housing as it was on the Corvette three-speed box. And the ratios were the same as those of the three-speed except for the addition of another ratio of 1.66 to one between the former first (2.20) and second (1.31) gears. This became a $188 option, generally available after May 1, 1957.

Bill Mitchell's long-nosed, high-finned SR-2 was used on the road and in motor shows as well as in competition at Daytona, Sebring, and Road America.

As the first experimental examples of these new goodies became available they were built into two Corvettes in November, 1956. Now preparations for the new racing season were beginning well in advance as Chevrolet gained momentum under Cole's direction. Acting as liaison between Engineering and field operations in this sphere was Walter Mackenzie — Chevy's racing manager without the official title. John Fitch was still an active participant on the sports car side, as were Fred Warner, Red Byron, Jim Rathmann, and Dick Doane.

The two 1957 racing prototypes were readied for testing, with many new design ideas incorporated. "We experimented with them at Sebring," Dick Thompson says, "and for the first time since I had started racing in 1953, I had my fill of driving. I would take one Corvette out and pound it until something gave way. Then I would trade it immediately for the other one. It was fatiguing but fascinating."

For a competition shakedown the cars were taken to the Bahamas for the Nassau Trophy Races starting on December 7. "The results, while hardly spectacular," admitted Thompson, "showed us that our problems were no longer of the major variety.

Now only the details needed working out. Our overheating problem was traced to bad head gaskets. The balance arm in the fuel-injection system was redesigned for greater strength, and we altered our piston design slightly. We were ready."

They learned a number of useful lessons in the preparation for racing of the already outstanding injected 283-cubic-inch engine. A cold-air intake was provided, from the grille to the fuel-injection air inlet. Stainless-steel high-tension ignition wires were used. The generator was mounted on the right side instead of the left of the engine, to give the tension side of the fan belt a firmer grip on the water-pump pulley. And a mechanically-driven 8,000 rpm AC tachometer was mounted on the steering column, where· it couldn't be overlooked.

Also spawned in the pre-season tests was RPO 684, a $725 package of chassis options that no would-be Corvette racer could afford to overlook. It included the following items:

1. Heavier front springs, with a rate of 340 instead of 300 pounds/inch, increasing the wheel rate from 105 to 119 pounds/inch.

2. Rear springs with five instead of four leaves, raising the

Corvette number 4 won GT class at Sebring in 1957, driven by Dick Thompson and Gaston Andrey. Ed Cole posed for pictures in the pits with the SR-2.

wheel rate from 115 to 125 pounds/inch.

3. Front anti-roll bar increased in diameter from eleven-sixteenths to thirteen-sixteenths inch.

4. Shock absorbers with firmer valving, enlarged in diameter from one to one and three-eighths inches.

5. A bolt-on adapter that extended the length of the central idler arm enough to reduce the overall ratio of the steering linkage from 21.0 to 16.3 to one, reducing the number of steering wheel turns from lock to lock to 2.9 from a former 3.7.

6. A clutch-type limited-slip differential, built by Spicer and dubbed Positraction by Chevrolet, with such extra-low axle ratios as 3.70, 4.11, and 4.56 to one.

7. Transversely finned cast-iron brake drums, and ventilated backing plates fitted with screens and large air scoops.

8. Brake linings composed of segments of Cerametalix, the ceramic-metallic compound originally developed by Bendix to stop heavy aircraft.

Considering that a Corvette thus equipped could be ordered right from the factory, virtually in race-ready condition, this was a remarkable plan. Also recommended were rims five and a half

inches wide, half an inch wider than standard, to take 7.10/7.60 x 15 six-ply racing tires. Corvettes built with these options — indeed even those in street trim with the full-house injected engine — were stunningly fast cars. Road tests during 1957 showed these results:

1957 Corvette Acceleration Tabulation			
	2 x 4 bbl. carburetion 3-speed	fuel-injected 3-speed	fuel-injected 4-speed
Nominal power	270 bhp	283 bhp	283 bhp
Final drive ratio	3.55:1	3.70:1	4.11:1
0-60 mph	6.8 secs.	6.6 secs.	5.7 secs.
0-80 mph	10.7 secs.	10.7 secs.	10.2 secs.
0-100 mph	17.6 secs.	18.2 secs.	16.8 secs.
Standing ¼ mile	15.0 secs.	14.2 secs.	14.3 secs.
Terminal ¼ mile	95 mph	93 mph	96 mph
Maximum speed	122 mph	125 mph	132 mph

Production Corvettes were first away from the Le Mans start of the 1957 Sebring 12-hour race, in which they finished an honorable 12th and 15th.

No longer was there any question as to whether the Corvette was faster than its American sister sedans, as many felt a sports car should be. It was in fact faster in acceleration than anything else that could be bought for use on the road. Said *Road & Track* flatly, "The data are unequalled by any other production sports car."

"The cold figures," commented *Sports Cars Illustrated*, "are pretty phenomenal. Injected and carb-fed Corvettes are closely comparable in performance, and both qualify as the fastest-accelerating genuine production cars SCI has ever tested. In fact, up to 80 they're not so far from the data posted by the Mercedes 300SLR coupe, which is generally regarded as the world's fastest road car. In low, the Corvettes zoomed up to 55 mph in a shade over five seconds, and in another nine they surged to 95 in second with very exciting verve."

The acceleration was also put to the test on the sands of Daytona Beach in February, 1957. Among production sports cars of three to five liters the Corvettes were dominant in the standing-start mile runs, Paul Goldsmith the quickest with a 91.301 mph average. Johnny Beauchamp and Betty Skelton placed second and third with averages of 89.798 and 87.400 mph. Skelton and Beauchamp reversed their order behind Goldsmith in the flying mile runs, Paul winning the class with an average of 131.941 mph.

The beach runs marked the debut of another special SR-2 Corvette built by GM Styling Staff, running in the modified class. Its extended nose and extra-light nacelles under the headlamps were like those of the first SR-2. A large finned headrest was added, striped in red and white like the rest of the car. For Daytona it was fitted with a Plexiglas enclosed canopy, pants for the rear wheels, and Moon discs for the front ones, fairing cones for the front lamps and Plexiglas covers for the sides of the grille.

Dynamometer tests of the injected engine for this car had yielded a peak of 310 bhp, not including the effects of the individual straight-pipe exhaust headers that were used on the car at Daytona Beach. But there wasn't enough time in Florida to allow optimum final tuning. In the hands of Buck Baker it went quickly nevertheless, winning its modified class in the standing mile with an average of 93.047 mph and covering the flying mile at 152.866 mph, second-best to a D-Type Jaguar.

Dale Duncan, John Kilborn, and Jim Jeffords drove number 3 to 15th at Sebring '57, after which Ed Cole joined GT winners Andrey (left) and Thompson

During the Speed Weeks, musician Paul "Pops" Whiteman organized a road race over a 2.4-mile course at nearby New Smyrna Beach airport, a "pro-am" event open to both paid and amateur drivers. Potent factory-backed Ford Thunderbirds were threatening strong opposition so the Corvette entries were strengthened by bringing over one of the cars that was then being tested at Sebring in preparation for the twelve-hour race. Though beaten by O'Shea's 300SL in the production race, Paul Goldsmith's Corvette qualified third fastest behind two Ferraris for the main event and had a magnificent battle for second with Marvin Panch's T-Bird in the race until Paul had to pit for a fresh tire. The former motorcycle racer placed fourth.

All this activity was prefatory to the main event, the 12 Hours of Sebring on March 23. This time Chevy was well prepared. A huge hangar housed its operation, which included five GT Corvettes. Two were practice cars; no Lambretta was needed for the drivers this year. One of the three race cars was the SR-2, less its Daytona Beach fairings, and the others were very trim production coupés. In spite of many interruptions by well-meaning Chevrolet engineers, competition veteran Red Byron managed to

have these cars in excellent shape for the race.

A promising experiment with one of the practice cars misfired but laid a foundation for the future: A strip-chart recorder was installed to trace the engine speed and manifold vacuum on the track, but it failed to work because the surface was too bumpy. Eventually Chevy engineers would become leaders in the use of on-board tape recorders and the telemetry of data from racing cars.

Olivier Gendebien's Ferrari Europa coupé was the only serious GT challenger to the Corvettes, and in fact had a three-lap lead after seven of the twelve hours. It retired, however, and the coupé driven by Dick Thompson and Gaston Andrey was the first GT car of any size to finish, in twelfth place, with a twenty-lap margin over the best-placed Mercedes-Benz 300SL. The other coupé was fifteenth, shared by Dale Duncan, John Kilborn and Jim Jeffords. Two laps behind it in sixteenth was the SR-2, plagued by excessive pit stops. It might have been showing its irritation at being driven by that arch-rival of the Corvettes, Paul O'Shea, paired with Pete Lovely.

The development work that achieved these results paid off in full with the confirmation of the Corvette — with injection and

After a frustrating twelve hours of pit stops, Pete Lovely took the checkered flag at Sebring in 1957 in 16th place in the massive SR-2 Corvette special.

Slightly modified '57 models at the 1969 NHRA Pomona Winternationals.

Don Yenko, above, and Bob Mouat in their '57's at Watkins Glen in 1963.

RPO 684 — as a bulletproof racing machine. Jim Jeffords and Fred Windridge were among those who started to campaign these satisfying cars in SCCA racing. Dick Thompson won the SCCA Class B Production championship with the Corvette in 1957, beginning an eight-year span during which that category was dominated by the fiberglass flyers. Early in the 1960's the 1957 models were still in Class B, and they were still being raced to championships by Corvette devotees like Don Yenko.

During 1957 sports car enthusiasts were beginning, at last, to warm to the Corvette, and though sales were not spectacular they were at least satisfactory. The Chevrolet sales department started publishing *Corvette News,* "a magazine for owners of Chevrolet Corvettes." The professionally produced quarterly became an invaluable conduit to and from owners, especially as clubs of Corvette drivers began to form. Through *Corvette News* they could contact each other and the division's first sales promotion man for Corvettes, Fred Warner. Chevrolet does not, as a rule, spend more time and effort to sell a car than that car strictly justifies, and the Corvette was no exception. In 1957 it began to deserve

Owners of these Corvettes turned to George Barris for instant identity.

Barris Kustom City's '57 Corvettes ranged from the racy to the rococo.

some attention and support, and it began to get it.

The stylists, of course, had always been Corvette-crazy. For auto show display and for the SCCA convention in Detroit in January, 1957, they built a special-trim version of the new car. It had a double-bubble windshield like that of the first SR-2, airscoops in its brushed aluminum fender coves, a glittering interior and a radically changed dash with the tachometer above the steering column and a prominent grab handle. These foreshadowed design ideas that were then already incorporated in a new production Corvette that the public had not yet seen. For there were future Corvettes in the works, and very exciting ones. No longer was there any doubt about the destiny of this car.

Edward N. Cole had wanted to make the Corvette a success, and now it was well on its way. The successes at Sebring, he felt, had made a big difference: "That was the turn of the tide. That was when the car started to attract attention in the areas where we had to have visibility. It began to take off and go, to confirm our original premise: that there was a demand for a product that recaptured the sport and fun of motoring."

Chapter 6

CORVETTE SS

One of the few men working in Detroit in the early 1950's who was able to speak with real authority on the subject of sports and racing cars was Zora Arkus-Duntov. He knew intimately what the European sports car was, how it was made, and by whom. The general attitude of the leaders of the American motor industry was and is that they know best how anything should be done; that nothing conceived anywhere else, and especially overseas, is any good.

Zora was able to see the situation differently. Unlike many, he knew that the Jaguars, Ferraris and Maseratis were conceived and built by very few people under conditions so difficult that American firms would deny that it could even be done. He knew also that the people who made those cars were experienced, clever, and determined. And the knew that they put their trousers on — just like Americans — one leg at a time.

In September, 1953, Zora addressed an SAE group in Lansing, Michigan. on the subject of sports cars. He showed how they'd developed over the years, what they were used for, why people bought them, and how those made in one country tended to differ in their characteristics from those built in another. He also stressed a point he considered very important: "All commercially successful sports cars were promoted by participation in racing with specialized or modified cars." Of such makes as M.G., Jaguar, Alfa Romeo, and Porsche this was undeniably true.

"Even if the vast majority of sports car buyers do not intend to race them," Arkus-Duntov continued, "and most likely will never drive flat out, the potential performance of the car, or the recognized and publicized performance of its sister — the racing sports car — is of primordial value to its owner. The owner of such a car can peacefully let everybody pass him, still feeling like the proud king of the road, his ego and pride of ownership being inflated by racing glory."

Zora was explaining what the K3 Magnette had done for the standard M.G., the 550 Spyder for the normal Porsche, the first racing 300SL for the street Mercedes-Benz, and the C-Type Jaguar for the production XK120. He continued to believe that this was the best approach for Chevrolet and the Corvette also. That's why Zora was not very much involved with the first spontaneous decision to race stock Corvettes at Sebring in 1956 and the follow-up effort in 1957. He recalls: "I was not the driving force in 'Let's Go Racing.' I was reluctantly pushed into it."

Duntov's philosophy was given added credibility by the 1956 Sebring event. Watching the race, it didn't take Ed Cole long to realize that no modified version of the stock Corvette would ever be able to challenge for the outright lead against the specialized sports-racing cars; Jaguar and Ferrari were the chief protagonists that year. He began to come around to the view that a special Corvette would be needed, one that bore the same pace-setting relationship to the stock Corvette as the Corvette itself did for the Chevrolet production models.

Many more weighty matters were on Ed Cole's mind, however, during that summer of his ascendancy to the general managership of Chevrolet. He could hardly have been expected to give high priority to the design and construction of a special racing car, a thing no major American car manufacturer had attempted since Studebaker built a team of five cars to race at Indianapolis in 1932. Cole had other problems, including startup troubles with production of a new truck line and the engineering of an all-new Chevrolet passenger car for 1958.

Once again Harley Earl entered the Corvette picture. Earl was a consummate strategist and tactician who knew how and when to use the Big Bluff to achieve his goals. When he felt GM was lagging in gas turbine research, for example, Earl conceived of the first Firebird, that delta-winged single-seater, and threatened to power it with a Boeing gas turbine. When it heard about this, the GM Research Laboratories turned to and built a suitable turbine for Earl's dramatic dream car.

Now, in the spring of 1956, Earl borrowed a D-Type Jaguar. It was one of the cars that had been built in a small series for sale, the property of Jack Ensley of Indianapolis, who had co-driven it

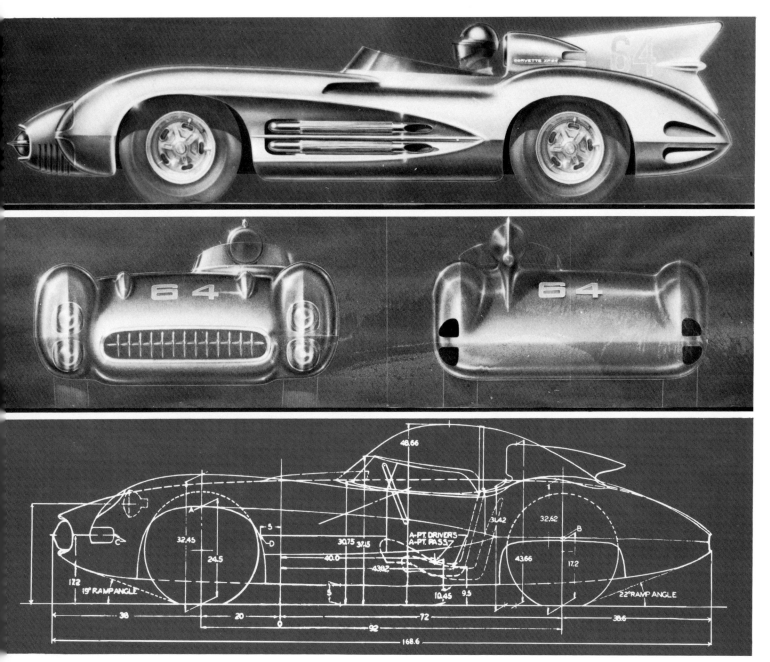

From full-size airbrush renderings of early August, 1956 (at top), design of XP-64 racing car was refined to precise specifications of the Corvette SS.

with Bob Sweikert, Indy winner in 1955, to third place at Sebring in 1956. Shortly after the twelve-hour race the engine had been destroyed by overrevving and the bright yellow D-Type arrived at Styling Staff minus engine, which was the way Earl wanted it. It was his idea that the car should be fitted with a Chevrolet engine, altered in its appearance, and raced at Sebring as an experimental Corvette.

First the D-Type went to Bob McLean's Research Studio, where both the engine and styling aspects of the conversion were studied, Then, in June, it was reassigned to Studio Z. One of the stylists there, Bob Cumberford, recalled: "We were supposed to figure out how to install a Corvette engine, convert the steering to left hand drive, and disguise the body so no one would ever guess that it was a Jaguar — all without changing the aerodynamic qualities!" The appropriate plans and sketches for this transformation were duly prepared.

It wasn't long before Chevrolet heard about this radical idea. Zora Arkus-Duntov was in New York on holiday when he received a call from Harry Barr, Chevy's new chief engineer: "Harley Earl wants to put one of our engines in a Jaguar and run

SS body shape approached final form in Chevy studio in September, 1956. Wool tufts helped evaluate air flow over a mockup body in wind tunnel tests.

it at Sebring. What do you think about it?" Zora expressed immediate reservations. After returning to Detroit he looked into it further, and found there were serious drawbacks to such an engine swap. Making the first sketches of a possible new chassis, he wrote a persuasive proposal recommending the design and construction of a special sports-racing Corvette. It was in due course accepted.

Was this exactly what Harley Earl had intended from the beginning? Would he in fact have persevered with the Corvette-Jaguar hybrid? His bluff was never called. The D-Type was eventually returned to Ensley, having fulfilled its apparent mission. It is not without historical irony that Ensley, in the course of the next two years, did install an injected Chevy V-8 in this D-Type. His mechanic, Joe Silnes, had anything but an easy time of it, justifying thereby the reservations of the GM men.

In July of 1956 a clay model of a sports car on a ninety-inch wheelbase was begun in the Chevrolet Studio at Styling, under the direction of Clare MacKichan. Its rounded contours, he recalls, were influenced by those of the D-Type, which was a much-admired car among the stylists. A first showing of the

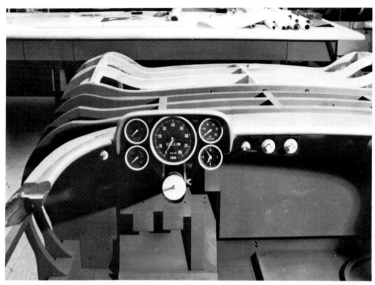

Chevy interior studio prepared buck for evaluation of gauges and seating.

Mockup of SS used for aerodynamic trials also served for comparison in December, 1956 of racing car design with slightly customized standard Corvette.

Engineers worked next to growing SS chassis mockup, left. Details of tubular space frame and de Dion rear suspension showed exceptional workmanship.

model and full-size renderings of the front, rear, and left side met with an enthusiastic reception from Ed Cole and the other members of top Chevy management who were given a look late in July. "There's your 1957 Sebring car," they were told, and they liked that idea very much.

Developed under Styling Staff's XP-64 designation, the original body design concept kept the standard car's front fender coves but filled them with two exhaust pipes/mufflers on each side. They reflected mirror-image symmetry about an horizontal plane, as did the shrouded headlights at the front and fender vents at the rear. A substantial fin trailed from a circular headrest. From this first version to the final one, the XP-64 kept a grille pattern that was much like that of the stock Corvette.

In mid-September the firm orders were written for the fabrication of the car, to the following precedent-setting requirement: "The XP-64 will be a competition racing car with special frame, suspension, engine, drivetrain, and body." The initial schedule called for one car to be ready for an auto show in New York in December, with three more to be finished "at some later date to permit testing prior to the Sebring race in March." These ambitious goals were slashed by a severe shortage of both time and manpower; the final approval was for one car, and *only* one car.

By October the styling development of the XP-64 was essentially final. The tailfin disappeared, while the teardrop-shaped headrest (concealing a strong rollover bar) remained. Rear wheel houses, which had been open from the beginning, were made very handsomely semi-enclosed. Conventional driving lights under the nose gave way to something new: cornering lamps flush with the front fender surfaces, operated by a lever in the dash at the left of the steering wheel. An engine air inlet was recessed below the main body surface, between two hood bulges that recalled those of the production 1956 Corvette. The Corvette SS — as it was formally dubbed — shaped up as an exceptionally good-looking racing car, spectacular by 1957 standards but none the worse for that, a machine of great individuality and character.

In a corner of the Chevrolet Engineering Center walled off by curtains and unpainted sheets of plywood, Zora Arkus-Duntov was working around the clock with a hand-picked crew toward the almost impossible goal of designing and building a raceworthy car for Sebring. They did it all right there, with desks and drawing tables next to mockups, trestles, and surface plates. Masterful fabrication work in the prototype shop followed their drawings, work done by men who might not have built a racing car before but were nevertheless among the most talented and versatile metal craftsmen in America.

Fuel tank was of GRP, left, deeply grooved to fit down over frame tubes. Special SS engine, center, had aluminum heads and elaborate magnesium oil pan.

Of course the SS had to be powered by the basic 283-cubic-inch Corvette V-8 engine, with its brand-new Rochester fuel injection. Instead of the stock cast injection doghouse, a special manifold had been built with straighter ram pipes that crossed each other to separate plenum chambers, each fed by its own air-metering venturi. This manifold was mated to the flush air inlet in the hood of the SS. When a mockup of this body was tested in the Harrison wind tunnel at the GM Technical Center on December 28, however, the pattern of wool tufts showed that the flow around the duct wasn't favorable. It might have been rectified, but there was literally no time for any kind of experimentation, so Duntov decided to use the normal injection manifold and give up the hood-top air inlet.

Instead of being attached directly to the aluminum doghouse, the injection-metering venturi faced forward and was connected to it by an elbow. Air was delivered to it by a duct from the grille, which added enough ram effect to produce an additional ten brake horsepower at 150 mph. The engine's dynamometer output was 307 bhp at 6,400 rpm. At Sebring it was red-lined at 6,800 rpm, leaving a margin of 200 rpm below its maximum safe revs of 7,000. The injection gave the V-8 excellent throttle response from the lowest speeds reached at Sebring, and contributed to the engine's flat torque curve. For the sake of relia-

bility the compression ratio had been limited to 9.0 to one.

Lightness was added to the engine by casting special cylinder heads of aluminum. Valve sizes were unchanged, but "at a quick glance we thought we could improve the ports," Duntov notes, "so they were improved." Apart from giving the valve heads a mild tulip contour, the valves themselves and the valve gear remained essentially the standard high-performance package. Special head studs were necked down in diameter to compensate for the aluminum's greater rate of expansion with temperature increases. Valve seat inserts were used for the exhaust valves but not for the intakes, which seated directly on the aluminum. In the running before, during and some testing after Sebring this was fully satisfactory, with no more than 0.001 inch of seat depression from valve pounding.

Aluminum was also used for the housing of the otherwise stock water pump, driven by a pair of belts. Magnesium was chosen for the special oil pan, which had several special features. Within a two-piece finned bottom cover were labyrinthine passages that helped cool the oil. Two lateral baffles were cast into the sump, which was the first to use the one-way swinging doors to capture and control oil flow that were later introduced on Corvettes. The complete engine weighed only 450 pounds, some eighty pounds less than standard.

Finned brake drums were fully recessed into front wheels of racing SS.

There were other contributors to lightness. One was the tubular steel exhaust system, with primary pipes that measured thirty-eight inches in length before blending with the flaring collector pipe; this system was credited with adding twenty brake horsepower. Mufflers were fitted under the door sills when the car left Detroit but at the track they were replaced by straight pipes. Aluminum was used for the clutch housing, the transmission case, and the radiator core, which also incorporated a section for oil cooling. The radiator was steeply inclined forward, which required the presence of a cylindrical coolant header tank just forward of the engine.

Hydraulic actuation controlled the clutch, which was a normal single-disc design bolstered by stiffer springs and heavy-duty disc facings. Special ratios for the four-speed box were 1.22, 1.54, and 1.87 to one. Bottom gear was selected to be just right for the slow hairpin turn at Sebring, to allow shifts in and out of the gear to be made in good time, without unruly and excessive haste, before and after the turn.

Design and build time were saved by basing the final drive on a Halibrand quick-change casting. Chevy made its own ring and pinion gears and quick-change gears, which were crown-shaved and shot-peened for highter fatigue resistance. The selection of overall final-drive ratios ranged from 2.63 to 4.80 to one, with 3.55 being the choice for Sebring. An open drive shaft with two

SS builders: Duntov with mustachioed MacKichan, left, and jacketed Jim Prem

universal joints took the drive from the gearbox to the frame-mounted final drive.

A limited-slip differential was readied for the SS, but wasn't installed at Sebring, for several reasons. One was that there hadn't been enough time to develop the hoped-for roller-splined half-shafts to the drive wheels, conventional sliding splines being used instead. Knowing that the limited-slip could sometimes direct almost all the drive torque to a single wheel, Zora Duntov didn't want to subject those splines to that kind of impact. In addition, he felt that a driver with a sensitive touch would be able to corner faster in the SS without the limited-slip differential.

From front to back this was a drive train that could be expected to work, but one that offered no margin of superiority over its competitors. The engine's peak power, for example, was about the same as that of the 1957 fuel-injected D-Type Jaguar, and the four-cam racing engines of both Ferrari and Maserati were more powerful. Thus did the SS reverse at the outset the traditional image of an American competition car as a blend of brute force and ignorance. But how was Duntov planning to make up the difference?

One advantage the designer sought for the SS was light weight. This would be especially valuable at Sebring. The other was low drag, which was expected to pay off in full in June, 1957, at a French track named Le Mans. Considering the lightness objective, Duntov had first to decide what kind of frame to use. A monocoque frame like that of the Jaguar D-type was undeniably attractive. Such a structure must be developed as well as designed, however, and there was no time for development. And with the skin serving as part of the structure, frame changes might have adversely affected the aerodynamics, and vice versa. This barred the monocoque from consideration.

For the XP-64 a tubular space frame was chosen. With time at an absolute premium, the frame of a Mercedes-Benz 300SL was obtained and used as a basis for the new car's design. In its final form it was vastly different from the German example, resembling it mainly in the pyramided tubes at the cowl and the truss structure under the doors. At the front and rear the mounts for the coil spring/shock units were connected transversely by substantial tubes. Where parts like the brake servo cylinders were attached the frame tubes were square, to make mounting easier, but otherwise they were round, of chrome-moly steel tubing about an inch in diameter. The weight of the complete frame, with all its brackets, was not excessive at 180 pounds.

To give the SS front end inherently high resistance to roll without having to resort to excessive spring or roll-bar stiffness, Zora Duntov elevated its roll center three and a half inches above ground level. Looking like pressings, the wishbones were hand-fabricated of sheet steel and fitted with ball joints to the forged-

Views of stages of Corvette SS final assembly flank the jig at GM Styling on which the magnesium body panels were checked for conformity to the frame.

steel steering knuckles. Instead of the metal-to-metal bushings that were to be fitted later, the chassis pivots of the wishbones were rubber-bushed. A small-diameter anti-roll bar crossed the chassis under the suspension and was connected to the bottom wishbones by short links.

Concentric assemblies of coil springs around tubular shock absorbers handled the springing at all four wheels. Hard mountings, spherical bearings of Teflon, were used at both ends of these assemblies to assure their prompt response to the slightest wheel movement — an aspect of design not widely appreciated at that time. The springs were retained by cups attached to the body of the damper and its rod, which provided a built-in bump stop. Fabric limit straps controlled wheel rebound.

All the SS coil springs were wound so that they began to bottom at one end as they were compressed, giving a progressively increasing spring rate with jounce. This worked so well that Duntov later found it was possible to run the SS on the banks at Daytona with the same springs that had been used at Sebring. These had been the softest of the three coil/shock sets prepared for the car. Another set had springs that were ten percent stiffer, while a third set had similar stiff springs with shocks that had firmer settings.

Independent rear suspension was seriously considered for use on the SS. Zora felt full independence was the best choice for the bumpy, twisty Sebring track, but he also preferred the de Dion

layout for Le Mans. Again with an eye on the long-term requirements and on the lack of time for eradication of errors, Duntov decided to place his faith in the fewer unknowns offered by the de Dion axle. Yet one aspect of this axle was to prove to be the Achilles' heel of the Corvette SS at Sebring.

The one-piece steel tubular de Dion axle curved around behind the quick-change section of the differential. Using a means of axle location which he attributed in part to Maurice Olley, Duntov relied on four tubular trailing rods. Each was ball-jointed to the axle and rubber-bushed where it pivoted from the frame. One rod at each side was attached above the hub and traveled forward and slightly inward. The other two were in a plane below the axle, converging toward the centerline of the car as they trailed rearward, attached to the underside of the axle close to its center.

The lower pair of rods gave the necessary lateral location for the axle, and conferred upon the car a rear roll center that was not more than seven inches above the ground. All the pieces needed to locate the de Dion axle weighed very little, all four struts and fittings adding up to about six pounds. Duntov also set up the axle as he had while working at Allard, giving it small amounts of fixed negative camber and toe-in. Taking effect quickly, before the suspension's designed-in roll understeer geometry could come into play, this gave the chassis improved stability on the straights.

Compact design of SS shows above and below nearly-completed car. Interior featured adjustable and removable wheel, and integrated rear-view mirror.

GM's Saginaw Division produced a special recirculating-ball steering gear for the SS. Mounted low on the left-hand side of the chassis, it operated a three-piece track rod with its lengths and idler-arm radii carefully worked out to avoid the steering wheel fight that's often a by-product of a front suspension geometry giving a high roll center. The overall steering ratio was 12.0 to one. Adjustable for height, the deeply dished steering wheel was also quick-detachable for easy entry.

Knowing there was no hope of proving a suitable disc brake in time for Sebring — though Delco Moraine was already experimenting with them — the Chevy men designed drum brakes for the SS. They knew they could get good results from the sintered Cerametalix linings used at Sebring in 1956, but they wanted a two-leading-shoe brake mechanism, one that would give more consistent response than the usual American duo-servo brake. The necessary components — pressed steel shoes, pivots, retractors and wheel cylinders — were all available off the shelf but unfortunately, not a GM shelf. They were 1956 Chrysler Center-Plane front-wheel brakes, used at all four wheels of the SS. This set the brake size at a twelve-inch diameter and a two-and-a-half inch width.

Brake drums made of aluminum with a molybdenum-sprayed braking surface were tested in advance, but did not give good results. Duntov might then have gone to an aluminum drum with an iron liner bonded in place by the Al-Fin process, but he had

had some experience with such drums and knew that there was a danger of cracking of the iron liner under high-heat stresses. He approached the design differently, conceiving the drum as an iron braking surface carried by a sheet-steel face piece, with an aluminum cooling muff bonded by the Al-Fin method to the outer surface of the iron portion. With this arrangement, he reasoned, the cracks were more likely to appear in the aluminum — which would not be crippling — than in the iron.

The rear brakes were mounted inboard, on special side castings made to fit the Halibrand center section, while the front ones were fully recessed inside the Halibrand magnesium wheels. Transverse finning of the drums encouraged the centrifuging of cooling air across the outer surfaces of the front drums. Air was ducted to the internals of each front brake from inlets at the sides of the grille, and the grillework across the rear of the body was designed to let air *in* at that location, to help cool the rear brakes.

One of the most experimental features of this advanced sports-racing car was the special power-boosted system developed in cooperation with an outside supplier to help control the braking force distribution between the front and rear pairs of wheels. This made use of two separate vacuum-servo brake boosters, sharing space in the rear of the chassis with the lightweight battery and twin electric fuel pumps. The conventional cowl-mounted master cylinder had a direct hydraulic connection to the right-hand servo cylinder, which in turn power-braked the two front wheels directly. This required two chassis-length hydraulic lines which were coil-wrapped for protection. The front wheel braking provided by this arrangement was always directly proportional to pedal pressure.

The hydraulic output of the left-hand servo cylinder was piped straight to the rear brakes, but the vacuum section was so linked to that for the front wheels that the two operated sympathetically. In other words, the front brake force was directly controlled by the pedal, and the rear braking was kept proportional to that at the front by an air link between the respective vacuum cylinders. The basic front/rear braking distribution for the SS was set at 70/30.

The air pipe that connected the two vacuum cylinders could be sealed off by actuating an electric valve which left the cylinder for the rear wheels completely isolated in whatever position it was when the valve closed. The necessary electric impulse was triggered by a mercury switch, mounted in the cockpit. The glass tube enclosing this switch was inclined forward so that the mercury would slide up toward the end a given distance for a

Stylists MacKichan (left) and Ed Donaldson flank Duntov for XP-64 discussion.

given quantity of car deceleration. When the mercury hit the end, in a stop of a preselected negative g., the circuit and valve were closed and rear braking force was held just as it was then. Front wheel force could continue to rise in proportion to pedal pressure, but the rear wheels remained isolated from the circuit until the mercury switch and the valve opened up again. With that mercury switch at just the right angle, braking at all four wheels could be fully used, without the ultimate deceleration being limited by rear-wheel locking. The switch angle could also have been changed during a race to compensate for lessening fuel load, a wet track, or changes in the road surface material.

Featuring swing-up sections at the front and rear, the body was fabricated superbly of sheet magnesium — surprising, perhaps, in view of Chevrolet's pioneering role in the use of fiberglass. GRP was used, however, for the intricate forty-three-gallon fuel tank. During the wind tunnel tests in late December of a full-size mockup of the SS, lift was shown to be moderate. Drag was found to be about the same as that of the Ensley D-Type, which was

checked in the same tunnel during the same test program. That was a fully satisfactory result.

These were the tests that ruled out the hood-top air inlet for the engine. Its removal allowed Duntov to release the warm air from the radiator through the upper surface of the hood. Ducting of the air upward had been a feature of the M.G. record-breakers designed by Reid Railton and of the 1955 Cooper 1100 cc sports car, but Duntov may have been the first to choose this layout with the additional objective of delivering a downward aerodynamic force component to the front of the car. Carefully shaped ducts fed the air from the grille to the radiator and exhausted it through louvers located in a low-pressure area on the hood.

As the components began to come together and the carefully checked lists of weights were compiled, it was evident that the SS would be satisfactorily light for a long-distance racing car: 1,850 pounds dry, about one hundred pounds less than the D-Type Jaguar. Though only one car had been approved for construction, Zora managed to wheedle enough duplicate pieces through the

shop to make a running automobile out of a chassis that had, to his management, been passed off as an "assembly mockup." He felt he needed a test bed to check out some of the car's design features before the racing SS was completed, and this was the way he got it.

Actually, to call that test SS an "automobile" was a form of flattery. Its interior was a mass of tubes and mismatched instruments; its body was rough fiberglass with no doors and no rear-deck cover, mounted over a one-inch plywood firewall. The "Mule," as it was known, was 150 pounds heavier than the race car and was down on horsepower, but it had its full quota of Chevrolet/Duntov engineering. "In short," John Fitch wrote, "the car was a combination of the ugly duckling and the poor little rich girl who had never been to finishing school, but she *flew!*"

Construction of the actual race car took so long that without the Mule little would have been learned about the design before Sebring. The Mule disclosed some faults in the cooling and braking systems, in time to rectify them in the race car. At one point

Arkus-Duntov's unauthorized "Mule" test car, running at first with a carbureted engine, performed yeoman service before Sebring. At far left Zora gives writer Ken Rudeen a demonstration at the GM Tech Center. At left Moss greets Duntov after Sebring laps, and above Zora confers with Fon Portago and John Fitch. Fuel-injected Mule engine is shown below.

its aluminum cylinder heads were cooked by overheating caused by an incorrectly made radiator header tank, and were replaced by stock iron heads. All in all, some 2,000 test miles were put on the Mule in Florida, most by Zora himself.

During the Friday practice session before the race a sensation was caused when both Juan Fangio and Stirling Moss took out the Mule for a few laps. Watches up and down the pit lane were brought to the ready as Fangio clambered into the Mule, quickly and efficiently checking the essentials: shift, pedals, mirror. After two exploratory laps (his manager gesturing from the sidelines that, being contracted to Maserati, he should not go *too* fast) he turned the quickest lap the SS design ever clocked at Sebring: 3:27.2 (or .4 or .6, depending on where you were standing). This was faster than Fangio's own lap record of the previous year, 3:29.7 in a Ferrari, and it was one of the best times set in the 1957 practice session. The Mule had previously gone no faster than 3:33.

Fangio spoke very highly indeed of the car's roadholding and steering response, likening it to the Maseratis in the way it could be throttle-steered through and out of corners. Rather than being

Getting final touches in the paint shop and being photographed in the Styling viewing yard, the SS revealed herself as a very handsome automobile.

critical, though, Fangio was famous for his utter indifference to whatever happened to be under him. He just made it go as fast as he had to. Moss, however, was known for saying just what he thought, and after the SS ride he said he was pleasantly surprised. After being flagged in once for a tire check he got his time down to 3:28, feeling that if needed he could cut two or three more seconds off that. Stirling was initially repelled by the rough and dirty conditions of the much-flogged "bucket of bolts," about which Duntov was touchingly embarrassed, while Fangio had taken it with a sly smile of sympathy. He had, after all, driven far less professional machinery in his early days in Argentina.

"The moral of this," the author wrote at the time about the Fangio/Moss test, "is that (A) the SS Corvette is potentially one of the fastest sports cars in the world and (B) it won't do a bit of good unless they can sign up some Class A drivers." Only later did it become known that Chevrolet had been acutely aware of this vital fact and had been trying hard to do something about it. In fact Juan Mañuel Fangio had signed a contract to drive the SS at Sebring, conditioned, understandably, on his approval of the

A removable plastic canopy was built for the SS to satisfy 1957 rules that required racing sports cars to have tops. Rear grille passed brake cooling air.

car. As race day approached there was still no car to try, so Fangio had been released to Maserati.

As co-driver to Fangio Chevrolet had wanted Stirling Moss, who was interested in the machine but had already made conflicting arrangements for 1957. Instead a contract was signed with Carroll Shelby. As Sebring grew closer and closer, with no finished SS in evidence, Shelby grew restless and asked to be freed from his commitment. He, like Moss, drove for Maserati at Sebring that year.

After these defections, Chevrolet called in John Fitch, who had already been retained to manage the 1957 team of stock and semi-modified Corvettes. Fitch, in turn, suggested as his co-driver the veteran Italian Piero Taruffi. The last-minute character of this assignment was well expressed in Taruffi's book, *Works Racer*: "At two o'clock in the morning on March 19, 1957 (the Tuesday before the race), I was awakened by a telephone call from the United States. Still half asleep, I managed to gather that the American caller wished me to drive a Chevrolet Corvette in the Sebring 12-Hours. As I never refuse a trip to the States I replied that if I found two return tickets to Miami waiting for me at the Rome office of Pan-American Airlines next morning, I should be happy to go. Pan-American phoned a few hours later saying that reservations had been made; and that is how my wife and I went to Miami and from there on to Sebring where we had the pleasure of meeting the folk from General Motors."

Taruffi would travel 6,000 miles to drive the SS a bare handful of laps in practice and only one in the race. The full-blooded Corvette SS arrived in Florida at the absolute last minute, the men of Styling and Chevrolet laboring inside the van on the way down, in the tradition of the cars for the Motoramas, to ensure that it met "GM standards of appearance." The SS was a beautiful machine, by anybody's standards, but when it arrived it was still not a finished racing car.

Even though the race SS was never really pushed in practice, one feature of its design was immediately evident: it was sizzling hot in the cockpit, "intolerable," to quote Duntov. Its magnesium body conducted heat, while the fiberglass of the Mule had insulated it, and the rough-built Mule was far better ventilated. Mechanics rushed to cut away the lower body panels along the exhausts; insulation was packed inside the cockpit, and scoops and ducts were added to the doors on both sides. It was still unbearably hot in the car. One shudders to think what it would have been like if they had been obligated to use the transparent bubble canopy, fitted to meet that year's requirement for a removable top.

Realizing that they had a very fast new car but an untried one, Chevy technicians did all they could to encourage the SS to last the twelve hours. They enlisted the help of Alfred Momo and his portable machine shop for last-minute changes and pinning and jam-nutting of every possible fitting.

The very intricate braking system had worked fine on the Mule, but it was far from right on the race car. In his book, *Adventure on Wheels*, John Fitch looked back at some of the panic of those last minutes before the start: "On the morning of the race, under a sunny blue tropical sky, I arrived early to test the brakes on the SS and see if we couldn't cure the trouble that had plagued us the previous afternoon in practice.

"When I reached the pit, Zora told me that he had tried the car and that no improvement was noted. The brakes were still operating well below racing standards — while they had been exceptional on the faithful Mule. After a minor adjustment, I took the car out for a run to see if they were any better. Down the airport straight the brakes were bad; I tried again, braking hard

Duntov, above, and Taruffi, below, drove SS in hectic final pre-race tests.

on the perimeter of an abandoned taxi strip, avoiding race officials who frowned on our late efforts. Now the front wheels were alternately locking.

"Back at the pits we suspected the power boost was not right and inspected the lines. We found that a junction was leaking and raced back to the hangar to remove the one from the Mule, feeling sure we had at last solved the problem. But no, they were no better — and we had run out of time. In just 15 minutes the cars would be flagged away, so we pushed the SS up to its number one position on the line. I practiced jumping into the cockpit twice, then found myself ringed by photographers and curious spectators, all shooting questions at Zora and me as the final minutes ticked away.

"The clear-grid order was given and I lined up across the sun-white concrete with the other drivers, warning those nearest me (O'Shea, Thompson and Hawthorn) not to stand on their brakes in front of me because mine were very erratic. Then the 10-1 countdown began over the loudspeakers.

The p.r. side: Fitch and Duntov pose and Ed Cole (plain cap) quizzes Fitch.

"Waiting anxiously there, on the line for the running Le Mans start, listening to the count, I felt that we had somehow been cheated, that if we had only been allowed another month the bugs would have been ironed out of the SS. Now with its malfunctioning brakes and many non-race-tested components, I was very much afraid of failure — in fact, it was almost a certainty. The huge crowd was solidly behind this 'supreme effort' on the part of Chevrolet — as evidenced by their wild cheers for us during practice. They wanted to see a Detroit car in the circle of champions and the sleek-looking SS seemed to hold immense promise."

Fitch got off to a good start in the race, but the SS didn't. During those last-minute violent stops to test the brakes, the right front tire had been flat-spotted in two places and this caused the car to vibrate at speed. For the first two laps John managed to hold sixth, behind a storming pack of three Ferraris and two Maseratis. After the third round he pulled in to have the front two tires changed.

Pressing on, in spite of brakes that were still not predictable, the SS began to reduce its lap times, clocking 3:32.8 more than once and cutting one at 3:29.8, a clear indication that the race SS was an even quicker car than the Mule prototype. Out of the corners it could pull away from the D Jaguars. Acceleration was slightly better than the 3.5 Ferraris and about par with the 3.8's, but it couldn't match the violent pull of the 4.5-liter Maserati V-8 that went on to win.

Before many more laps were recorded by the pit staff, which included Bill Milliken, Isabella Taruffi, John and Elaine Bond, and many other friends of GM, Fitch rolled into the pits with a silent engine. The terminal troubles were beginning. A quarter-hour was lost tracing a fault in a coil connection, and shortly afterward John had to replace the coil out on the circuit. By this time the rear suspension began to feel distinctly odd, to the extent of letting the tires touch the body and chattering uncontrollably after bumps. Undrivable and overheated, the Corvette SS retired officially after its twenty-third lap, turned by Piero Taruffi following a conference in the pits with Zora Arkus-Duntov and Ed Cole.

The main cause of the car's retirement, the handling deterioration, was traced to failure of a rubber bushing at the chassis end of one of the lower rods that provided the de Dion tube with lateral location. As Duntov later said, "It was doomed to fail." If the fitter was not familiar with the installation procedure for these bushings, he could split them during the assembly of the joint. This one had been split in just this way and thus became a

Short and not-so-sweet race appearance of the SS saw Fitch (white-banded helmet) behind the wheel. He shared the track with Hawthorn's D Jaguar (5)

built-in focal point for failure. The design itself had not been to blame.

In spite of the early retirement, Ed Cole had been sufficiently impressed by the potential the SS had shown at Sebring to approve the construction of a team of three cars to race at Le Mans. In fact, entries for three Corvettes had been requested and granted before Sebring, through the offices of a certain "M. St. Giles," this alias being the name of the place in Belgium where Zora Arkus-Duntov was born. And for a month and a half after Sebring Briggs Cunningham still hoped to be able to field at least one such car at Le Mans, on behalf of Chevrolet.

After Sebring, in fact, Cole passed along very specific thoughts on what he wanted done to the SS for future events. A high-priority item, he felt, was the further development of the engine with desmodromic (springless) valve gear, allowing it to turn to 8,000 or 9,000 rpm and to develop 400 bhp. In March and April of 1957 plans were well advanced for the 1958 version of the SS, for special SR models of both the Corvette and, for stock car racing, the new Chevrolet sedan, and for separate yet subsidized

teams throughout the United States to keep Chevrolet cars in the forefront of all important phases of competition.

But just as the SS program began with a call to a vacationing Zora Duntov, so it ended in exactly the same way. Zora had stayed on in Florida for a well-earned holiday after working beyond the point of exhaustion to get the SS ready. There he received a call that advised him that the Automobile Manufacturers Association was considering the adoption of a resolution to stop taking part in racing and publicizing racing successes. At Chevrolet this was all that was needed for an anti-racing faction to seize the controls again. Even before the official enactment of the famous AMA ban of June, 1957, the word was passed down to begin the termination of all Chevy's racing agreements and activities.

The ban, which had originally been recommended to the AMA at its February board meeting by Harlow Curtice, president of GM, "recommended to member companies that they take no part in automobile racing or other competitive events involving tests of speed and that they refrain from suggesting speed in passenger

Zora Duntov opened the new Daytona track in 1959 with some fast laps in the SS, now with covered front lamps and a windscreen for the driver alone.

car advertising or publicity," according to the official AMA news release. It was unanimously adopted by the heads of the major motor companies, who felt that the industry's escalation of the "horsepower war" was getting them into areas potentially irritating to legislators, areas which they had successfully avoided for decades without doing any harm to their business. Unanimous acceptance of the resolution reflected the always painful fact that while some will win in automobile racing, others must by definition be losers.

The Corvette SS was the most ambitious and sophisticated program to be so suddenly and, in this case, tragically cut down. Early in May the order was transmitted to scrap every fragment of the SS project except for the race car itself. At that time, three chassis frames were in existence as well as the race SS, the Mule, and many other components. Rescued from enforced oblivion, the Mule came to glorious life again two years later, as Chapter 8 will reveal.

When the Daytona International Speedway was officially opened in February, 1959, the fastest first laps were turned at 155

mph by Zora Arkus-Duntov, wearing his familiar yellow helmet, at the wheel of the Corvette SS. He was lapping the two-and-a-half-mile track at a higher speed than he'd reached on the five-mile beach straightaway three years earlier with his fin-tailed Corvette. And at GM's Phoenix five-mile circular track the SS was lapping at no less than 183 mph, its 283-cubic-inch engine of 315 bhp turning at 6,800 rpm, in a series of tests conducted in December, 1958.

Even if Chevy had still been racing, the Corvette SS wouldn't have been eligible to run at Le Mans after 1957. In 1956 and 1957 there'd been intense controversy over the high speeds the prototype sports cars were reaching on the classic French track, and in 1958 and 1959 a displacement limit of three liters, 183 cubic inches, was imposed. Duntov, reflecting on the events of those years, is certain that the failure of the three-car Corvette team to run as promised in 1957 was the final straw that provoked the Automobile Club de l'Ouest to ban the big-engined cars. In 1960 they lifted it again, but only for Grand Touring cars. That year Corvettes were entered again. That time they didn't fail to race.

Chapter 7

ALL-ROUNDER: 1958-1960

Many forces form a new automobile. Stylists, engineers, marketers, dealers, and advertising experts all have their say in the creation of a new model. Top executives of the auto companies also have much to contribute to car design, even when they're not necessarily highly qualified to do so. As one frustrated industry underling complained, "That's really all the fun those guys have in this business!" And where there is indecision there is much more room for conflicting opinions. There was to be a future for the Corvette. That bridge was crossed in 1955. But no one was quite sure of that future beyond 1957.

Styling Staff, which had taken the lead in the original creation of the Corvette, did so again in the planning of a totally new car for 1958. During the fall of 1955 a new dream car, the Golden Rocket, was designed and built for display by Oldsmobile in the 1956 Motorama. It had a sheer, grille-less front end, fender pontoons of virtually tubular section, and a tapering fast-back coupé canopy flanked by vestigial fins. Extra entry headroom was provided by a flap above each side window which lifted automatically when the door was opened. The Golden Rocket project inspired virtually concurrent design work on a new Corvette.

The impact of the first production Mercedes-Benz 300SL had been so strong that the GM designers were willing to conceive and build this new Corvette solely as a coupé, no roadster version to be offered. This made it easier to engineer the car as a unit-construction vehicle, with no separate frame, making extensive use of aluminum body and structural panels. Design work on this new car started in September, 1955. The clay model that was completed in midwinter retained the general lines and proportions of the Golden Arrow but had a completely different front end, with four headlights — the rage that was then sweeping the industry, led by GM — above two large oval nostrils as air inlets.

As the racing Corvettes were making their trouble-plagued debut at Sebring, in March of 1956, a fiberglass styling model of this proposed new 1958 Corvette was brought to completion.

Much more engineering work remained to be done, however, before such a radically-changed car could be readied for production. A crisis in the manufacturing development of a new Chevy truck line drew away the needed engineers, as did the heavy work load demanded by the all-new 1958 Chevrolet production car. Corvette as Son of Golden Rocket was shelved for 1958, and as it turned out, for good.

Styling had begun early in 1956 on a heavy facelift of the existing Corvette as a backup to the all-new car. Carried out in the normal Chevrolet Studio, this was clearly aimed at giving·the Chevy sports car more external glitter and gloss, which would allow it to exert the kind of superficial appeal that was felt, at that time, to have so much to do with the successful selling of cars. Four headlights were fitted, faired into the fenders, and surrounded by a chrome bezel from which a chrome strip trailed back atop each fender.

In the facelift the two nostrils that had been the sole air inlets of the originally planned new car became smaller inlets flanking the main opening, which kept the characteristic Corvette oval outline. All three openings had heavy chrome surrounds. Simple grille patterns were tried, honeycomb designs and fine mesh, but in the final design the familiar "teeth" were again featured in the central grille.

These were the main changes planned until the spring of 1956, when the car's quota of non-functional styling features was suddenly elevated. A pattern of washboard-like ridges appeared atop the hood in simulation of air outlet louvers. Dummy outlets were also tucked into the fender coves, behind the front wheels. The two air scoops aside the main grille were dummies, on normal production Corvettes. The rear deck sprouted twin chrome strips like those used on the one-off car for Sweden's Prince Bertil. If the objective was, as one designer said at the time, to make the Corvette look like a Cadillac, that aim was certainly achieved.

The new body increased the length of the Corvette from 168.0 to 177.2 inches, mainly at the front end, and widened it also from

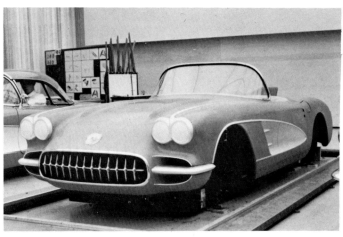

After final design of 1958 Corvette was frozen, in August, 1956, the front end above was being evaluated in the Chevrolet studio. It may have been a proposal for a special show car, or an option for the factory racing programs which were then still flourishing.

n January and February of 1956 the 1958 Corvette was maturing in e Chevrolet studio of GM Styling as above, below, and below right. Behind car above is split front-end motif that was also considered, on a completely new body with a rounded tubular cross-section.

Spectacular photography was hardly needed to show the changes in the '58 Corvette, which were not greeted with enthusiasm by the sports car purists.

70.5 to 72.8 inches. Instead of being attached to the body as they had been before, the more substantial bumpers were now braced directly to the frame by long steel brackets. Inside the body, cowl supports of aluminum had been added during 1957, and these were supplemented in the '58 model by a metallic backing along the rocker panels, below the doors. The GRP body material itself had been steadily improved and was now stabilized in design; the final change in the specification was made on April 21, 1957. All these body changes increased the Corvette's weight, which in a fully equipped 1958 car was over 3,000 pounds for the first time, some 200 pounds more than the 2,880-pound '57.

So extensively reworked was the new Corvette's interior that the only familiar items remaining were the steering wheel, shift lever, and the little white pull-knobs that opened the doors. Now the instruments were all grouped in front of the driver, dominated by a huge 160-mph speedometer. At its base, above the steering column, was the 6,000-rpm tachometer. It was flanked by the other four dials, all in deeply recessed cowlings. The clock, radio, and heater controls were carried by a central console, making the Corvette one of the first American cars to put this console motif, so often projected by dream cars, into production. Facing the passenger was a grab handle across an otherwise unused recessed area.

Improvements in the Corvette's instrumentation were owed in large measure to the increasing official involvement with the car of Zora Arkus-Duntov. "In 1955," Zora recalls, "Harley Earl invited me to Styling, assembled his entourage, and said, 'Let's do the car like this man says.' You recall that the 1953 Corvette had a tachometer at the center of the dash. I said, 'There's no way that you can monitor that.' Subsequently it was mounted above the steering column. It was not a very good location, but at least it was in the field of view." Seat belts became standard equipment in the 1958 model.

High-speed experience at Daytona and Sebring showed up under the hood of the '58 Corvette. Now all models had the generator mounted on the right-hand side so the fan belt wrapped more fully around the water pump/fan pulley. The heavy-duty chassis option was carried over from 1957, including built-in ducts which carried cooling air from the two nostrils at the front of the car through the rocker panels, to the rear brakes. Better fuel metering resulted from redesign of the nozzles in the fuel injection, which also had a more sensitive diaphragm controlling the mixture during warm-up. A new paper-element air cleaner was used with the injection, and was fed cool air by a front-end duct when the f.i. was married with the Duntov camshaft in RPO 579D. A new combination for 1958 was RPO 469C, mating the

On the road, however, serious drivers found that the 1958 model was even better than before, with an impressive-looking new instrument panel design.

high-rev Duntov cam with two four-barrel carburetors. It was rated at 270 bhp at 6,000 rpm, while the peak injected output was now quoted as 290 bhp at 6,200 for the 283-cubic-inch V-8; this engine came with a mechanically-driven tachometer reading to 8,000 rpm.

Options like these made it obvious that Chevrolet had given quite a lot of thought to the Corvette's competition potential before the ban on factory-backed racing took effect. It decided to continue offering these options on the Chevy sports car, reasoning that it was in the business of selling what people wanted to buy, and if some of their customers seemed interested in buying these "heavy-duty" items, that was entirely their business. Sports car racers suddenly became aware that they could order from their local Chevrolet dealer what John Fitch called "a relatively low-priced American-made bomber that goes like hell. The car's been the despair of a number of foreign manufacturers — Porsche and Jaguar, to mention two. And it's certainly a contender with the $10,000 and $12,000 Ferraris."

Corvettes came back to Sebring in 1958, without direct factory backing. Chevy dealer Dick Doane co-drove his car to twelfth overall and first in his GT class with Jim Rathmann. That year Nickey Chevrolet in Chicago prepared the Corvette that, by its distinctive color and vivid performance became known as the

"Purple People Eater," echoing the popular song of the day. Milwaukee ad man Jim Jeffords piloted it to an SCCA Class B Production Championship that season, and backed up that performance by winning the same Championship in 1959 again.

Corvettes were also being expertly race-prepared in California by, among others, Bill Thomas, who became a certified expert on the subject. For *Sports Car Journal*, that great British-born driver Ken Miles recorded his impressions of a 1958 Corvette set up for competition by Bill Thomas. "Once behind the wheel," wrote Miles, "there is no doubt whatsoever that this competition model is a very different kettle of fish from the 'street' machine. Chevrolet states quite firmly that this car is not intended for use on the highway, and how right they are!"

Ken's main reservation about street use of this car concerned the brakes: "When cold, the cerametallic lining is ferociously unpredictable; from low speeds the slightest touch on the brake pedal almost pitches both driver and passenger through the windshield; at normal freeway speeds incautious application of the brakes results in a hasty and unexpected change of lane, but at high speeds the brakes really come into their own and haul this great big automobile down from maximum speed with no sign of fade whatsoever, time and time again."

Miles found himself "pleasantly surprised by the ease with

which a comfortable drift could be maintained" through turns at on Firestone Super Sport tires inflated to 40 p.s.i. He noted: "Most drivers will appreciate the car's stability in a fast turn and the easy way it can be maneuvered 'round a tight turn by judicious use of the throttle. How good is the Competition model as a racing car? The results speak for themselves. Except on some unusually tight courses where its weight is a handicap, it is unbeatable."

How much progress the Corvette designers had made in some directions, and how little in others, was illustrated by Ken Miles's concluding remarks: "The ride is still at least as good as that of the majority of imported sports cars and better than most; the body is free from rattles and drafts, the gearbox is an enthusiast's dream, and there is something satisfying about sighting along that long brutal-looking hood. In only two respects does the car fall short, and whilst the styling department is undoubtedly responsible for the miserably illegible instruments I feel that the engineering department is probably to blame for the totally inadequate seats which are neither comfortable to ride in nor give any lateral support at all so that there is a constant temptation to drive round corners hanging on to the door with one hand in order to stay behind the wheel."

In some auto companies complaints like the latter would be dismissed as the ravings of a speed-crazed maniac. Chevrolet's Zora Arkus-Duntov, however, knew just what Miles was talking about, pointing out to writer Steve Wilder that seat design poses a difficult compromise in a dual-purpose sports car: "In a racing car, the seat is 100 percent for working, just like a stool by a lathe. But in a passenger car, you're lucky if it's a 'work chair' more than ten percent of the time. It must be easy to get in and out of, and comfortable for lounging in. The high sides of a real bucket seat are just right for holding you in place but they don't meet these other requirements."

The production Corvette's seats *were* reshaped slightly for the 1959 model car which was given many detail improvements but was necessarily outranked in the corporate pecking order by the crash program staged by GM to bring out new '59 body styles across the board to meet the challenge of Chrysler's "Forward Look." Responsible for the Corvette changes was Zora Duntov, who for some time had either originated, cleared or approved all the alterations to this car. His special status with regard to the Corvette, made official by a Chevrolet Engineering memo in

Operations at the St. Louis Corvette plant were moving more smoothly now, with 1958 bodies in the paint booths and being married to the chassis.

August, 1957, had informally been in effect well before that.

Duntov also moved those inner door-opening knobs farther forward on the 1959 car. Driving an earlier model on a rainy day, he'd noticed that the strap on the sleeve of his raincoat tended to snag on the knob and open the door when he made a left turn. The 1959 Corvette was also the first to have the T-handle on the gear-shift knob to serve as a positive lockout for reverse gear. On the passenger's side of the dash, an open stowage bin below the grab handle was a welcome addition. The clutch linkage was made easily adjustable, in the shop, to give either a six-and-a-half-inch travel with low effort or a more responsive four-and-a-half-inch travel with higher effort.

As *Road & Track* remarked, "The appearance of the 1959 Corvette has been improved by the simple expedient of removing the phony hood louvers and the two useless chrome bars from the deck lid." The wheel disc was also changed for the first time since 1956, acquiring ten small rectangular slots around its periphery to permit some cooling air to flow through them and the vents in the steel wheels. Cars with the full competition suspension/brake kit went even farther in being fitted with no more than the standard small Chevy hub cap.

In response to requests from the field, that famous RPO 684 was given even stiffer springs for 1959. The rates of the optional springs themselves went up from 340 to 550 pounds per inch in front and from 125 to 145 in the rear. The option continued to include the finned drums and ceramic-metallic linings. New in '59 was another option, RPO 686, to give better braking in hard over-the-road driving. It used new sintered metallic linings developed by GM's Delco Moraine Division. Each brake had three pairs of lining segments riveted to the primary brake shoe and five pairs of segments, slightly thicker, riveted to the secondary shoe. Special brake drums had no fins but were flared at their open end to prevent bell-mouthing and were honed to an inner surface finish as smooth as that of the cylinder bore of an engine. These linings were less harsh on the drums than the ceramic-metallic type, were far less sensitive when they were cold, and cost only $26.90 if they were ordered with the car.

Major additions to the rear suspension of the 1959 model were trailing radius rods from the frame to attachment points above the axle at each side. Working in tension to oppose the axle's torque reactions, these helped suppress the rear-axle chatter under acceleration from low speeds that had been an obvious fault

Coming down the line in St. Louis, and leaving the plant for shipment, the 1958 Corvettes looked as impressive as the Chevy stylists hoped they would.

Removal of the hood "louvers" and rear deck chrome strips cleaned up the lines of the '59 model, also given slotted wheel discs and rear-axle radius rods

ever since the power had been stepped up in the '57 model. The presence of these rods allowed the lower mounts of the rear shock absorbers to be relocated so they would experience longer travel with wheel movement, giving better spring damping. Fluid foaming in the shocks was discouraged by the insertion of a nitrogen-filled bag to occupy volume that otherwise would be attractive to air that could form bubbles and impair the efficiency of the damper.

All the good things it was possible to buy on a Corvette were gradually elevating its price. The base figure in 1959 was $3,875.00. With desirable options like the 290 bhp engine ($484.20), station-seeking radio ($149.80), heater ($102.25), hardtop ($236.75), as well as folding top and four-speed manual transmission, the car tested in 1959 by *Sports Cars Illustrated* priced out at $5,127.80, not including taxes and transportation. And it *did* perform. It accelerated to sixty in 6.6 seconds with the 4.11 axle, to eighty in 10.1 and to one hundred in 15.6 seconds. It reached ninety-eight miles an hour in the standing quarter-mile and covered it in 14.9 seconds. It accelerated from rest to one hundred and braked to a stop again in 26.4 seconds.

Reports on the '59 Corvette were enthusiastic, hailing it as by

Fifty-nines in action, above in a B Production race at Road America in 1962 ahead of an AC and Jaguar, and below in the 1969 Winternationals drags.

far the best of its breed yet, stressing that it was light-years away from the Powerglide six of only half a decade earlier. Yet they held out the promise of even better things in the future, specifically in 1960. "We predict that this will be the year of the big changes for the Corvette," said *Road & Track* in January, 1959, "and most of them for the better." They'd heard from former GM designers that there was a radical new Chevy sports car in the works for 1960. And indeed there was.

As always, the components available for use in the Corvette chassis depended very much on those being planned for passenger car use by GM. The small sports car production volume and the desire to hold the car's price at a reasonable level didn't permit the cost of tooling for manufacture of special units for the Corvette like engines, transmissions, and suspension components. Now, in 1957, it seemed that something might be coming that could transform the Corvette: a new General Motors passenger car for 1960 featuring a rear-mounted transmission combined with the differential, a "transaxle," in concert with an independent rear suspension. Carrying the code name "Q," this advanced program offered a transaxle that held high appeal for Corvette use. It carried rear brakes mounted inboard, reducing

Lines of full-size Q-Corvette were refined in 1957 from scale model at top.

the unsprung weight, and was to be available in both manual and automatic versions. In some instances the transaxle also carried the starter motor, and there were provisions for an hydraulic-retarder brake built into the assembly. This was an exotic piece of machinery that just begged to be built into an equally advanced new sports car.

In the Research Studio at GM Styling Staff a new Q-Corvette for 1960 began to take shape in the late fall of 1957, under the direction of Bob McLean. This time McLean didn't have to make the chassis layout himself. It was provided by Zora Arkus-Duntov, to Styling's requirements. The removal of the bulk of the transmission from the back of the engine allowed the car's conception to be extremely compact: wheelbase and track of ninety-four and fifty-three inches, and overall height of only forty-six inches (almost two inches lower than the lowest-ever model introduced in 1968). This compactness was achieved with an interior roominess that was greater than before, not less.

For power the fuel-injected 283 V-8 was specified, with some important changes. One was extensive use of aluminum, then being actively explored by GM and Chevrolet. The aluminum cylinder heads had been tried on the racing SS earlier that year. Planned not just for the Corvette but for all Chevrolets, Duntov recalled, were "ultimately aluminum engines, in which valves would be running without guides, without seat inserts, and the

Arrangement of components and unusual method of door opening were checked in Q-Corvette space buck. Transaxle was similar to those proposed for the

pistons would be running in aluminum. That was the only way it was thought of; Corvette could not support a program to have an aluminum engine for itself [though a decade later it would, in a limited way]. And there was some metallurgical development which indicated that that was possible." It would have contributed to the car's estimated dry weight of only 2,225 pounds.

To permit the lowest possible placement of the engine it was to be fitted with a dry-sump lubrication system. It also required a small-diameter flywheel and a twin-disc clutch to keep the bottom end of the engine as short as the shallow pan of the dry sump system permitted. In an aluminum case at the rear of the chassis, the main transmission assembly was placed at the front of the differential. Independent rear suspension was proposed, a modified swing axle design which used the universally-jointed half-shaft as a stressed member. Concentric coil/shock suspension units were indicated at the rear and also for the front suspension, inside the parallel wishbones.

Slimness outside and more room inside the Q-Corvette study pushed the designers toward a steel platform frame not unlike that of a Porsche in principle. With a production target of more than 10,000 units a year, consideration was also given to forming the main body panels of steel. Its structural concept was very advanced for the time, being that of a fastback coupé with a permanent arch behind the cockpit, supporting a removable roof

section between the arch and the windshield. The screen was split down the middle and had no pillars at the corners, each half of it swinging up and forward with the door as it hinged from an unique diagonal pivot near the center of the cowl.

These features were tested full-scale on a wooden space buck built under the direction of studio engineer Byron Voight. Among the stylists working under McLean were Bob Veryzer and Pete Brock. John Bird and a crew of five modelers carried out their ideas in clay, first in quarter-scale in October of 1957, and then in full scale in November. The ideas were fresh and revolutionary. They drew inspiration from Bill Mitchell's suggestion that the car might have some of the slimness of the early Boano and Pininfarina bodies built on Abarth chassis, those with a strong horizontal motif relieved by bulges above the wheels in the upper body surfaces. The nose became so low and wide that only driving lights could be fitted at the sides of the grille. The main headlights were designed to pop up, manually operated, from the front surface of the hood.

Before the end of 1957 the Q-Corvette was fully rendered and modeled in natural size for executive evaluation. It was a very handsome car with an exciting new shape, but it had the disadvantage of being costly to tool and produce. Zora Arkus-Duntov realized that this cost factor might well keep the Q-Corvette from ever being built. He favored a frame-mounted differential,

cember 2, 1957 comparison between Q-Corvette and 1958 model showed dramatic transformation stylists were proposing for the Chevy sports car in 1960.

for ten seconds
try to imagine
what owning a
Corvette
would be like . . .
you're close,
but it's better
than that!
how much better? your Chevy dealer can show you. . . . Chevrolet Division of General Motors, Detroit 2, Michigan.

Music without words was the theme of an ad that appeared in April, 1960 in the car magazines and in Sport, Sports Illustrated, The New Yorker, *and the* A.M.A. News

Instead of radical styling changes there were none externally in the '60 car.

but felt the extreme dry-sump engine approach was needlessly costly. He also felt it might be useful to keep a separate frame instead of the proposed unit-body construction. Zora wrote his chief engineer, Harry Barr, in December, 1957: "I feel that having a separate frame construction will enable us to take the decision as to body material on merits of economics of manufacture at a somewhat later date. . . . Actually our past body complaints can be classified as quality complaints rather than fundamental objection to fiberglass."

As 1957 became 1958, it became more and more evident that the auto industry was headed for relatively hard times. Exotic programs like the Q-series sedans with their transaxles were cancelled, and with them went most of the hopes for a radically changed Corvette. Chevrolet engineers also had their hands full getting the radical Corvair ready for the market. The last had not been seen, however, of the dramatic new sports car styling ideas developed with such speed, sureness, and enthusiasm late in 1957.

Knowing now that his 1960 model Corvette was going to be the best car he could make out of his 1959 model, Zora Duntov began applying himself to this problem. The research work on aluminum led to clutch housings of that material for the manual-transmission models, effecting an eighteen-pound weight saving.

More readable instruments with flat faces helped the 1960 Corvette driver keep track of the higher output from larger ports and better fuel injection.

This was an innovation that had been proven on the Corvette SS, as was another 1960 change that saved an additional fifty-three pounds on the fuel-injected engines: aluminum cylinder heads. These were destined to have a very short life, however. As Zora recalled, "We did them, they worked fine, we released them but we couldn't make them because we couldn't cast them."

Following the work done on the Corvette SS aluminum heads, the 1960 production items had important design changes that contributed, with an increase in compression ratio from 10.5 to 11.0 to one, to the jump in power from 290 to 315 bhp. The intake valve head diameter was enlarged from 1.72 to 1.94 inches, and matching improvements were made in the intake port. It couldn't be enlarged all the way through because the pushrods passed close to the ports near their outer ends, so each port was necked down to a venturi shape adjacent to the pushrod holes, then allowed to expand smoothly on its way to the combustion chamber. Subtle changes in the chamber itself included more gas-flow area around the intake valve, a slightly lower roof, and new thicker-crown pistons with a higher dome and deeper recesses for valve clearance.

The aluminum alloy used for these heads contained a high percentage of silicon, a forerunner of that used more than a decade later for the cylinder block of the Chevy Vega. The silicon strengthened the alloy enough to eliminate the need for valve-seat inserts. The heads were cast by the same low-pressure system that was then being introduced for the Corvair, in which the molten alloy flows up into the old from below. The high-silicon alloy of that time tended to be difficult to handle, however, and the casting itself was not a simple one. The unfortunate result was that there were frequent faults in the castings and a high rate of rejection that automatically increased their cost.

Sometimes heads managed to conceal their internal flaws through all the inspection stages and smuggle them aboard a Corvette; this was one of the two prime causes of the field failures that gave the aluminum heads a poor reputation in the early 1960 models. The other was overheating. If for some reason a Corvette's cooling system failed or lost water, the aluminum heads, with their lower melting point, were much more likely to be damaged than ordinary iron heads. In combination these were reasons enough to stop making and supplying the aluminum heads before the 1960 model year was really under way.

To satisfy the big-valve head's appetite for air, the internal volume of the fuel-injection plenum chamber was enlarged without changing its twelve-inch ram pipe length. Injection was offered both with the RPO 579D Duntov-cammed engine and a new combination, RPO 579 with an hydraulic camshaft and aluminum heads (for a while) producing 275 bhp. Something new was also added with the two Duntov-cammed engines in the range (RPO 469C as well as 579D): an aluminum cross-flow radiator by GM's Harrison Division. The fan was moved several inches closer to the radiator in all models, and a power-saving temperature-sensitive viscous fan drive became optional.

Duntov decided to give the Corvette suspension a rethink from the top down for 1960. He was well aware that he'd no longer be able to create special pure racing models like the SS. "Since we could no longer build two kinds of Corvettes with different characteristics," he reasoned, "we decided to give the buyer as much of *both* worlds as we could — to use our racing experience to combine in one automobile the comfort of a tourer and the ability of a racer. A big order, yes, but an interesting and worthwhile one. The 1960 Corvette was the first to reflect this thinking."

Zora threw out of the option list the ultra-stiff, heavy-duty springs. He sought instead to control the car's roll and handling with two anti-roll bars: a new one at the rear, pioneering this application in modern American cars, and a thicker-diameter (0.70 inch) bar at the front. Rear-axle travel in jounce was also increased one inch to reduce the chance of bottoming. These changes gave the '60 model a more agreeable ride and a handling feel that was nearer neutral, on the highway, without the former strong understeer. Though the new springing wasn't ideal for racing, it did give the buyer of a street Corvette the best combination of ride and handling he'd ever experienced.

The main racing option in 1960 was RPO 687, which combined the fast-steering adapter with an improved application of the Moraine sintered-metallic brake linings. In this RPO (Regular Production Option) they were married to the finned drums and vented backing plates that were formerly used with the now-obsolete ceramic-metallic linings, and given a new wrinkle, a twenty-four-blade sheet steel cooling fan built into each brake drum. It circulated enough air to reduce the brake operating temperature by as much as twenty percent.

All these improvements in the 1960 Corvette were internal; apart from some new color choices the car was unchanged externally. The cockpit was refined in detail with better-quality fit-

Corvette production broke the 10,000-unit level for the first time with the 1960 model, which had better suspension, now with a rear anti-roll bar.

ted carpeting, seats that were deeper, a new 7,000-rpm tachometer that eliminated the old rev totalizer that had been used since 1953, and flatter faces for the smaller dials that made them much easier to read. Duntov realized that even greater improvements than these in interior roominess and luxury would be needed if the Corvette were to be a serious competitor for the market for two-seater "personal cars" which Ford abandoned when it converted its Thunderbird into a four-seater car in 1958.

There'd been high hopes at first for heavy fallout from the T-Bird market in favor of the 1958 Corvette; a production schedule of 11,000 units was set, nearly doubling the 1957 level. Reality fell short of that, with 9,168 '58 models being built, but that was enough of a step up in relation to the modest cost of retooling the new body in fiberglass to allow Chevrolet to make money on the Corvette for the first time that year. Production continued a gradual climb toward the level originally visualized for the St. Louis plant, reaching 9,670 for the 1959 model and 10,261 for the 1960 Corvette.

The '60 model was the instrument for one of the proudest occasions in the history of the Corvette, its entry by Briggs Cunningham in that year's Le Mans twenty-four-hour race. Taking

Cleaner though the 1960 Corvette had become, in comparison with the '58, George Barris was (for once) able to dechrome it even further, as at top.

Their finest hour: Corvettes head the line at Le Mans in 1960, three Cunningham-entered cars ahead of the Camoradi entry driven by Lilley and Gamble.

The Cunningham team garage at Le Mans was the scene of the final preparation of the three Corvettes and a Jaguar prototype in June of 1960.

advantage of a liberalization of the race rules that allowed big-engined Grand Touring cars to compete, Cunningham entered three Corvettes and Lloyd Casner's Camoradi team nominated a single car. Preparations began very early, enough so for a single car to be sent to Le Mans for the pre-race test day on April 9. There the white hardtop's best lap time was 4:28.3, the car looking so alarming doing it that some of the officials reported to the Cunningham pits that parts of the suspension seemed about to fall off. They had never seen a Corvette at speed before.

The cars were prepared by Alfred Momo at his shop on Long Island with active assistance from Zora Duntov, Frank Burrell, and others at Chevrolet. Stripped of their grille inserts and chrome trim they were handsome brutes in white with blue striping, riding on the familiar Halibrand magnesium knock-off wheels. The hardtop was bolted in place, its rear window pierced by a big fuel filler. Special instrumentation and racing bucket seats were installed, as were adjustable steering columns to suit the different drivers. Engine oil was circulated through a cooling radiator by an electric pump. Standard cylinder heads were used on the test day prior to the event, and for the race itself new cast-iron versions of the aluminum heads, with their big valves

The Thompson/Windridge car (2) suffered damage before retirement, while the Fitch-Grossman entry (3) soldiered on to an honorable eighth place overall.

and improved porting, were produced.

The three Cunningham cars weighed in at about 2,980 pounds, while the Camoradi car was lighter at 2,830 pounds. It was not as quick as the Momo-prepared machines, however, and though it went far enough in the race to place tenth it didn't complete the minimum qualifying distance for its class, and so it wasn't officially a finisher. One Cunningham car was out after only thirty-two laps, spinning and crashing in a rain squall. Another retired in a manner *The Motor* described thusly: "After one of the most gallant and eventful drives that have been seen at Le Mans, the Thompson/Windridge Corvette (it had much of its bodywork removed early on Saturday and spent a long time during the night being unditched from the Tertre Rouge sandbank) suddenly belched smoke on its way past the pits for the 207th time, at 11:15 a.m. Smoke poured from everywhere; the bonnet, the cab, the exhaust. Showing great restraint the driver took to the escape road, stopped with tantalizing slowness, and leapt out to safety, as the smoke subsided." Fred Windridge had been at the wheel during this dramatic moment, which was not, incidentally, entirely unexpected because the car had been low on engine oil and hadn't yet completed the twenty-five laps that were manda-

tory at Le Mans between fills of water and oil.

That had been the fastest Corvette, reaching 151 mph on the straight and recording a best lap of 4:26.2, equal to 113.12 mph. Only marginally slower was the car co-driven by John Fitch and Bob Grossman, which had been in seventh place in the race as early as the eighth hour. It ran into engine trouble late in the running, however, and the rules against adding water had to be circumvented by packing ice by the bucketful around the engine during the final hours. They managed to bring their number three coupé home in an official eighth place, covering 280 laps and averaging 97.92 mph for the day-long race.

Eighth place at Le Mans. What did it mean? It was better than ninth place at Sebring, the best a Corvette (also co-driven by John Fitch) had done on its first attempt in a race half as long, far less important and far closer to home. And they had impressed the Europeans. *The Motor* remarked on the Corvettes' "brave and immaculate show at scrutineering" and, at the start, "the massive block of four white and blue Chevrolet Corvettes at the head of the line looking most imposing." If any proof were needed that America's only production sports car had come a long way in a few short years, it was provided by Le Mans, 1960.

Chapter 8

STING RAY RACER

In 1934 a twenty-two-year-old Pennsylvanian was a commercial illustrator for an advertising agency in New York City. He'd arrived there by way of Carnegie Tech and the Art Students League and an appreciation for the exciting things in life that were far more evident in New York than in his home town, where his father sold Buicks. This, however, had interested the young William L. Mitchell in automobiles, and in New York he'd spend hours outside and inside the Park Avenue showrooms of the great marques, admiring, absorbing, and later sketching the elegant custom-bodied cars of the day.

Mitchell pinned some of his automotive drawings on the wall of his cubicle at the Barron Collier Company. They drew the attention of the sons of the senior Collier, who by chance were among the greatest enthusiasts in America at that time for road racing in the European style. Barron, Jr., Sam and Miles Collier invited Bill to their family estate, "Overlook," near Pocantico Hills, New York, where they'd raced with powered buckboards that were the go-karts of those days, and also to the three-quarter-mile Sleepy Hollow Ring, a dirt track they'd carved out of some land owned by their father.

Caught up by the enthusiasm of the Colliers, Bill Mitchell made sketches of their racing events at the "Ring" with M.G.'s, Amilcars, and Willys and Ford specials, lively and spontaneous drawings that greatly pleased the youthful racers by making their totally informal events seem more established and mature. At their request, Mitchell designed an emblem for the Automobile Racing Club of America, as their group became known. And when Harley Earl, on the lookout for talent to expand his Art and Colour Section at General Motors, saw some of Bill's drawings, a new career was born. Mitchell was hired by GM as a stylist, and soon showed he was one of the most energetic and able men in this new profession. When Harley Earl retired on December 1, 1958, William L. Mitchell was named his successor, at the age of forty-six, as the head of G.M.'s Styling Staff.

Mitchell enjoys driving powerful cars and he can handle them well, but he's never been in a position where he could race himself. That doesn't imply that he ever lost his deep-seated enthusiasm for racing cars and the men who drive them. Before he had the top job at GM Styling he was a motivating force, starting in 1956, in the creation of modified Corvettes like the SR-2 that were entered in road racing. An SR-2 that was Mitchell's personal pride and joy saw a lot of competition action through 1958, handled by Jim Jeffords, among others.

As sometimes happens, Mitchell and GM Styling were able to obtain, in 1958, an experimental Chevrolet chassis that was no longer required for its original purpose. It was a famous chassis, that of the Corvette SS Mule that had seen so many pre-race laps at Sebring in 1957 and had, in its moment in the sun, been test-hopped by Juan Fangio and Stirling Moss. After Sebring the Mule chassis was completely cleaned up and refurbished, in a first stage of preparation for a planned assault on Le Mans. But with the cancellation of all Chevrolet racing plans the erstwhile Mule had never been fully bodied as an SS. It sat waiting for more than a year for Bill Mitchell to figure out how to acquire it.

If it were to be raced privately the car would have to be rebodied, so it couldn't be immediately recognized. Mitchell had no shortage of ideas in that direction. Under Bill's supervision, the main motif for the revived SS was adapted by stylist Larry Shinoda from the imaginative new design created in the Research Studio in 1957 for the stillborn Q-Corvette. It had the same low, wide grille and sharp-edged cross-section with prominent bulges for clearance above the wheels. A long, tapering central hood bulge was added to clear the fuel injection, and a conventional headrest containing a roll bar was added at the rear. A full-width windscreen was part of the design.

During the winter of 1958-1959 a fiberglass body was hand-laid for the car in the GM Styling fabrication shop. Given bonded-in reinforcements of annealed aluminum, the skin was conservatively heavy at 0.125 inch thick, about the same as that of a stock Corvette. Ducts at the sides of the wide front grille were ar-

During the June Sprints at Elkhart Lake's Road America in 1959, John Fitch battled with brake problems in Bill Mitchell's striking new Sting Ray racer.

The flying dentist, Dr. Dick Thompson, became the driver most closely identified with the Sting Ray. In its first season the car was a brilliant red.

ranged to feed fresh air to the fuel injection and also to the front brakes, and flush inlets in the rear deck admitted air to ducts that cooled the inboard rear brakes.

For engine cooling a prototype of the new Harrison aluminum radiator for the standard Corvette was used, angled sharply forward. Of the warm air departing from it, about one-third was deflected up through outlets atop the hood, while the rest flowed back through the engine room and the vents for the exhaust pipes to flush out the heat that had been so debilitating to the drivers at Sebring. The exhaust headers were grouped more closely together so they were less effective as radiators, and were given additional shielding. As a final heat barrier the firewall was carefully sealed and covered with a half-inch layer of Microquartz insulation, held in place by wire mesh.

The Sting Ray, as the rebodied SS was aptly named, became Bill Mitchell's personal property and its racing activities had to be financed out of his pocketbook, which had expanded with his elevation to a GM vice-presidency but was by no means unlimited in size. For this reason, as well as the fact that high-performance engine development at Chevrolet had been momentarily braked, the Sting Ray raced with an engine much like that used by the SS in 1957. Still 283 cubic inches in size, it was rated at 280 net horsepower at the clutch, installed, at 6,200 rpm. Peak torque was at 4,400 rpm, and the normal shift point was 6,500

revolutions per minute with 6,800 permissible in top gear.

Experimental aluminum heads of several different types were used successfully on the Sting Ray engines, with an 11.0 to one compression ratio. Set toward the rich side for reliability and cool running, the Rochester fuel injection unit dated from 1957 and delivered about six miles per gallon in competition. The cooling system included a 180-degree thermostat and a drive ratio of 0.7 to crank speed for the aluminum water pump instead of the usual 0.9. Heat was extracted from the seven quarts of SAE 30 Shell X100 oil by a special bypass-type oil cooler, an experimental Harrison unit designed for a truck transmission. It was sensitive to the oil viscosity (when the oil became thin it passed more of it) in such a way that it kept the lubricant at a virtually constant 240 degrees without a separate thermostat. Oil foaming was eliminated by a Dow-corning additive known as "200 Fluid."

In all its drive line and chassis details the Sting Ray was essentially identical to the SS. In the cockpit this was betrayed only by the deep-dished three-spoke steering wheel. Otherwise the panel was very simple, unlike that of the highly styled SS. While the car was raced it carried a Sting Ray emblem and nameplate, but nowhere was there an obvious reference to Corvette or Chevrolet. This car was anything but a stalking horse for a covert GM return to racing; in fact Bill Mitchell had to put on record for GM management a passionate yet plausible written argument in

Anatole Lapine, now head of the Porsche styling office, was a GM stylist when he co-drove with Dick Thompson in the 1959 500-mile race at Road America.

favor of his being allowed to enter the car on a personal basis before they would permit him to proceed.

Proceed Bill Mitchell did, entering his glossy red Sting Ray for the President's Cup Race at Maryland's twisty little Marlboro Raceway on April 18, 1959. Dr. Dick Thompson was the nominated driver, and Zora Arkus-Duntov was also in reluctant attendance — reluctant because he knew the chassis he had helped create would be competing in a kind of racing for which it had not been designed, and without the level of factory support it was intended to have. He could see only disadvantages to Chevrolet Engineering in this undertaking, and he never gave it his backing at any level. One of Zora's top mechanics, Eddie Zalucki, did, however, devote many of his off-duty hours to the maintenance of the Sting Ray during 1959.

Called "futuristic-looking" by one onlooker, this startlingly different car was the center of attention at Marlboro in its debut. During practice the complicated twin-servo brake system started playing its usual tricks, locking the wheels unpredictably and fading the brakes it didn't lock. A temporary cooling scoop was added to the rear deck and the right-hand half of the windscreen was sliced off to let the air get to the scoop. The hood louvers that exhausted air from the radiator were also cut out, leaving two unblocked rectangular openings. Carrying number eleven, which was seen most frequently on the car, the Sting Ray came

to the line for its first race after no more than a quarter-hour of practice.

In spite of the rain showers that dampened the track during the main event, Thompson took the lead at the start and held it again briefly later when the leading Lister-Corvette retired. Dick was battling with wheelspin (no limited-slip differential was fitted) and with the erratic brakes, and lost half a lap with a spin. He got rolling again and was placed fourth at the finish behind two RSK Porsches and a Lister-Jaguar.

Never lacking in verve behind the wheel, Dick Thompson was the object of the wrath of Marlboro's chief steward that day. After a later hearing, his SCCA license was suspended for ninety days. Reported *Auto Sport*, "Thompson was suspended for metal-to-metal contacts with other competitors! The tapped drivers swore it was all their fault — but the Contest Board seemed to feel that Thompson just was charging too hard."

For a new car the performance at Marlboro hadn't been bad at all. "The Sting Ray is no longer a show car," said a happy Bill Mitchell. "Now we're ready to race." Observed Duane Unkefer in *Sports Cars Illustrated*: "Judging from its brief but promising performance there's going to be a lot of action when some of the handling difficulties are worked out, and it's quite logical to assume that the Sting Ray will be whetting its barbed tail with a diet of dung-beetles in mind." This last reference was to the

Chevy-engined Scarabs that had been built and raced by Lance Reventlow and Chuck Daigh in 1958, and had been sold to private teams for 1959. The Sting Ray was in fact destined to engage in several epic battles with these California creations.

Several months elapsed before the Sting Ray appeared again at Elkhart Lake for the June Sprints, this time with John Fitch behind the wheel instead of the suspended Thompson. Fitch, of course, had lapped Sebring many times with the same chassis in its original SS Mule incarnation. Now he found its brakes to be just as troublesome as they'd been two years before, if not more so. The red machine had been cleaned up in the meantime, with grilles fitted to the air outlets in the hood, a tonneau cover for the right side of the cockpit, and the provisional rear air scoop removed. It had also acquired a permanent team manager/development engineer, Dean Bedford, Jr., a youthful and urbane engine specialist who had driven in the first race ever held at Watkins Glen in 1948, placing ninth in his M.G. TC.

Fitch was among the leaders at the start of the thirty-five-lap main event at Elkhart Lake, and settled down to fourth or fifth place. The unpredictable brakes took their toll on the nineteenth lap, however, causing a nasty spin and retiring the Sting Ray. "Fitch was in and out of the pits several times during Saturday's practice complaining about the brake setup," reported Jack Brady for *Road & Track*, "but evidently to no avail."

"A gauge of the Sting Ray's performance capabilities has been rather difficult to establish," Brady noted. "True to the Detroit tradition, the car weighs more than you would expect in a racing machine. It took two men to handle the lever jack during pit stops, with the jack itself sinking into the pit surface. Weight is probably a contributing factor to brake problems." The car wasn't all *that* heavy, but it did weigh quite a bit more than the magnesium-bodied Corvette SS at 2,154 pounds dry in its original early-1959 form.

The representative of *Sports Car*, Budd Blume, made an observation at Elkhart Lake that was also interesting: "Coming up the front straightaway the upturned body 'styling' appeared to lift the front wheels nearly off the pavement." This was not what the car's designers had intended; by making the body relatively flat on top and rounded on the bottom they had hoped to create an inverted airfoil, a huge wing that would push the car down against the track. They'd even conducted some wind tunnel testing to try to validate this concept, discovering in the process that the car's drag coefficient was between 0.43 and 0.45.

Realizing that high lift definitely existed and that it was hampering the car's high-speed cornering, Bedford found he could reduce it by shimming the rear coil springs to give the body a more forward rake. The shimming also helped keep the suspension from bottoming on bumpy tracks. For more twisty

At Road America in 1959 the Sting Ray was not quite the equal in speed of the Lister-Jaguar, trailing here, which was disc-braked and lighter in weight.

circuits, a smaller-diameter front anti-roll bar was obtained and fitted. The rubber bushings used in the radius rods to the rear de Dion axle began to show the same fragility they'd revealed in 1957, and were replaced regularly after every three races.

After Elkhart Lake the original ceramic-metallic brake linings were replaced by the latest Moraine sintered-metallic linings, riveted to the shoes and running inside normal Corvette finned brake drums. These, it was hoped, would behave more consistently, and they were put to the test at Lime Rock on July 25 in a professional race staged by USAC, which Dick Thompson was free to enter with or without an SCCA license. In this three-heat event, the one in which Rodger Ward's midget scored a cage-rattling victory over the best the sporty-car set had to offer, the Sting Ray placed ninth.

In another USAC event at the infamous Meadowdale track near Chicago, Dick Thompson faded the Sting Ray's brakes and failed to negotiate a slow turn. Sliding off to the side, the car's wheels were tripped by a sand bank and it executed a ground-level barrel-roll. The body itself wasn't badly damaged but the attachment points to the chassis did need some attention. Back at Elkhart Lake in mid-August, Dick Thompson was partnered by GM stylist Anatole Lapine in the 500-mile race. With lap times in the low 2:50's the car was not so quick as the best in its C-Modified class, the Lister-Jaguar that lapped in 2:47. The Sting

Ray put up a reasonably good show in the race until it retired. Brakes were again the main problem.

After Elkhart the Sting Ray was given a major overhaul. The complex double-booster braking system was discarded and replaced by a single Hydrovac power assist, modified by Bendix to allow the required pedal pressure to be adjusted. A complete changeover, for example to disc brakes, was ruled out at that time by the cost and the amount of engineering that would be needed. The only later change in the brakes was the welding of the linings to the shoes after Bridgehampton in 1960. But they were never as good as they should have been: "In every race I'd be out of brakes — and I mean *no* brakes — by the halfway mark," Thompson recalls, pointing out that the Sting Ray moved at much higher speeds and lacked the same degree of built-in head wind that helped slow down the stock Corvettes that gave satisfaction with similar brakes.

During October and November a completely new body was also made. Besides being slightly raceworn, the original body was heavy and tended to crack and split, its aluminum reinforcements being inadequately strong. The new panels were laid of three layers of fiberglass silk, adding up to a skin only 0.060 inch thick that was more resilient. The panels were reinforced with balsa wood and given heat-treated aluminum attachment brackets bonded in place. Where Dzus fasteners retained the body sec-

Dick Thompson handled the potent Sting Ray with an abandon that was exhilarating, taking it to an SCCA National Championship in its class in 1960.

After its retirement from racing the Sting Ray's debut as an auto show attraction was in Chicago on February 18, 1961, at McCormick Place.

tions, the GRP surface was increased in thickness locally to keep their screw heads from pulling through.

Seventy-five pounds were removed from the Sting Ray by the new skins. With the braking system changes this reduced the car's dry weight to about 2,000 pounds. Sporting a new metallic silver paint job the revised car first saw action against strong international opposition in the Bahamas in December, where Dick Thompson took it to tenth place in the Nassau Trophy Race. After that, in preparation for the 1960 season, the chassis was fitted with the set of ten-percent-stiffer springs that Duntov had originally produced for possible use in the SS. They seemed to suit the Sting Ray much better than the original springs.

For the 1960 campaign, run from a rented shop in the back of a woodworking company in Roseville, Michigan, the chief mechanic was R. Ken Eschebach, a Styling employee when not away from home racing. Ken's skills and unfailing good spirits were indispensable to the team's success. Ken, Mitchell, Thompson and Dean Bedford planned a major attack on the SCCA's National Championship in the C-Modified class, for cars with engines of from three to five liters. In this they were highly successful.

It was obvious in the first outing at Marlboro on April 16 that the car was vastly improved. It placed third behind two RSK

Porsches and defeated a very quick Type 61 "Birdcage" Maserati. On May 1 it finished second in the main event at Danville, Virginia, behind Bob Holbert's RSK, and two weeks later at Cumberland, Maryland, it won its class the third time running, being outraced only by two RSK's and two Type 61 Maseratis. The Cunningham-entered Maserati of Walt Hansgen was the sole machine to stay ahead of the Sting Ray at Bridgehampton, New York, on May 30, where Dick Thompson threw the silver sports car around that track's bumpy turns with flair and daring that were breathtaking.

The quick-change final drive provided a wide ratio selection for the tracks where the Sting Ray ran. The highest set was 3.70 to one for Bridgehampton and Meadowdale, giving the car a top speed of about 155 mph. For Danville and Elkhart Lake 3.86 gears were used, 4.20 for Cumberland and 4.39 for Marlboro. For those slower tracks the Firestone 6.70 x 15 tires used at the front could also be fitted at the back instead of the normal 7.10 x 15 size, on the 5½K x 15 Halibrand wheels.

The problem of finding a suitable differential for the Sting Ray was solved in a forthright manner. Running without some form of self-locking differential, the car hadn't been able to deliver its power to the ground on the typically twisty American tracks. A Powr-Lok limited-slip unit was tried, but didn't do the

Spruced up as a showgoer, the Sting Ray kept the metallic silver finish it had adopted during the 1960 season and was given a new windscreen.

When Bill Mitchell started using it on the road, the Sting Ray was given a windscreen for the passenger and much longer grilles for the two-hood vents.

job consistently. Finally the differential gears were welded together and the Sting Ray was run with a locked rear end. That took care of applying the power; all Dick Thompson had to do was steer a little more. He could do that with either the throttle or the steering wheel.

In June and July Thompson had memorable battles with the "Meister Brauser" Scarab driven by Augie Pabst of Milwaukee. On both occasions Bill Mitchell's silver car came off second best, but the sports car world knew it had been there. The June 18 duel was at Elkhart Lake, where the Sting Ray could take the lead in the back sections but was passed by the Scarab before the pits on every lap but the fateful thirteenth of the thirty-five-lap event. Thompson led that one, then made an unplanned departure from the road surface. He was twenty-four seconds behind the Scarab at the flag. During their struggle Pabst had set a new lap record at 2:44.8; after the race both drivers said they'd only been running on seven cylinders!

The rivalry was renewed at Meadowdale on July 24, where the two cars sat side-by-side on the front row of the grid. Pierre Perrin was there for *Sports Car*: "Pabst outdragged Thompson down the long descending straight, and when they appeared at the Monza Wall three miles later they were only a car length apart. The next lap found Thompson in the lead, with Pabst three car lengths back on this Monza Wall — the Monza Wall, in case you

haven't been there, is a highly banked 180-degree turn that can be taken by all but the fastest cars flat out.

"Thompson was driving the race of his life," Perrin continued, "and the Sting Ray was slowly increasing its lead over the Meister Brauser, when suddenly Pabst came by all alone with his left front fender pointing toward the sky, the result of coming too close to the Sting Ray on one of the many tricky corners. Thompson came into the pits, and after a routine inspection plus some water for the thirsty radiator the car went out and continued to burn up the track, although at the time he was almost a full lap behind the leader.

"Due to the roughness and irregular surface on the Monza Wall," wrote Perrin, "the Sting Ray appeared to be on the limit of adhesion. This spectacular performance overshadowed Pabst's fine drive, but soon the spectators groaned when the flying dentist came past and slowly coasted into the pits, retiring the car with a blown water pump gasket." Pabst and the Scarab were the winners, but those at Meadowdale that day will never forget the sight of the Sting Ray apparently "on the limit of adhesion." When Thompson drove it, that's the way it always seemed to be.

Thompson by now had easily clinched his Championship in C-Modified, piling up forty-eight points by the end of the season — thirty more than his nearest challenger. He and the Sting Ray were early leaders in the Elkhart Lake 500-mile race in Sep-

Before it was returned to its original appearance, the Sting Ray had a transparent hood scoop covering four dual-throat Weber carbs on a 427 CID engine.

tember, but were slowed by troubles that had his crew raiding the tow car for spare parts. They finished twenty-third overall and second in class. Practice troubles with the rear end at Watkins Glen later in the month persisted in the race, Thompson having to retire on the second lap of the Grand Prix.

Bill Mitchell's compact racing team went west in October of 1960 for the two professional events in California, well-attended by some of the world's fastest drivers and sports cars. At Riverside on the sixteenth the Sting Ray was the ninth-quickest qualifier, part of a topmost group of ten cars whose times were all within six seconds of each other. Brakeless at the finish as usual, Thompson finished eleventh in the race. A week later at Laguna Seca in the first of two heats Walt Hansgen — who should have known better — made the error of passing the Sting Ray, which at the time was holding down an excellent fourth place, and then immediately braking hard for a corner. There was nothing Dick Thompson could do to keep from hitting Hansgen's Maserati. Dick finished both heats but was well to the rear in this, the racing swansong of the Sting Ray.

In 1961 the racer reverted to a show car. Now Styling Staff could spruce it up with a flush-fitting tonneau cover and a wrap-around canopy for the driver's side. It was given "Corvette" and "Fuel Injection" emblems and painted and polished to a fare-thee-well for its official debut on the show circuit at Chicago's McCormick Place in February, 1961. This marked the return to the Chevrolet fold of their prodigal motorcar. When it ceased being a novel show attraction it was equipped with a passenger-side windscreen, a speedometer, and a rear license-plate mount, in which form — locked differential and all — Bill Mitchell drove it to and from work when the weather was fair.

The veteran chassis was given several technical transplants during the sixties. Dunlop disc brakes were somehow fitted in. It was powered by a larger-displacement small-block engine, then by a Mark IV 427-cubic-inch V-8 with quadruple Weber carburetors under a transparent plastic air scoop. It was bright red again, for a while, until Bill Mitchell decided he wanted to return it to the silver, smooth-hooded shape that had thrilled so many racing fans during two years of open competition — years that Mitchell had unashamedly enjoyed.

Carried in the cockpit of the Sting Ray during those years and many that followed was a shield-shaped emblem that drew quizzical stares from those enthusiasts who could get close enough to this extraordinary car to see it. It carried the letters "ARCA," and a lively drawing showing a front view of a vintage sports car approaching at high speed. The enthusiasm that had been born at the Sleepy Hollow Ring in 1934 was still burning with life at the GM Styling Staff more than three decades later, as part of the car that we now think of as the original Sting Ray.

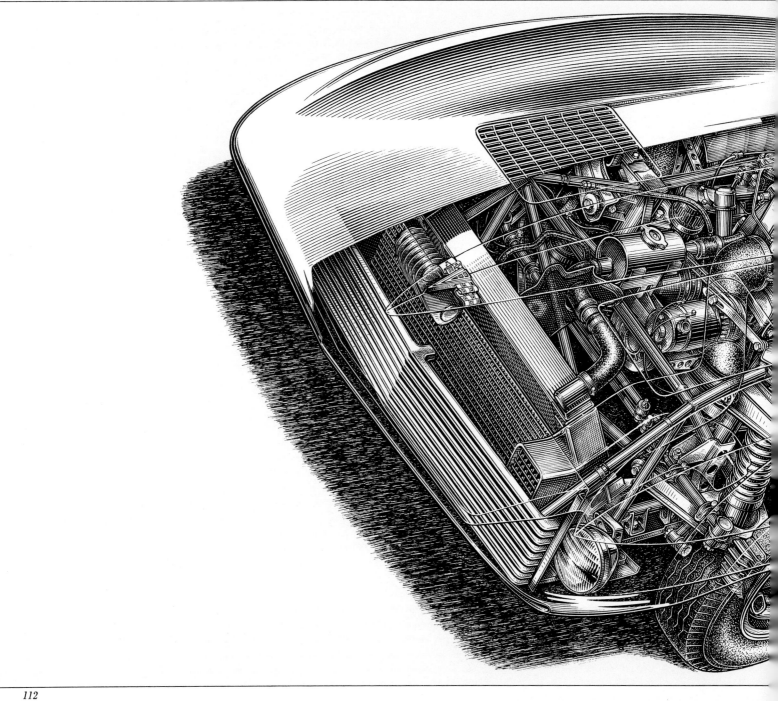

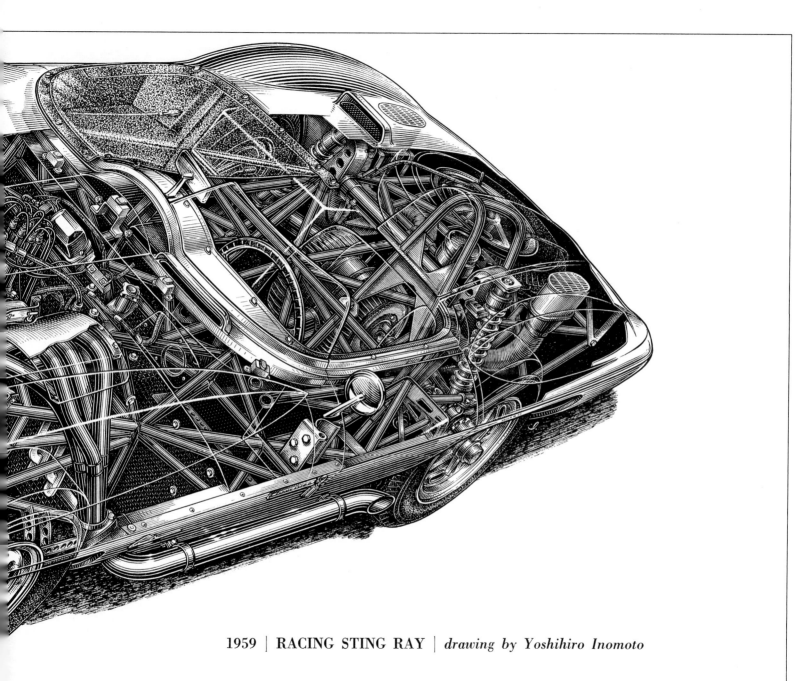

1959 | **RACING STING RAY** | *drawing by Yoshihiro Inomoto*

Chapter 9

MATURE MACHINE: 1961-1962

When the Sting Ray racer made its first appearance at Marlboro early in 1959 it was accompanied by a customized '58 Corvette road car that was, in its way, just as impressive. This had been created during the summer of 1958 as personal transportation for the soon-to-be chief of GM Styling, Bill Mitchell, and it embodied many ideas that he wanted to explore for possible future use not only in Corvettes but also in other GM cars. The late Fifties were years of turbulence, ferment, indecision and transition in automobile styling in Detroit. This experimental/personal car was one of the probes put forth by Mitchell to test the validity of new shape and proportion concepts.

This long-nosed, duck-tailed Corvette was eventually designated the XP-700, marking it as the first in a completely new series of design studies under the Mitchell regime. It also initiated a new policy, that of building true running experimental cars whenever possible, rather than the mockup "dream cars" that had populated so many of the Motoramas of the early fifties. There was always plenty of power under the hood of any special car that Bill Mitchell drove on the highway.

Through its midsection the XP-700 was much like the stock 1958 Corvette on which it was based. Its interior had special metallic floor trim and a steering wheel without the familiar lightening holes in its spokes. The fuel filler cap was exposed on the left-hand fender instead of being concealed, and air inlet scoops grew from the skin just behind each door. The rocker panels were sliced away to make room for an exposed muffler and twin-pipe exhaust system along each side, exhausting ahead of each rear wheel. Small circular rear-view mirrors were held by bullet-shaped housings, and cowl scoops similar to those on the first Corvette dream car made a reappearance.

The rear of the XP-700 was given a much lighter, fresher look, swept up from the rear spring hangers to a high break line that curved around the corners to windsplits trailing from the tops of the wheel openings. Its upper deck was flat, with a central windsplit through a circular Corvette medallion. Twin circular taillights were inset into the tail at both sides, flanking a heavy chrome surround for the recessed license plate. This rear-end shape was adopted almost intact for the facelift of the production Corvette for 1961, the main difference being the use of wraparound horizontal bumpers instead of the skimpy vertical bars used on the XP-700.

This personal Mitchell machine had a front end that broke radically with the heavy, blunt styles that had been typically GM through 1958. It was inspired in part by the work that was being done concurrently at Styling on a car that Harley Earl was to take with him into retirement, the Oldsmobile F-88 Mark III. This was a very low-built two-seater, using some chassis components from the abandoned "Q" passenger car project; it had an extended oval nose between horizontal pairs of headlamps. This concept was carried even farther for the one-off XP-700.

Mitchell's car had a high nose in the form of an exceptionally slim oval air inlet. Serving as a front bumper was a chromed ring inserted in the oval, mounted in a manner that allowed it to float rearward and absorb small impacts. There were other air-inlet scoops below the oval nose and at its sides, below the recessed headlights, which were Lucas spotlights, in fact, when the XP-700 was an auto show attraction. The lighter look of this special car was further enhanced by its chromed Dayton knock-off wire wheels and by triple louvers behind each front wheel opening.

In October of 1959 the XP-700 was overhauled to amplify its value as a special attraction at auto shows. Its tail was extended, deliberately exaggerated, in fact, so it wouldn't tip off too literally the design of the coming production car. It was also given a spectacular double-bubble hardtop of transparent plastic. Solar rays were deflected by a vacuum-deposited film of aluminum above the occupants, on the inside of the plastic. Also carried by the top was a periscopic rear-view mirror and a row of air vents down the metallic strip dividing the two transparent bubbles. Internal refinements included a cockpit-mounted chronometer, an experimental manual overdrive unit, and an

Mitchell-inspired XP-700 set new rear end shape for 1961 Corvette in its early-'59 form, above left. Rear was later reshaped, above right, with result below.

XP-700 departed radically from established Corvette styling lines with sharp nose, double-bubble roof, and outside exhaust pipes. Bill Mitchell personally designed the light, slim front end with its integral cushioned bumper-grille. Detail trim of both interior and engine room (far right) of XP-700 was painstakingly exact.

engine room that was chromed and crackle-finished to dazzling perfection.

The revised XP-700 had slots in the steering wheel spokes instead of the familiar lightening holes; the slots were scheduled for use on the 1961 production Corvette and the publicity pictures were taken with a slotted steering wheel, but the original holes reappeared on the actual 1961 Corvette spokes. Formerly optional items like the parking-brake warning light, dual sun visors, windshield washers and an interior courtesy light were made standard equipment on the 1961 model. With a change in the biggest body mold, the one for the floor panel, the transmission tunnel was narrowed several inches to the benefit of foot room.

In addition to the change in the tail, which added a small amount of luggage room with no increase in overall length, the 1961 model received a front-end cosmetic conversion. The hallowed grille teeth gave way to a simple mesh screen not unlike some of those considered for the '58 front end. This improved the looks of the Corvette, which regained any lost identity by having its name spelled out above the grille in large letters. The new car's cleaner appearance was given further emphasis by painting the formerly chromed headlight surrounds in body color.

Some of the mechanical improvements introduced as options in 1960 were made standard on the 1961 Corvette. One was the aluminum radiator, which weighed half as much as the copper

one it replaced, in spite of having a thicker core and ten percent more cooling capacity. It was altered in design on the basis of 1960 experience, given a separate header tank, a barrel-shaped container on the left side of the engine. Also standard was the viscous drive for the fan, which limited its maximum speed to 3,200 rpm and which imposed no drag on the engine until it was required for additional cooling.

Though the power units were carried over unchanged for 1961, there were refinements in the transmission department. Another technique first tried on the SS in 1957 made its way to the production line: an aluminum case for the four-speed transmission. It effected a weight saving of fifteen pounds, bringing to forty-five pounds the total amount of lightness added by the use of aluminum in the transmission, clutch housing, and radiator.

Buyers of Corvettes with the base three-speed transmission (30.9 percent of the customers in 1960, 22.6 percent in 1961) received a bonus in the new models with a wider range of ratios that gave better urban acceleration in combination with a higher standard axle ratio, 3.36 instead of 3.70 to one, to give easier highway cruising. The new ratios were 2.47 in first gear and 1.53 in second. The four-speed continued to be a close-ratio transmission, favored by 64.1 percent of Corvette buyers in 1961. The remaining 13.3 percent opted for the Powerglide automatic transmission.

Magazine road testers found it difficult to be critical of the Corvette in its ninth model year. "Continual refinements since 1954 have made the Corvette into a sports car for which no owner need make excuses," said *Road & Track*, adding, "It goes, it stops, and it corners. The Corvette is absolutely unmatched for performance per dollar in terms of performance machinery." Observed *Car Life*, "Its very high performance and general character have established it firmly as an exceptional prestige automobile, the car chosen by the true connoisseur, driven by those who know and appreciate the finer points of automotive engineering." Their tests and others gave results along these lines:

1961 Corvette Acceleration Tabulation			
	4 bbl. carburetion Powerglide	2 x 4 bbl. carburetion 4-speed	fuel-injected 4-speed
Nominal power	230 bhp	270 bhp	315 bhp
Final drive ratio	3.55:1	3.70:1	4.11:1
0-60 mph	7.7 secs.	5.9 secs.	5.5 secs.
0-80 mph	15.1 secs.	10.3 secs.	8.9 secs.
0-100 mph	24.0 secs.	16.5 secs.	14.5 secs.
Standing ¼-mile	16.5 secs.	14.6 secs.	14.2 secs.
Terminal ¼-mile speed	83 mph	93 mph	99 mph
Maximum speed	109 mph	131 mph	128 mph

These new Corvettes kept high the marque's reputation for competition suitability, though supremacy in the SCCA's A Production class wasn't reasserted until the extra-stiff springs were reinstated as an allowable racing option in 1962, when Dick Thompson became the A Production champ in a Corvette. He'd collected the most points in B Production in 1961, an honor that had fallen to Bob Johnson's Corvette in 1960. Denverite Danny Collins was an active Corvette campaigner during these seasons, after driving some more exotic modified machinery, which he compared to the favorite car of the readers of *Corvette News*, the magazine that Chevrolet had started in 1957 for owners of their sports car:

"The basic difference between the Corvette's handling and the handling of the Ferrari and the Mercedes Special was this: the Ferrari plows or pushes the front end off the outside of a corner very easily (this is called extreme 'understeer') ; the Mercedes Special was just the opposite — the slightest bit of throttle would

Fuel-injected engine, above, was carried over to cleaned-up '61 model.

send the tail end 'into orbit' or oversteer. The Corvette, bless it, goes where you aim it. You can slip the tail in or out at will with the throttle. The torque that the Corvette has goes a long way in helping the driver 'place' the rear end of the Corvette where he wants it.

"The Corvette could be set up in a variety of attitudes in the corner. You could 'drive through,' in a sort of crossed-up attitude, or you could 'slip through' on the verge of this crossed-up position, which placed your nose into the inside of the turn and your tail out with all your wheels pointed straight ahead. The latter invariably proved to be the quickest method. The Corvette is the first car I've raced that had such a wide choice!"

Five Corvettes were entered in the Sebring twelve-hour race in March of 1961, looking exceptionally clean with their newly abbreviated tails. It resulted in the best-ever showing for a strictly stock GT Corvette, an eleventh place overall finish in the race. The car was entered, prepared and co-driven by Dallas Chevrolet dealer Delmo Johnson, partnered by Dale Morgan of Tulsa, Oklahoma. They ran a carefully paced race, never exceeding 6100 rpm and averaging 81.76 mph for the half-day event over the difficult Sebring course. With extra-rich injector settings that favored reliability rather than power they averaged six miles per gallon of fuel from their thirty-six-gallon tank, and used only one quart of oil to cover 981.2 miles of racing. Don Yenko's two en-

tries were professionally prepared but more aggressively driven, one retiring and the other finishing well back.

During 1960 and 1961 another Texas enthusiast took a different approach to the Corvette, radically transforming it for use on the road. With the help of Carroll Shelby, wealthy enthusiast Gary Laughlin of Fort Worth shipped several new chassis to Modena, Italy, and commissioned the building of special bodies for them by Carrozzeria Scaglietti. This firm produced a fastback coupé body in aluminum that virtually duplicated the berlinetta it was then building for Ferrari while cutting some 400 pounds from the weight of a stock Corvette. The first car kept the typical Corvette grille; later ones that were imported and sold by Laughlin had a more Ferrari-like front end.

American buyers were happy enough with the improved looks of the normal Corvette to allow a further slight increase in the model-year production for 1961, to 10,939 units. Just about half of these were ordered with the detachable hardtop, a ratio that was typical for the time.

At the end of 1961 a new hand took over the tiller at Chevrolet, as Ed Cole moved up the GM corporate ladder. Semon E. Knudsen moved in from Pontiac, which he had brought from sixth place in sales to third, to head Chevrolet as his father, William S. Knudsen, had during the thirties. "Bunkie" Knudsen came to Chevrolet with a solid record of accomplishment behind

Corvette bodied in Italy by Scaglietti closely resembled the Ferrari coupé.

excitement is standard equipment! The small blue car lurking behind that '61 Corvette is a 1927 Bugatti. It was as exciting as any car can be, but it was a little short on creature comfort and only the best coordinated and most sinewy could hope to drive it. The Corvette, on the other hand, guarantees unstinting devotion to all the details of driver-passenger comfort and accommodation with *no* sacrifice in flashing performance or impeccable handling. Anyone who can drive well can drive a Corvette; the only thing that really sets it apart from today's automobiles is the absolutely ecstatic way it goes down the road. Built into every Corvette is a lifetime supply of pure sports car excitement such as you've never known before. Corvette by Chevrolet

Promotion continued to appeal to the escapist in us all with the 1962 model, refreshed in styling and monotone in exterior color.

him and a strong record for expertise in product development and in the use of racing to promote car sales. In fact it was Pontiac's highly successful covert support of stock car racing teams that helped push Ford into open disavowal of the AMA ban on racing promotions.

At Pontiac, Knudsen had taken full advantage of the ability that a GM divisional general manager had at that time to act independently. He worked through outside firms, like those of Ray Nichels for stock car racing and Mickey Thompson for drag racing and record breaking. The public at large wasn't aware that Pontiac parts and money kept these companies going, though it was known well enough to auto racing insiders. And Knudsen reported not at all on his actions to the men who had succeeded Curtice at the top of GM in 1958, Frederic Donner as chairman of the board and chief executive officer, and John Gordon as president and chief operating officer. Neither felt that racing was of the slightest value to any General Motors products.

Under Knudsen the throttle was opened on Corvette production. By adding a second shift at St. Louis, for the first time, half again as many sports cars were driven off the line in the 1962 model year as they had been the year before: 14,531, to be precise. Acceptance of the Corvette by sports car people had reached very high levels. Early models were enjoying excellent resale values, not only because there had been few radical styling changes but also because the fiberglass bodies were holding up

Introduction of the 327 CID V-8 engine was the most important chassis change in 1962, giving the car even more formidable racing potential.

extremely well, and word of this was getting around. Sales promotion activities were stepped up under the direction of Joseph P. Pike, an early Corvette enthusiast who took over sales responsibility for the car in April, 1960. Joe launched the model with a small phonograph record of its exhaust sounds and comments by Zora Duntov distributed with a copy of *Corvette News.*

Increased production in St. Louis was also possible because operations there and in Ashtabula were now running smoothly at close to the number of cars per hour that had been targeted back in 1953. To ensure that each body was as dimensionally precise as possible, the underbody was locked onto a special master-body truck and carried by it through the whole process of bonding and assembly. With its extensive steel reinforcements for the cowl and fenders, the complete 1962 body weighed 405 pounds — actually six pounds less than the equivalent 1953 figure. Down the final Corvette assembly line there were nine major inspection stations, followed by a test run indoors with the wheels on rollers and then a drive around the plant that included a stop on a roller rig that checked whether the optional limited-slip differential was working right. A final four-minute water spray at 18 p.s.i. pressure from twenty-eight nozzles, equivalent to a severe thundershower, was applied and passed without leakage before the new Corvette was cleared from the plant. Not until after the water test were the seats and the interior trim panels installed — just in case.

Since 1958 various Chevrolet passenger cars had been offered

Dick Thompson became 1962 SCCA National Champion in Class A Production with a '62 Corvette. He's in action above in a special event in Puerto Rico.

Sebring 1962: Bill Fuller, above; Black/Wyllie 18th-place car below.

More Sebring '62: Johnson/Morgan entry above; Black leading Fuller below.

with a new "W" V-8 engine of 348 cubic inches, a compact engine but a heavy-duty one as indicated by its weight of over one hundred pounds more than the 283 V-8. Some thought was occasionally given to using it in the Corvette. "The weight penalty is high," Zora Arkus-Duntov emphasized late in 1957, "but the cost of 350 H.P. or more will be the lowest." Fortunately, most Corvette fans felt, this installation was never made. At a very early date Chevy had started experimenting with large-displacement versions of the 283, 300-cubic-inch units which in fact pre-dated the design of the "W" engine. This work finally bore fruit in 1962 with the introduction of a 327-cubic-inch version of the small-block engine across the board in the Corvette. This was the foundation of an outstanding new range of engines that powered the Corvette virtually without change through 1965.

By introducing this enlarged engine Chevrolet was making official what the hot-rodders had been doing to the little V-8 for quite a while. The very successful Scarab sports cars of 1958 had engines bored and stroked to 339 cubic inches, for example. Ed Cole and Harry Barr increased the bore of the 283 by one-eighth inch to an even four inches, and lengthened the stroke by a quarter-inch to three-and-a-quarter inches. Though the rod length and bearing sizes remained unchanged, the rod of the 327 did have a heftier shank section to take the higher stresses of the bigger piston. For the same reason all the 327 V-8's had the heavy-duty Moraine aluminum bearings that were only used in the hot 283's before.

The special big-port head, with its 1.94-inch intake valves, was fitted to three out of the four new engine types offered in the Corvette. Only the base engine had the 1.72-inch intake valves, fed by a single Carter four-barrel carburetor, and opened and closed by a new hydraulic-lifter camshaft with more duration and overlap. It developed 250 bhp at a modest 4,400 rpm. The next hotter engine stayed with the hydraulic cam but moved to the big-port head, fed by an enlarged (1.25-inch primary venturis instead of 1.06-inch) Carter carburetor instead of the famed dual-quad carb layout, which had looked impressive but was costly and complex. Its output was 300 bhp at 5,000 rpm; both it and the lower-powered unit were offered with optional Powerglide, now with an all-aluminum housing.

Both these engines carried a double layer of head gaskets for a compression ratio that was officially 10.5 to one, official in the sense that the actual mechanical ratio was nearer 10.2 to one, a higher number being quoted — as was customary — to take into account the buildup of combustion-chamber deposits during the engine's early lifetime. For the two top-rated engines one gasket

was removed from each bank to raise the c.r. to a nominal 11.25 to one, actual 11.1 to one. The Duntov solid-lifter cam remained in use, output being 340 bhp at 6,000 rpm with the big Carter four-barrel and 360 at the same speed with injection.

The Rochester fuel injection went into its sixth year of production with a major change to adapt it to the deeper breathing of the bigger V-8. Instead of its original relatively complicated cold-start enrichment system it was given a simple choke valve in a new port right through the center of the conical "plug" that formed the fuel-metering venturi for the injection. When this valve was closed, as it was automatically for a cold start, it had a definite choking effect although the venturi itself — necessary to provide metering — remained fully open. With the valve open, once the engine was warm enough, it made available enough total air inlet area to meet the greater appetite of the new engine. Optional enlarged exhaust outlet area was also available in the form of RPO 441: straight-through mufflers.

Offered only with the two hydraulic-lifter engines was another new drive line, taking its lead from the wide-ratio three-speed launched in 1961. This one brought to the Corvette the wide-ratio four-speed transmission gears that had already been offered in Chevy sedans. Dubbed RPO 685, it had indirect ratios of 2.54, 1.92, and 1.51 to one. A specially recommended axle ratio for use with this box was a brand-new one, 3.08 to one, offering lazy top-gear cruising with an overall low ratio of 7.83 to one, which, with the added torque of the new engine, was multiplication enough for a fast break from a traffic light. The close-ratio four-speed transmission with the 3.70 to one axle was the normal (optional) pairing with the solid-lifter engines.

The effects of the forty-four additional cubic inches of displacement weren't felt so much at the bottom end of the acceleration range, where the street 1962 Corvette was limited by its tires and by its rear leaf springs, which hopped and chattered in spite of their radius rods. It became a bear over the quarter-mile distance, however. Here's what various magazines recorded in their road tests for the standing quarter:

	Axle Ratio	Elapsed time	Terminal speed
Car Life	4.11	14.0 secs.	100 mph
Car and Driver	3.70	15.0 secs.	95 mph
Motor Trend	3.70	14.9 secs.	102 mph
Sports Car Graphic	3.70	14.5 secs.	104 mph

SCCA 1962 Champions seen at Road America that year were Don Yenko in B Production, left, and Dick Thompson in A Production, in a 1962 model, at

No matter which magazine you were reading, you had to conclude this was one of the faster street machines you could buy at that time. Corvette base price was now at the $4,038 level, and a fuel-injected car could carry a price tag like the one *Car Life* tested: $4966.

Bolder looks made the '62 stand out as clearly as the black lines it could etch on the pavement. The mesh insert in the grille was now anodized black. Along the rocker panels, serrated strips of anodized aluminum added brightness, and provided a transitional touch to the motif of the all-new 1963 Corvette, which had already been designed by the time the changes on the '62 were settled. Finely-finned inserts in the fender coves replaced the three prominent chrome strips, and for the first time since the coves became part of the Corvette styling, in 1957, they couldn't be painted to order in a contrasting color. They were given more shapely raised edges without a chrome surround.

A potential challenger to the Corvette on the tracks of America had appeared during 1961: the Jaguar XK-E. One of the best American drivers, Bill Krause, handled one of the new all-independently-sprung Jaguars at Santa Barbara, California, over Labor Day weekend in 1961. First Bob Bondurant and then Paul Reinhart, who went on to be the Pacific Coast Divisional Champion in Class B Production in 1962, dealt easily with the English intruder. On only a few occasions did the Jaguar XK-E ever seriously challenge the pride of St. Louis.

Bob Bondurant had recorded many of his early racing laps in Corvettes, to begin with in a 1957 model of his own. He was very successful and soon moved up to driving somebody else's '59 model, a fast machine with a '61 engine entered by Santa Barbara's Washburn Chevrolet. This was even raced as a B Modified car with an engine opened out to 340 cubic inches, in which form it raced at Riverside and Laguna Seca in 1961 without bringing embarrassment to the marque of the bow tie.

On that Riverside weekend in 1961 a rematch of the Corvette-Jaguar battle was staged. The British car came off second-best again, this time losing to a factory-fresh '62 Corvette bearing an unusual "00" designation, piloted by Dave MacDonald. Dave got his start in competition with a string of Corvettes in drag racing, then switched to road courses in 1960 and came up a winner on his first attempt. He won the B Production Championship of the California Sports Car Club in 1961. Starting off that season with nine straight wins, Dave said, "At the April 16 race in Stockton, California, I was protested after winning the production race. When my engine was torn down, the inspectors found that I needed a valve job, had a leaking head gasket and an out-of-balance engine!"

At the end of 1961 the "00" numerals appeared on a most unusual "Corvette," another creation of MacDonald and his long-

Corvette cavorts ahead of a Daimler Dart at Danville and Frank Dominianni hustles his '62 model past a Morgan at Watkins Glen during 1963 season.

time backer, Jim Simpson. Seeking to mate the known virtues of the Corvette's power and handling to a lighter and handier chassis to run in modified events, they had Max Balchowsky build them a ninety-five-pound frame on a ninety-two-inch wheelbase, with suspension like that of his famous Old Yaller Mark IV. Around this they wrapped an eighty-five-pound fiberglass replica, shorter, narrower, and lower, of a '61 Corvette body. With power from a virtually stock 1962 fuel-injected engine, this amazing amalgam won its first time out at Cotati at the end of the 1961 season. Dave MacDonald's career was all too brief, cut short by a fatal crash at Indianapolis, but he had been for several seasons a brilliant jewel in the Corvette's crown.

Not unlike "00" in concept but built for a different purpose was Jack Lufkin's Corvette special, which staggered its rivals several years running at the Bonneville National Speed Trials. Based on the frame of a wrecked '62 Corvette, Lufkin's car had a solid front axle and suspension by Frank Kurtis, and a replica Corvette body also made at the Kurtis shops. In addition to proving useful at the drags, the Lufkin car set a D Sports-Racing record with a destroked engine at Bonneville at 187.659 mph in 1963, and shattered the C Sports-Racing mark the following year with a sizzling 204.248 mph two-way average.

Even though open Chevrolet participation in racing was barred, Corvette bits and pieces were still able to account for themselves remarkably well. This was owed to sound basic engineering, to the fierce loyalty and enthusiasm that the Corvette inspired, and to careful spadework behind the scenes. In January of 1962, for example, Zora Arkus-Duntov took a red fully-optioned hardtop Corvette to Daytona and Sebring for extensive trials with both Firestone and Goodyear technicians in attendance.

Why would a non-racing company take such pains with its products? That's what Jerry Titus asked Zora, eliciting this reply: "Many of our customers race and I therefore feel a responsibility to know our product's capabilities and limitations under such conditions. On the basis of our findings we can develop the vehicle with maximum safety and reliability designed into it. We are also evaluating components and obtaining data what will enable us to make logical improvements in future models."

Those "components" and "future models" were also in evidence at the early 1962 tests. One was a prototype of a brand-new Corvette that would be introduced later that year, disguised for the moment in a '62 body. The other was a blue-and-white single-seater with its engine in the rear, perhaps the most extraordinary Chevrolet ever to be seen by the public, once described as "looking like an eyeless, gill-less fish from the depths of the sea, or like a frozen scream." Its official name was far less exotic: CERV I.

Chapter 10

THE CERV STORY

It was one of the most unlikely scenes in the history of world motor sports. Here we all were at Riverside, California, for the second running of the United States Grand Prix in November, 1960. It was the last race of the 2½-liter G.P. Formula and all the major teams were there with the exception of Ferrari. Lotus, B.R.M. and Cooper were on hand in force and Scarab and Maserati were represented too. The motor press of the world had come to this track in the California desert to report on this historic curtain-closing event. And there, right in the middle of it all, was the most exotic-looking experimental single-seater car imaginable, though its engine was much too large to qualify for the race, built by devoutly non-racing Chevrolet.

It's hard to conceive how they dared to build it, let alone bring it to Riverside and show if off, in view of the prevailing GM attitude toward racing. There was Zora Duntov explaining its features to car builder John Cooper, and turning over its controls to Stirling Moss for a few demonstration laps of the track. Detailed photos and carefully worded news releases describing the CERV I as "a research tool for Chevrolet's continuous investigations into automotive ride and handling phenomena under the most realistic conditions" were being distributed to the press by Walter Mackenzie, former manager of racing for Chevrolet and now the Division's director of product information. There was a surreal quality about the sight of these men and this fantastically racy open-wheeled car in the midst of the Grand Prix crowd at Riverside. It was a big, powerful, sleek, blue-and-white question mark.

Even for its builder CERV I remained something of a question mark during its several active years of testing, modification and more testing. During those months and years of the late fifties and early sixties Zora Duntov and his crew were concentrating on one objective and then another for the single-seater, surviving the corporate highs and lows of changing personnel and points of view: One week it was "Let's go racing"; the next week it was "Cut out that talk about racing." CERV I went through it all.

Only now can we see that it survived these vicissitudes to keep alive the concept of exciting cars at Chevrolet, and to serve as a vital link between the Q-Corvette and racing SS and the new production Corvette that was unveiled for 1963.

Some of Zora's first thoughts about building a rear-engined racing car came to him at Sebring in 1957, when he was battling the surprisingly intense cockpit heat problems of the SS. "Why not at least put the engine behind me," he thought, "so I can be rid of that much of the heat?" Not until 1959, when Chevy's internal freeze on racing had begun to thaw, did he have a chance to start building a car that would embody that idea. This was the year of the emergence of the rear-engined Corvair. One of the successful internal sales points in favor of the CERV I was that it could be used to stage performance demonstrations that would spectacularly validate the soundness of the high-performance rear-engined car, of the Corvair taken to its ultimate limit, so to speak.

Duntov kept several criteria in mind when he and his senior engineers, Harold Krieger and Walt Zetye, sat down to design Chevrolet Experimental Racing Vehicle I. There existed the possibility of running it someday at Indianapolis, so its chassis dimensions had to conform to those required by that event. The wheelbase was fixed at the Indy minimum, ninety-six inches, and the track was set at fifty-six inches front and rear. Overall length became 172 inches, the maximum body width fifty-two inches.

CERV I was also intended to perform with virtuosity on the twisting gravel road to the top of Pikes Peak. This had already been the scene of several triumphs for the Cole-Duntov team, and it was the primary objective for this new car. In the beginning, in fact, before it had an official designation CERV I was referred to around Chevrolet and GM Styling as "the Hillclimber." It was suited to this use by its rearward weight bias — approaching sixty percent — as well as its low polar moment of inertia, achieved by grouping the engine, driver and fuel tanks close together in the center of the car, and by its upright seating position, af-

Riverside Raceway resounded to the booming exhaust of CERV I as Zora Duntov put it through its paces before the U.S. Grand Prix in November, 1960.

Conceived as a blend of hill climb record-breaker and Indy racer, CERV I did neither but explored new techniques with mid-engine layout, aluminum block

fording excellent visibility in all directions.

Chevy V-8 power was, of course, at the heart of "the Hillclimber." It took to the greatest extreme possible at that time the idea of an all-aluminum Chevrolet engine, building it around the stock 283-cubic-inch dimensions. The heads were aluminum, as briefly produced early in 1960, and that light material was also used for the water pump housing, flywheel, clutch pressure plate, and the starter motor body. Most startling was the use of an aluminum cylinder block made of a high-silicon alloy that required no cylinder liners. The standard Corvette pistons ran directly in the aluminum bores, just as they did a decade later in the production Vega and in Chevy-based Can-Am racing engines. CERV I was one of the pioneers along this trail, its block weighing ninety pounds less than the stock cast iron part.

Magnesium was also employed, for the clutch housing and the special inlet manifold for the fuel injection. Taking advantage of the engine's location behind him, where it didn't interfere with the view forward, Zora gave it a taller injection manifold with ram-pipe lengths increased from twelve to sixteen inches to enhance the mid-range torque that would be all-important in hillclimbing. A finned plenum chamber at the top was fitted with a metering venturi at the rear, where it was fed air by scoops in the sides of the car's tapering headrest.

Better than one hundred percent volumetric efficiency at certain engine speeds was achieved with this manifold, whose ram

pipes gradually decreased in cross-sectional area as they approached the critical port dimension, the section adjacent to the pushrods, then expanded again on their way to the valves. The exhaust pipes were also individually tuned with forty-inch header lengths, enclosed at the rear in groups of four by large tubular collectors.

The engine was otherwise similar to the stock 315-bhp Corvette V-8 of 1960, with the same Duntov cam, solid lifters, and stock crankshaft, bearings, rods, pistons, and rings. The light alloys had, however, cut the weight of the engine by more than 175 pounds. Complete with starter and generator it scaled only 350 pounds. The breathing refinements had allowed the V-8 to develop no less than 353 bhp at 6,200 rpm, so it actually delivered more than one horsepower per pound, a remarkable achievement, and one-and-a-quarter horsepower per cubic inch. The generator was a very small unit with an output of five amperes, driven by the same belt that (thanks to a smaller crankshaft pulley) drove the water pump at one-third less than the stock speed ratio to reduce the chances of cavitation at the high speeds the engine would consistently be reaching.

The drive was taken from the hydraulically-operated clutch to the basically stock four-speed transmission, which was placed between the engine and the final drive gears. Though not the most compact arrangement theoretically possible, this positioning ideally suited the general architecture of the CERV I. The

ar brakes were mounted inboard, and wheel drive shafts served as upper lateral links in CERV I's independent rear suspension, a very neat arrangement.

transmission was made as short as possible in its special aluminum housing by bringing the reverse gears — normally overhung to the rear — inside the main case. Indirect ratios were the standard ones: 2.20, 1.66, and 1.31 to one. A remote linkage ran forward to a shift lever on the right-hand side of the cockpit.

Reworked Halibrand components from the SS project were used for the CERV I final drive, encasing a 3.55 to one ring-and-pinion combination. The available quick-change gears gave thirteen different overall ratio increments from 2.63 to 4.80 to one; for some tests at Sebring a 3.28 overall ratio was used. As on the SS, the rear brakes were mounted inboard. This time normal Corvette mechanisms were chosen, with Moraine sintered iron linings. Brake diameter was eleven inches and the lining width two and a half inches in front, two inches in the rear.

For the uses Duntov had in mind for this car, extraordinary braking was not a critical requirement. The drums were completely special: all-aluminum with fine finning, vented faces, and cast-iron liners bonded in by the Al-Fin process. Front/rear braking proportion of 57/43 was effected by a single master cylinder with dual pistons, an early example of the type we use today in which a failure in one brake circuit won't affect the other one.

Zora had not given up on the idea of some form of variable control for the rear brake pressure. An experimental device tried on road courses in CERV I continued to use a dash-mounted mercury switch (as previously described for the Corvette SS) to sense the amount of deceleration the car was performing. When a pre-set peak was reached, the switch operated a solenoid valve that isolated the rear brake circuit, preventing the rear wheels from locking. The driver could vary the angle of the mercury switch to suit the prevailing road and car conditions. CERV I also had two brake pedals operating the same master cylinder. One was in the usual place and the other was on the left side of the cockpit, ideal for the left-foot braking that Duntov would have used if he had ever run this car at Indianapolis.

Duntov, Krieger and Zetye designed an admirably simple independent rear suspension for CERV I. Camber change was controlled by two lateral links, one being the universally-jointed drive shaft to the wheel and the other being a tubular link below it. An eccentrically-mounted inner pivot for the lower link served to adjust the normal camber setting. The hub carrier was fabricated of boxed sheet steel and was made integral with a radius arm that went forward to a frame mount. Allowing an adjustment for toe-in by shims at its pivot point, this arm applied the drive thrust from the wheel to the frame. These rear suspension concepts were not unlike those that had been projected for the Q-Corvette.

No new front suspension design was needed because a complete Corvette SS assembly was available and well suited to the needs of CERV I. The same progressively-wound variable-rate coil springs were used, carried by hard-mounted Delco shock absorbers of special "take-apart" design that allowed fast changes of the internal valving by substitution of components. The spring rates at the wheels were one hundred pounds per inch in the front and one hundred forty pounds per inch in the rear, where similar coil-shock units were used. An eleven-sixteenths-inch anti-roll bar was fitted at the front.

SS steering linkage used on CERV I was driven by a special fast-ratio Saginaw recirculating-ball steering box. The ratio of the box was 12.0 to one and that of the entire system 13.5 to one. With a universal joint at its base, the steering column rose at a rather steep 45-degree angle, its exact position being adjustable at its upper mounting bracket in the cockpit. Capping the column was a stock Corvair steering wheel, needing two-and-a-quarter turns from one lock to the other.

All this machinery was connected together by a tubular space frame of chrome-molybdenum alloy steel. Except for the major front and rear crossmembers all the tubes used were unusually small, being either seven-eighths-inch with 0.050-inch wall thickness or five-eighths-inch with 0.040-inch walls. The design was a very rigid triangulated truss from front to back, with torsional stiffness added by the three-dimensional structure built out to the sides past the cockpit and the engine bay. With all attachment brackets the frame weighed 125 pounds.

A body for "the Hillclimber" was styled in a special subterranean studio at GM Styling. There Larry Shinoda and Tony Lapine, under studio head Ed Wayne, worked on this and other private projects close to the heart of Bill Mitchell. Their shape for this car was of mirror-image symmetry about a sharp break line that encircled the body, which was fully enclosed on the underside. Twin inlets flanking the oval air inlet were to have been used for small oil coolers supplementing a front-mounted oil reserve tank, but these were never put to extensive use in CERV I. Instead, ducts ran rearward from inlets in the fronts of the side sponsons to carry cooling air back to the engine oil pan. This did the job, tests proved, and was much lighter besides.

A fiberglass tray inside each of the side sections of the frame supported a ten-gallon fuel cell made by U.S. Rubber, giving a total fuel capacity of twenty gallons. At the front a special aluminum radiator was backed by a duct which, as on the SS, carried the warm air up and away. A substantial windscreen kept most of it from being dumped directly into the cockpit. Hand-molded of only two layers of glass-fiber cloth, the complete CERV I body weighed about eighty pounds. Complete dry weight of the single seater was commendably low at 1450 pounds.

During the early part of 1960 Zora Duntov's spare-time energy was concentrated on the massive Cunningham Corvette attack on

Sturdy dyno stand was needed for the engine tested for CERV I in 1962 with twin turbo-superchargers, below, and observed by Duntov on the opposite pa

Le Mans, so it was not until later that summer that he and his crew had a chance to complete CERV I mechanically. In September, 1960 the white car with its metallic blue upper surfaces went West for its first trials on Pikes Peak. There was intermittent snow on the mountain above 10,000 feet, but the road below was clear enough for Zora to test the car extensively and to take interval times to find out how well it might be expected to perform over the entire climb.

"As far as we could tell," Duntov remembers, "the times were terribly disappointing. There were no official records, and it was a matter of hearsay. Somebody would say, 'Well, Unser did that stretch in such-and-such and we're off his times by so much'." This was a crushing blow for the plan, which had been for Firestone to sponsor and publicize an attempt on the hill record. "Chevrolet was not to be involved," said Zora, "except as a moving platform for the tires." Lights were green from Harvey Firestone on down until they flickered yellow and then red at the news of the slow test times.

"Firestone got cold feet," recalls Duntov, "and in my own mind I was disappointed because it felt like we were really flying. But, as far as we knew, we were doing poorly. Then we decided no go. I didn't run the Peak officially. But then, when we got back, we find out that the time was splendid and on every stretch I was

knocking off from the record. But at the time I did not know that. It was a shame that we accepted as gospel what we were told at the Peak."

To salvage the time and effort spent in Colorado, Duntov and the Firestone crew took CERV I to nearby Continental Divide Raceway for some road-course testing. Many changes were rung on the wheels and tires in these early weeks of experimenting, made possible by the knock-off magnesium Halibrands available in diameters of fifteen, sixteen, seventeen, and eighteen inches and widths of five and a half, six, and eight inches. Firestone worked with Zora on the tires, the initial problem being to get rubber on the rear that was adequate to take the car's accelerative and cornering powers simultaneously. This was a time of great ferment and transition in the design of racing tires and the CERV I became an important experimental tool for both Firestone and Goodyear in the development of the modern wider tire.

After these first trials CERV I was brought back to Detroit for overhaul and changes, then scheduled for two weeks of testing at Riverside early in November. As it happened, the U.S. Grand Prix was set to be held at that California track on November 20, so permission was requested and given to keep the car there for the G.P. and show it to the public for a few demonstration laps.

MC Roots-type supercharger at center below was tested for CERV I but found wanting. Unblown "mailbox" manifold at right was used in '62 Daytona tests.

In the news releases drafted for the occasion its experimental nature was very successfully emphasized and the significance of its name altered to "Chevrolet Engineering Research Vehicle." This was enough of a public-relations curtain to permit this showing to pass with some very favorable publicity and surprisingly little comment on what a pro-racing gesture CERV I was on the part of anti-racing Chevrolet and GM.

At Riverside Dan Gurney had assisted Zora with the tests of CERV I. Both Dan and Stirling Moss lapped the 3.3-mile road circuit in 2:04, not far from the Grand Prix lap record set by Moss in a Lotus at 1:55. The car's top speed, properly geared, was in excess of 170 mph, as Zora had discovered on the new banked track at the GM Proving Grounds. Duntov switched his sights to take aim at another challenge: the 180-mph lap at Daytona. In 1960 NASCAR's Bill France had deposited $10,000 in a Daytona Beach bank, to be turned over to the first man to lap his two-and-a-half-mile banked track at better than 180 mph. The track record then stood at 176.887 mph, to the credit of George Amick in an Indy car.

Knowing that he'd need more horsepower to reach that speed, Duntov started some development work in that direction. Then he took CERV I along to Florida in January, 1962 to establish some baseline data on its behavior on the bankings. It had been fitted in the meantime with a tachometer mounted in a faired housing atop its cowl, and had been repainted with three blue stripes flowing from the nose to the cockpit. Thus adorned it had appeared in full color in the November, 1961 *Esquire* with none other than Ed Cole behind the wheel. The magazine had quoted Duntov on the CERV I:

"CERV I is design without limit. It is very fast. It is very sensitive. It amplifies all disturbances of steering and driver control, and all problems of transmitting power to the road. It is an admirable tool. It tells us, for example, what to put in Corvette, for the highest margin of safety to the driver."

Duntov has often shown a disregard for his own safety at the wheel that curls the hair of his associates. "We've gotten used to him here," a Daytona official told Jerry Titus. "He tells us that there's no need for the ambulance or fire trucks as he doesn't drive that fast. A couple of years ago, during a Corvair test, he was about to get on the track when a call from Detroit came in. He said he'd call them back after a couple laps, then proceeded to break a rear axle and dump the car. After we cleared away the debris, he called them back. They calmly told him not to run the car — they'd found the axles were defective. Now Zora answers his calls immediately!"

Stylists had given CERV I front oil cooler "nostrils" which were never used.

Titus was there in January of 1962 when Zora took CERV I onto the Daytona high banks: "He was soon lapping at 162 mph, then pulled in to comment that rear-wheel camber was excessive, the final-drive ratio was wrong, a rear brake was partially locking, and that he felt the tire profile was wrong! Eventually he was consistently lapping at over 167 mph, felt this was fast enough for his evaluations and that more horses would be needed to exceed this figure." The horses in question were already being corraled at the stables back in Michigan.

In subsequent tests at Sebring, Jerry Titus had a chance to handle CERV I and thereafter gave a report on this unique opportunity in the pages of *Sports Car Graphic*: "Very obviously a bundle of dynamite, it was to be treated with caution. Wheelspin could be incurred at the top end of third gear — roughly 135 mph — even though adhesion was excellent. We ran the back straight at Sebring backwards from a standing start, exceeded 172 mph long before we used up its 3800-ft. length. Although the seat upholstery is only one inch thick, this bear's acceleration

Tail tapered sleekly, thanks to relatively forward placement of mid-engine.

could really bury the driver in it.

"Hard application of the brakes in corner approaches merely squeezed the chassis further into the road. In fast sweepers much the same effect is achieved — the harder the throttle is applied, the more the car squats and sticks. The ride was exceptionally comfortable and even bordering on soft. At no time was any real physical effort necessary to control the car. Brake and clutch pedal efforts were on the high side, but steering and shifting were very light.

"As with many rear-engined machines," Titus continued, "it was critical to braking in tight corners, where hard deceleration gives it a tendency to plow or go straight. Once aware of this, it's a simple matter for the driver to make sure he has all his stopping accomplished before entering a tight or hairpin type corner." Zora himself was even more unhappy about this behaviour of his brainchild: "The car does not turn well. Really contemptible. CERV I was a lumbering car in some ways, but it had unlimited potential. The Peak would have refined it."

Low-speed handling faults were no barriers to high speed at Daytona, but for this more power was clearly needed. One experiment was made with a supercharger assembly using a GMC 4-53 Roots blower driven by a cogged rubber belt. Inhaling through two downdraft Rochester injection metering units, it produced 420 bhp at 6000 rpm. Even more productive was the work done with turbo-supercharging, using twin Thompson-Ramo-Wooldridge exhaust-driven blowers. Each was directly fed by a stock Chevy cast-iron exhaust manifold, mounted upside-down so it also served as a main mounting for the blower.

Air pressured to a peak of 17 p.s.i. was piped from the two compressors to both sides of a normal Rochester injection doghouse. At first the injection system was used to squirt fuel into the inlet eyes of the compressors, but this didn't give cylinder-to-cylinder distribution that was accurate enough. Fuel was injected at the ports thereafter, the system being equipped with special non-return valves that allowed the port nozzles to deliver fuel against boost pressure, without losing their air-aspirating ability when the engine was run at low speed and boost. Each TRW turbocharger was fitted with a long straight-through fuel-metering venturi of the type first developed at Engineering Staff by Duntov.

On the dynamometer the engine had to be run with its long exhaust stacks pointing toward the front of the engine. Mounted in CERV I, the whole system was reversed in position so the air inlets would point forward and the exhausts would trail to the rear. Testing uncovered failures in the cylinder heads, at first, and then in the pistons. Finally the program managed by Denny Davis attained reliable running for this spectacular engine at speeds of up to 6,000 rpm on a compression ratio of 8.5 to one. The output? Just on 500 horsepower. Not until the Mark IV "porcupine" V-8 came along did the Chevy dyno rooms resound again to this level of power.

Only tentative trials of this super-potent small-block engine were made in the CERV I chassis, without its body being fitted. "It was so strong," Zora recalls, "that it lifted the front wheels off the ground!" No all-out run for maximum speed was ever made with the turbocharged engine, but CERV I was further modified with such an attempt in mind. Perhaps, thought Zora, a chance might arise to set a 200-mph lap speed at a tire testing track like Firestone's. Like any good executive, he didn't want to be caught without a plan if his general manager should suddenly show a strong interest in going fast.

A new nosepiece was made for CERV I that eliminated the side nostrils and provided instead long fairings trailing back to the upper and lower front suspension members. The cooling ducts in the side sponsons were closed off, as being redundant for runs of very short duration, and the leading edges of the sides of the body were tapered back more sharply. Later-model Halibrand wheels and Firestone Indy tires were fitted.

In the engine bay of the altered CERV I, circa 1964, a bored and stroked V-8 of 377 cubic inches was installed. Fed by Hilborn fuel injection on a cross-ram manifold, it had enough horsepower to push the single-seater around the five-mile circular banked track at GM's Milford Proving Ground at an average of 206 mph. This was one of the last official acts of this amazing experiment, which was retired officially in 1972 as an inhabitant of the Briggs Cunningham Automotive Museum in Costa Mesa, California.

In 1964 another Chevrolet Experimental Racing Vehicle was built, the four-wheel-drive CERV II. But two years earlier a proposal for a quite different kind of CERV II had been put before Bunkie Knudsen, who had made it clear that he would welcome rational suggestions - for ways that Chevrolet might get con-

structively involved in racing again. Zora and his team met this demand with a plan for an open sports roadster built to the four-liter (244-cubic-inch) displacement limit that had just been adopted for prototype cars qualifying for endurance races like Sebring and Le Mans.

"It is the consensus of Chevrolet engineering management," said their proposal of mid-June, 1962, "that the CERV I and its progenitor, the Corvette SS, have established a valuable engineering lineage that should be perpetuated by the proposed CERV II." With this new and special car, Duntov hoped to reawaken the Corvette SS concept of a separate and parallel line of experimental/racing Corvettes whose achievements and developments would contribute to the improvement and promotion of the standard model.

The mooted CERV II was to be a mid-engined sports-racer, with a simple truss-type frame of thin-wall aircraft steel tubing, weighing seventy pounds. Made of fire-resistant fiberglass about 0.08 inch thick, the body and its mounts were to contribute another 192 pounds. Planned around a ninety-two-inch wheelbase

CERV I was tested at Daytona in 1962 with cowl-mounted tach, larger vents in headrest to admit more air to the fuel injection, and fresh paint scheme.

and fifty-two-inch track, with tires and rims that were wider than those normally used at that time, this CERV II would have scaled 1,378 pounds dry and 1,798 pounds ready to race with the driver aboard, fifty-eight percent of the latter amount being on the back wheels.

Brakes would have been disc-type with aluminum calipers, and the fuel tanks two eighteen-gallon rubber bladders in the side sills. As planned the rear suspension was like that of CERV I while the front end had new tubular wishbones and several pieces related to the Corvair, including the steering gearbox and linkage. Very advanced for 1962 was the suggestion that titanium should be used for the front and rear hubs and for the exhaust manifolds. This light yet strong metal was also recommended for use inside the special 240-cubic-inch V-8 engine for the connecting rods and possibly for the valves. Both aluminum and magnesium would have been tried for the special cylinder block casting, with cast iron liners.

The main dimensions and features of the small-block Chevy engine would have been kept to provide a proven foundation for

As it lapped Milford at 206: nose fairings, 377 CID and Hilborn injection.

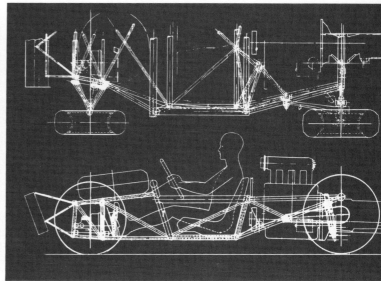

Tubular steel space frame was to have been basis of CERV II prototype, begun in 1962 for racing in 1963 season. Design was straightforward.

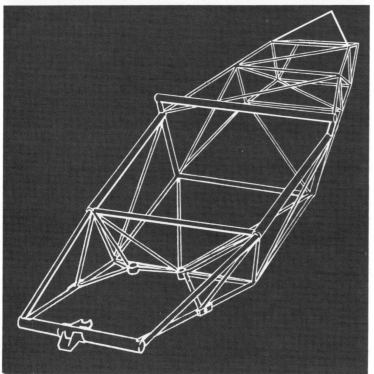

this four-liter edition. Bore and stroke were to be 3.66 x 2.88 inches, capped by an advanced version of a three-valve cylinder head that Zora had been developing, first on the 283 block and then, late in 1961, on the 327 engine. This had shaft and bevel drive at the front to a single overhead camshaft along each bank of cylinders that operated the valves through individual rockers. The head, with two inlet valves and a single exhaust, was one that Zora once hoped to make an over-the-counter high-performance bolt-on kit for all Chevy small-block engines.

For the four-liter engine, fed by an injection arrangement like that of CERV I, a peak speed of 8,500 rpm and a maximum output of 400+ bhp were stated objectives. This car was to have its engine next to the final drive and the transmission overhung to the rear, so a special transaxle design was needed. Duntov's designers came up with some remarkable concepts. One was a four-speed manual box using gears from the production transmission inside an aluminum case. Its countershaft ran on needle bearings around an input shaft that went through the box from the clutch, at the front, to a set of quick-change gears at the extreme rear. Rotation of the countershaft and the input shaft were in the same direction so the needle bearings would only have had to deal with the speed differential between them. This

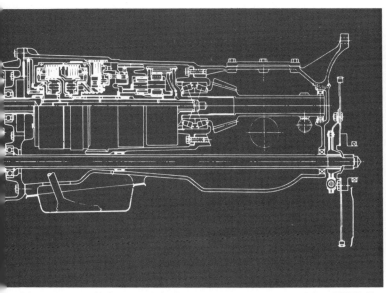

Manually-controlled power-shifted transmission was proposed for CERV II, as were 3-valve cylinder heads, which were being dyno-tested in 1961.

transaxle was to weigh ninety pounds, and the engine was to scale 332 pounds bare, 382 in fully dressed condition.

Quick-change gearing was also a feature of the alternate transmission, an automatic unit that made use of planetary gear sets and multi-disc clutches adapted from a production Chevy automatic transmission. No input torque converter or hydraulic coupling was to have been used. Instead, the internal multi-disc clutches and brake bands were to be used to start the car from rest and to switch from one gear to the next, with fully manual control, through three forward speeds.

Knudsen approved the CERV II plan and by the late summer of 1962 the necessary drawings were virtually complete and the fabrication of suspension components was already under way. About that time, however, Bunkie was given a rap on the knuckles by top GM management, which had sensed that he was a leader among the Divisional heads who were getting ready to go racing again. Regretfully he had to cancel this CERV II program. There had been an alternate proposal, however, one less overt, which he now okayed. It was based on a brand-new production Corvette, and though it was destined to fall short of its objectives, it was to leave on road racing proof positive that Chevrolet had been there.

Chapter 11

TOTAL TRANSFORMATION

CERV I had been swept into being by the same wave of enthusiasm at Chevrolet for new kinds of cars and rear-engined cars in particular that had brought the Corvair to life. A Corvette with its engine behind the driver had very nearly come into existence at the same time. It was the first of the "mid-engined "concepts — those with the engine ahead of the rear axle but behind the cockpit — that would tantalize and intrigue Corvette enthusiasts for more than a decade to come.

Zora Arkus-Duntov's first serious thoughts about moving the engine to the rear arose in 1958. Rear-engined racing cars hadn't then gained the prominence they enjoy today. Mid-engined Coopers had won that year's first two Grand Prix races, but these were thought to be exceptions rather than the rule, and front-engined racers continued to hold sway that season and most of the next. The mid-engined message began to reach the Grand Prix crowd when Jack Brabham won his first World Championship with a Cooper-Climax in 1959, and by 1960 the conversion to cars with engines in the rear, for Formula 1 and sports car competition, was well under way. But in 1958 it had barely begun.

In considering what had been accomplished in the design of the chassis for the Q-Corvette, the all-steel prototype of the late fifties with a transaxle from a projected new line of production GM sedans, Duntov wondered if the transformation of the Chevy sports car had gone far enough to make all the effort worthwhile. In terms of weight distribution, he felt, "We had not gained so much by moving the transmission back. It was like moving the battery around, or the spare tire." The car had been shaping up as a very expensive one to build at a time when GM needed to think about saving money. Did it go far enough to justify its cost?

"Getting good handling and performance in a car is simplified," wrote Duntov later in explaining his philosophy of design, "if vehicle masses are so disposed that the suspension and steering improve the effect of mass disposition rather than compensate for basic inequities. It is desirable for vehicles with a high power-to-weight ratio to have a weight distribution in the range of 47% front — 53% rear to 40% front — 60% rear. This distribution assists traction and reduces steering effort." Zora knew about earlier mid-engined racing cars, the remarkably successful and widely misunderstood German Auto Unions of the 1930's. They had shifted their weight sharply rearward to good effect, and Duntov felt the Corvette could well do likewise.

Zora's argument to Ed Cole was, in essence: "We have all this special suspension equipment and the transaxle already, for the Q cars. Why don't we make even better use of them by connecting them to an engine placed in the back, ahead of the rear wheels?" Receiving Cole's enthusiastic assent, Duntov and his men went to work on the first mid-engined Corvette design. A new assessment of the production situation had shown that the Chevy sports car could still be built economically with a fiberglass body, even at a rate of more than 20,000 a year. So they laid out the mid-engined car with a separate frame and a GRP body, carrying over most of the suspension ideas from the all-independent Q-Corvette.

One of the main aims of the new concept was to take advantage of the absence of an engine in front to improve visibility while lowering the profile and the center of gravity. But a certain conflict arose with the stylists, who were loath to give up the long-nosed look that still spelled "sports car" to many. Their proposed shapes for the new car did not, in Duntov's opinion, take full advantage of the radical new layout. Unlike the Q-Corvette, this one had conventional doors, and a doghouse of substantial size on the rear deck to contain the induction equipment.

There were other problems, too: To get sufficient interior room, the car's wheelbase had to be made uncomfortably long. And finally the transaxle and rear suspension pieces vanished when the Q sedans were cancelled. There'd also been a Corvair-powered version, this having a louvered rear deck and deep air inlet gills behind the doors on each side. It was still being evaluated in the form of a fully detailed clay model early in 1960, but it too fell by the wayside. For by that time plans were well advanced for a new front-engined Corvette — firmly based on the

Vestiges of the Q-Corvette styling concept (Chapter 7) were visible in the extensive facelift of the existing body that was being considered in late 1958 and early 1959. A possible 1962 model, it would have added all-new exterior paneling without changing the inner structure or the chassis.

Transitions to crisp new styling idioms were being made in the late 1950's, as indicated by the beveled front end of this early 1960 proposal for a rear-engined Corvette using a Corvair power train. Vee-eight-powered version was similar in profile with a large rear-deck bulge for the carburetors.

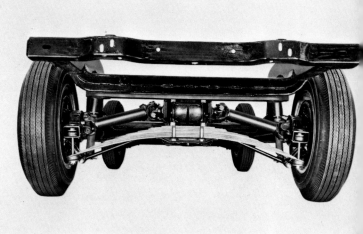

Chassis for new XP-720 Corvette looked simple but was in fact highly sophisticated, including new independent rear suspension, seen from rear at right.

popular form of the racing Stingray.

The motif originated for the Q-Corvette and further developed for the Stingray had taken unshakable hold of the stylists at the Technical Center. They knew they would someday apply it to a production Corvette. They first attempted to make that change during the 1958-59 winter as a major facelift of the existing car for the 1962 model year. Built around its cowl and windshield structure, and to a certain extent the restyled rear end that was to be launched in 1961, it carried a prominent break line all the way around the body as did the Stingray, which was under construction at that time.

As an adaptation of the earlier body, this proposal couldn't bring to life the crispness that was one of the best features of the Q-Corvette and Stingray. Its upper surfaces were too soft, its proportions too bulky and its front end too heavy, beetle-browed above four headlights that were inset below the break line. It represented a compromise, a car that could be built if Chevrolet were willing to settle for something less than the best Corvette. That was not what Ed Cole had in mind.

In the fall of 1959 a new project was begun at Styling to design from scratch a new Corvette based on the Stingray. It was assigned the code number XP-720, and put in work in the same windowless basement studio where the sports-racing shape had come into being. Such a car does not grow in a vacuum, however. Styling needed guidelines from Chevrolet for the wheelbase,

engine position, general substructure of the new car. This was forthcoming from Zora Duntov, who in the meantime had been working on a completely new chassis for the XP-720.

In a memo to Harry Barr, his chief engineer, Zora had outlined in December, 1957 some of his thoughts about the standards that should be set for the successor to the Corvette as it was then known. "We can attempt to arrive at the general concept of the car," he wrote, "on the basis of our experience and in relationship to the present Corvette. We would like to have better driver and passenger accommodation, better luggage space, better ride, better handling and higher performance."

"Superficially," Zora continued, "it would seem that the comfort requirements indicate a larger car than the present Corvette. However, this is not so. With a new chassis concept and thoughtful body engineering and styling, the car may be bigger internally and externally somewhat smaller than the present Corvette. Consideration of cost spells the use of a large number of passenger car components which indicates that the chassis cannot become so small that they cannot be used. I feel that considerations of ride, handling and stability dictate a frame-mounted differential."

These principles were realized in the design of the completely new chassis for the XP-720, which took place during 1960 and 1961. The only components that were carried over without major changes to the new 1963 model were the engine and drive train

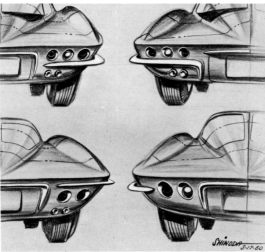

Bill Mitchell, at far left, closely followed the development of the new car's shape with Irv Rybicki and other stylists. Sketches are by Larry Shinoda.

combinations. Otherwise it was completely rethought from the ground up. Duntov later related to the SAE some of the reasoning that led to the final design:

"The passenger compartment was placed as far back as possible and the engine centerline was offset one inch to the right, taking advantage of the fact that passenger footroom requirements are less than those of the driver. This offset also reduced the width of the driveshaft tunnel, because the crankshaft and offset rear axle pinion were now on the same centerline.

"The task of attaining a good ride and handling combination is lessened as the C.G. is lowered. Therefore, the ground clearance line was set at five inches and all major masses were placed as close to this line as possible. The frame and underbody went on the groundline, and the occupants were placed within the frame rather than on top of it as before. The engine and transmission were placed as low as compatible with safe ground clearance, and as far back as possible without reducing footroom comfort.

"The spare tire was moved to a compartment accessible from the outside and the fuel tank set above the spare tire. Luggage storage space was increased by using the area behind the seats in the new closed body design instead of a trunk as in former models. As a result of these various changes, the new design weight distribution is 47% front and 53% rear, compared to 51% front and 49% rear on the 1962 Corvette. The height of the

C.G. above the ground is 16.5 inches versus 19.8 inches on the previous model. The new wheelbase of 98 inches, four inches shorter than the previous Corvette, was accomplished with occupant comfort being enhanced rather than impaired."

The X-member frame that had remained much the same since 1953 was replaced by a new ladder-type design, composed of two boxed side rails joined together by five crossmembers. Two tubular inserts in the second crossmember from the front allowed the dual exhaust pipes to pass through an area that otherwise would have been very troublesome. The cross-section of the side members was tailored to suit the needs of styling: the shapes of the outside tumble-home of the body and the sides of the cockpit inside. Computer analysis helped settle the main design features of the frame, including the steel thicknesses and the section designs, before the first actual frames were built. This advance work meant that few changes were needed from these first test frames.

No weight was saved in the new frame, which like the previous one weighed 260 pounds, with brackets, and its bending stiffness was about the same as the earlier design. The torsional rigidity, very important in a sports car and especially one with all-independent suspension, was increased from 1,587 to 2,374 pound-feet per degree. "In the course of the frame development," recalled Kai Hansen of Chevrolet, "the point arose that if stiff was good, stiffer was better. Consequently, a frame was built with torsional

New XP-720 GRP body had steel inner structure to support cowl, doors.

Concealed headlights caused Chevy body engineers many sleepless nights.

stiffness considerably greater than the production design." This had been of similar layout but with tubular members, compromising less with the needs of production and interior room. "Evaluation of a vehicle equipped with the stiffer frame proved the ride to be unacceptable," Hansen reported. "This approach was quickly abandoned."

The suspension for the XP-720 posed an economic challenge. There was to be independent rear suspension, but now there was no Q-series sedan to provide the hardware. It would have to earn its own way. "Now at that time the sales figures were low," said Zora, relating his efforts to sell the car's concept to his management. "So, every time you come out and say, 'Well, it has to have independent suspension,' they say, 'Boy, you cannot do it! How will you pay for it?' Well, I'd say, 'We're going to sell 30,000 cars.' And we can afford something like that.

"Ultimately," Duntov continued, "by adapting from the existing axle and parts, it came out that we could afford independent. And, as a matter of fact, by using passenger car front components — just rearranged — we were saving money and product cost. As far as the chassis would eventually go, we would save more money in the front than we put into the rear." The rearrangement at the front consisted of swapping certain suspension members from side to side, though retaining the

Complete space buck at left was built early in 1960, showed other headlight scheme and rear-view periscope. Dash design dates from November of 1960.

pressed steel wishbones and ball-jointed upright that were then used on the big Chevy sedans. Though ounces could have been saved here and there with a new design, these ready-made parts were fully tested, proven and ready to go, which saved both time and money.

Experience with the Corvette SS and the CERV I had helped prove a new arrangement for the front suspension pieces that sharply departed from passenger-car practice. The inner pivots of the upper control arms were lowered, which had the effect of raising the front roll center to what Duntov called "an uncommon height" of 3.25 inches above the ground. "This causes considerable camber change during vertical movement of the wheels," he explained. "The advantages of this arrangement are higher resistance to roll for a given ride rate, and lower increase of positive camber; that is, lower loss of cornering power. The changes in lateral forces associated with changes in camber during vertical motion of the wheel are compensated for by appropriate toe changes during the same motion."

This change was not without its compensating drawbacks, however. Noted Zora: "Such an arrangement is more sensitive to correct wheel alignment and under unfavorable conditions more wheel-fight prone than a conventional arrangement, but improvement in ride and handling and steering response were

Early XP-720 study of October, 1959 resembled racing Stingray with roof.

Comparison made in April, 1960 between XP-720 clay model and 1960 Corvette showed new car's lower, slimmer lines and still-provisional design details.

143

deemed to be well worth the extra care." A hydraulic damper was added to the steering linkage to soak up such kickback as the new geometry might transmit from road wheels to steering wheel.

The steering linkage was behind the suspension instead of ahead of it, as it was on the Chevy sedans, and it was given a built-in quick-steering adjustment. Each steering arm was drilled for two positions for its ball joint, offering overall ratios of either 17.0 or 19.6 to one. The faster ratio was to be supplied from the factory with an option that was new to the Corvette in 1963: linkage-type power steering. For the first time a recirculating-ball steering gear was made part of a Corvette, having an internal reduction of 16.0 to one. At the upper end of the column the steering wheel was made adjustable for distance over a three-inch range.

Without any compromise of principles, the careful use of pieces from the parts bins for the front suspension saved enough money to allow Zora Duntov and his designers, Harold Krieger and Walter Zetye, to devote their full attention to the best possible independent rear suspension concept. The principles already tested and proven on CERV I were directly applied to the XP-720 rear suspension design: the use of the drive shaft as an active member of the suspension; control of forward thrust from the wheels, and in this case, rear brake torque reaction as well, by massive radius arms extending forward to the frame.

Most sophisticated independent rear suspensions, those that became increasingly popular on racing cars in the late 1950's, didn't make use of the drive shaft as a stressed member. They set the desired wheel movement pattern with control arms and links, then gave each drive shaft a splined coupling to allow it to vary in length as the wheels went up and down. The trouble was that these couplings didn't always slide freely in and out, especially when heavy drive torques were being applied to them, with the result that the wheels were sometimes locked in place, the rear suspension immobilized by the balky couplings. Hence it was an appealing idea to eliminate the sliding splines (since friction-free roller splines would have been too expensive) by using the drive shaft, with its two universal joints, as part of the suspension linkage.

Duntov, Krieger, and Zetye carried out the very careful geometrics needed to use the half-shaft as part of the suspension. They laid it out so the tension stress on the axle of the outside wheel in a corner was minimized, reducing thereby the forces applied by the axle to the tapered-roller bearings retaining it at both ends. Struts below the axles completed the wheel-locating parallelogram, as seen from the rear, and had eccentric ad-

XP-720 clay model was painted and foil-chromed for April, 1960 review.

justments at their inner pivots for setting the camber. Each hub was carried by a boxed steel arm that swung from a forward frame pivot; a shim adjustment at this point allowed the rear toe-in to be altered. At a height of 7.56 inches, the rear roll center was lower than that of the live-axle Corvette.

This advanced suspension had what Zora Duntov called "an anachronistic feature": a transverse leaf spring. Even within Chevrolet it was seen as a step backward. Zora remembers the reaction of chief engineer Harry Barr: "Transverse leaf spring! Model T!" The spring had nine leaves, seven of them separated by polyethylene liners to reduce the friction between the leaves. It was attached at the center to the cast iron differential case and connected at the ends to the trailing arms by tension rods. "It did the job very well," said Duntov. "It was the cause of much conversation here, but nobody could produce anything better for that particular car at that particular moment."

In addition to the standard springs, special ones were developed for racing the new Corvette as part of a new Z06 option package. Testing of the new chassis and these springs was conducted with prototype pieces disguised by a cobbled-on 1962 body, its nose replaced by panels like those of the new car, all painted blue. It was put through its paces at Daytona and Sebring in January of 1962, while the CERV I was being groomed

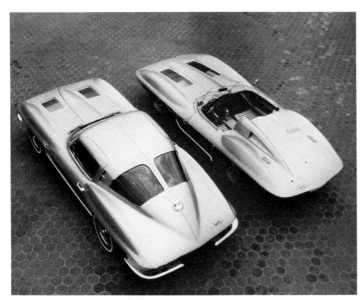

Sting Ray coupé of '63 showed amazing fidelity to Sting Ray concept.

for its attack on the 180 mph mark at Daytona. "The results were astonishing," said Dick Thompson. "At Sebring the car put up times five seconds faster than a comparative 1962 standard model and at Daytona was five miles an hour faster than the '62." The two different suspension systems compared as follows:

	1963 Corvette standard	1963 RPO Z06
Front spring rate	260	550 pounds/inch
Front anti-roll bar dia.	0.75	0.94 inch
Rear spring rate	162	305 pounds/inch
Rear shock absorber dia.	1.00	1.375 inches

Very precise wheel control was designed into the XP-720 without the excessive harshness that independent rear suspension can sometimes provoke. "At the rear," engineer Kai Hansen reported to the SAE, "rubber is used at eight locations at the suspension links. It is also used at both ends of the shock absorbers, at either end of the rear spring link and between the spring leaves. The nose of the differential carrier is attached to the frame through large rubber pucks on both the compression

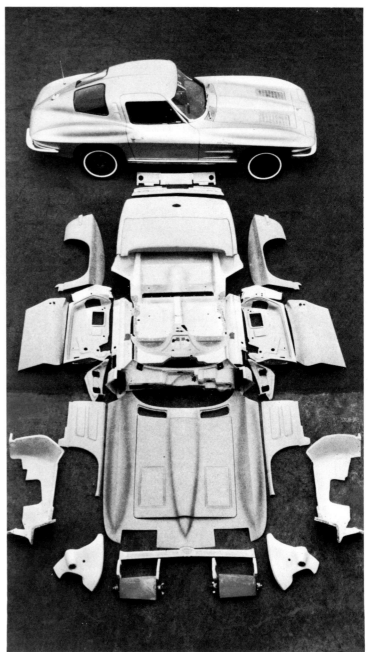

Display of panels used in '63 roadster shows ingenious design for GRP.

and rebound side. The complete rear suspension, including the differential carrier, is attached to the differential carrier crossmember, which in turn is bolted to the frame through huge rubber isolation mounts." These mounts were shrewdly designed to allow generous movement vertically but very little laterally.

Also under test early in 1962, especially at Sebring, were the new brakes of the new Corvette. These were adapted from the current big Chevrolet passenger car, having the same eleven-inch diameter as before but more width, carrying linings two and three-quarter inches wide in front and two inches in the rear. The standard brakes with organic linings adjusted themselves automatically every time the car was braked in reverse. With the Z06 option, the adjustment of the sintered metallic linings took place while the car was moving forward — an obvious requirement for racing. A vacuum brake booster, optional for the first time in 1963, was part of RPO Z06, as was a dual-circuit master cylinder.

During the brake development period, Duntov related, the test car "was equipped with brakes that were instrumented to measure heat generation between the secondary lining facings and the drum. These instruments (thermocouples) were connected to a four-position switch in the center instrument console and then to a direct-reading gauge that read brake temperature

Kent Kelly handled both drill and mike in XP-720 wind tunnel trials.

in degrees Fahrenheit. During the design and testing program, we were able to compare various lining recipes and determine which was most suitable to the Corvette's requirements." The mercury-switch control for varying the front/rear brake effort proportion was also used during the test period to arrive at the best fixed ratio.

An adventurous new option resulted directly from a request by Grady Davis, Gulf Oil executive and enthusiastic Corvette campaigner. He wanted a lightweight road wheel with a genuine knockoff hub that would ease the task of changing wheels and tires on a Corvette during a long-distance race. The wheel was developed as an aluminum permanent-mold casting with a handsome radial-rib pattern and a wider rim than standard, six rather than five and a half inches. The wheel was lighter than the stock steel part but the added weight of the center-lock adaptor counterbalanced that saving.

Although it was the spectacular appearance of the '63 Corvette that made the initial impact (before enthusiasts had a chance to find out how much better the new chassis was), it's fair to say that the stylists had an easier time fulfilling their XP-720 assignment than did the engineers. For the new car was clearly a direct translation of the basic shape of the racing Stingray. From the start the new car was seen as a fastback coupé; in fact the stylists were quite happy to contemplate the complete abandonment of the roadster model in favor of the coupé — a continuation of the thinking that had gone into the Q-Corvette.

When the designers rolled their first clay model of the XP-720 out into the open-air viewing yard on October 20, 1959, it was seen to be the racing Stingray with a rounded, tapered hardtop grafted on. At this early date the motif of a split rear window was already developed, divided by a rib down the centerline of the car. Enhanced by a windsplit line running from the windshield to the tail, this rib gave the coupé an organic unity that was especially close to the heart of chief stylist Bill Mitchell. This divider came close to splitting apart the often troubled relationship between Mitchell and Zora Duntov, whose main interest was in being able to see out the back window of his new car. Mitchell won that point, saying, "If you take that off you might as well forget the whole thing."

Through the 1959-60 winter the shape of the XP-720 was gradually refined to meet the needs of the production model. A marked change from the lines of the Stingray was a nipping-in of the car's waist, making it look less bulky. It was also clear that hidden headlights would be essential if the distinctive Stingray front-end look were to be preserved. This was a bold decision, for the last American production car with hidden lights had been the

Dr. Peter Kyropoulos checks print made by Kelly of airflow patterns during model tests in GALCIT tunnel that resulted in static pressure data shown.

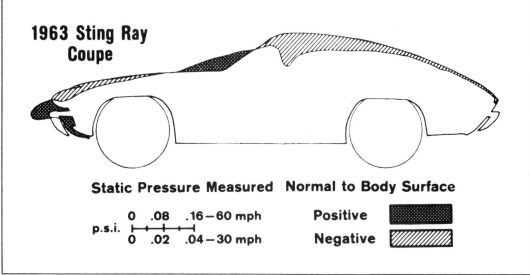

1963 Sting Ray Coupe

Static Pressure Measured Normal to Body Surface

p.s.i.

| 0 | .08 | .16 — 60 mph |
| 0 | .02 | .04 — 30 mph |

Positive

Negative

1942 DeSoto, not exactly a landmark automobile.

Chevy body engineers worked especially hard to perfect a system for rotating the lights into position. Had this not worked properly it would have done permanent damage to both the Corvette and the hidden-light principle. "We designed and built five different types of mechanism to control the lamps," reported body engineer Carl Jakust. "These ranged from a simple rod and cable design up through a complicated Rube-Goldberg that handled all motion with a single switch. We finally settled on a two-motor electrical system that required two switches to operate but has no little dogs running on treadmills" — the trademark of the fantastic mechanisms created by cartoonist Goldberg.

A wood-framed "space buck" helped the stylists work out the entry and exit arrangements, including another novelty: doors that extended a substantial distance into the roof to give more entry room. Like the hidden lights, this was a fillip that GM Styling had hoped for some time to have a chance to introduce. Also incorporated were functional air vents in the hood like those of the Stingray. These had to be made inoperative when it was appreciated that warm air flowing back from the engine room would go directly into the cowl inlets for interior cooling air.

At GM (and at most other large companies) the designs of exteriors and interiors are carried out in separate studios. Unfortunately this was all too obvious in the instrument panel created for the XP-720, which related not at all in its contours to the lines of the hood ahead of it. The instrument layout was a strong step forward, as was the roomy glove box, but the double-cowl motif of the dash had a distinctly dated look in a car that was otherwise uncompromisingly advanced.

With the design of the XP-720 coupé substantially complete by the spring of 1960, not until the fall did the stylists turn reluctantly to a convertible model and, still later, to a detachable hardtop. During the few working days between Christmas and New Year's of 1960, fully detailed fiberglass styling models of both cars were put on display in the Styling auditorium, along with the original Stingray, for the approval of Chevrolet and GM management. In its detail trim the car had not yet reached its final form. Surface vents were concentrated fore and aft of the rear wheel opening; these were later moved to the front fender. Simulated louvers along the rocker panels would not be used. Fuel filler caps would be concealed beneath the rear-deck emblem. For cost reasons the opening deck lid shown on the coupé model would not be seen in production.

During 1961, after the details of the XP-720 had reached their final form, the car's shape was subjected to a searching analysis

Early Shinoda sketch for Shark show car was too close to planned '63.

In March and April of 1961, clay model of XP-755 Shark was developed.

Shark had pop-up rear-deck mirror-lights; left one is shown activated.

Supercharged Shark was complete and running as shown by June of 1961.

in the GALCIT wind tunnel of the California Institute of Technology. GM Styling was then embarking on a fundamental study of vehicle aerodynamics, under the direction of Dr. Peter Kyropoulos, using painstakingly detailed three-eighths-scale models for tunnel tests, to be correlated later with the performance of the cars on the road. Surface pressure readings and air flow patterns were exhaustively studied by Kyropoulos, assisted by Kent Kelly and H. J. "Jud" Holcombe. Though the car's shape (like the original Stingray) developed lift, the amount was felt to be within acceptable bounds. And neither the hazards of excessive lift nor the means to combat it were very well understood at that time.

Another proposed variation of the XP-720 never made it to the wind tunnel, though it was built in the form of a completely trimmed styling model. Hedging the substantial investment he would be making in new tooling for this car, Ed Cole pushed hard for the addition of a four-passenger model to the line. This the stylists reluctantly made ready as a stretched version of the coupé, with longer doors and some limited space for two seats in the rear. It was an ungainly-looking car, perhaps as much so as the designers could make it. Allied against Cole in opposing this model were Mitchell, Duntov and salesman Pike, all of whom argued that it posed a dangerous devaluation of a concept that had finally proven itself as a money-maker, that of an exclusive and genuine two-seater sports car. Cole capitulated and the four-seater was set aside.

Completing the engineering of the body, the Chevy men gave the new car a steel structure around the doors, designed in place from the start, an improvement on the reinforcements that had grown like Topsy within the original body. Instead of forty-eight pounds, as before, the new body had eighty-two pounds of steel in the central "birdcage" support, as it was known. This allowed a reduction in the weight of the plastic used to 300 pounds in the convertible model, whose complete body, ready to install, scaled 397 pounds against 405 pounds for the 1962 body.

Though it was smaller in every exterior dimension, the new Corvette came through its prototype build phase (two convertibles and one coupé were made) weighing about the same as its predecessor. This was a disappointment to Duntov, who had hoped that the car could be significantly lighter. One reason the blue test car with the modified '62 body had gone so well in early racing trials was that it was in fact lighter than the old solid-axle car. "However," Zora reflected, "it must be realized that several additions were made to the vehicle.

"For instance," he elaborated: "The exhaust system has

thicker walls for durability; the new retractable headlights are heavier than the former conventional design; the new 20-gallon tank is heavier than the old 16-gallon tank; the 1963 brakes are bigger. Torsional stiffness of the 1963 convertible is 10% above its 1962 counterpart, and the sport coupé is 90% stiffer than the 1962 convertible." These were useful gains. Also important was the reduction of unsprung weight effected by the new suspension. It was cut by eleven pounds in the front end and eighty-nine pounds at the rear. This increased the ratio of sprung to unsprung weight — so important for good ride and handling on bumpy roads — from 5.27 to 7.98 to one. Because the new car's weight distribution had been shifted rearward, the ratio worsened slightly at the front end, going from 7.55 to 7.45 to one.

Duntov was able to experience the improvements he'd made, driving his disguised prototype chassis on race circuits and on the street for a thorough evaluation. John Fitch, Jerry Titus, and the author were among the "outsiders" who were given a preview of things to come with a turn at the wheel of this blue car. Bill Mitchell, on the other hand, was denied a comparable pleasure. He'd personally supervised the styling of a spectacular new sports car, but now he'd have to wait almost two years before he could be seen in it on the road. This he was not willing to do. He decided to build an exaggerated replica of the new Corvette

as a show car and a personal car, a successor to the XP-700.

The first sketches by Larry Shinoda of the new car, the XP-755, showed only minor alterations and the addition of the double-bubble canopy from the XP-700. This was dangerously close to the actual form of the XP-720. A radical new "cover" theme was needed, and this was supplied when Mitchell hooked and landed a shark during a deep-sea fishing holiday off Bimini. The aggressive look and graded coloration of the mounted shark's head set the styling motif for the car that became the Corvette Shark.

From inspiration to realization took no more than a few months, the aim being to debut the Shark during a race weekend at Elkhart Lake in the summer of 1961. The shape was developed to fit a 1961 Corvette chassis, its frame raised at the rear to suit the show car's upswept tail. By mid-April the clay model of the Shark had been approved by Mitchell and construction of the car's fiberglass body had begun. With slight modifications, including a new prismatic periscope for rear vision, the twin-bubble roof from the XP-700 was carried over to the Shark. It still looked spectacular, at the expense of giving the show car an excruciatingly small amount of headroom. The outside exhausts were similar to those on the XP-700, made even more visceral in appearance by exposing the four header pipes on each side.

During its long lifetime the Shark has been given a new interior, at left, and a 427 CID Mark IV engine, shown, among its many power transplants.

The Shark's headlights were hidden (well below legal height) behind grille sections at the sides that rotated to bring them into position. Gill-like forms flanking the grille contained cornering lights that came on when the turn signals were actuated, a feature that was then being planned for introduction on the 1962 Cadillac. The rear turn signal lights were recessed in the deck lid, flashing their glow rearward through mirrored surfaces in the lids that popped up when they were actuated. The lids lifted one at a time for turn signals, and popped up together to beam a bright eye-level warning when the driver of the Shark braked abnormally hard.

Painted in an iridescent blue that blended into a white underbody, like its namesake, the Shark caused a sensation when it toured the course in its Elkhart Lake debut and when it was displayed officially by Chevrolet for the first time at the New York Show in April, 1962. It usually appeared with chromed Dayton knock-off wire wheels, though polished Halibrand magnesium wheels had also been tried but found not to suit the car's appearance so well. Small bumperettes at the tip and corners of the nose and a circular emblem at the center of the grille were added after the car had been on the road for a while.

Under the bulge in the Shark's bonnet was a special engine built for the car by Leonard McLay and his crew in Styling's

Detail changes to Shark added bumperettes and different side mirrors.

mechanical assembly department. Leonard had been nursemaid to Harley Earl's Le Sabre dream car, a supercharged V-8 which could be highly temperamental, learning enough in the process to build a practical supercharger for the Shark's 327-cubic-inch Chevy V-8. The blower was a small GMC 4-53 Roots-type unit, driven by vee belts to deliver a boost pressure of about 8 p.s.i.

McLay fitted the blower deep within the engine's center vee on a manifold made from a two-inch aluminum plate in which the gas-flow passages were routed to a depth of one and a half inches, covered by a three-quarter-inch plate that carried the supercharger and its pressure-relief valve. Four side-draft carburetors like those on the first Corvettes fed the blower through a shallow plenum chamber, two of them being on each side of the chamber. An early tendency to backfire when the throttle was opened suddenly was overcome by fitting a special high-pressure pump that reacted to throttle movement by injecting gasoline directly into the manifold below the supercharger.

As newer and bigger Chevrolet engines became available, they were tried out in the Shark. For a while it had an experimental Rochester timed fuel injection system, followed later by a 427-cubic-inch Mark IV Chevrolet engine. Features that weren't available on pre-1963 Corvettes crowded the Shark's engine room: air conditioning, power steering and power brakes.

Originally the Shark retained the 1961 instrument panel, in an interior embellished with tight-fitting bucket seats and a Ferrari steering wheel, a gift to Bill from Enzo Ferrari. Later the Shark was given a completely new panel, one stressing stark efficiency with severe lines, circular dials, a black crackle finish and six central instruments angled toward the driver. Lower, wider seats gave as much headroom as was possible beneath the sloping, silvered canopy. Changes like these helped keep the Shark current as a useful experimental car and show car; more than ten years after it was built it was still in use and in demand for auto show and parade appearances.

Broad hints by Bill Mitchell and GM public relations men left no doubt in the minds of most magazine editors that the Shark foreshadowed in some way the shape of the 1963 Corvette, though the writers could not know that the Shark had been built after that shape had been finalized and was not a true predecessor of the coming Corvette. *Car Life* made this comment about the racing Stingray and the Shark: "They are unique, copy no trend and are exceedingly handsome and graceful in the bargain. If followed through on the '63 Corvette, they will make it truly a car apart." How right they were.

Chapter 12

THE YEAR OF THE STING RAY

Guards, engineers, test drivers looked at one another with knowing smiles. That high, harsh howl was unmistakable. It echoed from the concrete of the high-banked track at Milford, resounded from the open exhausts of a new Corvette under test. They'd heard it before; they knew it meant that Zora Arkus-Duntov was on the five-mile circular track, his right foot pressed to the floorboard of a new model, extending it to its absolute limits.

The car was a Corvette Sting Ray, as the XP-720 had been officially named. Its dual exhausts fanned out to the sides, opening ahead of the rear wheels. These carried oversize 8.20 x 15 tires, which the coupé — which it was — had been designed to accommodate. Fitted with a 3.08 to one axle ratio, the test car was timed at a maximum speed of 161 mph. In another trial a roadster was clocked at 156 mph. These final validating runs showed that the new shape was much the same in its overall drag as the old one, for there were few changes in the engine room for 1963.

All the engines for the new model year had a positive crankcase ventilation system, revised cooling water circuitry giving better heat distribution during warmup, and a more sensitive vacuum-advance mechanism for the distributor, phased in during the 1962 model year. Otherwise the main improvements were concentrated on the Rochester fuel injection, to make it both easier to produce and more precise and effective in operation. This was the first major overhaul of the design of the injector since its introduction six years earlier.

The aluminum plenum chamber was newly cast in two parts, having a finned cover that allowed the main body to be designed and cast with less compromise. Its individual ram pipes to the cylinders were slightly larger and more smoothly faired to speed the flow. The plenum chamber itself was enlarged in volume, and supplied with cool air from a duct alongside the radiator through a larger cleanable oil-wetted polyurethane filter.

At the inlet venturi, the throttle shaft was mounted horizontally. The by-pass air supply for idle conditions was deleted, idle air being supplied instead through the main throttle valve. Electric operation of the choke was eliminated in favor of direct vacuum control, signaled by heat from the left-hand exhaust manifold. A new high-pressure fuel-delivery pump was built in, composed of five spring-loaded pistons driven by a rotating wobble plate. Offering a higher output at cranking speeds than the earlier gear-type pump, the new design gave more consistent starting. Hot starting and idling were improved by a fuel return line that helped keep vapor out of critical parts of the system.

There were sharp finishing touches to this extensively improved 360-horsepower engine. Chrome plating was applied to the fuel lines, fuel filter fittings, dipstick, and oil filler tube and cap. The driver of an injected Sting Ray also had something new in the way of an aid to control: a warning buzzer that sounded when the engine revs reached 6,500. So quickly did this engine reach high speeds and so smoothly did it behave when it got there that the buzzer was useful as a precautionary warning to the inattentive.

Engines, frames, brakes, body panels, special fixtures began arriving in St. Louis in the early spring of 1962. In an area of the plant specially cleared for that purpose, a pilot line was set up where the first of the radically changed '63 Corvettes could be built, testing the incredible jigsaw puzzle of pieces that comprise a new car, while the 1962 models were still rolling down the line. Twenty-five pilot-line Sting Rays were thus manufactured, cars that were used for photography, for dealer previews, for a promotional film starring Dave MacDonald and Dick Thompson, and for the first impressions gathered by the press at the Milford Proving Ground as early as June and July of 1962.

Most of those impressions were very good indeed. "Tricky, twisting roads are this Corvette's meat," reported *Car Life*. "With its new suspension it seems to lock onto them, going precisely where directed and sticking to the tightest corners without the shadow of a doubt. Where the old Corvette had an annoying penchant for swapping ends when cornered vigorously, the new

One of three hand-built prototypes of the 1963 Sting Ray Corvette completes its test runs at GM's Milford Proving Ground with 1962 wheel discs.

Dramatically divided rear window was a controversial feature of the 1963 coupé. Roadster and hardtop models were also part of the new Sting Ray line.

one just sticks and storms. This suspension is the best thing since gumdrops!"

"We were a bit spoiled, perhaps," suggested Jerry Titus of *Sports Car Graphic*, "by testing the prototype first, as it had all the heavy-duty suspension items included and added up to a fantastic improvement over the '62 that was similarly equipped. The showroom model can't, quite naturally, perform the same tricks on a racing circuit, but it can come darn close. The ride and handling are great. We won't elaborate on how great; you've got to drive one to believe it."

"Whether you slam the car through an S-bend at 85 or pop the clutch at 5,000 rpm at the drag strip, the result is the same — great gripping gobs of traction." That was the first impression of *Road & Track*, which concluded: "As a purely sporting car, the new Corvette will know few peers on road or track. It has proved, in its 'stone-age form,' the master of most production-line competitors; in its nice, shiny new concept it ought to be nearly unbeatable."

Said *Car and Driver*, "One glance at the new Corvette tells you that it is faster and sportier than its predecessors. Hiding independent rear suspension under its sculptured tail, the Corvette is now second to no other production sports car in road-holding and is still the most powerful." *C/D's* New York-based editors

knew that GM Styling people had measured the Jaguar XK-E coupé inside and out when it made its world debut at the New York Show in April, 1961, and surmised therefrom that the Jaguar had inspired the creation of the Sting Ray coupé. In fact, of course, the styling of the new Corvette had then been virtually frozen, and the GM men were merely curious to find out how the new British car — sure to be an important competitor — compared with their own handiwork.

Backing their original conviction that the coupé body was the only one that was needed, the stylists were confident that this would attract the lion's share of the buyers at its suggested retail price of $4,252. Chevrolet sales promotion, on the other hand, in the person of Joe Pike, felt that the roadster would assert its traditional role in the Corvette picture. It was more favorably priced at $4,037. There was support for both sides in the 1963 sales pattern, which saw the coupés attract the overwhelming majority at first, followed by a late-season demand for roadsters. The result was an almost exact balance for the model year of 10,594 coupés and 10,919 convertibles. This level of output, either figure representing a full year's production a couple of years earlier, was only possible with the St. Louis factory working two complete shifts.

Proper scheduling of the new options was also a challenge,

Production dash differed in detail from styling car shown. Engine's at right.

since there was no way to judge how heavy the demand for them would be. Power steering was $75.35 extra, power brakes $43.05, and power windows (which had been offered before) $59.20. About one-sixth of the 1963 models sold had these options, and one-eighth were equipped with Powerglide transmissions ($199.10 extra). The detachable hardtop continued to be ordered on slightly more than half the convertibles delivered. Pricing for the engine options was $53.80 for the 300 bhp unit, $107.60 for the solid-lifter 340 bhp engine and $430.40 for the Ramjet Fuel Injection. The four-speed transmission was $188.30 extra.

When it launched the Sting Ray, Chevrolet knew well that there were some 60,000 Corvette owners out there to whom it had never really made a strong appeal to trade in their cars on a new model. It expected brisk sales, and it got them. "The waiting period is at least 60 days," reported *Motor Trend* in May, 1963, "and dealers won't 'deal' a bit on either coupés or roadsters. Both are going for the full sticker price, with absolutely no discount and very little (if any) over-allowance on trade-ins."

Motor Trend, making an extensive evaluation on the road with a production car, found that it had some reservations about what Chevrolet had wrought. "From the important styling and all-around performance angles," it noted, "the new Sting Ray is an even greater car than its predecessors. But for a car that sells in

the $4,500-6,000 range, it doesn't reflect the degree of quality control we feel it should."

The magazine criticized the body panel fit and surface smoothness, and the way the interior trim was installed. These were partly the result of the inevitable start-up problems at Ashtabula and St. Louis, and partly endemic to the unique status of the Corvette: a high-performance luxury sports car, a contender for the highest rank among the world's automobiles, built by the division of GM that rose to fame as a mass builder and merchandiser. Bill Mitchell, perceptive as always, put it another way: "An alarm clock and a chronometer both tell time, but it's the way they do it that makes the difference." He kept after Chevrolet, urging it to keep the Corvette's quality as high as possible, and it did improve substantially in the next few years.

Motor Trend observed that both the coupé and roadster tended to be noisy on the road. The array of instruments met with their approval, "but their design is such that at night, with the instrument lights on, they're hard to read. The brushed aluminum backing of each gauge tends to glare." There was little but praise for the handling: "We thought the old model cornered darn well, but there's no comparing it to this new one. At high cruising speeds — and even at maximum speeds — nothing but an all-out competition car will equal it in stability. It's completely comfortable without being mushy, and it takes a large chuck hole to induce any degree of harshness into the ride."

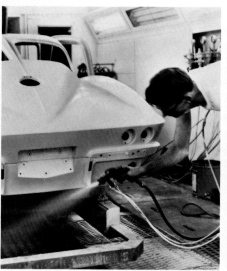
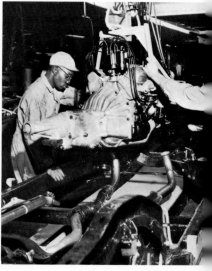

Photo sequence beginning at the upper left shows beginning of body assembly of '63, completed body, spraying in paint booth, and engine installatio

Putting a 300 bhp coupé through its Road Research Report procedure, *Car and Driver* was not so pleased with some specifics of the Sting Ray's handling: "The new all-independent suspension has completely transformed the Corvette in terms of traction and cornering power, but it still has some faults. The standard setup on the test car seemed a bit more suitable for race tracks than for fast back-road motoring. A rigid front anti-roll bar in combination with a relatively stiff transverse leaf spring in the rear reduces the resilience and independence of the suspension of each wheel with the result that even on mildly rough surfaces the car does not feel perfectly stable.

"On bumpy turns it's at its worst, veering freely from one course to another," said *C/D*, "but on a smooth surface it comes incredibly close to perfection. There is some understeer but the car has such a tremendous power surplus, even with the next-to-bottom engine option, that the tail can be slung out almost any old time, and after a while throttle steering seems the natural way of aiding the car around a curve." Calling the new power steering system "every bit as good as those used by Rover and Mercedes-Benz in terms of feedback and road feel," *C/D* nevertheless felt the manual steering of the new car was light enough to make the power option almost superfluous. Not until 1968, in fact, was power steering specified by more than a quarter of the Corvette buyers.

"As an American car it is unique," *Car and Driver* concluded,

Finished 1963 model leaving the line at upper right passed through (left to right) body drop, installation of seats and trim, and polishing of paint.

"and it stands out from its European counterparts as having in no way copied them but arrived at the same goal along a different route. Zora Arkus-Duntov summed it up this way: 'For the first time I now have a Corvette I can be proud to drive in Europe.' We understand his feelings and are happy to agree that the Sting Ray is a fine showpiece for the American auto industry, especially since it is produced at a substantially lower price than any foreign sports or GT car of comparable performance."

This premise was put to the test late in 1963 when a Sting Ray coupé was sent to Europe, specifically for tests by publications there. This wasn't done for sales promotion reasons; Chevrolet couldn't meet its domestic demand and had no interest in fanning the enthusiasm of European buyers. The car, a red coupé with fuel injection and a 3.70 axle, was shipped over to satisfy the curiosity of the continentals about this colonial challenger to their artistic pre-eminence in the world of sports cars.

The career of this Corvette was anything but untroubled. After it had been carefully prepared and approved by Zora Duntov, its clutch was burned out by the driver taking it through the Holland Tunnel in New York's rush-hour traffic to a New Jersey port for shipping. So the order of the day when it arrived at GM Continental in Antwerp, Belgium, its home base, was extensive repair — not a very auspicious beginning.

Later, when it was being picked up by Britain's *Motor Sport* for a test, one of the drive shafts broke next to the outer universal joint, thrashing around to shatter various underbody parts while the affected wheel leaned inward. The driver was able to keep control because the trailing torque arm was held in place by its rubber-bushed forward pivot; this was a possible failure which Zora Duntov had not expected to happen but for which he had nevertheless designed and tested in advance. But the red coupé was in for another round of time-consuming repairs.

London's *Motor* was the first to test the Sting Ray and report on its results. It accelerated faster than anything they had ever tested, offered fuel consumption that was "not unreasonable" for its performance, and had a gearbox that was "one of the best we have ever encountered in such a high-performance car. The change is smooth, fast, and astonishingly light, and the synchromesh can only be beaten by the most brutal methods, and then only in the lower two gears.

"In most respects," *Motor* summed up, "the Chevrolet Corvette Sting Ray is the equal of any G.T. car to be found on either side of the Atlantic. It falls down on refinement (which is surprising in a model from a country where the most unpretentious cars are notably refined) and wet-road behaviour, a shortcoming for which the cure might be found in the choice of tyres. The silhouette is good, but some of the styling details both inside and out seem fussy. The car is not free of gimmicks, but the performance needs no flattery, the handling is good, and the brakes superb."

Coming second, Britain's *Autocar* was entitled to be more critical, and was. One car in its experience, a Zagato-bodied Aston Martin DB4, had accelerated faster than the Sting Ray. And the magazine observed that "the refinement, particularly in respect of engine and transmission noise, is inferior to that of most of its European competitors and this gives the impression of the car being more powerful than it really is. To the purist, some of the false styling features, such as dummy grilles and air vents in the body, appear unnecessary.

"The performance is certainly vivid," admitted *Autocar*, "but if more attention had been given to such items as tyre adhesion in the wet and wipers that clear the screen effectively above 80 m.p.h., instead of some gimmicks which only attempt to give an impression of engineering thought, the Sting Ray would be a better car." Editors used to high thirst with high performance were again impressed by the Corvette's restraint in this regard, and also with respect to oil (in a country where high-output engines normally guzzled their lubricant): "It was even more surprising that no oil was added to the sump throughout the 1,440-mile test."

Autocar signed off with these views: "Judged by the Sting

Show-car version of stock '63, displayed in Chicago, had Shark-type exhausts.

Ray, the American manufacturers are still behind those of Europe when endeavouring to build a car combining real performance and refinement — rather surprising when their more normal road cars are so good in the latter respect. No doubt the less highly tuned versions would be preferred by the majority of owners and give enough performance for them." This was actually the case, the much smoother and quieter hydraulic-lifter engines being chosen by most Sting Ray buyers. But for the ultimate in performance there was nothing like the instant response and wide rev range of the injected V-8.

After it finally got the repaired Sting Ray, *Motor Sport* didn't find the engine so offputting: "Indeed, there can be few people who would willingly go back to a 'buzz-box' after sampling the torque of a big V8. The unit is not at all noisy except when running near its rev. limit, and in this respect is undoubtedly quieter than the E-type Jaguar's twin-camshaft engine, although, strangely enough, the American V8 is not as smooth in its delivery of power as the venerable straight-six of the Jaguar.

"Fortunately for British enthusiasts who may be regretting the price of the Sting Ray, the car falls short of the standards set by the E-type in respect of handling, steering and braking." (The car's price in England was close to $10,000.) *Motor Sport* was not happy with the Firestone Super Sport tires, especially on wet or poor surfaces, with the extreme ease with which the tail came around when the throttle was opened, and with the tendency to pull to one side when cold, caused by the sintered iron brake linings.

Nor did the styling details impress: "It is the external appearance and internal layout of the Sting Ray that the British enthusiast will find most distasteful, for it is as vulgar and over-ornamented as the E-type is simple and functional. The basic shape of the car is quite pleasing but it is completely spoiled by dummy louvres in the bonnet, and false vents in the front wings and body sides, while various insignia are scattered over the body announcing that the car is a Sting Ray, has fuel injection and is made by Chevrolet; in addition, the opportunity is taken several times to place crossed flags in prominent places, including the large petrol tank flap.

"Naturally, the emphasis of the Sting Ray is on performance," the magazine continued, "and perform it certainly does. Other cars which are travelling quite quickly disappear to a dot on the horizon in an incredibly small space of time once the Sting Ray is past, and there are very few cars which can attempt to hold the Sting Ray for any length of time. Within a few seconds of leaving a built-up area it can be cruising at 100 m.p.h. at a modest 4,500 r.p.m., and at this speed the car feels like most other cars do at 50 m.p.h., for engine and wind noise is kept to a minimum.

"Despite its various shortcomings," *Motor Sport* concluded, "it is impossible to ignore the appeal of the Sting Ray for it offers tremendous performance even by American standards, and while it falls below the ideal in respect of ride, handling and braking, it is still an impressive piece of machinery by any standards. At present Jaguar have little to fear from the Sting Ray but in America development seems to go ahead very rapidly and next

Pininfarina Rondine was built on the new Sting Ray chassis for display at European shows in late 1963. It retained the standard instrument panel.

year's Sting Ray may well be a vast improvement. Now if only Jaguar had that engine and gearbox!"

There was one point on which almost all the road testers on both sides of the Atlantic seemed to agree. Their comments:

Road & Track: "Our only complaint about the interior was in the coupe, where all we could see in the rear view mirror was that silly bar splitting the rear window down the middle."

Car Life: "The bar down the center of the rear window makes it all but impossible to see out via the rearview mirror."

Motor Trend: "The rear window on the coupe is designed more for looks than practicality, and any decent view to the rear will have to be through an exterior side-view mirror."

Car and Driver: "Luggage space is surprisingly roomy but central window partition ruins rear view."

Autocar: "Nothing can be seen of the tail through the divided rear window, which makes reversing in confined quarters rather precarious."

Motor Sport: "The test car was actually a 1963 model but the 1964 models have slight modifications, including the deletion of the central dividing strip in the rear window, which allows some measure of rearwards vision."

On a car that was as attractive as this one to policemen in cars and on motorcycles, the rear-window divider was a substantial deterrent to a confident and relaxed attitude behind the wheel. It did indeed survive only the 1963 model year.

First race for the Sting Ray was at Riverside on October 13, 1962. Dave MacDonald drove No. 00, Bob Bondurant No. 614, and Doug Hooper No. 119.

There was agreement also on the vivid performance of the Chevy sports car. The relevant figures were as follows:

1963 Corvette Acceleration Tabulation			
	1 x 4 bbl. carburetion Powerglide	1 x 4 bbl. carburetion 4-speed	fuel-injected 4-speed	fuel-injected 4-speed
Publication	Car Life	Car and Driver	Sports Car Graphic	Autocar
Nominal power	300 bhp	300 bhp	360 bhp	360 bhp
Final drive ratio	3.36:1	3.36:1	3.70:1	3.70:1
0-60 mph	7.2 secs.	6.2 secs.	5.6 secs.	6.5 secs.
0-80 mph	13.0 secs.	9.6 secs.	10.1 secs.	10.2 secs.
0-100 mph	22.9 secs.	14.8 secs.	14.1 secs.	14.9 secs.
Standing ¼ mile	15.5 secs.	14.5 secs.	14.2 secs.	14.6 secs.
Terminal ¼ mile speed	86 mph	98 mph	102 mph	96 mph
Maximum speed	130 mph	118 mph	151 mph	146 mph

The editors of *Car Life* and their editorial director, John R. Bond, thought enough of the Sting Ray to present it their Award

...oper won that debut race, but the Ford-powered Cobras had been menacing.

for Engineering Excellence for 1963. In justifying it they ventured one prediction which unfortunately did not come true: "The Corvette, purely and simply, has the best suspension and chassis mass-manufactured in the United States today. In fact, the use of independent suspension for all four wheels offers so many advantages we feel it is a safe prediction that most U.S. production cars will have it within five years." The trend actually went the other way, with the Pontiac Tempest dropping its independent rear suspension after 1963, though the Corvair did change from a less sophisticated design to the Sting Ray rear suspension geometry in 1965, at the suggestion of Zora Duntov.

"In all," their Award report concluded, "we at *Car Life* would say that the Corvette has finally achieved the refinement needed to match its great brute strength. The Sting Ray represents leadership in automotive design. It is tomorrow's car, on the street today." This citation was in a sense a gift from Ed Cole, who had supervised the engineering development of the Sting Ray until his departure from the Division late in 1961, to his successor Bunkie Knudsen. It was Knudsen who was managing Chevrolet when the Sting Ray was introduced, and who was in charge of its manufacturing, sales promotion and further development.

Unable to resist tampering with their new toy, the GM stylists produced a show-car version of the convertible for display at the Chicago Show in February, 1963. It had external headers and mufflers like those of the Shark and functional air outlet grilles in the hood. With its aluminum wheels it was a very handsome car, finished in light pearlescent blue with an outlined white stripe down the hood and rear deck.

A supplier of plastics to the auto industry, Rohm & Haas, chose a Corvette convertible as a Trojan horse to carry some of its new applications ideas into the fortress of Detroit. Dubbed Explorer II, it had many special features of acrylic plastic adapted to the existing styling by a Detroit industrial design firm, William M. Schmidt Associates. Acrylics were used for a transparent hardtop, fairings for fixed headlights, metal-finished wheel discs, an injection-molded instrument cluster, and a fender-to-fender lighting strip across the rear end.

Considerably more ambitious was the work done on a 1963 Sting Ray chassis by Pininfarina. This great Turinese coachbuilder had enjoyed a warm friendship with Harley Earl that carried over to Bill Mitchell, a friendship that had moved GM from time to time to ship a chassis to Italy for Pininfarina to custom-body in any way they wished. This was done also with a Sting Ray, which was not seen again until its arrival at the Paris

At Sebring in '63 the best-placed Corvette was the Johnson/Morgan No. 3, in 16th position. Johnny Allen and Jef Stevens were 17th overall in No. 6.

Corvettes of 1962 and 1963 vintage jousted in late-1962 Puerto Rican GP.

Salon in October, 1963, little more than an hour before the official opening. It had been transformed into the svelte metallic turquoise Rondine.

Bearing the Italian name for the swallow, in honor of its fleet and distinctively shaped tail, the Rondine kept the Sting Ray instrument panel and offered a variation on its wheel-disc theme — but that's about all. Otherwise the hardtop coupe was a stunningly fresh and stimulating exercise, its theme a beveled surface along the usual highlight line that wrapped around the front of the car and along the doors, then reversing its angle to a dihedral slope as it passed the rear door edges and formed the upper surfaces of the rear fenders.

Other features of the Rondine were clever: small "eyelids" above the fixed headlights that lifted up when they were switched on; a reverse rake to the rear window, which could be rolled up and down. But it was the fender line that was fundamentally fresh, and to no one's great surprise Pininfarina found a home for it in the company's design for the Fiat 124 Sport Spider, which was introduced at the Turin Show in 1966 and was still in production, in slightly modified form, six years later.

Scoring successes with the buyers and the critics, the new Sting Ray had its work cut out for it on the race track. Hopes had been initially high, as Zora Duntov recalled: "When we came out with the Sting Ray, the car had superior handling than the previous model, lower drag than previous model. While it was growing, I thought that this car would not only snap at Ferraris

No. 2, a Grady Davis 1963 Sebring entry, reached 5th place overall driven by Lowther/Black/Yenko, but then fell back to 25th after twelve hours.

— I mean GT-type Ferraris; at that time production car racing was a popular type of racing — but this car's chassis can take increases in power, as subsequent development proved. We can work on that, I felt, and we would be the very top dog, better than Ferrari in this type of competition. The calculation was made without Carroll Shelby!"

The famous road racing driver from Texas who wore bib overalls when he was behind the wheel, co-winner at Le Mans in 1959, had considered for some time the building and racing of a car of his own. That had been Shelby's thought when he worked with Gary Laughlin to have several Corvettes rebodied by Scaglietti in Italy: "What I wanted was a little 2,000 to 2,500-pound car. We could have done that by putting a lightweight body on the Corvette chassis, but the guys in charge of the Corvette program didn't think that was such a hot idea. They got real cranky when they found out about it and they shot it down. However, it wasn't Zora Duntov who shot it down. He's not the sort of guy who'd be against something like that."

Discouraged by Chevrolet, Shelby turned to Ford, who backed him financially to build a car, the Cobra, with an English AC chassis under a new small Ford V-8 engine. It was small and light and it went like a rocket. "My idea," said Shelby, "was to build a car that would outrun the Corvette and Ferrari production cars. Production car racing was a lot bigger then. Well, soon enough, we got about three Cobras built and we decided to see what one would do on a race course." The chosen occasion

was the Times Three-Hour Invitational Race on October 13, 1962, the day before the Times Grand Prix at Riverside. It happened also to be the racing baptism of the 1963 Corvette.

Four of the new Z06-optioned Sting Ray coupés had been built in St. Louis and driven west, for break-in mileage, to be run in this event. Three were assigned to West Coast drivers who'd enjoyed Corvette successes, Dave MacDonald, Bob Bondurant, and Jerry Grant, while the fourth went to hot-rodder Mickey Thompson, a long-time friend of Bunkie Knudsen, to be driven by Doug Hooper. Though there hadn't been much time for preparation, the cars were fully race-equipped except for the knock-off aluminum wheels, which weren't yet available.

After the Le Mans start on the back straight, the race became a hard-fought duel between Bill Krause in the lone Cobra and Dave MacDonald's Sting Ray. This ended around the one-hour mark when first the Corvette and then the Cobra shed their left rear wheels. Two more Sting Rays were stopped by engine failures, leaving a lonely Doug Hooper in the lead with the race half over. Hooper's sinister-looking black coupé made one 20.5-second pit stop for thirty-one gallons of gas and a quart of oil, then held off a late-race challenge by Jay Hills's Porsche RSK to take the victory for Chevrolet. Mickey Thompson was jubilant: "I don't think it's ever been done before . . . a new production car winning the first time out!"

Zora Duntov was less sanguine about his future prospects: "Although we won the first race, as far as I was concerned the

Arch-rivals on the starting line at Road America in June, 1963: Bob Johnson in No. 33 Cobra (winner) and Dick Thompson's ZO6 Corvette (placed th

writing was on the wall. Shelby will suffer loose wheels, loose axles, loose this and that, but ultimately he has the configuration which is no damn good to sell to the people, except very few, but by the looks of it will beat Corvette on the tracks unless we do something." Cramped and uncomfortable, with traditional British side curtains for weather protection, the Cobra was indeed uninviting to the public at large. Only some 900 AC-based Cobras were manufactured in all. But its weight of 2,020 pounds gave it an insuperable competition advantage over the Corvette.

In a June, 1963 cover story titled "Corvette vs. Cobra: the Battle for Supremacy," *Road & Track* reported that "the domination of Corvette in its racing category came to an end" in another race at Riverside that followed their first encounter. Said *R&T*, "Dave MacDonald [switching from Corvette to Cobra] and Ken Miles, driving Cobras, beat all of the Corvettes (and there were some good ones there) so badly that it was not even a contest. Indeed, just to add insult to injury, Ken Miles made a pit stop after his first lap, ostensibly to have the brakes, or something, inspected, and after all of the Corvettes had gone by, he set out in pursuit. Whittling away at the Corvettes at the rate of about five seconds per lap, on a 2.6-mile course, Miles caught his teammate,

MacDonald, and relegated the first Corvette to third place in what seemed like no time at all.

"The next confrontation," the magazine continued, "was at the Daytona 3-hour, where a vast comedy of errors prevented the Cobras from defeating the GTO Ferraris and Dick Thompson, in a Sting Ray, beat back the faltering Cobras to one-up them in that race." In the testing Sebring 12-hour in 1963, three of seven Corvettes finished and three of six Cobras completed the race, the best one in eleventh place, ten laps ahead of the first Corvette back in sixteenth, the car of Delmo Johnson and Dave Morgan. It was a pattern that would persist. In 1964 the Corvette was shut out of Divisional SCCA Class A Production Championships completely by the Cobra, and not until 1969 would it again win an A Production National Championship.

Corvette owners and enthusiasts were understandably incensed over this state of affairs. One of them wrote Chevrolet's Joe Pike and asked him what he intended to do about it. He replied in part as follows: "As far as the Sting Ray versus Cobra competition is concerned, I am afraid the Corvette is not going to be competitive. As a fellow Corvette enthusiast as well as the individual responsible for the national promotion of this car for

Competition at Marlboro featured Ralph Salyer, No. 25, en route to a Divisional Championship in SCCA's Class A Production for the 1963 season.

Chevrolet, I do not like to see Corvettes being beaten by a Cobra either.

"When SCCA classified the Cobra as a production car," maintained Pike, "they goofed. Only five or six hot Cobras have ever been produced, and the few dozen street versions are no more competitive with the Corvette than the Corvette is with the factory racing Cobras. You cannot give away a thousand-pound weight disadvantage with similar horsepower and expect to win, even if the Corvette does out-handle the Cobra. The Cobra is no more of a production car than the GTO Ferrari and should have been in C Modified at the very beginning, where it not only belongs but where it has demonstrated its ability to compete with other modified cars.

"Over the years Chevrolet has improved and refined the Corvette as a true production dual-purpose sports car designed to be driven on the street and competitive with other similar vehicles on the track. We want to continue to build a production sports car designed primarily for street use and grand touring that a lot of people can afford to buy and that a few who wish can race. If we were to compete directly with the Cobra," Pike continued, "I am sure the car would have to cost in excess of $10,000 — and

there really aren't 100 people in the entire country who can afford to buy such a car strictly for racing."

The era of Cobra dominance on the track was demoralizing but not damaging to the Corvette, in the view of Zora Arkus-Duntov: "Fortunately, we did not suffer any to speak of. We did still win some races. But the car became recognized as a good value, good product, on its own. Even if it doesn't win the races right now, it's still the best thing you can buy. So this lack of racing success, I think, at that point did not result in a drop of sales. And a different type of people got attracted to the car. It was a vastly improved car. It had only one problem: It did not win the races against Cobra, yet Cobra did not compete with the car in the marketplace."

There was a possible solution to this problem. Zora had begun working on it in 1962 with the blessing of Bunkie Knudsen. It was a solution that would have tested the question of just how many people *would* buy a $10,000 Corvette mainly for racing. And it would, on a bright and sunny day in the Bahamas, demonstrate how a fully committed Chevrolet could have dealt with the Cobra menace, with the Ferrari GTO, and with almost anything else on the track.

Chapter 13

GRAND SPORT ADVENTURE

"Lots of us still felt Corvette should be winning races." That, simply put, was the view of Arkus-Duntov and others above and below him at Chevrolet. "Since we cannot build special vehicles and since our production vehicle is not capable of competing, then maybe we should have a limited production of some lightened version." This was the idea, compelling in its logic and simplicity, behind the Grand Sport Corvette.

The arrival of Bunkie Knudsen on the Chevrolet scene had triggered a new round of activity on the part of those interested in abnormally high performance. As a new man in the division, Knudsen had several things going for him, and he knew it: Having just been granted the assignment by GM management, a certain amount of initial latitude would be given him to get the job done his way; he was not hamstrung by preconceived ideas about what could and could not be done at Chevrolet; his good performance at Pontiac had given his superiors confidence in his ideas. There were other advantages that were uniquely Knudsen's: His substantial personal wealth gave him an independent outlook (as he later proved with his surprise move to Ford), and he was just as willing to place his trust in talented individuals as he was to rely on the internal machinery of a giant corporation.

Knudsen put in hand the work on a new stock car racing engine, the Mark II or "porcupine" 427-cubic-inch V-8 that rocked the balance of power in the NASCAR fraternity when it first appeared at Daytona early in 1963. Of the two Corvette-related programs offered him by Duntov, he had initially chosen the more exotic CERV II (Chapter 10) as a sports-prototype entry in the major long-distance races. But before many parts for it had been made in 1962, one of the periodic waves of discouragement of racing swept downward through the strata of GM management from Frederic Donner, at the very top. The CERV II project went into the dustbin during this housecleaning.

GM general managers do not give up easily, however. Often the ones who succeed are those who challenge corporate policy in order to gain their ends; they never cease testing the limits of their authority. Now Knudsen bought Duntov's other recommendation, one closely related to the new Sting Ray. This had certain distinct advantages. As part of the existing Corvette program, a special car could be brought into being without the need to expose it to the critical gaze of the GM Engineering Policy Committee, the group that meets monthly to approve new divisional product developments. And so, with a minimum of fanfare internally, Chevrolet Engineering started working in the summer of 1962 on the car they came to know best as the "lightweight" Corvette.

The premise was a simple one and did not differ greatly from the reasoning that had led Ford to back Shelby's Cobra. In 1962, the F.I.A. had realigned its World Championship for Manufacturers to make Grand Touring cars eligible to win, those being cars that were approved or "homologated" by the F.I.A. as having been built in a quantity of at least one hundred in a twelve-month period according to a single specific design spelled out in the official "homologation papers" submitted by the manufacturer to the F.I.A. For 1963 there was to be no upper displacement limit on the engines of such GT cars. This was an open invitation to American GT car builders, most clearly to the Corvette, to compete for Manufacturers Championship points in the qualifying events like Sebring, the Targa Florio, Le Mans, and the 1000 Kilometers of the Nürburgring.

Those who had backed the idea of the "lightweight" Corvette were audacious enough to believe that it could not only beat the other GT cars but could also be made capable of taking overall wins. It was to be founded on the brand-new suspension geometry of the Sting Ray, the car to be a replica of the new coupé built to the lightest possible weight consistent with reliability. The relatively high aerodynamic drag of the coupé was to be overcome by the installation under the hood of a truly formidable amount of horsepower for that time. And 125 of these Grand Sport Corvettes were to be built and sold on a first-come, first-

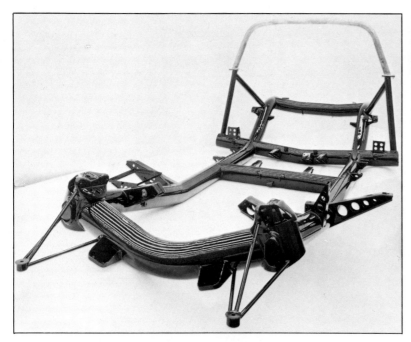

Gradually growing chassis of first Grand Sport is seen from front above and from rear below. Frame's tubular side members ran dead straight in plan view. Transverse leaf spring layout was used, along with standard car's geometry, for rear suspension.

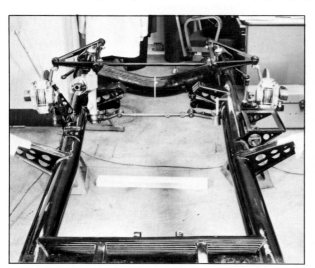

Special aluminum differential housing was centerpiece of Grand Sport rear suspension assembly, attached to the main frame tubes at three points.

Rear suspension radius arms were made specially for the GS with holes drilled for lightening. Inside the rear brake discs were the small shoe brakes, shown, which were applied only by the hand brake lever.

served basis.

In the Grand Sport, Duntov was able to realize the kind of Sting Ray he had wanted to build all along — only moreso. A completely new frame was designed, still a ladder-type pattern but now· an utterly classical example of the style, its side members extending dead-straight from front to rear in plan view. These were steel tubes of substantial diameter, connected at the rear by three crossmembers of similar size and at the front by a huge crossmember half a foot in diameter. As seen from the side, the frame was level through its central portion, sloping gently upward to the front suspension mounts and rising sharply at the rear to leave room for the rear suspension.

Making the main frame members straight meant that their strength, both in beam and in torsion, was at a maximum, but they could no longer be detoured around the passenger compartment. A bulge down the center of the floor on each side of the cockpit made room for the tubes on their way from front to back, and the seats were mounted flush with the top of the frame, each attached to four brackets provided for that purpose. This made the Grand Sport seating position an inch or two higher than that of the standard car, for which there was sufficient headroom, offering the driver a better view. Mounts integral with the rear of the frame accepted a bolted-on tubular roll bar, and other

The same fine detail work evident on the Corvette SS was visible again in the exquisite fabrication of the GS front suspension and steering links.

brackets, triangulated tubes or thin sheet steel drilled for lightness, held the body on at two points in the front, two at the sides and two at the rear. With all its attachments the frame weighed 160 pounds.

Though there were many references at the time to these cars as the "aluminum-bodied" Corvettes, Chevrolet had remained true to fiberglass as a body material. They were fabricated entirely by the Chevy Engineering prototype shop of GRP hand-laid with three layers of glass cloth to a thickness of 0.040 inch. As a central armature the stock model's steel "birdcage" was replaced by a hand-hammered sheet aluminum framework around the doors and windows. Bonded together, the complete body lifted on and off the chassis as a single piece.

Zora had deleted the center divider from the Grand Sport's rear window without waiting for permission from Bill Mitchell. He also mounted the headlights in fixed positions behind fairings of plexiglass and added a removable deck lid at the rear for access to the spare tire. The large fuel filler cap for the thirty-six gallon tank was built into the right rear quarter of the roof. All the windows except the windshield were plexiglass, those at the sides being raised and lowered by means of straps which retained them in the desired position.

The Grand Sport interior was made remarkably civilized, as

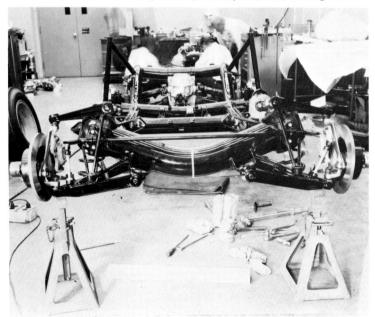

Stands had to be placed just right beneath the GS front suspension to avoid bending the thin sheet steel from which they were made. Solid brake discs were later replaced by ventilated discs for better cooling.

169

befitted a production model from Chevrolet. It made use of the stock model's instrument cluster, a plastic molding, with some substitutions: an oil temperature gauge instead of the gas gauge, and the installation of a 200 mph (!) speedometer. The floor and center tunnel were neatly carpeted, and all the interior surfaces were professionally finished off. Not unlike those in the Corvette SS, the deep bucket seats were of fiberglass molded to a tubular framework. Their position could be changed but bolts had to be removed and refitted to do it.

A stock steering wheel guided the Grand Sport through a special recirculating-ball steering box, similar internally to the standard Corvette unit but with a faster ratio, giving two turns from lock to lock, and with an aluminum housing. The three-part track rod linkage was the same as that of the stock Sting Ray. While the front-end geometry resembled that of the standard car, the pieces were entirely different. The beautifully slender knuckle, carried by two ball joints, was of chrome-nickel-molybdenum steel alloy, shot-peened to build its resistance to fatigue failure. The wishbones were fabricated of sheet steel that was heavy enough to take the design stresses but so thin that they could easily be bent if a jack were slid into the wrong position to lift the car.

Large-diameter coil springs with concentric Delco high-performance shocks supported the front end, and an anti-roll bar was bracketed to the front face of the chassis frame. At the rear, the transverse leaf spring still proved to be the best for the job at hand. With nine rubber-separated leaves, like the standard spring, it was bolted solidly to the bottom of the differential casing, which in turn was rigidly attached to the rear frame crossmember. There needed to be no flexible rubber mounts in this rear suspension; noise was not a problem. Delco dampers were mounted vertically to attachments outboard of the frame.

The rear half-shafts were similar to the stock parts, acting as suspension members, but were larger in diameter. Standard rear spindle carriers of cast nodular iron were used in the GS, mounted in fabricated sheet metal trailing arms akin to the stock ones but lighter in weight, pierced with lightening holes. Forward thrust and brake torques from these arms were taken by large rubber bushings on outboard extensions from the frame crossmember just behind the seats.

Since the GS was to be substantially lighter than the production Corvette, it was possible to equip it with an existing type of British Girling disc brake. (When shown both the weight and performance figures of the stock Corvette, the Girling engineers admitted that at that time they had no disc brake system they could recommend for it.) The aluminum calipers had two pistons

The completed fiberglass body for the GS had a central armature with hand-formed sheet aluminum framework around the doors and windows.

outboard and one inboard, pressing against lining pads that measured 3.30 x 2.04 inches in front, and 3.06 x 1.55 inches in the rear. A vacuum booster for the brakes was standard equipment.

Brake discs measured eleven and a half inches in diameter and were deeply offset from their mounting flanges, giving the discs a "hat-section" design, a reference to their appearance. The smaller diameter of the "hat" in the rear discs was used to solve a difficult problem, that of providing an effective hand brake with a four-wheel disc system. Within the center of each disc a small conventional expanding-shoe brake was fitted, of duo-servo pattern, with normal organic linings. These brakes were applied by a typically British fly-off lever placed on the right side of the driver's seat, between it and the central tunnel.

Some liberties were taken in the molding of the body for the Grand Sport to be sure that it had enough fender room for the widest suitable tires that were then available. It was supplied with Halibrand magnesium wheels of 15.0-inch diameter and 6.0-inch rim width, weighing 16.5 pounds apiece. Knock-off hubs with three-eared retaining nuts were provided. There was room for tires of up to 7.10/7.60 section in front and 8.00/8.20 in the rear. Keeping the standard ninety-eight-inch wheelbase, the GS was also close to the normal track dimensions at 56.8 inches in front, 57.8 in the rear. The "lightweight" was 172.8 inches long,

69.6 inches wide and 51.9 inches high, with 4.3 inches of ground clearance.

During November and the early part of December, 1962, Grand Sport number one was taking shape in a windowless cubicle along one of the back halls of the Chevrolet Engineering Center. For its first trials it was powered by a fuel-injected Corvette engine that differed from standard mainly in its aluminum cylinder heads and experimental aluminum block, identifiable by the "O-" prefix to its part number cast into the block surface. Of course the clutch and transmission housings were also all-aluminum. New to the Grand Sport was an aluminum case for the differential, which could carry the normal range of Corvette final-drive ratios as well as a Dana limited-slip differential.

The first serious outing for GS number one, after runs up and down the check road at the GM Technical Center to make sure nothing fell off, was a test session at Sebring in cooperation with Firestone on December 15 and 16. The white Grand Sport accompanied standard and experimental Sting Rays to Florida for a thorough shakedown and tryout of tire and brake equipment.

During these tests, with Masten Gregory and Dick Thompson assisting with the driving, it became clear that the half-inch-thick solid brake discs used on the GS didn't offer enough heat-dissipating ability. Later, new discs were made that were one inch

Chassis of first Grand Sport was complete as shown before body was fitted on. Seats differed: driver's was adjustable and passenger's was fixed.

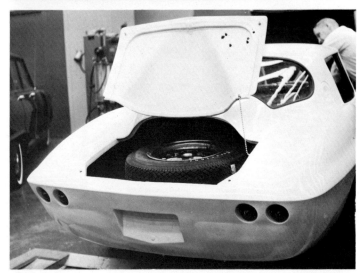

First GS, during completion, showed one-piece rear window, fairings for fixed headlights, and rear access door for spare and "luggage."

thick but weighed only a quarter-pound more, because they had internal ventilating passages that acted to pump air outward, like a centrifugal blower. These reduced the brake lining temperatures from more than 400° F. to the 300° F. level during a series of stops from 100 mph to rest at 0.8 g. deceleration. The Grand Sports were changed over to these discs and to the wider modified Girling calipers to suit them, as they became available.

Before the end of 1962 the specification of the Grand Sport had been frozen to allow the homologation papers to be prepared, for submission to the ACCUS-FIA, the American organization affiliated with the F.I.A. in Paris. They stated that the car's curb weight was 1,908 pounds. As is customary in such applications, this represented the lowest possible weight at which the car might be entered in a race. The actual weights of the Grand Sports ranged from 1,900 to 2,100 pounds, depending on the type of engine and amount of equipment they were carrying.

The application also described the special engine that was under development for the GS. It was to be founded on a cylinder block of the basic 327 pattern, cast in aluminum with dry iron liners. The four-inch cylinder bore was to be retained, but there was a possibility of using a stroke as long as four inches, which would have brought the displacement to 402 cubic inches. Experimentation showed that the longest stroke the engine was happy with at that time was three and three-quarter inches, which displaced 377 cubic inches. Even this required special clearance notches in the block and specific connecting rods so they wouldn't bump into the camshaft. At this size it was also difficult to attach enough counterbalancing mass to the crankshaft. But the bottom end was sound enough, running to a tachometer redline of 6,500 rpm, with a nine-quart oil supply.

Zora Duntov, who with his brother Yura had created the Ardun hemispherical-head kit for the Ford V-8 of the forties, now created a new cylinder head design for the Chevy V-8 that powered the Grand Sport. It retained pushrod valve operation, using rocker arms to open valves that were mutually inclined to suit hemispherical combustion chambers instead of the normal Chevrolet wedge-shape chamber. This in turn allowed much larger valves, the heads measuring 2.20 inches for the inlets and 1.72 inches for the exhaust valves.

No chances were taken with the ignition, which was supplied by two spark plugs for each chamber. It was difficult to find room for these among the rocker gear to the valves, but Duntov's designers managed it. Sparks came from a single distributor at the rear of the engine, powered by two coils. Rochester constant-flow injection delivered the fuel, the system being altered to allow the use of individual ram pipes to the respective cylinders. These were shown as rising vertically in the artful paintings, supposedly showing one of these engines installed in a ˙Sting Ray, that were prepared to accompany the homologation application.

Had this sixteen-plug engine been operable at its maximum displacement of 402 cubic inches, the Chevy men had allowed themselves to hope for an output as high as 600 horsepower. At the 377-cubic-inch level the figure was 550 bhp at 6,400 rpm allied with a maximum torque of 500 pound-feet at 5,200 rpm. These were numbers with which to conjure. No GT or sports-racing car had yet been built with more power than this. And with the large valves and generous cam timing (inlet 55°/117°; exhaust 106°/44°; lift 0.46 inch) the maximum output was distributed toward the high-rpm end of the power curve where it was most needed to overcome the Grand Sport's high aerodynamic drag. It was forseen that the engine could be built with compression ratios of 10.0, 11.0 or 12.0 to one, according to the fuel quality available and the length and type of race envisioned.

This, then, was the Grand Sport Corvette that Chevrolet had described in the request for homologation that it submitted to ACCUS-FIA, stating that it would build one hundred such cars between July 7, 1962 and June 1, 1963. Judging by the performance of the F.I.A. in the past, it seemed likely that the car would be accepted before construction of the full one hundred cars had been completed, especially since Chevrolet was hardly a small, backyard operation. So five cars were built initially. Authorization was then obtained to build twenty additional cars and forty of the special sixteen-plug engines. This would have been enough matériel for the 1963 racing season; as these were being completed the series of one hundred cars would have been scheduled for manufacture at the plant of an outside contractor to Chevrolet.

The first unofficial reaction from ACCUS-FIA to the Chevrolet application was a warning that the F.I.A. was now being much more critical about verification of production since it had accepted the Ferrari GTO early in 1962 before the full one hundred had been built, only to have Ferrari stop building the model when he was still well short of that number. But such setbacks were the least of Chevrolet's worries in January, 1963. Both internally and through the press, GM's top management had become increasingly aware that certain of its divisions were actively testing the limits of GM's allegiance to the AMA ban, which had been repudiated by Ford, followed by Chrysler, the previous May. Did GM still intend to abide by the terms of the

A normal Rochester-injected V-8 was installed in the first Grand Sport.

This special 16-plug engine was built for the GS but never used in it.

Shirtless Bob Clift talks with Masten Gregory at December, 1962 tests of a white GS at Sebring. First race appearance was at Marlboro in April, 1963.

agreement of June 6, 1957? The answer came on January 21 from Frederic Donner and John Gordon in an internal policy letter: GM was sticking to the agreement and the respective divisions would kindly comport themselves accordingly.

Not until a reporter asked GM about it, on February 16, did it become public knowledge that the corporation had cracked down on its would-be racers. Quizzed on the subject at a press conference that month, GM chairman Donner said: "Ever since the AMA adopted — I think you can term it a recommendation — back in 1957, we have had a policy on our books, and we haven't had any change in it." Hadn't his divisions frequently violated that policy since then? "Very often you run into interpretations of policies that to an outsider might look like violations — that distance between interpretation and violation is a very delicate one."

Donner had radically narrowed that distance in his private communications to his divisional chiefs. Performance programs throughout the company came, as Zora Duntov would say, "to a screeching halt." The ax fell on the Grand Sport Corvette after the parts for only five cars had been completed and before any significant development work had been done on the sixteen-plug engine. A golden era in the history of the Corvette seemed over before it had even begun.

But the Grand Sports were not allowed to become expensive museum pieces for the Chevrolet Engineering garage. Two of the completed cars were loaned to very close friends of the division, men who could be counted on to put them to use without talking about them too much: Dick Doane and Grady Davis. They went out the door in identical trim, painted white and powered by a normal 360 bhp 327-cubic-inch fuel-injected engine. Detail changes since they were first built included a narrow spoiler across the hood, scoops atop the rear fenders to pump cool air to the rear brakes, and vent slots low in the rear of the body to help keep the differential cool.

It was patently impossible to expect these two cars to do anything of significance during 1963. They had been released with engines offering nothing like the power for which the GS had been designed. Their entrants could get only the most limited kind of technical help from the cars' makers. And though they were designed as GT cars they had to run in the SCCA's C Modified class, which was inhabited by the likes of Scarabs and Chaparrals, cars built without compromise for racing. Yet run they did, and without disgrace to the Corvette name.

Dick Doane's Illinois-based car saw relatively little action in 1963. He fitted it with a long-stroke engine and entered it in the Road America 500 on September 8, but it was never in the run-

Thompson drove Grady Davis's GS in its Marlboro debut (shown) and also to an overall win at Watkins Glen, 1963, with special dual-inlet injection.

ning and spent much of the race in the pits. Gulf Oil's Davis was much more active in campaigning his GS, though his main aim with Dr. Dick Thompson that season was to challenge the Cobras in A Production with the Z06 Sting Ray, a quest that proved fruitless.

History repeats itself, they say, and the adage was proved when the Grand Sport made its racing debut at the first SCCA National Championship race of 1963 on April 7 at Marlboro, Maryland. The same race meet four years earlier had seen the baptism of Bill Mitchell's racing Stingray with the same driver at the wheel, Dick Thompson. And this time, as before, there were problems. Thompson was left behind at the start when an injector part failed, then took off again, after a twenty-minute stop for repairs, to see what the car could do. On the twisty Marlboro track it was three to four seconds a lap slower than the race winner, Roger Penske's Cooper-Climax, which is to say about three seconds a lap faster than Thompson's best times in a Z06 Sting Ray with a similar engine.

On April 28 at Danville, Virginia, the Davis GS was handled by Ed Lowther in the hour-and-a-half-long Governor's Cup race. In spite of valve bounce problems that limited its power the coupé placed fourth overall and third in its C Modified class. Dick Thompson took it over again for the Cumberland, Maryland, Na-

tionals on May 12, in which he was third in class and fifth overall in the main race for modified cars. Always a challenger at Elkhart Lake, Thompson contended for the lead with the GS in the main 160-mile race in June. Troubled by a balky cylinder, he placed third behind a Chaparral (front-engined) and a Scarab. Also in June, Thompson took fourth overall at Bridgehampton with the "lightweight."

July and August seemed likely to be less productive for the Davis-entered GS. It failed to finish at Lake Garnett, Kansas, where it was to have challenged the Shelby-backed Cobra of Ken Miles, and it was also among the DNF's at Meadowdale, Illinois. In that August 4 event Dick Doane took his Grand Sport through to a sixth-place finish. In the next several weeks the Davis GS was given a thorough overhaul and several evil-looking scoops on the hood, the larger of which fed air to a new downdraft induction system composed of two Rochester air-metering venturis, each supplying air to a group of four cylinders. The sides of the front fenders were also cut away to vent more warm air from the engine room.

With these changes the GS appeared for the Nationals at Watkins Glen on August 24. There it proved to be entirely competitive. In his thirty-lap race Dick Thompson led from the start, then gave way in traffic to Harry Heuer's Chaparral on lap seventeen. Thompson kept pressing the front-engined Chaparral until its rear end blew with a gout of smoke on the twenty-seventh lap, leaving the way clear for the dentist from D.C. to score the first overall victory for the Grand Sport Corvette. His winning average was 90.82 mph, fastest of the day. On September 15 the Thompson/GS combination looked strong in a 500-kilometer race at Bridgehampton until it was sidelined by brake problems. Thompson found himself fourth in C Modified Championship points at the end of the '63 season.

The winningest sports-racing car in the SCCA Nationals that year was the Cooper-based Zerex Special, built originally by Roy Gane for Roger Penske and entered in 1963 by John Mecom, Jr., who had acquired the car and with it the services of Gane and Penske. The younger Mecom, who has since become nationally known for his ownership of teams in major sports, was a Houston, Texas, resident and the scion of a family dedicated to adventurous oil exploration. Tall and good-looking in the Rock Hudson mold, at the age of only twenty-three, John Mecom, Jr. bought his first racing car in mid-1962 and by the following year was running one of America's most prominent teams from a huge garage at the Houston International Airport.

Young Mecom had money, machinery, talented people and class. All his racing cars and much of his equipment had been refinished in his official racing color, a Cadillac light metallic blue. His team emblem, very professional, showed a map of Texas flanked by the Texas state flag and the checkered flag. In addition to Penske, he had hired Augie Pabst and A. J. Foyt as drivers during the '63 season, men of unquestioned ability. In short, Mecom had made a tremendous impression in a short space of time; he had the equipment and the money to go racing the right way; and he was not aligned with any manufacturer. This made him an ideal ally for Chevrolet when the Division decided to risk an escalation of its Grand Sport activities late in 1963.

There's no doubt that the successes of the Cobras in sports car racing had the Chevy men, from Bunkie Knudsen on down, hopping mad by the time the '63 season ended. Shelby and his drivers had lost no chance to rub in their successes with such devices as mock gravestones engraved "R.I.P Sting Ray." Blocked by GM policy from building the 100 Grand Sports, Chevrolet nevertheless felt an overpowering urge to use the cars it did have to show Ford what it would be up against if Chevy were seriously in racing. It chose to do so through the Mecom Racing Team, the first target being the Nassau Speed Week events early in December.

Special Chevy engines were supplied to Mecom for a Cooper

Monaco, a Lola GT coupé and a rear-engined Scarab sports-racer he had bought from Lance Reventlow. In addition, the two Grand Sports were brought in from Davis and Doane and, along with a third car that had been in Warren, prepared for Nassau. There was much to be done. To make use of the latest low-profile Goodyear tires, new Halibrand wheels eleven inches wide were fitted. These had to protrude outward, so deep fender shrouds were added to the body to provide the covering for the wheels called for by F.I.A. rules.

Among other body changes, eight holes were drilled across the back between the taillights to allow more air to circulate around the rear brakes and differential. Air vents at the sides of the engine room were made official, and fitted with neat grilles. Opaque shrouds were made for the headlights, which were not needed at Nassau. And new hood panels were made, with two forward-facing grilled air inlets, to cover the closest thing that Chevrolet could provide to the engine originally envisioned for the production Grand Sport.

The 377-cubic-inch displacement was chosen, encased in an aluminum cylinder block with aluminum cylinder heads. Between the heads was a special light-alloy intake manifold in which the inlet pipes crossed between each other to the opposite side of the engine, like intertwined fingers. Bolted to flanges on the

After reworking, three GS Corvettes arrived at Nassau on November 30, 196.

manifold were four twin-throat Weber carburetors with 58-mm bore diameters, the two carbs on the right side of the engine feeding the left-hand cylinders, and vice versa. The result was a light, simple and serviceable power unit that delivered 435 pound-feet of torque at 4,000 rpm and 485 bhp at 6,000 rpm.

Painted by Chevrolet in Mecom's Cadillac blue, the three Grand Sports arrived in Nassau aboard the *Bahama Star* on November 30, the day before their first event. With the addition of numbers, Mecom and Goodyear stickers and a tape stripe on the nose to help tell one car from another, they were ready to race. These Sting Rays with hormones were magnificent-looking cars with an air of forbidding malevolence. Now they *looked* like competition cars, and Chevy engineers were in Nassau *en masse* to see that they had the performance to match their looks. Most of them professed to be in the Bahamas on holiday, and when one of them was asked a question, said writer Leo Levine, he prefaced his reply with: "You realize, of course, you're talking to a man who isn't here."

The Grand Sports were there, as they showed in the five-lap qualifying race that preceded the December 1 Tourist Trophy event for GT cars and prototypes. Along with Pabst in the Chevy-Lola, the two GS's driven by Dick Thompson and Jim Hall ran off and hid from the Cobras and the Ferrari GTO to get the

m left: John Mecom, Augie Pabst, Roger Penske, Dick Thompson, Jim Hall.

front-row grid positions. The Lola won the subsequent ninety-nine-mile Tourist Trophy over the potholed four-and-a-half-mile course laid out on an abandoned airfield, but the Corvettes ran into rear-end trouble, both retiring. The Chevy men had work to do before the next event, the Governor's Cup on December 6.

There were several rear-end problems, not all of which were entirely clear at the time. One was that the ring and pinion gears were installed with too much pre-load, which can overheat and overtax the axle lubricant if the gears aren't carefully and patiently broken in. Another was that the Dana limited-slip differentials were "green," again not broken in, and in their design not entirely suited to the needs of the GS. Yet another problem was that the axle lubricant didn't have enough resistance to scoring of the rubbing surfaces.

The final drives were set up as carefully as possible. In addition, a cooling system was installed that used a pump to circulate the axle oil through a radiator carried under a shroud on the back deck, just below the rear window. The changes worked, as demonstrated by the results of the 112-mile Governor's Cup race. All three Grand Sports were entered and all three finished. Roger Penske's was third, on the same lap as the winning Scarab-Chevy of Foyt and the runner-up Ferrari 250P. Augie Pabst was fourth and Dick Thompson, slowed by difficulties, was sixth. Arch-rival Shelby placed his best Cobra no better than eighth.

In the longest and most important race of the Speed Week, the 252-mile Nassau Trophy contest on December 8, another hitherto hidden problem manifested itself on the two Grand Sports driven by Dick Thompson and John Cannon, a new recruit to the Mecom team. Air pressure building up under the hoods was too much for the hold-down fasteners at the trailing edge, which came adrift. The blue coupés, which had been running in third and fourth places behind the same two cars they'd trailed two days before, had to make a series of stops to have the hoods taped down. This dropped them to fourth (Thompson) and eighth (Cannon). The best Ford-powered finisher was a Cobra in seventh place.

"We don't know what it proved," wrote Al Bochroch in *Car and Driver*, "but Chevy shot Ford right out of the sky at Nassau." It didn't really prove much, except that Shelby's team could have a terrible week just the way others could, but it did send a lot of Chevy men home from their "vacations" deliriously happy, which was worth something, and it gave a much-needed lift to the spirits of Corvette owners and enthusiasts.

On the day after the main race, John Mecom gave journalist Bernard Cahier the keys to John Cannon's Grand Sport and turned him loose with it for an hour on the Oakes Field course. Cahier wrote in *Sports Car Graphic* that "my first impression was of how docile the car was at low speed, how light and direct the steering was in spite of the enormous Goodyear tires. The car was big all right, but did not feel it. For a competition machine the brakes, clutch, throttle and gearbox were particularly pleasant to use, in a way like a refined GT car, and I was hardly expecting that."

Putting his foot down hard, Cahier "was breathless with the stupendous acceleration of the car. If you really want to show off you can leave rubber marks for a quarter of a mile, as you still get wheel spin when putting it into third gear. Needless to say, no acceleration time could be taken, but I understand that this Grand Sport Corvette will do zero to 100 mph in nine seconds flat and the standing quarter-mile should be under 12 seconds.

"The handling seemed free of any major vices and the car was equally at ease in slow, medium or fast bends. However, I noticed that at high speeds on the straight the combination of power, acceleration, and the not-too-good aerodynamics of the car make the front of the car lift and the steering becomes light indeed. Also, on fast bends the car was not too happy with the very rough surfacing of the track and was wandering enough to keep me fully alert.

"It is a very large car," summarized Frenchman Cahier, more accustomed to automobiles on the European scale, "but quite easy to drive, immensely powerful but very controllable, and having general performance and handling which put it well ahead of the Ferrari GTO and Ford Cobra. Granted, the Corvette Grand Sport is not homologated as a true GT car (and it is a pity), but it is a true GT machine in every sense of the word."

Happy enough with their GS coupés and the sweep of all three races at Nassau by Chevy power, the engineers brought the Grand Sports back to Warren for some further massaging with future races in mind. Similar entries were planned for the Daytona Continental in February and Sebring in March, in which the cars would run as prototypes, hopefully again causing consternation in the Ford camp. Carroll Shelby in particular was livid at these phantom appearances by obviously factory-prepared cars from devoutly non-racing General Motors. "I hope that Ed Cole will be the next president of General Motors," he said late in 1963, "because at least he is honest and when I am up against him, I won't have to be fighting a ghost."

The very real spirits at Chevrolet Engineering began changing the GS design based on the experience at Nassau. In the future a timed Rochester fuel injection system was to be used, with a new

Late-1963 changes to Grand Sports included new hoods, wide wheels, flared fenders, additional body venting, and aluminum-block 377 CID power units.

Grand Sports led away from the start of the Nassau Tourist Trophy, above. Below, Jim Hall's GS chases Pabst's Chevy-engined Lola GT, the race winner.

design of cross-ram intake manifold; this called for a change in the hood design. To accommodate this and also to relieve the pressure that had popped hoods at Nassau, a new panel was made with a set of lateral louvers in front solely for venting warm air from the radiator up and away to the rear. Two sets of longitudinal louvers along the sides were to admit fresh air to the injector ram tubes. The hood was also more positively retained.

To make servicing easier during the long-distance races, a pneumatic jacking system was installed that would lift the entire car when an outside compressed air source was plugged in. Fittings were also added to allow extra cooling water to be added against the pressure of the system.

While the three Nassau coupés were being updated along these lines to be used as Sebring entries, something quite special was being cooked up for the 2,000-kilometer Daytona Continental on February 16, 1964. Since this was to be run over the 3.81-mile Daytona combination of an infield road course with a long run on the high-banked tri-oval track, it was clear to Zora Arkus-Duntov that the highest possible speed would have to be reached and maintained on the banking. This would be frustrated, however, by the high drag of the GS coupé. Yet there would be no point in doing a new body design, for then it would no longer resemble the Sting Ray.

Analysis and testing showed that higher speed would be reached if the frontal area of the Grand Sport were reduced by making it into a roadster. Hence the two remaining GS chassis from the five that had been built were bodied as open roadsters, given low windscreens with a raised portion in front of the driver, who also had a faired headrest. A rollover bar remained in position, enclosed with some style by a fiberglass fairing. How specifically these cars were tailored to Daytona is revealed by the placement of the fuel filler and air-jack attachment on the left-hand side, where they'd be closest to the pit wall at that particular track. Right-hand access is required at most other road-racing tracks, including Sebring and Le Mans.

Once more, however, hopes had blossomed only to be left withering on the vine. Early in 1964 Bunkie Knudsen received a comprehensive dressing-down from his corporate superiors. They had seen the headlines, such as the New York *Herald Tribune*: "Don't Look Now but That's a Chevy Tooling Up in the Pits." They knew something was up and they stopped it summarily, probably rolling up their ultimate weapon: the threat of a sharp cut in the year-end bonus. Even for the wealthy Knudsen the GM bonus, which at his level of pay would have matched his yearly salary, was not something to be scorned.

The ax fell sharply on any further Chevrolet exploitation of the Grand Sport. Knudsen also withdrew the help he had been giving Mickey Thompson, who had entered Chevy-powered cars at Indianapolis in 1963 with some success. The only program to survive this cutback — and that because it was so clandestinely conducted — was the steadily growing cooperation between Frank Winchell and Jim Musser of the Chevrolet Research and Development Department and James Ellis Hall of Midland, Texas, whose rear-engined Chaparral 2 models were becoming more and more Chevrolet-colored beneath the skin. And in 1964 the indefatigable Duntov was creating another racer, the four-wheel-drive CERV II, about which more will be learned in Chapter 18.

What was to be the fate of the Grand Sports? The three coupés were sold for unspecified amounts, one to Jim Hall and two to John Mecom, Jr. They left Chevrolet with the equipment that had been contemplated for Sebring with the exception of the engines, which were identical to those used at Nassau apart from the substitution of iron cylinder blocks for the aluminum ones. Mecom in turn sold one of his cars, the much-raced machine that Grady Davis had fielded in 1963, to Delmo Johnson of Dallas.

Grand Sports understandably suffered various teething troubles, in their revised form, during the Nassau outing in 1963. At the wheel in the Tourist Trophy and in early practice sessions were Dick Thompson, No. 80, Jim Hall, No. 65, and Roger Penske, No. 50. The last two later became GS buyers.

This car played a role in a surrealistic drama acted out in Texas in February, 1964.

In conjunction with the SCCA Convention, which was held in Dallas February 6 through 8, a regional race was scheduled at Green Valley Raceway, a little 1.9-mile track about forty miles away. Texan Carroll Shelby caused a stir by entering two Ford-powered cars, a Cooper and an A Production Cobra, in this minor race. Then Johnson entered his Mecom GS Corvette, and asked that it be allowed to run against the Cobra in A Production. Shelby recoiled: "I had to go to the bank and borrow money to build 100 Cobras so I could race against the Sting Rays. John Mecom is one of the richest young men in Texas. Let him build 100 of those cars and I'll run my production car against them." The race was an anticlimax as Shelby pulled his Cobra out and Johnson's GS was hobbled by clutch and cooling problems, but the controversy and the promise of a Ford-versus-Chevy clash had drawn a record crowd of 12,000 souls to Green Valley that day.

Getting down to more serious racing, all three coupés did appear at Sebring on March 21. Delmo Johnson's car was in trouble on and off the course from the fall of the starter's flag. He and his co-driver Dave Morgan kept it in the race, with long spells at the pit for rebuilds, completing 144 laps and finishing thirty-second. Not quite up to his usual standards of preparation, Mecom's coupé was handled by John Cannon and A. J. Foyt, who was getting the hang of this new kind of racing, lying eighth early in the race. He and Cannon fluctuated between eighth and tenth place until a wheel came adrift after the ninth hour, dropping them to a twenty-third-place finish with 168 laps completed.

The star GS performer was Hall's white coupé. Co-driver Roger Penske took the first turn at the wheel and Le Mans-started with such vigor that he was the race leader after the first lap. Only the four factory Ferrari prototypes passed him during the initial hour. Penske and Hall changed places several times with the leading Cobra Daytona coupé, driven by Dan Gurney and Bob Johnson, but seemed to have the measure of it on speed. During the sixth hour, however, the GS had the bad manners to break a rear half-shaft. Another hour had passed by the time an axle had been taken from an unsuspecting Sting Ray parked along pit row and installed in their car. They placed eighteenth overall.

After Sebring there weren't many places where a car like the

John Cannon, No. 65, and Dick Thompson, No. 50, placed eighth and fourth respectively in the main event, the Nassau Trophy Race, on December 8, 1963. Oil coolers mounted on their rear decks helped cool their rear axles, but nagging troubles with hood fasteners dropped them from fourth and third places.

Chevy Engineering converted two Grand Sports to roadsters with the Daytona Continental in mind, deciding that the open body offered lower air drag.

GS could go. So fast had been the pace of racing development among the prototype and modified cars, now almost entirely rear-engined, that the "lightweight" coupés had no chance to shine in those categories as they had, so briefly, in 1963. Delmo Johnson continued to run his in the southwest, including a revival of the Mexican Road Race late in 1964, and entered it at Sebring in '65 with a Mark IV engine he had pulled from a new '65 Sting Ray and enlarged from 396 to 427 cubic inches only days before the race. Understandably it didn't do too well. At this writing, Johnson still has his Grand Sport.

Jim Hall was so busy during 1964 winning the SCCA's professional United States Road Racing Championship with his Chaparrals that he had little time for his GS, which carried chassis number 005. He entered it, however, in the Road America 500 on September 13 along with a single Chaparral 2, with himself, Hap Sharp, and Roger Penske as a team of three drivers for two cars. The Chaparral ran into trouble so they concentrated on the Grand Sport, which was holding down a solid second place behind a Mecom Ferrari 250LM. A late-race call at the pits to attend to a loose wheel let a Miles-driven Cobra sneak into second place, the GS placing third.

After that outing Roger Penske bought the Grand Sport from Hall and decided to enter it in the Nassau Tourist Trophy in December. "We tore the gearbox apart," he recalled, "completely disassembled the rear end and installed a new ring gear and pinion, rebuilt the brake calipers, and took the suspension off and Magnafluxed it to make sure there weren't any cracks. We Magnafluxed the wheels, put on new wheel bearings and new spinner knock-off nuts. We found the threads were worn on the old ones and that was why we were having a problem losing the wheel. To reduce weight, we took out the automatic jacking system and our pressure water system. The Grand Sport weighs in at about 2,100 pounds, but ours was a lot lighter."

The preparation was done by Bill Scott in his shop at Newtown Square, Pennsylvania — which later became the headquarters of Penske Racing. And the engine rebuild was done by Jim Travers and Frank Coon at Traco Engineering in Culver City, California, who continued as major engine suppliers to Penske Racing almost a decade later. So in a sense this Grand Sport venture set the style for Roger Penske's subsequent racing activities, and it did so in its performance too. Roger fought off challenges from Miles in an experimental 427-cubic-inch Cobra and Jack Saunders in John Mecom's Grand Sport Chevy to win the Tourist Trophy event. It was the first third of an unprecedented hat trick that saw Penske win all three major Nassau races, the last two with a Chaparral. It was another great week for Chevrolet and another poor one for Ford, which saw its Cobras and GT40's humbled by the Chevy-powered cars.

Penske's friend and fellow Philadelphian George Wintersteen became the next owner and driver of this highly successful GS,

Roadsters racing in 1966: Dick Guldstrand at Sebring in Penske entry, No. 10, and George Wintersteen at the Bridgehampton USRRC in his own No. 12.

and entered it at Sebring in 1965. For power he used a Traco Chevrolet V-8 of 365 CID, which had a stroke one-eighth-inch shorter than the 377 to ease some of the bottom-end building problems. In the rainy 1965 twelve-hour event the Wintersteen coupé, with co-driving help from Peter Goetz and Ed Diehl, covered two laps less than it had the year before but finished better, fourteenth overall and second in its prototype class. When Wintersteen later sold the car, less engine, it was bought by collector David Erwin of Painted Post, New York.

Penske, Wintersteen and the Grand Sports had not seen the last of each other. Early in 1966 the dust sheets came off the two Daytona roadsters. Penske took delivery of both of them and engaged Californian Dick Guldstrand, an expert in Corvette racing matters, to prepare one, chassis 002, for Sebring. It was fitted with a 427 Mark IV engine, its front springs shimmed to hold the extra weight, and during practice aluminum heads were tried for the first time on a Mark IV. The car raced with the proven iron heads, however, driven by Guldstrand and Dick Thompson (Penske had retired from driving after his Nassau triumph). Engine trouble retired it after five hours at Sebring.

George Wintersteen bought the other roadster, chassis 001, from Penske in the spring of 1966. Fitting it with bolt-on American Racing magnesium wheels instead of the troublesome and heavier knock-offs, he installed a 427 Mark IV engine and ran it in eastern events, including several USRRC's. It was a

finisher but not a high enough placer to gain any points for George. Early in 1967 he sold it to an enthusiast in the South, where it was still being raced at the end of the sixties. Like most who have parted with their Grand Sports, Wintersteen wishes he'd never sold it. The other roadster, 002, became the property of John Mecom.

Some gratifying successes are part of the Grand Sport saga, though not the overall wins in major European events for which the car had been conceived. Yet running under wraps the GS Corvette was a reminder to Ford, then on the way up in its historic assault on the racing world, that the way would not always be easy. It was also a marvelous morale-builder for the engineers of Chevrolet and the others in GM who felt that racing was not among the seven deadly sins. In this they differed from board chairman Frederic Donner, who expressed himself on the subject in May, 1964:

"Racing cars are built for sheer speed and for endurance extending over very limited periods. They are very different, however similar their names, from the cars built for sale to the general public. Their specifications must be determined by the demands of racing. Thus, they must possess qualities which aren't the same as those that the majority of the buying public seek in a car for personal and family use."

Someone must have been telling Mr. Donner about the Corvette Grand Sport. He couldn't have described it better.

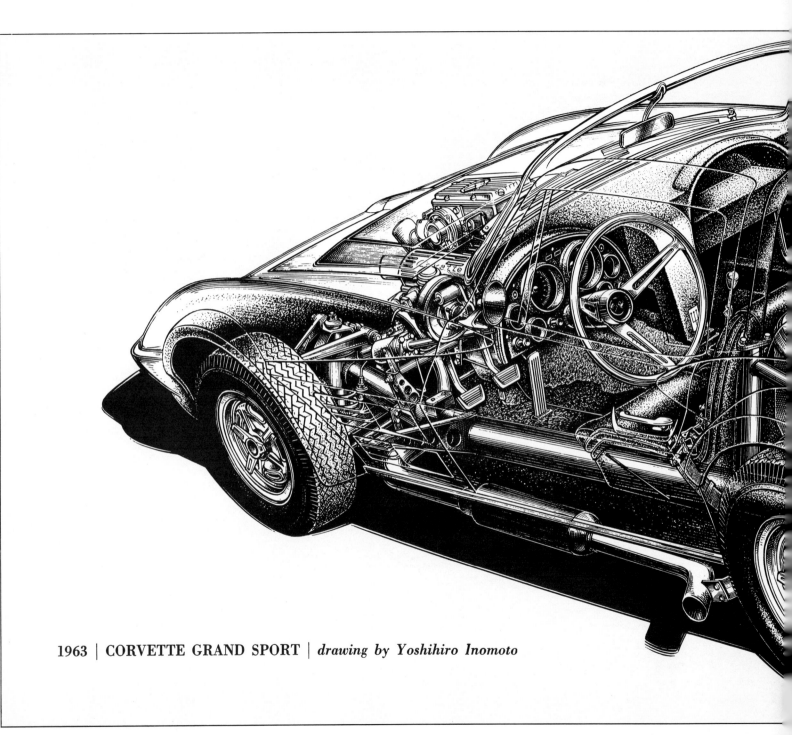

1963 | CORVETTE GRAND SPORT | *drawing by Yoshihiro Inomoto*

Chapter 14

POWER TO STOP AND GO:
1964-1967

It was an axiom of the soaring, sporty sixties in the American automobile business that no matter how good your car was one year, you had to change it for the next year, even if you made it worse. In 1964, '65 and subsequent seasons one might with reason have expected to find the Chevy engineers and stylists resting after their labors had brought forth the Sting Ray. But they did not lie idle; indeed each year brought changes of great significance, few of which could be counted as retrograde. Instead of adding gingerbread to its basic form, the stylists year by year removed it, much as they had with the 1958 model. One wonders whether they planned it that way in advance.

Nineteen sixty-four was, in a sense, phase two in the introduction of the production Sting Ray. It saw many refinements both above and beneath the skin that changed the car fundamentally not at all but made it that next shade better in every aspect of performance, handling, ride and appearance. *Car Life*, which had liked the '63 model, loved the '64: "There is no more go-able, roadable, steerable, adjustable, comfortable, respondable, or stoppable car mass-produced in this country today." It found no new 1964 car that came up to Sting Ray design standards, so the magazine made no Award for Engineering Excellence that year.

Many if not all the objections of both sports car purists and 1963 Corvette owners to the first Sting Ray's styling were eradicated in the new model. Gone were the fake grilles in the hood (though the indentations remained) and the divider down the rear window. The rear glass was newly glued in place with a Thiokol adhesive, a method GM had first used the year before on the Buick Riviera. It allowed a very slim, tailored-looking chrome window molding to be used.

The small louvers in the rear quarters of the coupé were restyled. Those on the right remained dummies, while those on the left were made functional, to serve as outlets for an elaborate interior ventilation system. A duct inside the body led to the louvers from an electric blower mounted just behind the left rear wheel well, where it could draw air from the interior. A pull knob on the dash operated a flap valve in the duct, opening it one-third and turning the blower on at low speed in its first position, and switching the fan on high with the valve wide open when pulled fully out. It was an intriguing idea but it wasn't possible to perceive much circulation when the blower was used, and in fact it was too small to pump enough air to do any good. It remained through the 1965 model year and was removed thereafter.

Bolder-looking rocker panel moldings were fitted to the '64, and new wheel discs with nine radial slots in a smooth surface. Changes inside included all-black faces for the instruments, to reduce reflections, and a simulated walnut steering wheel rim. A frontal attack on what Detroit calls NVH (noise, vibration, and harshness) was made in the body with stiffer rear panels less likely to resonate, better sound damping in the coupé with layers of cotton fiber and mastic between the carpets and the floor, and rubber body mounts for both the coupé and convertible.

The NVH patrols also scouted the chassis. An annoying "sizzling" of the gear-shift lever was stopped with rubber bushes in the linkage and a new flexible boot for the lever. The stiffness of the rear engine mount was reduced by half. The exhaust pipes were newly attached at the front to the transmission instead of the frame, and hung at the rear more flexibly. And exhaust noise was reduced with changes to the muffler design.

Other chassis changes excised much of the ride harshness that critics had discerned in the previous model. Duntov's experience with the SS and CERV I was drawn upon to give the 1964 Sting Ray variable-rate springing, more pliable when lightly impacted but firm when committed to a corner. At the front the coil springs were more tightly wound at the top than at the bottom, the upper coils bottoming in jounce and thereby stiffening the spring rate. The same effect at the rear was achieved by forming the shorter spring leaves with less pre-set curvature, so the shorter ones only came into play as the spring was flexed upward. Shock absorbers were recalibrated to suit the new rates,

Enthusiasts welcomed the less cluttered look of the 1964 Sting Ray, with new slotted wheel discs. Restyled coupé roof vents are missing on this prototype.

"If there were people who doubted whether or not the large American companies knew how to build a real sports car or whether or not they were interested in building one, they all know differently now."

—Paul Frere, Auto, Motor und Sport

Noted European automotive journalist Paul Frere recently put a Corvette Sting Ray through its paces in a road test for the German magazine, Auto, Motor und Sport. The above is a summary of his findings. Below are a few detailed comments.

Speaking of Corvette's handling, Mr. Frere said, "The driving characteristics of the Sting Ray are by all means comparable with the best European sports cars. The suspension is soft but well adjusted, which gives you a high degree of driving comfort and a feeling of safety at high speeds on streets which are not particularly smooth. . . . The steering has to be called exemplary."

Mr. Frere found the Corvette transmission to his liking: "The shifting itself is an actual pleasure with the short, precise and smooth lever. All gears are absolutely foolproof synchronized and the shifting process takes place as fast as you can move the lever from one position to the other."

Of the Corvette Sting Ray's overall sports car capabilities, Mr. Frere concluded, "The Sting Ray in this respect is not second to any one of the best European sports cars. . . . It can compete with them in price, even in Europe, and it tops them all in one area which is very important to those drivers who do not use their sports cars for fun only: There is a wide-spread, well organized customer service available."

America hears a lot about European sports cars. It's interesting to hear what Europe thinks about our sports car. . . . Chevrolet Division of General Motors, Detroit, Michigan.

CORVETTE STING RAY CHEVROLET

Comments by Paul Frère quoted in this ad resulted from his test of the 1963 coupé sent to Europe late in 1962.

and the rubber bump stops at all four wheels gave a less abrupt cushioning rate.

There were no changes in the brakes, but in testing a '64 model *Car Life* had a chance to get acquainted with the full competition system, a $629 option, and found it excellent: "The harder these brakes have to work, the better they are. Dispensing with our usual crash stops from 80 mph, we called on them to halt the Sting Ray from 100 and 110 mph in quick succession. Then, as a matter of curiosity, the 0-100-0 test was tried and returned a 20.6 sec., better by far than anything we have ever tested."

The 0-100 part was covered in 15.0 seconds, thanks to the fuel-injected engine in the test car. It was newly rated at 375 bhp at 6,200 rpm, with 350 pound-feet of torque at 4,600 rpm. This was no less than 1.15 horsepower per cubic inch, the highest output that Chevrolet would ever offer from the 327-cubic-inch V-8. Its sister mechanical-lifter engine was fed by a carburetor new to the Corvette, a Holley model 4150 with four 1 9/16-inch throttle bores atop an aluminum intake manifold. It mixed enough air and fuel for 365 bhp at 6,200, and 350 pound-feet at 4,000 rpm.

While the two hydraulic-lifter engines remained the same (250 and 300 bhp), these two fire-breathers had been given their added power with new ports, valves, and cam timing. Revised heads accommodated 2.02-inch inlet valves and 1.60-inch exhausts, with ports to match. A new mechanical-lifter camshaft replaced the veteran Mark I Duntov grind that had served so nobly since 1956.

One-piece rear window of the 1964 coupé removed the main objection to the

It offered much higher valve lift, 0.485 inch, and the following timing:

Inlet opens	BTDC	61°
Inlet closes	ABDC	105°
Exhaust opens	BBDC	109°
Exhaust closes	ATDC	57°

To suit the higher lift, larger valve clearance cutouts in the piston crowns were needed, which had the net effect of reducing the nominal compression ratio to 11.0 to one.

As the craze for high-performance cars took a sharp upswing during the sixties, with big engines in small packages like Pontiac's GTO, the first of the "musclecars," four-speed transmissions proved equally attractive to enthusiastic buyers. This decided Chevrolet to start making its own four-speed boxes at its plant in Muncie, Indiana, instead of buying them from Warner Gear. Its design had, of course, been originally conceived by Chevy, which now widened the gears and beefed up the synchronizers when preparing the drawings for the Muncie version.

The professional road testers gave their stamp of approval to the 1964 Corvette, criticizing chiefly a certain lack of arm and leg room, the difficult access to the trunk space, and a tendency of prices of options to creep upward. *Road & Track* tried a 300 bhp car with the Powerglide transmission and found it "remarkably lively even if some of the keen edge of the really hot version was lost. We were able to draw an interesting comparison with a stick shift Pontiac GTO which we sampled at the same time. The Sting Ray tended to squat down on its rear suspension when leaving the line, with never so much as a chirp from its tires, and then gobble up the strip in 15.2 seconds after shifting itself smoothly into high range at 56 mph. In complete contrast, the GTO didn't want to leave the line at all, preferring to sit there burning rubber due to poor weight distribution and lack of an up-to-date rear suspension." But the Corvette, its laurels as the highest-performance street machine threatened by cars like the GTO, would soon have to think harder about doing some rubber-burning of its own.

Were the Chevy stylists satisfied with gradual changes in the shape of the Sting Ray? Not necessarily. It was their job to keep proposing new designs to the division management, to have something new ready at all times in case Bunkie Knudsen — then at the helm — wanted it. No sooner had the original Sting Ray been launched, for example, than Bill Mitchell and his men were hard at work on ways to obsolete it. One was a complete facelift of the front end, not easy to do because the original concept was so successfully integrated. This was a good try, however, with air inlets split above and below a slim bumper in the manner of the GM-X show car being completed at about the same time for the GM Futurama at the New York World's Fair.

Late in 1963 a completely new coupé shape was being studied by a special studio under sports car enthusiast Henry Haga, for possible use on the Sting Ray chassis. It was a super-slick full-size creation in clay with the flowing clarity of line of an advanced aircraft, from its leading-edge air inlet to its inset rear bumper. Automotive muscle was added by tough-looking exposed exhaust pipes and polished inserts in the Halibrand-style wide-rim wheels. This "wedge" Corvette conception (for which the time was not yet right) revived the entry idea of the Q-Corvette of six years earlier, with doors that extended forward to a central split in the windshield, hinged to swing up and ahead to expose the whole side of the cockpit for easy entrance.

Not knowing about these behind-the-scenes suggestions, Corvette buyers were entirely satisfied with the aesthetic changes made to their favorite car for 1965. There were the usual trim alterations: simpler rocker panel moldings, a three-bar grille now painted black with a chrome surround, and new wheel discs that closely simulated the look of the increasingly popular aluminum wheels being used on the street. Plusher vinyl upholstery appeared inside, along with new molded door panels, seat-belt retractors, and restyled instrument faces that were flat, clean, and free of gimmicks.

Exterior styling was also made more functional. Now the hood panel was smooth except for its central bulge, free of the depressions for the original fake air outlets. And there were now three vertical slots in each fender side, fully operational air vents from the engine room. New options included a steering-wheel hub that the driver could easily adjust over a three-inch range for the right amount of arm reach, and also a wheel with a genuine wood rim. This did not survive long as an option, being judged to come in conflict with some of the new safety rules concerning injury to occupants in a crash. Ignition switch and locking provisions were altered in the 1965 Corvette, which was also given a new gear selector for the optional Powerglide with straight-line movement of the lever instead of the earlier maze-like quadrant that had served as an excellent test of manual dexterity.

Those who'd been looking for an engine for a street Corvette with the performance of the big-port versions allied with the refinement of hydraulic lifters (and Zora Duntov had been among them) found what they were seeking in a new 350 bhp engine offered in 1965. It was basically a hydraulic-camshaft version of the 365 bhp engine with the Holley four-barrel carburetor, plus a new cam grind that provided valve lift of 0.447 inch and offered an opening pattern remarkably similar to that of the high-performance mechanical-lifter cam. Redlined at 6,000 rpm, the new engine reached its power peak at 5,800 rpm and produced 360 pound-feet of torque at a moderate 3,600 rpm. Dressed up with finned rocker covers, it was offered solely with manual transmissions and cost $107.60 extra.

There was no extra charge for the change in the '65 Corvette that most enthusiasts found the most welcome and exciting: disc brakes of advanced design on all four wheels (though for the early part of the 1965 model run drum brakes were still offered as a "credit option"). "The announcement that the 1965 Corvette would have disc brakes," recalled Zora Arkus-Duntov, "was greeted by the motoring press in unison with 'Finally.' This implied that we did something we should have done a long time before and were blind to facts which were obvious even to a casual student of the subject.

"In actual fact we were not blind, backward or obstinate. We had a considerable background with disc brakes which indicated that just slapping units of existing accepted design on the Corvette would not produce the desired results. What sets the Corvette apart from other sports cars is its unparalleled combination of weight and performance in a comparatively low-drag body. The effect of this combination was apparently not fully clear to most experienced disc brake makers [including Girling], who embarked on the Corvette project without a shadow of doubt as to the successful outcome," Zora concluded, "only to have to admit complete defeat."

As quotes from earlier road tests have shown, there was really precious little wrong with the Corvette drum brakes in their various option gradations. The heavy-duty drum system was able to survive twelve hours at Sebring without appreciable loss of performance, which was no small accomplishment. "Although brutal," said Zora, "this drum brake had the highest energy-dissipating ability and durability of all brakes we could visualize on our Corvette.

"However," admitted Duntov, "the Corvette, being an instrument of driving pleasure, could stand improvement in brake modulation" — the smoothness and progressiveness of braking in proportion to the amount of pedal effort applied. "For a vehicle of this nature, it is not sufficient to be steered, accelerated and braked. It is important how well the car responds to the driver in the performance of these tasks." There was also the need to keep

up with the competition: "We were aware of the 'sex appeal' of the disc brake, and the opinion held in some sectors that unless you have disc brakes 'you don't have a brake.'" These were the inputs that led Chevrolet to start serious work on discs with the aim of releasing them in 1965.

The inside track in the race for the Corvette brake business was held by GM's Delco Moraine Division — but it had a lot of ground to gain on the pioneers of discs, British firms that were working, in part, under American (Goodyear) patents. Delco first tried a disc brake in September, 1937, and found it "a dismal failure," according to the Division's Arthur R. Shaw. It tried many other designs after the war before arriving at a configuration in 1954 that seemed promising: a floating ventilated disc gripped by metallic linings. It was tried on the Corvettes of that time, during the pre-Sebring preparations of 1956, and was used on the Firebird II gas turbine car.

A lighter, cleaner Delco Moraine brake of the same floating-disc principle was tried at Sebring on a Sting Ray during the

Dial centers shown as silver in 1964 p.r. photos were actually black.

tests at the end of 1962, where the new Girling brakes of the Grand Sport were also being given a workout. Experience up to that time seemed to indicate that a power booster would have to be part of any disc brake package, because the brakes had no self-servo action — the very reason why their modulation was so much better. A vacuum booster was part of the Grand Sport system, for example.

"We did not believe that we would be able to design this brake to operate without power assist," Duntov related. "However, our management felt that we could not accept the cost penalty of power assist on the base brake." The manual brakes had to have satisfactorily light pedal pressure requirements for good stops without the aid of a booster. "This decision contributed to an orientation of design which, in retrospect, has proven most beneficial." It forced the Chevy and Delco men to think hard about the brake system efficiency and led them to some unorthodox solutions.

For a start, the Delco engineers gave up their floating discs

and designed a new caliper (the part that grips the disc) that was frankly patterned after the Girling brake. It had two operating pistons on each side of the disc in a cast-iron caliper that was split down the middle and bolted together. The cross-over hydraulic line from one side to the other was made an internal drilling instead of the British caliper's external pipe. Like the Girling, the Delco caliper allowed the brake pads to be pulled out through a slot in the back for inspection or replacement without the need to dismantle the brake.

Its most important departure from accepted American caliper design practice was the brake's abandonment of positive withdrawal of the pads, away from the disc, after the brake was applied. Instead, the pads were allowed to rest gently against the rotating disc. This gave instant brake response to the pedal, kept the pads as close to the disc as possible under all conditions of hard cornering and bearing misalignment, and made the brakes relatively immune to the effects of ice and rain. And it failed to bring the high disc and pad wear and the high rolling resistance

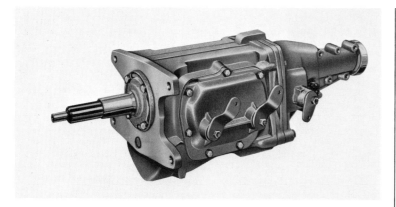

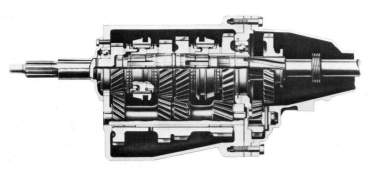

Four-speed Corvette gearbox, originally designed by Chevrolet, was also made by it in strengthened form at Muncie, Indiana factory starting in '64.

Among '64 Korvette Kreations by Barris, ex-Starbird Cosma Ray at bottom.

that most of the brake "experts" had forecast.

It was important, however, to pick the right lining to use with this type of brake. In looking for the proper compound, Delco Moraine ran 173 brake dynamometer evaluations of 127 different compositions from a dozen manufacturers. The material they chose lasted a minimum of 50,000 miles on the GM Proving Ground durability test. The pads were applied by caliper pistons which were one and seven-eighths-inch in diameter in front and one and three-eighths-inch in the rear. This gave a 65/35 distribution of braking effort in a front/rear ratio.

Radially ventilated discs were mandatory to meet the Corvette's need for high heat dissipation. This made them one and a quarter inches thick, and the final diameter was set at eleven and three-quarter inches; both dimensions were a quarter-inch larger than the discs used on the much lighter Grand Sport. The drum-type parking brake used for the GS was also carried over to the production Corvette, further simplified by combining its backing plate with the sheet-steel splash shield fitted to protect the brake from the effects of weather. Drum diameter and width for the parking brakes, hidden inside the rear discs, were six and a half and one and a quarter inches respectively. Slight changes in both the stock steel wheel and the optional aluminum wheels were needed to provide enough clearance for the outboard portion of the caliper.

"In view of established baselines," reported Chevrolet brake engineer Arnold Brown to the SAE, "the braking potential of the system appeared to be limitless." He found this out during the first road trip to evaluate prototype brakes: "The test course selected was mountainous roads in western West Virginia, specifically Peters and Potts Mountains. The schedule established through the years in this area has long been considered as severe a test of a brake system as is necessary for customer acceptance.

"With the Corvette's relatively light weight and good handling, however, the schedule quickly expanded itself into a sports car rally with speeds and decelerations well beyond the idiot limit for conventional cars. Other than a relatively obvious conclusion that splash shields would be necessary to control water sensitivity, no significant engineering data was obtained." A special brake abuse test had to be developed, just for the Corvette.

With the new four-wheel discs as standard, all 1965 and later Corvettes now were delivered with brakes which, except for the linings, were good enough to stand the toughest abuse test of all: twelve hours at Sebring. "You can put the proper lining in anytime," said Zora Duntov, "and go racing. We have insulators so the fluid is prevented from boiling, things normally not put in the run-of-the-mill street disc brakes. The benefit on the road is long life of the lining and no fade, in any condition." *Road & Track* testers did not disagree: "We grew bored, almost, with the ease and lack of fuss with which the car stopped straight and true. No lock-up, no fade, no muscle-straining increases in pedal pressure. Just good dependable stops. Wonderful."

R&T summed up its impressions of a 1965 fuel-injected coupé: "The entire car, and especially the interior, is keyed to the boulevardier sports/racey types who account for the great majority of its sales. It has enough pizzazz for a movie set, or crumpet collecting, or nymphet nabbing, or for the types who get their jollies from looking at all that glitter. It encourages the Walter Mittys to become Fangios or Foyts. Yet it also goes well enough to suit the driver who is sincere about going fast, and can handle that much performance with skill." Small wonder that sales of 1965 Corvettes rose to 23,562 units, up from the previous model year's record of 22,229. Coupés had by now settled down to a level of about thirty-six percent of production and sales.

Chevy had one more trick up its sleeve for the buyers of 1965 Corvettes, a surprise package it unwrapped early that spring, one offering no less than 425 horsepower over the counter for this two-seater sports car. It marked a watershed in the interpretation of the sports car idiom by Chevrolet. Since 1958, the Division had offered its "W" engine in its passenger cars, starting at 348 cubic inches and rising eventually to 409 and, in the Z-11 version, 427 cubic inches. But none of these relatively heavy and bulky engines had ever been offered in the Corvette. Instead, Duntov had successfully directed it toward higher and higher power per cubic inch from comparatively light engines, maintaining the advantages of handling and traction he had engineered into the Sting Ray.

"Earlier we had considered the big V-8 engine for the Corvette," Duntov reflected, "but in that I only saw more weight. Conditions were changing in the Sixties, however. The trend was toward more brute power, less 'sophistication,' in both sports cars and family cars. And as a two-seater, giving up the extra room and comfort of a larger car, the sports car must perform better in every respect — including acceleration. So we also needed more power for the Corvette, whose chassis was already designed with that possibility in mind. I was in favor of doing that." Work in this direction was pursued under the direction of Ellis J. "Jim" Premo, who had succeeded Harry Barr as chief engineer of Chevrolet. Premo was a lean, scholarly-looking engineer who had previously been overshadowed by the Cole/Barr team but who

GM Styling's own Korvette Kustom: a late 1962 suggestion for a facelift.

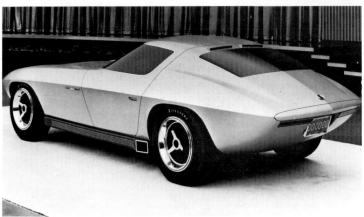

Possible all-new body was styled by GM group under Henry Haga late in '63.

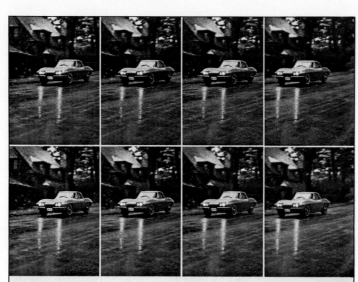

American sports cars all look alike.
'65 CORVETTE

Corvette is America's one true sports car—has been for years.

But Corvette is also two body styles. Five engines and three transmissions available. Plus enough other equipment you can order to make any kind of sports car you want.

For aficionados, there's the snarly Corvette. Ordered with a 375-hp Ramjet fuel-injected V8, 4-speed fully synchronized shift, Positraction, cast aluminum wheels, special goldwall tires, genuine wood-rimmed steering wheel, telescopic steering column,

special front and rear suspension and special exhaust system.

For boulevardiers, there's the plush Corvette. Ordered with a 300-hp V8, Powerglide, power brakes, steering and windows, tinted glass, genuine leather seat trim, AM/FM radio, and air conditioning.

And if you're a bit of both aficionado and boulevardier, you can get all kinds of in-between Corvettes, part snarly and part plush.

Every Corvette gives you 4-wheel disc brakes, fully independent suspen-

sion, retractable headlights, and a sumptuous bucket-seated interior as standard. At a very reasonable price compared to any car near its class.

Now you know why America has only one sports car; with all those different Corvette versions, who needs any more?

Corvette Sting Ray

CHEVROLET

Chevrolet Division of General Motors, Detroit, Michigan

Ad placed in Sports Illustrated, The New Yorker, *and* Sport *promoted the "plush" car for the "boulevardier" and the "snarly" Corvette for the "aficionado."*

Cleaner rocker panels and triple hood vents identified the 1965 Corvette.

now came into his own under Bunkie Knudsen. Premo and Zora Duntov enjoyed a particularly warm and constructive relationship that directly benefitted the Corvette.

The Corvette escaped an association with the "W" engine, however. Instead it was allowed to wait until there was a production version of the "mystery" V-8 with which Chevy had knocked the stock car racing world on its ear at Daytona early in 1963. Based on the bottom end and the bore/stroke proportions of the Z-11 engine, Don Keinath of Duntov's high-performance engine group had directed the creation of a new cylinder head concept that took advantage of Chevy's stud-mounted rocker arms to incline the valves so the shapes of the inlet and exhaust ports could be dramatically improved.

Known at Chevy as the Mark II, this 427-cubic-inch engine was nicknamed the "porcupine" for the seemingly random pattern of its valve stems protruding from the cylinder head. It had been built at the urging of Bunkie Knudsen strictly for stock car racing; there were no plans for any appreciable production of the engine when it made its record-smashing first appearance at Daytona. Any future it might have had in racing was radically diminished by the early-'63 clampdown on competition by GM's Donner and Gordon, the same suppression that had limited the Grand Sport production to five cars.

The first installation of record of the Mark II engine in a Sting

Corvette was credited with spurring mid-sixties rebirth of the fastback body.

Ray was made at the end of 1962 by Mickey Thompson, who was creating his own brand of "lightweight" car at his shop in Long Beach, California. He built several of these specials, one of which placed third in a 250-mile race at Daytona in 1963, driven by Bill Krause. But they remained rare birds, for not until a year or so later did serious work begin on the design of a production version of this exceptional engine, one which, like the small-block Chevy, seemed to have been touched by the magic wand of speed.

Production of the Mark IV, as it was designated, began in January of 1965 and by April it was being offered at three different horsepower levels for Chevrolets, Chevelles, and the Corvette. Because General Motors then limited its divisions to engines of less than 400 cubic inches in their intermediate models (such as the Chevelle), the Mark IV first emerged with dimensions of 4.09 x 3.76 inches for a displacement of 396 cubic inches. Down below were four-bolt caps for the 2.75-inch main bearings of this strong yet compact engine, which scaled 680 pounds with all accessories, some 150 more than the 327-cubic-inch engine.

In the Corvette the Mark IV replaced the 365 bhp small-block option as the car's most powerful carbureted engine. With an 11.0 to one compression ratio and a solid-lifter cam, it was rated at 425 bhp at no less than 6,400 rpm and 415 pound-feet of torque at 4,000. It breathed through a Holley four-barrel carburetor and

Chevy was allowed to mention the 1965 Corvette's four-wheel discs in ads but could make few claims for them because other Chevys were not so equipped.

2.19-inch inlet valves, with 1.72-inch exhaust valve heads. Nor did the 396 have power on paper only. "We can take one of those babies right out of the crate and we *know* it'll put out 400 horsepower," said California Chevy-tuner Bob Thomas. "However, we took one 396 that read 398 horsepower on the dyno and blueprinted it [trimming all parts and adjustments to exact factory specs], put it back on the dyno and got 442 horsepower! And that's an entirely stock mill!"

Due attention was given the Sting Ray chassis when this engine was specified. Front springs were made stiffer, and a nine-sixteenths-inch anti-roll bar was added at the rear end to supplement a seven-eighths-inch bar for the front suspension. A wider copper-core cooling radiator was paired with a larger fan. Clutch plate pressure was increased, and the rear axle shafts were made of stronger SAE 4240 steel and, with the universal joints, shot-peened to resist fatigue failure.

With the weight distribution now slightly to the fore at 51/49, there was some reason to expect that the Sting Ray handling might have deteriorated with the big engine, but *Car Life* vowed this was not so: "Response to small movements of the steering wheel feels slightly quicker, probably because of the lower slip angles of the new low-profile tires [7.75 x 15 U.S. Rubber Laredos] and new balance of front-rear roll resistance. Steering effort, surprisingly, does not seem to have been increased much by the added weight." The ride, the magazine's testers found, was slightly improved.

There was no mistaking a Sting Ray with the Mark IV engine. To make room for it a new hood panel was necessary, with a pregnant swelling expanding the outline of the tapered bulge down the center. Grilles along the sides of this air-cleaner container were functional. This gave the Corvette a more brutal look, entirely in keeping with the new engine, an impression of stark power that was further enhanced by another option for all the Corvette engines that was announced at the same time: side-mounted exhaust pipes.

The offering of this exhaust system was the realization of a long-cherished dream by Chevy's Corvette enthusiasts. "There was nobody in Styling or Engineering who did not want this exhaust system," remembers Duntov. Stylist Clare MacKichan traces serious consideration of it to the show 1963 convertible which was fitted with Shark-like outside exhausts. Then in 1964 another show car, a coupé, had outside exhausts with a finned pseudo-manifold emerging from each of the front fenders. This gave away the extent of the impact that had been made on GM stylists by Bertone's original 1963 body for the Chevy-powered Iso

Grifo, which also had a finned treatment of the exhaust headers.

"The amount of work that went into these pipes was staggering," says Zora of the final design, a fluted and slotted tubular housing around a chambered pipe that provided a modicum of muffling. "Jim Premo was challenged by the problem they presented. Their outside surface was to heat up no more than would the skin of the car in the sun of Arizona." This was achieved, at least to Chevrolet's own satisfaction, with a double-layer aluminum protective shroud which was ventilated for cooling on the outside and polished on the inside of the inner layer to reflect heat back to the pipe.

These pipes looked absolutely devastating and gave the Corvette a sound that was strictly business — even if it could be wearing on a long trip. Tests or no tests, there were also distinct hazards to the unprotected shins of those who showed insufficient respect for the pipes, which *did* get hot. The side-mounted exhausts were restyled to suit the 1968 Corvette, with which they looked even better. But local restrictions on noise, especially those of the state of California, finally made it impractical to continue offering what had become known as the "off-road" exhaust system. Order sheets for 1970 Corvettes no longer included it.

Disc brakes on all four wheels vastly improved the Corvette for 1965.

An almost predictable series of external changes allowed the discerning to recognize the 1966 Sting Ray. It had new rocker panel moldings resembling those used on the original '63 car, new wheel discs, an egg-crate grille pattern (like the show coupé of 1964), and a complete absence of vent slots in the coupé roof, with the removal of the air-exhausting blower. The coupé also had a sound-damping vinyl-covered foam headliner, and both 1966 models had new laterally pleated expanded vinyl seat panels. As in all Corvettes since 1963, leather upholstery was an optional extra.

The transition that began under the Sting Ray hood in 1965 was completed in 1966. Fuel injection was no longer available, and there were many, even within the Chevrolet and Rochester Divisions, who mourned its passing. Chevy men pointed to the fact that injection had cost $538 in its last year, while now the most powerful engine commanded a premium of only $313. The counter-protest came from Rochester that they'd gradually simplified the injection and reduced its price to Chevrolet, while Chevy had actually been raising the injected engine's cost to the car buyer, pocketing the difference. In any case the mid-sixties were the years of the big engines, and the Sting Ray was

Girling principles were followed by Delco in disc brake caliper design.

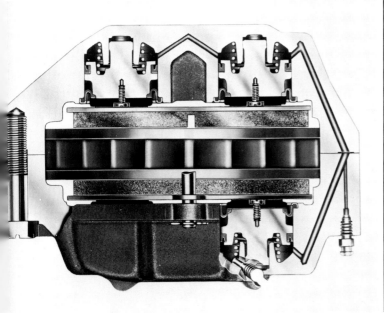

Corvette Sting Ray Convertible

New with 4-wheel disc brakes
'65 CORVETTE

Corvette for '65 offers 4-wheel disc brakes as standard equipment.

Disc brakes act smoothly, evenly. Resist fade even in the most brutal use. They're almost unaffected by water or heat.

They're self-adjusting. Need virtually no maintenance.

So what was always one of the world's greatest cars going is now one of the world's greatest cars stopping, too. But even that's not the whole story on Corvette for '65.

There's a new look—new grille styl-

ing, smooth new hood, sporty new wheel covers, and handsome front fender louvers for increased air flow through the engine compartment.

Speaking of engines, Corvette for '65 has a brand-new V8 to go with the standard 250-hp version and others, from 300- to 375-hp, that you can specify. This new V8 combines 350-hp sizzle with calm, cool behavior. Yours for the ordering in Sport Coupe or Convertible models.

Corvette's list of items you can specify to fit your taste is as long as ever:

4-Speed Synchro-Mesh or Powerglide transmission; power steering, brakes and windows; genuine leather seats—even AM/FM radio.

There's never been a sports car like Corvette. And there's never been a Corvette like this '65!

Chevrolet Division of General Motors, Detroit, Michigan

Drum brakes remained optional on the Corvette early in '65 model year until existing supplies were consumed.

197

powered by one of the best — even bigger for 1966.

Now the Mark IV was taken out to its full original size of 427 cubic inches by enlarging the bore to 4.25 inches. "This was done primarily to save weight," joked Zora Duntov. "You must remember that cast iron is very heavy, and by removing 30 cubic inches of it we have made a significant reduction in weight." Two versions of the 427 were offered. One was similar to the previous 396 apart from its added inches. It produced 460 pound-feet of torque at 4,000 rpm and, to avoid confrontations with critics of speed inside and outside GM, was rated for peak power at only 5,600 rpm: 425 bhp, as before. The power curve kept climbing beyond 6,000 to a 6,500 rpm redline, however, to an unofficial maximum of more than 450 horsepower.

Though the boost in performance with the 396 hadn't been too impressive, with the hot 427 it was that and more. "Compared to anything you might come up against," said *Car and Driver*, "unless you're unlucky enough to encounter a Cobra 427, it's the wildest, hottest setup going. With the normal 3.36 rear axle ratio it'll turn a quarter mile that'll give a GTO morning sickness, and *still* run a top speed of around 150 mph. The 327-engined version is still our favorite, but if you must go faster than anybody else, and you insist on being comfortable, this is a pretty wild way to go."

Most of the major car magazines put the 425 bhp 1966 Corvette through its paces, with the following results:

1966 Corvette Acceleration Tabulation				
Publication	Sports Car Graphic	Motor Trend	Car Life	Car and Driver
Body style	coupé	convertible	convertible	hardtop
Final drive ratio	4.11:1	4.11:1	3.36:1	3.36:1
0-60 mph	4.8 secs.	5.6 secs.	5.7 secs.	5.4 secs.
0-80 mph	7.3 secs.	—	8.7 secs.	7.8 secs.
0-100 mph	11.2 secs.	—	13.4 secs.	10.8 secs.
Standing ¼ mile	—	13.4 secs.	14.0 secs.	12.8 secs.
Terminal ¼ mile speed	—	105 mph	102 mph	112 mph
Maximum speed	140 mph	135 mph	130 mph	152 mph

No matter which magazine you favored, you found out that Premo, Duntov and Keinath had joined forces to build a veritable bomb for the benefit of the new general manager, Elliott M. "Pete" Estes, who arrived at Chevy in 1965 in time to help launch the new models. Estes, like Knudsen, had come up through the

Introduction of Mark IV engine option early in 1965 transformed both appearance (with a huge new hood bulge) and performance of the Corvette. Outside exhaust pipe was another new option, its multi-walled aluminum insulation the result of untold man-days of development work by Chevrolet Engineering

general managership of Pontiac, but he was an executive of quite different qualifications. He had solid engineering credentials after a duty tour with the GM Research Labs and a spell as Pontiac's chief engineer. More of a team player than Knudsen, the tall, mustachioed Estes soon involved himself in all aspects of the vast Chevrolet organization.

Sharing the Chevy stable with the 425-horse entry was a less potent version of the Mark IV engine. It had smaller inlet valves at 2.065 inches in diameter, a lower compression ratio at $10\frac{1}{4}$ to one, a hydraulic-lifter cam that raised the inlet valves 0.461 inch and exhausts 0.480 inch against 0.520-inch lift for both in the 425-horse version, an iron intake manifold, smaller carburetor venturis, cast instead of impact-extruded pistons and main bearing caps retained by two instead of four bolts. The output of this "mild" engine was still greater than the old fuel-injected 327: 390 bhp at 5,200 rpm, and 460 pound-feet of torque at 3,600 rpm.

There were other engine changes down the line in 1966. The 250-horsepower V-8 was dropped from the Corvette lineup, making the 300-bhp engine the base power unit with the 350-bhp version being the only other 327-cubic-inch unit offered. Also new was the base transmission, a fresh design produced at Chevrolet's Saginaw plant, providing synchromesh for all three forward speeds. It also offered fast engagement of a constant-mesh reverse gear. Like the Powerglide, this box was available only

For 1966 the optional Mark IV engine was enlarged from 396 to 427 CID, giving the Corvette the quite phenomenal performance cited above left.

with the base engine.

Had the Chevy men capitulated in the face of the racing challenge posed by the 289-cubic-inch Cobra and its successor, the 427 version? Not by any means. New "special-purpose off-road options" — the official euphemism for racing parts — were matched to the added power of the Mark IV engine. Checking RPO M22 brought a special four-speed gearbox with a magnetic drain plug, and reduced helix angles on the gear teeth that gave it more torque capacity but made it so noisy that the engineers named it the "rock crusher."

Option number F41 brought super-stiff front and rear springs and bigger one-and-three-eighths-inch-diameter shock absorbers. For comparison, front springs rated at 550 pounds/inch replaced the standard parts which offered a rate varying from 207 up to 380 pounds/inch at full jounce. At the rear the standard variation was from 140 to 168 pounds/inch; the F41 spring rate was 305 pounds/inch. With these springs came a heavier 15/16-inch front anti-roll bar, the rear bar remaining unchanged. The springs, dampers and anti-roll bar were essentially those of the Z06 option of 1963.

Under RPO J56 the would-be racer found a heavy-duty brake system that was just what he needed. Like all the Corvette disc brake sets, it had a dual-circuit master cylinder, now with the addition of a proportioning valve in the line to the rear brakes to reduce their tendency to lock up under severe braking. This was especially necessary in view of the greater forward weight bias of the Mark IV-engined car, whose increased speed and weight forced some of the other J56 alterations: stronger rayon-reinforced brake hoses, larger semi-metallic brake linings attached to wrought nickel alloy backing plates, flanged for strength and held by two retaining pins instead of one; a malleable iron brace for each of the front brake calipers.

The 1967 Corvette was a car that was not meant to be. That is, it wasn't supposed to appear in the guise in which it actually came to market. An entirely new body had been set for introduction that year but was delayed for a twelve-month period for reasons which will be outlined in a later chapter. So in styling and specifications the '67 was an interim model, as reflected also by the drop in production for the model year to 22,940 cars from the dizzying record output set with the 1966 model at 27,720 Corvettes.

Among the features which had been specially planned for use with a new body were the hand brake lever mounted on the center console, between the seats, and new ventilated steel wheels with a six-inch rim width as standard equipment. The now mainly decorative status of the optional cast aluminum wheels was acknowledged by making them bolt-on parts, eliminating the weight and cost of the knock-off hubs. The identity of the '67 Corvette was established by a central backup light in the rear and (again) new front fender louvers. The optional hardtop could also be ordered with a black vinyl covering, for the first time.

The role of the Mark IV engine grew even more in 1967, acknowledged by a new and aggressive-looking pseudo-scoop hood panel that covered all the 427-cubic-inch engines. The lower three engine choices remained unchanged, with the important addition of the Powerglide transmission as an option with the 390-bhp Mark IV V-8. At the top of the ladder were two more engines, both topped by a triangular air cleaner covering a new manifold fitted with three Holley two-barrel carburetors. These were interconnected by a system that sensed vacuum in the venturi of the center carburetor (not in the manifold, as with other multi-carb arrangements) to open the throttles of the two end carburetors gradually as the engine's need for additional air and fuel increased.

This new system, reported *Car and Driver*, "results in an astoundingly tractable engine and uncannily smooth engine response. As soon as it's rolling, say at 500 rpm, you can push the throttle to the floor and the car just picks up with a turbine-like swelling surge of power that never misses a beat all the way up to its top speed of over 140 mph. And you get the same response — instantly — in any gear any time you open the tap. On the whole,

the Corvette's three deuces are as smooth and responsive as fuel injection."

The lesser of the two 3 x 2-barrel engines carried a hydraulic-lifter cam and was rated at 400 bhp at 5,400; 460 pound-feet at 3,600 rpm. This too could be ordered with the Powerglide transmission. Only the close-ratio four-speed was fitted behind the mechanical-lifter version, which was again deliberately under-rated at 435 bhp at 5,800 rpm. This was a $437.10 option, to which another new $368.65 option could be added: aluminum cylinder heads. These chopped an important seventy-five pounds from the front end of the car and offered larger exhaust valves, measuring 1.84 inches across the heads.

This was the production debut of the aluminum heads for the "Mark" engine that had first been tried at Sebring during practice in 1966 on the Penske-owned Grand Sport roadster. They were one of the building blocks in the construction of a Corvette engine that became legendary, the L88 option announced in the spring of 1967. There was no hedging on the output of this engine; Chevy didn't say anything about it at all. But a reliably-reported power figure for the L88 was 560 bhp at 6,400 rpm on fuel of 103 research octane. It was as pure a racing engine as Chevrolet had ever supplied for the Corvette.

The L88 engine could only be ordered with all the other racing options, plus the K66 transistor ignition system, the G80 Positraction differential and option C48: deletion of the otherwise standard heater and defroster, "to cut down on weight and discourage the car's use on the street," said *Corvette News*. L88 design

Chevy in competition: Wintersteen in GT-Class-winning Penske Corvette at Daytona, 1966, and Duntov accepting 1967 SCCA Rally Championship trophy.

features included a 12½-to-one compression ratio, an aluminum intake manifold modified to form a plenum chamber under the single Holley 850 CFM carburetor, extra-heavy-duty bottom end and valve train to lift the valves as high as 0.559 inch with an overlap of 136 degrees, and a small-diameter flywheel fitted with a high-capacity clutch. Adjuncts to the L88 were an aluminum cross-flow radiator and an engine air intake from the grille at the base of the windshield, an area of high air pressure — the same inlet location used at Daytona for the spectacular debut of the Mark II engine in 1963.

Even with this new engine the heavy Corvette was still no match for the Cobras in the short sprint events on twisty tracks that typified most SCCA competition. But it helped. Corvettes had been shut out of the SCCA's Class A Production Divisional Championships in 1964, and had picked up only a single Divisional award in 1965. With the advent of the "Mark" engine, however, the outlook brightened. Two A Production Divisional cups were collected in 1966 and three in '67. Corvettes were still doing very well in B Production with a National Championship in 1964 (Frank Dominianni of Long Island, New York) and Divisional awards in duplicate in 1965, triplicate in '66 and quintuplicate in 1967.

The big-engined Corvettes really came into their own in the long-distance races. A comeback from the dark ages of 1964-65 was made in 1966 by a Sunoco-sponsored coupé entered by Roger Penske. Dick Guldstrand, George Wintersteen and Ben Moore drove it to twelfth overall and first in GT category at Daytona in

The car that was not meant to be: 1967 Corvette with subtle styling changes.

February, and in March Wintersteen and Moore placed ninth at Sebring, at long last equalling the finishing level (with the modified car) of the Corvette's first try in the twelve-hour ten years earlier. They won the GT class at Sebring too.

Four Sting Rays came to Sebring in 1967 and one of them, driven by Don Yenko and Dave Morgan, placed tenth overall and first among the GT's even though it spent the last forty minutes of the race wedged in a sand bank after a complete brake failure. That same year an L88 coupé was entered at Le Mans by a California dealer, Dana Chevrolet, with much behind-the-scenes Chevy help. In spite of being by 300 pounds the heaviest car in the race at 3,265 pounds wet, it easily led the GT category in the hands of Dick Guldstrand and Bob Bondurant. It was clocked at 171.5 mph on the Mulsanne Straight, twenty miles an hour faster than any Corvette had ever gone there before and twenty-two quicker than the Ferrari that finally won the GT class. The L88 engine came apart — as they have always had a tendency to at Le Mans — after eleven and a half hours of racing.

Record top speeds for Corvettes were set not at Le Mans but at Bonneville during these years. There the cars fell into a class known as A Grand Touring, which was assaulted every August during the week of speed on salt known as the Bonneville Nationals. The record was set at 155.132 mph in 1964 by Bob Hirsch driving a car belonging to Chicagoan Bill Scace. This was topped in 1965 by Michigander Barry Bock with his new 396 Sting Ray coupé. Bock averaged 169.654 mph across the salt lake in his first exposure to any kind of automotive competition.

Bock came back the next year with his engine enlarged to 427 cubic inches and fed fuel by Hilborn fuel injection. He overcame many tuning problems with the help of Bonneville veterans to set a fine new record of 180.138 mph. The Scace/Hirsch Corvette speedsters were not to be outdone, however, and regained a solid hold on the A Grand Touring record in 1967 with a two-way officially timed average of 192.879 mph. For a basically stock-bodied Sting Ray, that is really pushing the wind.

So great and so lasting was the impact of the original Sting Ray body style for the Corvette that it is surprising to reflect that it survived only five years. That makes it the shortest-lived basic body design in the car's history, if we accept the fact that its predecessors were all variations on the theme of 1953. They hardly qualify as rarities, with a total five-year production of 117,964, but those that have survived without abuse or modification will gain increasing recognition for what they are: genuine classic sports cars, the best America could build and, as such, commanding the admiration and respect of the world.

Chapter 15

MAKO SHARK II

"The car makes its impact through pure form, without applied decoration."
—*Motor (London)*

"Now there is a new show car which amply illustrates the 'surface entertainment' idiom. It consists of a particular talent to take something that is basically good and clean and pure, then embellish upon it with emblems or textures or patterns which have no relationship with function, but appear to."
—*Car Life*

"As an over-all design it kind of fills the mental outlines of the car Cato always had ready in that seemingly abandoned warehouse for the Green Hornet to rocket off into the night."
—*Hot Rod*

"It was an exceptionally beautiful car that had nothing to do with European nor, what is more, with American style, but just with simple, pure style, neat, aerodynamic and perfect. It was a demonstration of how, in a field dominated by chromed, oversprung dinosaurs, an absolutely new and functional car can be made with great ingenuity and simplicity." —*Style Auto*

"The overall shape and proportion is interesting and exciting — it's just that there are too many extraneous convolutions, such as the eight separate grilles spread forward of the windshield. Its coloration is attention-getting and the car no doubt will stir plenty of discussion, which is just what GM wants."
—*Car Life*

"It hasn't the functional beauty and purity of Pininfarina's Ferrari 275 Berlinetta, which anyone would be glad to be seen in, but let's give it full marks for showmanship and a taste of what's to come."
—*Autocar*

Functional? Beautiful? Embellished? Attention-getting? Aerodynamic? Extraneously convoluted? Perfect? Discussion-stirring? Exciting? It was all these things and more, which in itself was remarkable. When the Mako Shark II appeared, in the mid-sixties, it did so against background noise in the field of sports and high-performance cars that was at record decibel level. Ford was doing its best to monopolize the world of sports cars with its Cobras, Mustangs, and GT40's, while the "musclecar" era of Hemi-engined Plymouths, Olds 4-4-2's, and Pontiac GTO's was in full flower. It took something quite sensational to stand out in the midst of this corral of hyperthyroid horsepower. Only a car like Mako Shark II could have done it.

Among the Corvette-related dream cars and experimental cars the Mako Shark II was as significant in the history of the production model as the original racing Stingray. When it was designed and built it was no more than an idea, a concept, a product of the creative imagination embodied in plastic, plating and paint. It was one of a handful of different ideas for Corvettes of the future, ideas promoted by different and competitive factions within Chevrolet and Styling Staff. This one had a little something extra going for it: It was the personal project of William L. Mitchell.

Time does not stand still at the frontiers of automobile styling, especially where sports cars are concerned. In this respect the Corvette posed a paradoxical challenge to its creators. The world of two-seater cars was and is swept by sudden and impulsive fluctuations of taste and preference. Notes Italian coachbuilder Nuccio Bertone: "The so-called 'sports cars,' those automobiles which present more personalized features, are more subject to changes in fashion and have to be renewed more rapidly than production-model cars." Working with builders like Maserati and Lamborghini, Bertone could easily make those pace-setting changes. But the economics of the Corvette to Chevrolet were such that it could be profitable only if a given body style and chassis design were to remain in production a relatively long time, indeed even longer than a high-volume production car like the Impala.

Sensing the shifts in the shapes of sports cars, Bill Mitchell decided to extend exploratory probes in new directions. He did so literally the moment the 1963 Sting Ray was in production, for in

Mako Shark II was a controversial experimental car because some viewers saw only its lovely basic lines, while others saw only its busy embellishments.

that instant the earlier dreams, the Stingray racer and the varicolored Shark, became commonplace reality. It was time to forge a new dream of the Corvette of the future and, if possible, to create simultaneously a new and stimulating personal car for GM's top stylist.

One of the first steps in the evolution of this fresh vision of the future was a study in pure mechanistic form, a full-scale design of a single-seater, open-wheeled car code-named "X-15" after the famous experimental aircraft for its long nose, bulbous flanks, and at one stage, flat black paint. The X-15 was never publicly shown and it no longer exists, but it served its purpose as an extreme from which a retreat could be made toward practicality, a shatterer of preconceived notions about the limits of styling change. Its direct legacies to Mako Shark II included the square-section finned look of the cast exhaust headers (on the first version of the Mako) and the subtly elevated shape and finely finned grilles of the "power bulge" in the hood above the engine.

The X-15 was the stepping-off place for the brief given by Bill Mitchell in mid-1964 to a small styling group headed by Larry Shinoda. It had moved from the windowless room in the cellar of Styling Staff to another windowless cubicle in Styling's warehouse building, the repository of molds and models of the dreams of the past, across 12-Mile Road on the south side of the GM Technical Center. The studios there provided a refuge — like the partitioned-off corner of the Body Development Studio in which Harley Earl had created the first Corvette — where new ideas could be nurtured in an atmosphere of privacy that offered both honor for those judged fit to live and respect for those doomed to die.

Having begun with an open-wheeled single-seater, Mitchell now wanted to move one step closer to a usable road car. He sketched and described to Shinoda and his associates the characteristics he wanted: a narrow, slim, "selfish" center section and coupé body; a prominently tapered tail; an ·all-of-a-piece blending of the upper and lower portions of the body through the center, avoiding the look of a roof added to a body; and a sense of prominent wheels which, with their protective fenders, were distinctly separate from the main central body section, yet were grafted organically to it. This was the launching pad for the missile known as Mako Shark II.

Once a pathbreaking car is done it looks easy, logical, simple. Such was the Corvair of 1960, for example. It revealed none of the tortured dead ends that had trapped its designers before they found their felicitous way out of a maze of indecision. Nor did the Mako Shark II spring instantly, magically into being to suit Bill Mitchell's specifications. It had to be buildable on the existing Sting Ray chassis, which imposed certain constraints. There was also a plan to see it as a star attraction on the Chevy stand at New York's International Auto Show in April, 1965 — not too far in the future.

The last traces of a late snow were still on the ground in March when the Mako Shark II was rolled out to the Styling viewing yard to be photographed by Chevrolet's Myron Scott before its New York appearance. Though it was founded on an actual Corvette chassis, it was at this stage a full-size exterior/interior mockup rather than a running car. It had originally been simply dubbed the Mako Shark, but at the last minute the decision was made to rename the original Shark the

Shown in April, 1965, first Mako Shark II was a detailed non-running mockup with finned outside exhaust pipes and handsome new wide-rim knock-off ι

Mako Shark I and make the new design the second in the series. It was not the last time the new car's name would be changed.

Although some compromises had been necessary, Mitchell and Shinoda had come very close to achieving their aims in the Mako II. A greater seat inclination allowed the car to be three inches lower than the Sting Ray, with a steep tumble-home on the sides of the coupe's slender, enclosed canopy. An already narrow roof line tapered even more to a pointed tail atop the rear deck, its upper surface broken by a panel of six louvers, providing rear vision, that could be electrically closed or opened. The roof panel above the seats was hinged at the rear so it could swing upward when the door was opened to give more entry room, and was also planned to be completely removable for fair-weather motoring.

A look of severity and high surface tension was sought and found in the shape of the Mako Shark II, with sharp break lines atop the front and rear fenders, veed glass in the windshield, a tightly nipped-in waist, the subtlest of up-curving ducktails, and flared wheel houses that seemed just barely capable of reaching out to cover the outer edges of the tires. The wheels were similar to the optional aluminum ones for the Sting Ray but with rims much broader at a 7.5-inch width.

Twin air inlets were provided in a sharply pointed nose, and finely grilled outlets in the upper hood surface were proposed as outlets for warm air, with characteristic disregard of the possibility that this air might flow back into the engine again through the inlet grilles to the rear. The "power dome" was marked "MARK IV 396" in honor of the new optional engine that had just been introduced and which, in 427-cubic-inch form, would actually power the Mako II. Extra flash and flamboyance

were given this show car by the cast aluminum exhaust stacks protruding from the fender sides, painted crackle black except for the edges of the fins, which were buffed to a high gloss.

Around the faces of the existing Corvette instruments the warehouse-based stylists built a completely new instrument panel, recessing the gauges deeply into surfaces that sloped down and away from the occupants. A deep center console formed a "bundling board" between the seats and carried all the main switches and controls. The seats were fixed in position in the body, integrated with the interior design, and the headrests (hung from the roof) and the pedals (formed as part of the floor) were adjusted into the right position with electric motors.

As befitted a non-running display car the first Mako Shark II had a startling steering wheel. In outline and hand-grip position it was a modified version of the wheels used in light aircraft. Along its horizontal top bar were two controls to be thumb-rotated, that on the right for selecting the automatic transmission range and the one on the left for the turn signals. At the hub of the wheel was a knob marked "variable ratio steering," signifying that it had only to be turned to a different position to get faster or slower steering. A system like this had actually been used at that time on several variable-stability experimental Buicks built jointly by GM and the Cornell Aeronautical Laboratories.

Painted with the gradations from dark to light used on the first experimental Shark, and rolling on Firestones of 8.80 front section and 10.30 in the rear, the Mako II was indeed a powerful attraction on the Chevrolet stand in New York. When it returned to Michigan again it was changed in only one way: The paint was removed from the external "exhaust systems" and the aluminum surface was buffed all over. While this was being done, work was already well along on the completion of the running Mako Shark II — on which the external exhausts were not used.

Fully functional in every detail, the operational Mako Shark II was an utterly fantastic machine in the quality and extent of its advanced equipment. All this was explained to newsmen, when the car was previewed at the Technical Center, by Warren Olson, who had supervised its mechanical assembly with the expert crew that included Ken Eschebach and Art Carpenter. Olson had been general manager of Lance Reventlow's Scarab racing team and had also been with Shelby during the early Cobra days, before joining GM. Now he was helping launch the car in Michigan on October 5, 1965, before flying with it to Paris, where it would adorn the GM stand at the world-famous Automobile Salon, opening on October 7. Thereafter it became a temporary captive of GM's Overseas Operations Division, which displayed it in Lon-

Graduated light/dark paint scheme showed more vividly on fully operational Mako Shark II, which toured Europe's shows after its October, 1965 complet

don, Turin and, in the first months of 1966, Brussels and Geneva. It returned in time for the New York Show in April, 1966.

There was scarcely an enclosed cubic inch of the Mako Shark II that was not packed full of electronic or mechanical equipment. Its chassis was that of the Sting Ray with four-wheel disc brakes, powered by the 427-cubic-inch Mark IV V-8 that was just then becoming optional in 1966 Corvettes. A single four-barrel carburetor was fed by a special air cleaner whose inlet faced rearward beneath the fine-grilled hood bulge. Drive was through the three-speed Turbo Hydra-Matic transmission, which was then offered with the "Mark" engine in big Chevrolets but was not yet available in the Corvette.

The complete front end of the body tilted up and forward, in the manner of the XK-E Jaguar, to afford access to the crowded engine room. It was released by a handle at the lower left of the instrument panel, adjacent to the hand brake, the adjustment for the pedal position over a five-inch range and the trigger for opening the fuel filler cap, flush with the tail surface, by means of a remote-mounted vacuum servo. Two circular lids in the hood allowed fluid levels to be replenished without the need for lifting the entire panel; the left one was for coolant and the right-hand one was for engine oil. Both were held shut by magnetic catches. (Such external filling had been seen at least thirty years earlier, on the 1936 Cord.)

Chrome and black-crackle paint cosmeticized the engine compartment, from the cross-flow radiator to the air-conditioning compressor and the electronics boxes on the firewall. Mounted in the leading edge of the hood, behind "eyelids" that were electrically retracted, two headlight units each contained three

quartz-iodide beams. A foot control selected the beam combination that was right for the conditions. The lights were both too low and too bright to be fully road-legal but this was hardly an obstacle to their use in a one-off experimental car.

Operating the turn signal caused the relevant group of three round taillights to flick on in sequence, cycling from the inner light outward, and blinked a light in the corner of the grille at the front. At the same time a set of four "gills" ahead of the front wheel opened, if the headlights were on, to expose a cornering light. Fiber-optic strands led from each of the running lights to a tiny group of indicators on the center console that told the driver at a glance if any of his lights had burned out.

The turn signal control was a switch on a cylindrical extension to the left side of the steering column (another Cord-like feature). Next to it was another switch that extended or retracted two spoilers that curved up to a maximum height of about four inches out of slots in the upper edge of the tail. This feature was greeted with high good humor by some sectors of the motoring press, for the spoiler craze that swept the industry was still several years in the future, and only that fall had the Chevrolet-built Chaparral 2C introduced the concept of the variable-angle spoiler to the racing world.

Another cylindrical control on the right side of the column selected the Turbo Hydra-Matic operating range, using a vacuum-powered remote control developed by GM's Saginaw Division. Topped by a two-spoke wood-rimmed steering wheel of conventional round design, the column was adjustable for reach and angle in relation to the fixed and firmly-padded seats. Built into the seat supports were four-point safety harnesses of pure

Among Mako II features were retractable rear bumper and spoilers, digital clock, speedometer and fuel gauge, and tilt-forward hood/fender assembly.

racing-car pattern with a central rotating lock. A slide handle on the center console freed the harnesses for adjustment purposes; when it was released they were under the control of inertia-sensitive anchors.

Forward on the console were the digital clock and the trip and main odometers, and to the rear of these the four slide controls for the heater/air conditioner. Next was the radio panel with three prominent thumb-wheel controls. And to the rear were the ignition switch and a battery of nine rocker switches. The front row was for the road, instrument, and map lights. The second row controlled the rear-window louvers, the screen wipers, and the washers. These were hidden when not used under hinged lids in the cowl; the washer fluid was carried in a tube up each wiper arm to be deposited directly in the path of the blade.

The rear row of switches included one that was fairly ordinary: a lock for both doors. The others were unusual. One extended and retracted a rear bumper bar, which, when it was hidden, was completely flush with the body surface. The other could flip the rear license plate around and hide it from view, again behind a flush panel, at a touch of the switch. This was there for aesthetic and show purposes but Bill Mitchell preferred not to talk about it for fear that his motive for fitting it might be misunderstood. He was, after all, one of the more enthusiastic drag racers along Detroit's justly famous Woodward Avenue. The rear view of Mako Shark II was completed by rectangular exhaust outlets curving up from the underside of the chassis.

Instead of the ten round gauges of the Mako II mockup, the running car had a dash that was striking for its stark simplicity. The front of the cockpit was no more than a curved continuation

of the lines of the door panels, broken only by four outlets for ventilating and cooling air. Directly in front of the driver was a hooded binnacle, as close to eye level as possible. Within it were warning lights for oil pressure, coolant temperature, generator charging, turn indicators, high-beam indicator and seat belt.

The two main instruments in the binnacle were radically different and not easy to build. They were direct digital readouts for both the car speed and the fuel-tank level. In a special compartment behind the seats was a big box full of the tricks that GM's AC Electronics Division had to perform to convert velocities and levels into the readings given by instantly changing neon counter tubes, an achievement that was dramatic and practical at the same time.

Suspended from the roof, as in the mockup, the headrests now contained tiny speakers, two in each one, arranged to give stereophonic sound from the AM/FM multiplex radio. The roof also housed the machinery that swung the front panel up, at the press of a button in the door, to make it easier to get in and out. Pillars supported the windshield at the sides, but it was frameless across the top. Other rocker switches in the doors operated the side windows and also the door latches. All told, the Mako Shark II used seventeen small fractional-horsepower electric motors to run its power-operated goodies.

In its globe-girdling sorties the Mako Shark II was anything but an inanimate object being trucked from one show to another. In Italy, for example, special arrangements were made for Giovanni Agnelli of Fiat to try the firefrost-blue car at an airport near Turin. (It wasn't then registered for road use.) It took quite a while for Bill Mitchell to get it back, but when he finally did

By 1969 extensive customizing by GM Styling had transformed the Mako Shark II into the Manta Ray, with a longer tail, "sugar scoop" rear window, pop-up mirror lights in the rear fenders, and a low front spoiler. Built-in Endura front and rear bumper bars were body-colored.

he managed to put some miles on it as a personal machine and as a pace car for major racing events. But by the fall of 1967 the shape of the Mako Shark II began to be mirrored on the road by the new 1968 Corvette, and the Mako II no longer enjoyed its unique *avant garde* status. It was time, thought Mitchell, for some changes.

By 1969 this aquatic creature had switched its species, making a return to the undersea family that had been so successful a decade earlier. Now it became the Manta Ray, through a transformation made mainly from the cockpit to the rear of this elaborate car. Only the tapered "boat tail" motif remained with the addition of a new and considerably longer rear end in place of the abrupt duck tail. Now it tapered to a point in the side view, too, meeting at a high horizontal line protected by a self-colored Endura bumper pad built in.

Gone were the rear-window louvers, replaced by a very narrow rear glass in a scooped-out section of the tail. The fuel filler was moved to a central location, and the wide new fender surfaces were used for flip-up lights for signaling turns and panic braking in the manner of the Shark. The lights themselves were inset into the deck and reflected rearward by mirrors in the undersides of the pop-up lids. Nacelles below the rear bumper line carried the

Manta Ray made its 1970 appearance with faired-in outside exhaust pipes and tiny rear-view mirrors mounted high at the sides of the windscreen pillar

four main taillights flanking the license-plate holder, which was fixed in position.

The white-underbelly coloration was subdued along the sides of the Manta Ray but applied more heavily at the front. There the nose was given more protection with a bump-resistant guard ringing the narrow air-inlet grilles. The car's face took on a double-chinned look with an additional aerodynamic spoiler below the grille. Under the otherwise unchanged hood went a new engine, the ZL-1 all aluminum edition of the Mark IV V-8.

During the winter of 1969-70 the Manta Ray underwent subtle additional surgery. Its identification emblems were changed, and a crossed-flag medallion was added atop the fuel filler cap. Normal bullet-shaped rear-view mirrors were replaced by very small mirrors attached to the screen pillars high up at each side, almost at rooftop level. And a favorite Mitchell motif staged a comeback: The side exhaust system. It was artfully blended with the waist-nipping chrome inset below each door, a finned cylindrical bulge containing a muffling element that terminated at a down-turned outlet ahead of the rear wheel.

These were the last substantive changes to a dream car that had since become reality. Mako Shark II/Manta Ray was built at a time, not so many years ago, when an exercise in pure automotive form could be undertaken at its own pace, for its own sake. It had been built in the tradition of the great GM dream cars, the Le Sabre, the Firebirds, the first Corvette, as an automobile whose many advanced features were fully operational. It had not been cheap to do it this way. It had cost some two and a half million dollars to create the running Mako II, and probably close to three million as the car stands today.

How does a company like GM amortize an expenditure like that? At motor shows, races, plant openings, in editorial pages, the imagination invested in Mako II has repaid its creators, quite apart from its direct dividend in the form of the 1968 Corvette. But the price was high. That money in the early seventies has been flowing into experimental safety cars, show-car facelifts of existing vehicles, and advanced styling mockups whose value in terms of future production car design is often too great to allow them to be revealed to the world.

Does this mean that the Mako Shark II is the last of the big-time dream cars from General Motors? In a world as ephemeral as that of styling there are no absolutes; such a prediction would be rash indeed. But the controversial Mako II sets a standard that's hard to surpass. For the men who shape the Chevrolet sports cars that should be challenge enough.

Powered now by the aluminum-block ZL-1 engine developed by Chevrolet for Can-Am racing, Manta Ray is less a lithe beauty than a burly highway-hugger.

Chapter 16

TRANSFORMATION '68

The arrival of Estes as the new Chevrolet general manager wiped the slate clean again. As it had when Cole took over, and then Knudsen, the appearance of a new man at the helm was a green-light signal for the initiation of new projects and the revival of old ones that had met with rejection before. It was a honeymoon period, not only for the new man himself but also for those reporting to him. It saw another outburst of Corvette creativity that culminated in the introduction of the totally restyled 1968 model.

Pete Estes presided over a new era in which the Corvette encountered a sharp increase in competition from cars in its own division and corporation. The initial threat came from the Corvair, which recovered from its lukewarm debut as an economy car to score a marked success as the first of the small sporty cars. And the turbo-supercharged Monza Spyder version was a sharp-looking convertible that approached the performance of the original six-cylinder Corvettes, offering a cheaper alternative to Chevy's two-seater sports car. The much improved Corvair of 1965, with its Sting Ray-inspired rear suspension, possessed a potential for development to even higher levels of performance and handling, high enough to pose a strong challenge to the Corvette.

Before it had a chance to become dangerous, the Corvair menace was defused by Estes. All further development of the air-cooled flat-six was halted in the spring of 1965. The focus of design and sales effort in this size and price class was now to be the Camaro, Chevy's long-delayed answer to Ford's Mustang, a much cheaper car to build than the Corvair and therefore a better money-spinner for Chevrolet.

Powered by front-mounted V-8 engines, the Camaro was an even greater hazard to the Corvette's unique status among sports car enthusiasts. This was borne out in November of 1966 when Chevrolet announced the Z/28 option package for the Camaro to make it eligible for the SCCA's new Trans-American Championship and called the car, in its catalogue, the "closest thing to

a Vette, yet." In fact it was perilously close, for the Z/28 was and is an extremely competent and exciting road car. The reference to the Corvette was flattering, to be sure, but also threatening, for Estes and Chevrolet stood to lose much more if the high-volume Camaro were to be a flop than if the Camaro were to eat into Corvette sales. If a decision had to be made between the cars, there was little doubt which way it would go.

Against this ominous backdrop the drama of the next new Corvette was enacted. It included a subplot of intradepartmental conflict within the Chevrolet Engineering Center, for Frank Winchell's Research and Development group had ideas about originating the design of the next Corvette. Research work with both rear-engined and mid-engined Corvair-based sports car chassis had persuaded them that it might be possible to make an acceptable high-performance car with a water-cooled V-8 mounted back of the rear wheels, in the manner of the Corvair. Such a two-seater, with a coupé body styled much along basic Mako Shark II lines, was designed in 1965 and was test-running early in 1966.

This was a very compact car, with a short wheelbase made possible by the engine's rearward location, and a backbone-type frame down the center of the cockpit. Suspension was fully independent in the racing car manner, and the wheels were those used on the later models of the Chaparral 2. A 327-cubic-inch V-8 engine was placed in the duck-tailed "bustle" at the rear of the car and connected to a modified 1963 Pontiac Tempest transaxle unit. This arrangement put seventy percent of the car's less-than-2,700-pound weight on the rear wheels.

Winchell's aim with this car had been to get acceptable handling with the extreme rearward weight bias by using front and rear tires of the same diameter but markedly different widths, much wider at the back. "The car could be set up to handle properly on a skid pad in steady-state cornering," related former Chevy Research and Development engineer Paul Van Valkenburgh, "but the transient or dynamic response was nearly un-

Models show planned shape and proportions of mid-engined Corvette being considered by Zora Duntov's design group in 1965 for the 1968 model year.

Also thinking mid-engine, GM Styling created this radical shape concept early in 1966. It proposed replacement of the rear window by a periscope.

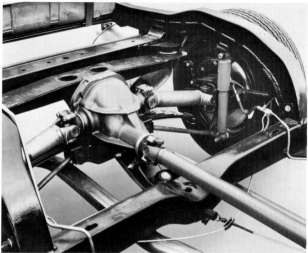

Sketch shows development of the actual 1968 Corvette form, intended at first for the '67 model. Suspension changes lowered the rear roll center.

controllable at the limit.

"At one stage," wrote Van Valkenburgh in *Sports Cars of the World*, "a test driver was trying high speed 'lane changes,' whipping back and forth across a two-lane test track, and the car got one step ahead of the driver's corrections. Although the guard rails were slightly more than a car length apart, the car was even more uncontrollable traveling sideways, and the beautiful color-matched urethane bumpers were put to a durability test." The stability problem was never satisfactorily solved, and with other difficulties, such as excessive cockpit heating from the upward-ducted front radiator, it ruled this concept out of consideration for production.

Meanwhile Duntov's Corvette engineering group had been working in parallel on alternate rear-engined designs. Their main proposal was founded on a ninety-nine-inch wheelbase with the engine placed ahead of the rear axle, there being room enough for the massive Mark IV V-8, if it were to be offered in this car. The rear suspension continued to use the axles as part of the mechanism guiding the wheels, but adopted twin parallel trailing arms instead of the single radius arm.

Taking shape in mockup form in 1965, this mid-engined Corvette was to be based on a steel platform-type frame, under a fiberglass body. Its radiator was to be mounted in the rear, behind the engine, with a forced draft at low speeds from two fans driven from the back of the transaxle. The latter was again a major obstacle to the adoption of a mid-engined design. Even if gear trains from existing Chevy transmissions were used, tooling expenditures in the millions of dollars would have to be made to supply special automatic and manual transaxles for a mid-engined Corvette.

Several body styles were suggested for this fairly conventional mid-engined car. One, proposed as the shape for the first engineering prototypes, showed again adaptations of the lines of the Mako Shark II to a car with the cockpit in the middle. It would have had a fixed "roll bar" at the rear of the cockpit and a removable roof panel over the passengers.

While Duntov's group was lining up its design arguments in favor of this car, Bill Mitchell's stylists were working on some possible aesthetic themes for it during the 1965-66 winter. One such was a very aircrafty study, shown as a painted and trimmed full-size clay model in March, which captured the feeling of separate nacelles fully enclosing each rear wheel. Large air scoops were set into the leading edges of these nacelles, which had wheel shrouds that would have hinged upward for tire changes. There was no rear window at all in the sharply tapering coupé roof, vision rearward being solely through a periscope.

The jauntily upswept nose and tail of this proposed Corvette were rimmed by Endura-coated steel members giving built-in bumper protection. Like earlier suggestions, this study showed a sweeping wrap-around canopy, which was split down the center

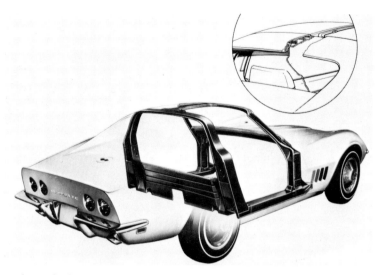

Steel "birdcage" concept for center body support was carried over to the 1968 structure. Hydraulic chassis shaker gave the new body a workout.

of the screen to permit each half to swing up with its associated door. The doors were exceptionally long, extending forward past the edge of the front-wheel cutouts. Room for luggage was found in the extreme rear of the tail.

The overwhelming cost burden of the required transaxle was the main obstacle that prevented this mid-engined car from getting any farther than the Q-Corvette had in the previous decade: to the advanced mockup and study stage, but no more. There was, as usual, an alternative on hand, a second "theme car" that had been styled in the warehouse studio slightly in advance of the model of the Mako Shark II. It met the same styling criteria as the Mako II but was more directly aimed at possible production on the existing front-engined chassis.

From Larry Shinoda's studio this theme model was taken to Styling Staff's main Chevrolet studio, which by now — with the rapid increase in the types of Chevy cars — had become a cluster of different groups reporting to chief Chevrolet stylist David Holls. Under Holls, Henry Haga's studio carried out final Corvette styling work for production. It did not dim the outlook for the new Corvette to know that both Holls and Haga were dyed-in-the-wool car enthusiasts and collectors of the first rank, men with "gasoline in their blood," in the phrase coined by Harley Earl. It was their responsibility to transform the Shinoda/Mitchell theme car into a final, practical new body design for the 1967 Corvette, an assignment welcomed by Holls: "This type of car is the real

frosting on the cake in our business."

The first '67 proposal retained the tapered, boat-tail roof line of the Mako Shark II. This was superseded for production by a "sugar scoop" treatment around a flat rear window glass, inspired in part by the roof design of the Porsche 904. "We just thought it was a newer configuration to be putting back there than that complete fastback type." Dave Holls told journalist Gene Booth; "we felt this was better. It was a natural, and it's a natural to do our three body styles — the roadster, the little hardtop that attaches on, and then this Aero-Coupé design where you can take off the roof panels, remove the back window and have a new-era convertible." In fact the removable roof combined with a fixed arch behind the cockpit was a realization, almost a decade later, of the idea first proposed for the Q-Corvette.

The initial styling model for the 1967 Corvette, the one used to mold a body for the first engineering test car, was much along Mako Shark II lines in its fender and side shaping, with a very low, spatulate nose and a substantial built-in spoiler at the rear. As early as the fall of 1965, in parallel with the several rear-engined studies, a car with this new shape was on test at the Milford proving ground. Since no major chassis changes were envisioned, the engineers were chiefly interested in finding out what effect the aerodynamics of the new body had on the performance of the car. Their initial findings were not favorable.

The existing 1965 Corvette was used as a baseline for the tests;

its body shape had a tendency to lift at both ends with increasing speed. At 120 mph, for example, the front end had lifted two and one-quarter inches above the static level and the rear had risen one-half inch. On the proposed new design the large rear spoiler held the back end down so firmly that at 120 mph the rear was *depressed* one-quarter inch, at the rear wheels. Pushing down the back tended to raise the front end up, which it didn't really need since the nose shape of the new car proved to be a very powerful lifter on its own. It rose two and three-quarter inches at the front-wheel centerline at 120 mph.

The increase in front-end lifting forces brought with it additional air drag. While a 1965 Corvette needed 155 horsepower at the wheels to move it at 120 mph, the new design demanded no less than 210 bhp at the same speed. The objective, of course, was not more drag, but less. To improve matters, the front fenders were first vented in a manner that had been helpful on the Chaparrals. This cut the front-end lift to about the same amount as the '65 model and reduced the power requirement at 120 mph to 175 bhp. Next, a spoiler under the nose was tried, another Chaparral-tested device that was to see use on the production Corvair. It slashed the power demand to only 105 bhp and reduced the nose lift to a mere five-eighths inch.

These fixes had been very effective but there were other problems with the new shape. The large rear spoiler and the roof design limited rear vision, and the view forward was partially blocked by the very high fenders. These and other considerations convinced Zora Arkus-Duntov that it would be premature to rush this body into production in 1967, and he carried this argument to Pete Estes, who bought it. The existing body was refurbished for '67 and 1968 became the year of destiny for the all-new body.

Back went the shape to Styling Staff, where both Shinoda and Haga were involved in its revision. They shaved down the front fenders, trimmed back the spoiler to a subtle lip, altered the contours of the rear fenders and the roofline to get better rear vision, raised the break line of the nose to bring the grille more prominently forward, and built a small aerodynamic dam into the underside, blending into the prominent lip around the front-wheel openings. For both cooling and drag reasons the vent louvers in the sides of the fenders were made larger too.

These changes were evaluated with detailed quarter-scale models in a wind tunnel and also with a first prototype of the actual car. This showed that there were still some structural challenges awaiting the Chevy light-car body engineers, who had responsibility for the Corvette body at that time. The lift-off roof panel was conceived as a single piece, clamped in at front and

back, but this wasn't working out well at all. Chassis and body flexing allowed too much relative movement between the top of the windshield and the rear "roll bar," making the assembly noisy and unreliable. This was solved with a last-minute change: the addition of a central strut joining the two together and the division of the roof panel into two pieces. So late was this modification made that it delayed the beginning of production of the 1968 Corvette coupé and forced Chevy's public-relations men to have most of the coupé press photos retouched.

New interior features required some special engineering and test work by the body men. One was the seat design, with the backs now inclined at thirty-three degrees instead of the previous twenty-five. Another was a direct carryover from Mako Shark II, the use of fiber optics to assure the driver that his running lights were working. These used fine strands of a DuPont plastic called Crofon, bundled together into shielded cables by GM's Packard Electric Division. A tiny lens at the console end of the cable magnified the light transmitted through the cable from the relevant bulb, showing that it was alive and well — if it was. Also new was the absence of quarter-windows and the addition of high-level fresh-air dash inlets and grilles in the rear deck to let stale air out.

Another Mako-bred feature was the concealment of the windshield wipers beneath a pop-up panel, lifted by a vacuum-powered actuator. This was mainly a styling feature — and an impressive one — that offered the added benefit of guarding the wiper blades from the hot summer sun. Vacuum power was also

Mister Muscle among 1968 engines was aluminum-head L88 Mark IV.

used for the new swing-up headlights, resembling the units used on the 1966 Olds Toronado. During tests both these devices had to prove that they had enough power to break a frozen-on sheet of ice three-eighths of an inch thick. If the ice were any heavier than that, reasoned the Chevy body men, the owner's main problem would be getting into the car!

With realignments of responsibility at Chevrolet Engineering, Zora Duntov was no longer in full charge of all aspects of Corvette design. During the 1966-67 winter, however, he'd begun testing and development work on the new model that had shown that special problems were posed by the engine-cooling provisions. This was especially true with the big engine, which had always been harder to cool than the small one. And now there were two added problems: The license plate blocked the center of the grille, and the retracted headlights hung down to impede the flow through the rest of the grille.

Zora's concern on this point was quickly followed, in the early spring of 1967, by a serious illness that resulted in his hospitalization in New York during most of May and June. When he was first stricken Zora called Jim Premo, told him of his concern about the cooling and asked Premo to take personal charge of that problem on the new Corvette. Premo assented, but before he could do anything about it he was transferred away from Chevrolet to another GM assignment and replaced by Alex Mair, who hadn't been briefed on what was, after all, a relatively minor problem in the total scope of Chevrolet car design.

When Duntov returned to action early in July he was assigned

With open exhausts the L88 easily delivered in excess of 500 bhp.

the job of preparing the prototype cars for the press preview of the '68 models for magazine writers, held in the middle of that month. The Corvette to be used was a metallic blue coupé powered by a Mark IV engine coupled to the Turbo Hydra-Matic transmission, which was optional in the Corvette for the first time in 1968. Zora tried it and realized his worst fears. The blue machine was more teakettle than car.

If the men of the fourth estate were to see and drive a new Corvette, some fast work was clearly required. Underneath the car's "chin," just ahead of the spoiler, Zora cut two oblong holes that admitted more air to the radiator. He also added a strip to the spoiler to make it twice as deep, increasing the local pressure in that area and encouraging the air to flow up through the holes. Then the spaces around the radiator were sealed off so the air had nowhere to go except through it.

Would these changes add enough cooling? Duntov frankly didn't know until the press day, when America's auto writers were unwittingly acting as test drivers for the world's largest auto company. The blue car was seldom at rest during a full day of driving in sunny 85-degree weather, and it worked fine. The temperature rose as high as 210 degrees but then stabilized there; this was considered the normal running temperature for the new car, whose cooling problems were exacerbated by the addition of forced-air manifold reaction for reducing exhaust emissions. The changes Zora made to the air inlet and spoiler were adopted at once for the production cars, but not until the introduction of the 1969 model was it possible to complete the job with the sealing of the gaps around the radiator. Nevertheless, Corvettes with this body style and the Mark IV engines have never had more than marginal cooling ability, and are not recommended for extensive use in traffic with the air conditioning switched on.

Except for the introduction of the Turbo Hydra-Matic, a much better automatic for the Corvette than the old Powerglide, the drive-train options for the new model were unchanged. In fact there were some changes to the intake manifolds of the Mark IV engines to squeeze the carburetors down lower to get them under the stylish hood of the new car. This threatened to reduce the power until some new induction tricks were tried and found successful in restoring the reluctant horses. A distinctive hood design was used for the Mark IV engines, and with the L88 option yet another hood was supplied that drew cool air from the high-pressure area at the base of the windshield. Duntov's tests showed that this hood alone reduced the L88's acceleration time from zero to 140 mph by seven seconds. L88 maximum speed was

185 mph with the new body, a slight improvement on the 183 mph maximum on the Milford banked track with the older shape.

To put this kind of power to work, Zora Duntov planned some subtle chassis changes for the new car. One fault with the existing model had been its tendency to lift its nose under hard acceleration, even at speeds as high as a hundred miles an hour. When the nose went up the resulting change in front-wheel alignment would allow the car to wander unpleasantly — the effect Bernard Cahier had noticed in the Grand Sport. Already close to their stress limits, the rear springs couldn't be made stiffer to counter this, nor would it have been desirable to do so. On some recent production Corvettes the rear springs had inadvertently been allowed to become too stiff, making the cars oversteer more than they should. This was to be avoided at all costs.

The chassis's resistance to pitching was increased by moving the rear springs to their highest allowable stiffness tolerance, a spring rate of 140 pounds/inch, and making the front coils of thicker wire on the Mark IV-engined cars for a spring rate of 284 pounds/inch, equivalent to ninety-two instead of eighty pounds/inch at the wheels. This increased understeer by shifting more of the roll couple to the front wheels, a change that was further promoted by lowering the rear roll center from 7.56 to 4.71 inches above the ground. This was accomplished by reducing the heights of the inner pivots of the two lateral suspension rods, those just below the half-shafts. The exhaust pipes passing under the rods had to be pinched to give enough clearance for the rods. "They're already squashed in three or four places along the line," said Zora, "so now there will be one more."

The lower rear roll center was more compatible with another change in the 1968 model: standard wheel rims seven inches wide, carrying low-profile F70 x 15 tires. The increased grip afforded by these wheels and tires helped counter any tendency toward excessive understeer the new spring rates might have caused. They stuck to the pavement so well that the new car could take corners with a lateral acceleration of 0.84 g. with normal tire pressures, a substantial improvement on the previous Corvette peak figure of 0.75 g. Wet-road performance was also markedly better. Tests had been run with radial-ply tires, even though they weren't then widely available in the United States, but they showed no increase in cornering power and were less predictable at the limit in a turn.

The wider rims and stiffer springs brought with them a ride quality that was perceptibly stiffer. "You pick up harshness with wide rims," confirmed Duntov; "there's no doubt about it. But stability is increased, so it's well worth it." These decisions ex-

Auto writers were unwitting testers of this blue '68 at the press preview.

emplified the uncompromising attitude that the Belgian-born engineer had been able to maintain toward this car. The suspension was tailored to cope with the Corvette's performance needs, and if the ride suffered, as it did in this instance, that was just the price that had to be paid. Since the Corvette was in other respects becoming "a luxury sports car," as one Chevy engineer called it, this firmer ride was a contradictory trend that marked an apparent schism in the car's personality: more like a racer in the chassis, and more like a Thunderbird, as *Road & Track's* Ron Wakefield remarked, in the elaborate body.

The new body increased the car's weight by some one hundred pounds, much of it distributed forward, where the front overhang accounted for the seven-inch increase in the overall length. With the new wheels the track was wider, now 58.7 inches in front and 59.4 inches in the rear. While the width was about the same as the previous model, the height was reduced by two inches. This reduction had the visual impact the stylists wanted. David Holls: "We knew how much higher the '63 was, but it was lines on paper, superimposed lines. When you actually see them out on the road, it's a lot more vivid. It's funny how, overnight, you can just blow 'em out of the tub."

On the road, said chief Chevy stylist Holls of the new Corvette, "they looked even better to us. Sometimes when you see them on the road, after announcement, it isn't just what you had wanted. But this one, to me, turned out even better. It's sneakier, lower — it's got sort of a hound dog look in the front, like it's sniffing for something. And the little tops on the convertibles are cuter than a bug's ear, in my opinion, really a small, selfish kind of upper."

The new car took on quite different personalities with the two

Zora Arkus-Duntov shows off the new-look interior of his 1968 Corvette.

wheel disc styles that were offered. One was a simple cap and trim ring for a bold, painted steel wheel, while the other was a very fine and elaborate radially ribbed wheel disc with the delicacy and interplay of the wire wheels of a Type 59 Bugatti. The choice of the two, said Holls, was deliberate: "My boss, Bill Mitchell, who is always very involved in Corvette programs, says you still have to design Corvettes so there is that black one that looks good when it pulls up in front of a night club. In other words, you can't design a car like a Chaparral, because too many people are buying them not for competition but just because they look so darn good."

This new one looked very good indeed. Those who tried them found out that the svelte and sporty appearance was bought at the cost of interior room, particularly shoulder room and trunk room. There was still no exterior access to the trunk, which was made much smaller on the new coupé and remained small on the convertible. Oddly enough there was no glove compartment in the dash. Instead there were three storage bins in a row behind the seats, the small central one being lockable. The left one contained the battery and the right one was for the jack and tools.

The spare tire remained slung underneath the rear of the chassis, where it had been moved during the 1963 redesign. Also the standard fuel tank remained in its location athwart the car at the extreme rear of the frame where its mass, when filled, was not too advantageous to the car's handling. As before, the optional larger fuel tank, intended for racing, was placed well forward in the chassis, where changes in its contents would have much less effect on the Corvette's handling characteristics.

The standard fuel tank location, chosen because it made the most of the trunk space that could be reached from the inside of the car, had also run through intense legal flak since the introduction of the Sting Ray. Suits had been filed against Chevrolet after accidents in which, reportedly, Corvettes had been struck from behind, starting fuel-tank fires which had then flashed all too easily and rapidly forward through the luggage compartment into the cockpit. The suits contended that Chevrolet had erred in designing the car in such a way that this could happen. Yet the 1968 redesign showed no changes that reflected an awareness of this problem on the part of Chevrolet.

As these new models (no longer carrying the Sting Ray name) started rolling off the line in St. Louis and into those Chevy dealerships lucky enough to get delivery of an early Corvette, Zora Arkus-Duntov was enjoying one of the less happy periods of his professional life. In the wake of his illness and the shifts in top management at Chevrolet, he found the development of the Corvette had been assigned to the same group that worked on the big Chevys at that time, while he had been made a special consultant to the chief engineer with little authority or responsibility. This was not to the liking of Zora, who in spite of various ups and downs had survived as something of a maverick in the politically highly-charged atmosphere of this very large engineering center.

In his "special consultant" role, Zora went to Europe to help introduce the Corvette to the press during the motor shows in the fall of 1967. He took along a manual-shift coupé with a Mark IV engine for demonstrations to leading writers in many countries. One of these writers was Belgian Paul Frère, a respected technician and former racing driver as well as an old friend of Zora's.

"One of the reasons why Zora was keen to have my opinion [about the Corvette]," wrote Frère, "was that on the occasion of the Frankfurt Show, the car had been tried on the Hockenheim track by the two testers of the German magazine [*auto motor und sport*] which had strongly criticized the 1967 version, and one of them had found the new model still a difficult car to drive. Well, to make it short, there is no doubt that it is easier to get the best out of an MGB than out of a 7-litre Corvette, but is this not just logical?"

Paul Frère found the body noisy and full of rattles, the brakes "extremely safe" and the gearbox "sheer delight to manipulate." With the tires pumped up to 29 p.s.i. at the front and 33 p.s.i. at the back, on the advice of Duntov, Frère put the Corvette through its paces over ten laps of the Zolder race circuit in Belgium. "Zora was very apprehensive of what I would think of the power steering at racing speeds but, frankly, I could find nothing wrong with it. Any action can be taken quickly and accurately, the return action is good and the power comes in very smoothly, so that it is in no way obtrusive. The Corvette goes round the bends very smoothly with little roll and excellent stability, on a line that is best controlled by playing the steering and the throttle against each other.

"After only a few laps" of Zolder, reported Frère in *Motor*, "I knew exactly what the car would do in most circumstances and I was lapping in the 1:57 bracket, much faster than I had ever lapped in a road car. As a basis for comparison, some other best times have been 2:07.5 with a Mercedes 250SL, 2:05.2 with a Porsche 911 (a 911S would probably take one second less) and 2:04.0 with a Mustang Hi-Performance, with handling kit. Even my best lap in 1:57.0 could probably have been improved by a second if the track had been completely dry."

This was a very good review for the restyled Corvette, gratifying to Duntov both as designer and "special consultant." When he opened his December, 1967 issue of *Car and Driver*, however, Zora read a quite different assessment of the new car from the pen of editor Steve Smith. "With less than 2,000 miles on it," wrote Smith in his editorial column, "the Corvette was falling apart." After a trip from New York to Watkins Glen and back, he decided it was "unfit for a road test."

"Few of the body panels butted against each other in the alignment that was intended," said Smith. "Sometimes the pieces chafed against each other, sometimes they left wide gaps, sometimes they were just plain crooked. In the rain, water leaked through a gap in the bolt-on hardtop and dripped on our left shoulder like the Chinese water torture. The surface of the fiberglass was as wavy as a home-built layup. The door locks were stiff enough to bend the key when we tried to lock the doors from the outside.

(The right-hand door refused to lock from the inside.)

"The windshield wiper arms were improperly installed," continued Smith's litany of disaster, "and collided against each other with a resounding crash that knocked them even further out of alignment, eventually causing the wiper blade on the driver's side to chatter uselessly across the glass. The car rattled and shook on mildly bumpy roads. There was a resonance at idle that made conversation sound like it was taking place underwater. Two knobs came off in our hands. The gas cap lid had to be pried open. Even the ash tray couldn't be emptied without jimmying it out of its receptacle with a screwdriver."

Smith also cited one of the car's "flaws in basic design," the placement of the latch that allowed the seat back to swing forward in a location where it couldn't be reached when the seat was fully rearward. "The engine was reluctant to start, it overheated in city traffic, the exhaust manifold leaked, and there was too much friction in the steering," *C/D*'s editor continued in his devastating recital of "the car's shocking lack of quality control." Nor was this an isolated example. The owner of a 1968 Corvette wrote, a year and a half later, that "it has been either inoperative or at a dealer's for repair over one-third of the time I have had it. Actually, there were 48 major items wrong with it the first week I owned it."

Any new car is entitled to its fair share of teething troubles but the 1968 Corvette had obviously collected far too many. Chevrolet had tried to integrate this sports machine into its normal engineering program and to treat it like "just another car." The unique Corvette, they found, didn't respond well to that approach. Nor, they discovered, were Corvette testers and buyers boundlessly tolerant of imperfections in what was, after all, Chevy's most expensive car by a wide margin. The 1968 base

Convertible '68 model shows standard wheel discs and coupé wears optional discs, shows roof panels removed. Both have special hood for Mark IV engine

prices were $4,320 for the roadster and $4,636 for the coupé; next down the division's price ladder was the Caprice three-seat station wagon at a base figure of $3,547.

The story in *Car and Driver* played a catalytic role in restoring the Corvette to its own separate and distinctive status in the engineering hierarchy of Chevrolet, with the head of that operation, in the post of chief engineer — Corvette, a certain Zora Arkus-Duntov. Various horizontal groups were still charged with work on portions of the car but in the vertical alignment Duntov had renewed authority over every aspect of the Corvette from advanced development to the quality of the finished product.

Later in 1968 *Car and Driver* was given the keys to a 400 bhp Corvette coupé, which it found good enough to test, and indeed, "a brilliant car with all of the virtues and all of the vices of American technology . . . an almost irresistible temptation to buy American." *Road & Track*, less convinced than *C/L* that the Corvette "stimulates all of the base emotion lurking deep in modern man," vowed that "for those who like their cars big, flashy and full of blinking lights and trap doors it's a winner. The connoisseur who values finesse, efficiency and the latest chassis design will have to look, unfortunately, to Europe." Such were the differences of opinion that the new Corvette inspired.

About the performance of the new car with the Mark IV engine there was general unanimity. "The '68 Corvette is a two-door rocket sled," said *C/D*. "LSD makes a great trip, but our choice is a few seconds of wide open throttle in a 427 Corvette." *Car Life* echoed the same sentiment: "Who needs LSD with something like this to get high on? Maybe it's noisy, rough and uncivilized; but you'd better believe that it takes a lot of car to catch this bear." *R&T* concluded that on the 435 bhp model "everything has been sacrificed to one cause — blinding acceleration. If that's all you need, buy one."

Some did buy the '68 model with exactly that requirement in mind, for the Corvette had not lost its appeal to racers. Chevy's paperwork experts had been busy early, gaining recognition of the new model with the L88 engine as a Group III touring car by the F.I.A., taking effect from January 1, 1968. In doing so Chevrolet certified that it had built 500 such hardtop roadsters, with a curb weight of 2,776 pounds, between August 1 and November 1, 1967. In fact no such car had yet been built, except for a mockup for photographs, and only three L88's were turned out by St. Louis in time to be shipped west to California for preparation for the Daytona twenty-four-hour race in February.

These were plenty potent machines. Duntov's development car for testing such L88 components as the new cowl-induction hood

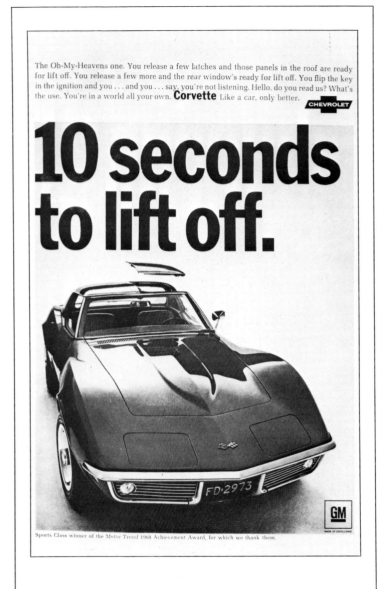

Campbell-Ewald enters the space age to dramatize the new coupé's removable rear window and separate roof panels.

was timed to accelerate from rest to 60 mph in 4.2 seconds, to 100 mph in 8.0 seconds and to 140 mph in 17.0 seconds. The three cars were the Daytona entries of the American International Racing Team, a new group backed by film star James Garner, who had taken more than a passing interest in real racing after his exposure to it while filming *Grand Prix* with John Frankenheimer in 1966. Two more new '68 cars were entered by a team sponsored by Sunray DX oil. But where had these other L88's come from? One was made from a new showroom-stock 1968 Corvette by Don Yenko, and the other was composed of new body parts on a 1967 race-prepared chassis, a Herculean task of poring through parts books and assembling a kit Corvette performed by Michiganders Jerry Thompson and Tony DeLorenzo.

This debut was not a successful one for the newly-shaped Corvettes, which were bested by a Sunray DX-entered 1967 model driven by Jerry Grant and Dave Morgan, placing tenth overall. At Sebring, however, it was another story. There Sunray DX fielded the only new Corvettes, a trio of them. One was driven by Dave Morgan and Hap Sharp, long-time friends who had taken their first plunge in racing together in 1958 with the joint purchase of a new Corvette. Their careful pacing through the twelve-hour race paid off with a record-shattering (for Corvettes) sixth place overall and first in GT category. Through the 1968 season in SCCA competition both Don Yenko and Tony DeLorenzo won divisional championships in Class A Production with the long-nosed new Corvettes.

Another car based on the new 1968 design emerged from Styling Staff in the spring of 1968 looking as though it was already halfway to Bonneville to break all speed records, but it was strictly a motor show special. Dubbed the Astro-Vette, it was a pearlescent white roadster that won the unofficial nickname "Moby Dick" from its creators. Its main styling features were all in the interest of reduced aerodynamic drag: fully enclosed rear wheels, a long, tapering tail, narrow wheels and tires, flush discs for the front wheels, and an extended nose with air inlets of minimum size.

Scribed in the sides of the Astro-Vette were locations for vent flaps that would open automatically when under-hood pressure rose to a predetermined level. Partial belly pans were fitted at the front and rear of the chassis to reduce underbody drag. A low plexiglass windscreen surrounded the cockpit, and a faired-in rollover bar was attached to the rear deck. The Chevy crossed-flag motif was painted on the hood of this car, which awakened distant memories of the Corvette's early speed triumphs at Daytona Beach and yet, because it never actually ran at high speed, mocked those accomplishments at the same time.

Was the new Corvette to be a useful competition car no longer? Not if enthusiasts like Don Yenko, Jerry Thompson, Henri Greder, John Greenwood and Zora Arkus-Duntov had anything to say about it. The once-menacing Cobras were now fading from the scene, and the future belonged again to the Corvette.

One of James Garner's A.I.R. entries rumbles by at Daytona, left, and Garner himself holds a trophy for Don Yenko at War Bonnet Raceways late in 1968

ts "Moby Dick" nickname unkindly but shrewdly suggesting a great white whale, the Astro-Vette was a pseudo-aerodynamic study built for show, not go.

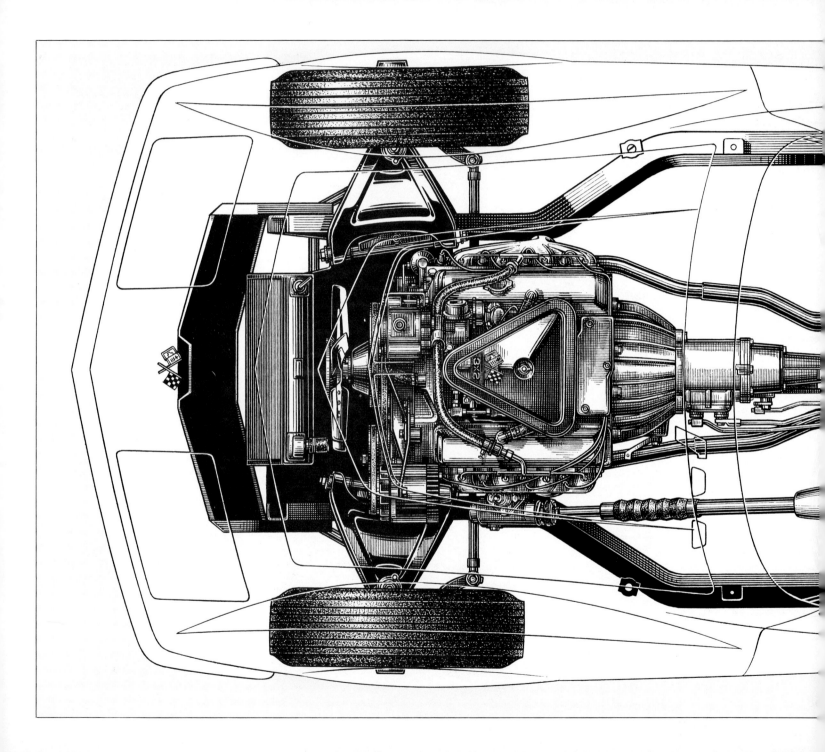

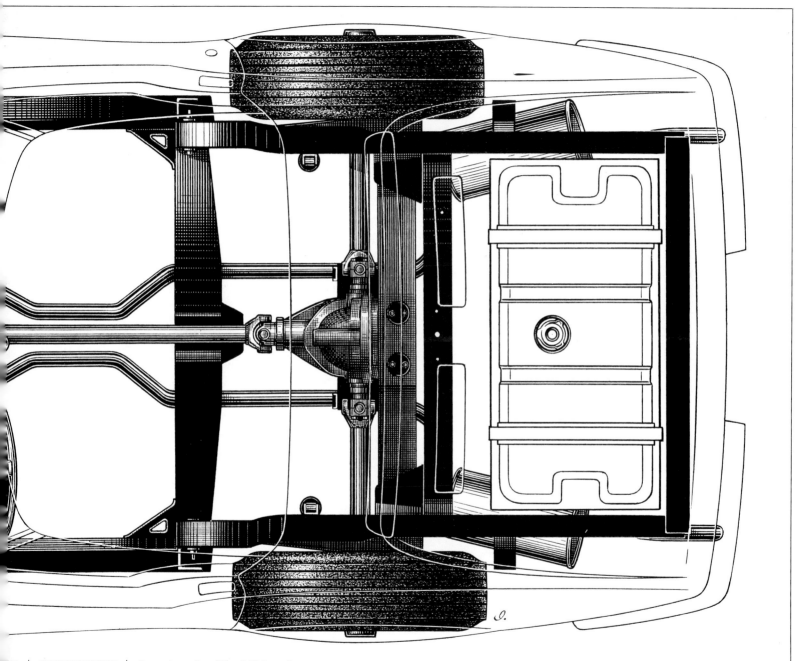

Chapter 17

'VETTE FOR THE SEVENTIES

It happened again in 1969. Just as the full transition to the production Sting Ray was a two-stage affair, spread over a period of two model years, so it was with the launching of the new body in 1968. Not until the announcement of the 1969 models was the changeover to a new kind of Corvette complete in every detail. Heralding it was the return of a famous designation to the front fenders, now in script and a single word: "Stingray."

Throughout the Corvette in the new model year there were many subtle touches that brought the promise of the new body style to fulfillment. The exterior door controls, for example, were as they were originally designed: flush panels that were squeezed down with the fingertips to release the door. These had only been simulated in 1968 by a combination of a pushbutton control with a recessed finger grip.

Black-painted grille bars replaced the chrome of the '68 front end, and at the back the reversing lights were integrated with the inboard taillight units. The road wheels didn't look much different but they were, significantly, going one more step toward race-car handling for the road with a rim width of eight inches. This was an unprecedented and uncompromising width of wheel for use on the highway, intended to extract as much adhesion as possible from the F70 x 15 nylon-cord tires. And if the ride was made harsher by the seven-inch rims in 1968, it became harsher still with the new rims. The suspension of this "luxury sports car" was tuned for the speed range between 80 and 120 mph, said Zora Duntov, adding that if it were changed in favor of a plusher ride "you'd penalize the man who's going to drive fast."

Shaking and shuddering of the 1968 models, especially the open ones, on bumpy roads was countered by additional stiffening for the rear of the frame. Specially helpful were diagonal braces from the crossmember behind the seats to the frame side members that arched up over the rear axles. The production balance was also shifted sharply in 1969 to favor the coupes, making them fifty-seven percent of the model-year production instead of thirty-five percent as they'd been the year before.

Extensive interior changes worked in favor of both safety and spaciousness. Door inner panels were reshaped, at no small expense, to build in desperately needed additional shoulder room. Steering wheel diameter was cut down by a single inch to fifteen inches, adding a little more room and underlining the fact that power steering was, for the first time, being installed on more than half the Corvettes produced. The optional adjustable steering column now tilted as well as telescoped.

To use the interior space better, the right side of the dash was equipped with pockets for maps and manuals. Seat back height was increased by legally mandated head restraints. Standard on the coupé and optional on the convertible was a new type of seat belt with an inertia-locking anchor, one that allows the wearer to move freely until it's "told" by sudden movement that a crash is in progress.

The Corvette's undisputed standing at the top of the Most Wanted list posted by the nation's car thieves was celebrated with another new option, a factory-installed horn-blowing alarm system that had become available during the '68 model year. Like other GM cars, the 1969 model had a new steering-column lock system that was a further deterrent to the light-fingered and heavy-footed.

The Corvette's console and panel, already rivalling that of a light plane in its intricacy and intrigue, became even more esoteric with the addition of a warning light to show that the headlight units were partially but not fully open. Under the steering column there was, as in '68, a separate control to lift the lights up without turning them on. Still wary of icing conditions, Chevy recommended to owners that they open the light units if the weather were snowy or icy. Among the other warning lights on the central panel was a signal that a door was ajar and a light, cancelled at will by a button beneath it, that reminded the passengers to buckle up their seat belts for safety.

Those who road-tested Corvettes were always impressed by the installation in each car of a tachometer with yellow and red dial

Press preview day for the 1969 models saw some special Corvettes in action: above an early LT-1, at right an L88 with off-road exhausts, and below a brutal ZL-1 set up by Zora Duntov. Not shown was Chevy Engineering's own development car for competition, at upper right.

Corvettes coming down the St. Louis line in 1969 had chrome-edged fender vents, stiffer frames, and wider-rimmed wheels for better cornering adhesion.

ranges that exactly matched the engine's peak recommended running speeds. Four different tachometers were needed to suit the six different engines that were offered at the opening of the 1969 model year. A new custom touch in this most personalized of all major American cars (the vast majority were built to suit a specific customer's requirements) was a plate at the base of the console that spelled out which engine displacement and power rating was in each car.

Corvettes continued to be offered with a mind-boggling choice of transmissions and axle ratios, the latter covering a range of almost two to one from 4.56 to 2.73 to one. Some of these were supplied on relatively few cars. In the 1969 model year, for example, only 230 cars in a record-shattering production run were built with the base three-speed transmission. Some dealers refused to order three-speed cars, even for buyers who said they wanted them: "If they backed out, we'd be stuck with the car! There's nothing wrong with it, you understand. It's just that it goes against the trend. Everybody wants the four-speed or the Turbo-Hydro." Also in the minority were buyers of the lowest axle ratio, the drag-racing-only 4.56 gear. Only twenty 1969 Corvettes had it.

The range of four different Mark IV engines, including the aluminum-head L88, was carried over intact from the late-'68 pro-

gram to 1969. The news this year was in the small-block category. The path pioneered five years before with the racing 377 CID engines was followed, part of the way, by keeping the bore at 4 inches and lengthening the stroke to 3 31/64 inches for a displacement of 350 CID in the base Corvette engines. The block used in the Corvettes was sturdier with heavier main-bearing bulkheads and four-bolt main caps, in addition to other detail improvements.

The power rating of the base engine remained the same with the added inches, 300 bhp, but it was reached at the lower peak speed of 4,800 rpm. Tachometer redline for this engine was at 5,300 rpm. With a 10¼ to one compression ratio, its peak torque of 380 pound-feet was reached at 3,400 rpm. Torque was also increased to the same level on the 11-to-one compression version of the new 350, at the higher speed of 3,600 rpm. Power remained at 350 bhp at 5,800 rpm, with a 6,000 rpm redline, from this hydraulic-lifter engine. Early indications were that there'd also be a new mechanical-lifter small-block engine in the line, the new LT-1 option, but this had to be postponed for one full model year.

Denied the LT-1 for twelve months or so, lovers of exotic Corvette engines still had something to look forward to. It was called the ZL-1. In the fall of 1968 the British-built McLaren sports cars stretched to two years the dominance in the SCCA's Canadian-

...num-block ZL-1 introduced in 1969 was perhaps the ultimate 'Vette V-8.

American Challenge Cup series that was to last for half a decade; they did it with a new Chevrolet engine that slid an aluminum cylinder block and a special dry-sump pan underneath and around the Mark IV L88 components. During 1969 this 520-pound engine was further improved and offered for sale by Chevrolet in the division's most exotic car: the Corvette. It was a mere $3,000 extra for one hundred less pounds above the front wheels.

In its final form the ZL-1 engine was improved in many details along with its iron-block sister, the L88. Connecting rods and bolts were beefier. Exhaust ports were enlarged to near-circular form and matched with valves increased in diameter to 1.88 inch. Inlet valve size was *status quo* at 2.19 inches but the port shape was improved, opening up a venturi just above the valve and filling in a pocket near the valve guide. The valve seat inserts were given a smoothed section that promoted air flow with the valves partially open. Only in the ZL-1 was a new camshaft supplied that increased the valve lift and shortened the open duration period, changes that the Chevy men found made the most of the head improvements. The new figures were 0.560 inch/347 degrees for the intake valves and 0.600 inch/359 degrees for the exhausts.

The famous and controversial "open chamber" cylinder heads for the L88 and ZL-1 also made their bow in 1969. With their

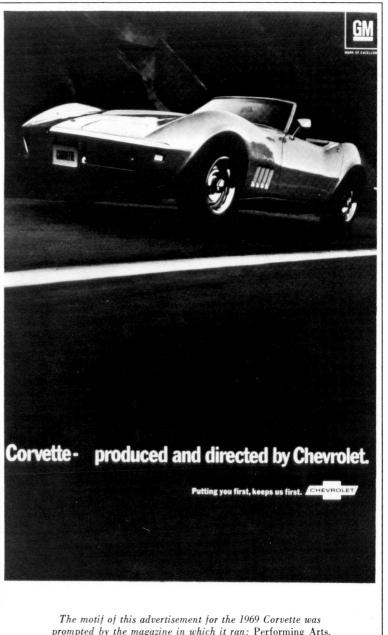

Corvette – produced and directed by Chevrolet.

Putting you first, keeps us first. CHEVROLET

The motif of this advertisement for the 1969 Corvette was prompted by the magazine in which it ran: Performing Arts.

combustion chambers opened up on the side toward the spark plugs and exhaust ports, they were believed by the racing crowd to be the last word in high-performance Mark IV heads. In reality, however, the chamber change was made to reduce exhaust emissions by cutting back, by about fifty percent, the "quench" area in the chamber where the piston and head approach each other very closely at top dead center.

The power output *was* better with the new chamber, not because it breathed better but because it had less surface area through which heat could escape to the coolant. But its reduced quench area made it more prone to the detonation that could destroy pistons, and demanded that the clearance between piston and head be set and maintained as close as possible. Ironically this was easier to do with the iron L88 block than with the ZL-1, whose aluminum block tended to expand more as it became hotter. For sheer power the L88 was the choice, while for power from a light engine and car the nod went to the ZL-1.

Tape-controlled machine tools at the Chevrolet engine plant in Tonawanda, New York, produced the ZL-1 blocks from castings of 356 T-6 heat-treated aluminum alloy. The block design was changed from the cast-iron original to pack in more metal, especially in the main bearing bulkheads, where required by the weaker aluminum. Provisions were made for two additional hold-down bolts along the inner edge of each cylinder head. For additional grip, bolts were made longer in the aluminum or provided with steel Heli-Coil inserts, where length couldn't be ad-

ded. The cylinder bore was protected by a dry cast-iron sleeve inserted from the top and held in place by a flange, clamped into a matching recess by the cylinder head.

These super-Chevy engines were selectively assembled and balanced in Tonawanda under conditions that Zora Arkus-Duntov described as "surgically clean." As delivered in a Corvette the ZL-1 was fitted with cast-iron exhaust manifolds, which the serious racer immediately replaced with lighter and smoother tubular headers that unlocked the engine's power. With a 12½ to one compression ratio, and tuned to the razor edge, the ZL-1 could inhale enough air and fuel through its single four-barrel Holley to deliver 585 bhp at 6,600 rpm. Mated with it in the racing Corvette was the ZL-2 hood, a special panel with a higher central bulge, drawing cool air at high pressure from the base of the windshield.

When asked what kind of man was likely to buy a ZL-1 Corvette, Duntov replied, "First, he will have a lot of money." It had to be a second or third car, because this was a Corvette that could scarcely be used on the street. Weighing only 2,908 pounds without fuel, and fitted with 3.70 gears, a ZL-1 set up for road racing covered the standing quarter-mile in an easy 12.1 seconds and reached 116 mph in the traps. A car prepared by Chevy engineers Gib Hufstader and Tom Langdon for drag racing, geared at 4.88 to one and driving through a special Turbo Hydra-Matic, reached 127 mph in the quarter after only 11.00 seconds from rest. Abusing the gearbox with a start from neutral into

Jerry Thompson, No. 6, won his class at Donnybrooke, left, and Michigan International, in 1969, ahead of Owens-Corning teammate DeLorenzo, No. 1.

drive yielded a time of 10.89 seconds and speed of 130 mph.

This was performance at a level almost unprecedented among quasi-production cars offered for sale to the public. "The ZL-1 doesn't just accelerate," reported Eric Dahlquist in *Motor Trend*, "because the word 'accelerate' is inadequate for this car. It tears its way through the air and across the black pavement like all the modern big-inch racing machines you have ever seen, the engine climbing the rev band in that leaping gait as the tires hunt for traction, find it, lose it again for a millisecond, then find it until they are locked in."

Road testers of the 1969 Corvettes found the Chevy sports machine to be very much a mixture as before. *Car and Driver* summed up its views succinctly:

"The small-engine Corvettes are marginally fast and extraordinarily civilized. The large-engine Corvettes are extraordinarily fast and marginally civilized." The latter judgement was perhaps unfair to the 390 and 400 bhp hydraulic-lifter Mark IV engine options, seldom tried by the magazines because they lacked the glamour of the triple-carb solid-lifter engines. But Corvette buyers preferred the less exotic Mark IV's, which *Car Life* called "very calm, very quiet."

The almost impossible task of testing a complete range of Corvette engines, transmissions, axles and accessories was achieved by *Car Life* in 1969. Allan Girdler summarized the magazine's impressions: "The Corvette isn't a perfect car. Nobody, especially Duntov, ever claimed it was. The Corvette is one heck of a big car for two people and almost no luggage. The styling is flamboyant, as if it were designed to be photographed rather than merely seen. The mechanical details are overdone in some places, underdeveloped in others. Things fall off, or don't work, or rattle.

"We don't care," continued Girdler. "The Corvettes we drove, and that's all the Corvettes the factory has plus one, varied so much in specification that it would be more accurate to draw conclusions on the basis of Corvettes, not Corvette. So we'll do it. Corvettes are for driving, by drivers. Winning races, going to the store or driving cross-country, the Corvette driver will be tired of smiling long before he's tired of the car."

But he did often smile through gritted teeth as he tried to keep all this car's complex systems operational. Pete Estes had added a third shift in St. Louis to produce an unprecedented 32,473 Corvettes in calendar 1968 — the last of the 1968 models and the first of the 1969's. The result was that quality control was barely able to hold its own, let alone improve. During these years it reached an all-time low.

In 1970 *Road & Track* surveyed 177 Corvette owners and found that "the worst thing about Corvettes, according to the owners, is the workmanship — or the lack of it. Whereas 18% of the owners of 1963-67 models considered workmanship the worst feature, an astounding 40% had that comment to make about the 1968-69 models! Seventeen percent of the owners of both series listed squeaks and rattles as the worst feature."

So rapidly did the Corvettes roll off the line that the car pro-

Immaculate and fast Owens-Corning Corvettes dominated their class in SCCA racing in 1969, and also placed No. 67 fourth in GT class at Daytona.

In the 1969 revival of the Tour de France, Henri Greder's No. 143 Corvette placed second overall. At the Nürburgring (center) his time was fastest.

duced at 10:32 a.m. on November 7, 1969, was the quarter-millionth made since it all began on June 30, 1953. It was still a 1969 model, though the normal time for changeover to the 1970 cars was long past. Taking over the helm of Chevrolet on February 1, 1969, John Z. DeLorean had decided to prolong the car's production, along with that of the Camaro and Firebird, into the 1969-70 winter to make up ground on an order backlog and a two-month strike at GM plants early in 1969. This extension accounts for the all-time record set by the 1969 model year production, 38,762 Corvettes.

George Dyer of Montebello, California, became the owner of that milestone 250,000th car. Others perhaps better known became owners of new Corvettes in 1969. The crew of Apollo 12, America's second mission to land successfully on the moon, took delivery of a trio of identical gold Mark IV-engined coupés. Pete Conrad, Dick Gordon, and Al Bean were all car enthusiasts — like many of the astronauts — with Conrad the most committed to his avocation as an SCCA road-racing competitor.

Others who bought 1969 Corvettes included Tony DeLorenzo, Don Yenko, Herb Caplan, H. C. Whims and Gerry Gregory — all winners of SCCA Divisional Championships in Class A Production. DeLorenzo, the son of GM's vice-president in charge of public relations, had earned his title after a season of exceptional success as a member of a two-car team sponsored by Owens-Corn-

ing Fiberglas Corporation. Tony won six of eleven races entered in his Central Division in 1969, leaving the other five victories to his teammate, Jerry Thompson, a Chevrolet engine development engineer. It was Jerry who went by them all at Daytona at the American Road Race of Champions on November 30 to be crowned the 1969 Class A Production National Champion — the first Corvette driver to win that honor since 1962. The long, dark years of the Cobras were over at last.

At its late February debut, the 1970 Corvette introduced new styling touches that prevailed through 1972 and a new pricing philosophy that marked a sharp break from the past. Both indicated a further shift of the Corvette away from the role of the pure sporting car (the ZL-1 notwithstanding) and toward its new orientation as a "luxury sports car."

The public had been given a sneak preview of the '70 styling changes a year in advance by a show car built by Styling Staff and dubbed the Aero Coupe. It had the egg-crate-pattern grille, matching louvers along the fenders, and more deeply flared wheel house openings that were part of the new 1970 body design. Some of the Aero Coupe's other features, such as its high, curved windshield, its Chaparral-type wheels and its remote control for the automatic transmission, weren't yet ready for production.

Parking lights were now squarish in shape and set into the cor-

...der also set the fastest lap time at Le Mans (night scenes) in the 1969 French Tour. Faulty ignition hampered him elsewhere, as at the Nogaro track.

ners of the grille. Mandatory side marker lights at the front and rear were larger and better integrated into the design. At the back, new rectangular exhaust pipe tips were recessed into the underside of the tail in a manner inspired by the running Mako Shark II. Detail refinements were made to the taillights and the stainless steel rocker moldings. Carried over from 1969 was the new washer system: spraying fluid on the windshield from the arm of the wiper, again like the Mako II, and jetting it on the outboard headlight lenses, when desired, to clean them.

Inside the '70 Corvette the seats were changed again to add an inch of headroom — urgently needed — and to integrate the headrests and build in a more accessible release button for the seat back hinge. The inertia reels for the shoulder harnesses were tucked away more neatly in the rear quarters, opening up more trunk room, and the belts were fed through slots in the seat backs that made them seem built-in.

A new option in the first year of the seventies was a "custom interior" that gave the Corvette a dressed-up look, a subtle touch of plushness that moderated the machinelike character of the interior. It was like having the cockpit of a Gemini spacecraft redone by an interior decorator. Leather-trimmed seats, cut-pile carpeting door to door and wood-grain trim on the console and doors added welcome warmth. The option even included a leather boot for the manual shift lever.

An earlier sixteen-dollar option, evenly tinted glass for all windows, was made standard equipment in 1970. This reflected the increase in the number of cars fitted with air conditioning, which rose from 30.6 percent of 1969 model-year production to 38.5 percent in 1970 and would continue to climb to 52.7 percent in 1971. Also made standard on the new car were the Positraction differential and the four-speed manual box, which could be wide-ratio or close-ratio or swapped for the Turbo Hydra-Matic on the base engine at no extra cost.

The general dressing-up of the Corvette and the making of these former options standard were part of a new pricing plan under John DeLorean that frankly took advantage of the car's unprecedented popularity. This was reflected by the annual poll of its readers conducted by *Car and Driver*, in which the Corvette had been chosen the Best Value for Money in 1965 and 1966 and then Best All-Around Car from 1967 through 1971 (it was just squeezed out of the latter category by the Datsun 240Z in 1972). Each year's production quota was usually spoken for, covered by concrete dealer and buyer orders, as early as March or April. Under these conditions, couldn't the price be a little higher? That was the reasoning, and that's what happened.

Corvette prices jumped sharply from the mid-$4,000 level in 1969 to more than $5,000 in 1970. Suggested retail prices for the 1971 model, with the addition of an evaporative emission control

GM Styling's one-off Aero Coupe (two views at top left) set the grille and interior styles for the 1970 model. Mechanical-lifter LT-1 V-8 finally made an official and firm appearance among the engine options.

system, were $5,299 for the convertible and $5,536 for the coupé. These base figures stayed at about the same level in 1972. Option prices were $115.90 for power steering, $47.40 for power brakes, $85.35 for power-operated windows, $464.50 for air conditioning and $283.35 for an AM-FM stereo radio. Small wonder that the delivered price of the Mark IV-engined coupé that *Road & Track* tested in 1970 added up to $6,773. The money was evident in the car, too: It scaled 3,740 pounds at the curb, only forty-seven percent of it on the rear wheels with the driver seated.

In 1970 the small-block engine lineup remained the same at the two lower power ratings, and the small solid-lifter engine, the LT-1, finally made its appearance. This resulted in a lighter Corvette, typically 3,335 pounds at the curb, distributed equally between the front and rear pairs of wheels. The new engine was identified by a special hood dome surrounded by striping and "LT-1" lettering, and also by the raffish ripsaw roar of its exhaust pipes and the tapping of its mechanical lifters.

The rumpety-rump of the LT-1's idle betrayed its generous cam timing. This checked out at 317 degrees of intake duration, 346 degrees on the exhaust side and 96 degrees of overlap. Valve lift was 0.459 inch intake, 0.485 inch exhaust. Unlike the other 350-cubic-inch units it used the same big two-and-a-half-inch exhaust pipe system as the Mark IV engines, and it also breathed through

a carburetor usually found on larger V-8's, the 850 CFM Holley four-barrel with vacuum-controlled secondary throttles. For reliable high-speed operation (redline: 6,500 rpm) it had transistorized Delco ignition and two-thousandths of an inch of extra skirt clearance for its impact-extruded pistons.

This was a lively engine in the tradition of Duntov cams and fuel injection that could push the LT-1 through the quarter-mile in 14.2 seconds with a trap speed of 102 mph. That kind of acceleration proved that the rating of 370 bhp at 6,000 rpm and 380 pound-feet at 4,000 rpm was on the conservative side by normal Detroit standards. For competition in the SCCA's Class B Production this engine was part and parcel of a special ZR-1 option package that included the cold-air hood and all relevant brake and chassis racing equipment.

A Production racers scanning the option lists of the 1970 Corvettes saw new magic numbers replacing the fabled L88 and ZL-1 (though the all-aluminum engines were still sold directly by Chevrolet Engineering to Can-Am competitors). Now the codes to conjure with were ZR-2, for the complete Mark IV racing kit, and LS-7, for the hottest version of the big V-8 engine, which was even bigger in 1970. For the first time since its introduction as a 396-cubic-inch engine in 1965 its stroke was increased, now to an even four inches to bring its capacity to 454 cubic inches. The

Handle with driving gloves.

Some cars you have to handle with kid gloves. Not so with Corvette.

Because under that sleek hull is a sports car capable of handling any road you'd care to put before it.

Behind fat F70 x 15 tires are disc brakes all around. And an advanced fully independent suspension. That glues Corvette down to roads most other cars just can't come to grips with.

Under that long stretch of hood: a standard 300-hp V8. Or order the 350-, 370-, 390- or 460-hp engine. All are backed up by a 4-Speed shift and Positraction rear axle.

And to help you keep tabs on all this, there's an instrument panel that reads out like Apollo 13. Big tach. Ammeter. Oil pressure gauge. Running light monitors—the works.

Corvette. Go ahead and try one on a road. It fits like a glove.

Putting you first, keeps us first. **CHEVROLET**

Campbell-Ewald pulled on its gloves and lowered its lens to dramatize the 1970 Corvette for a car magazine ad.

233

added inches in the Corvette resulted from Chevy's need to expand the engine's size to counterbalance the loss in performance in its regular passenger cars caused by the steady reduction in exhaust emissions to meet state and federal laws. Making the Mark IV six percent bigger was scarcely noticeable in the Corvette, whose performance was limited more by its tires than its engine.

There was more torque, to be sure, with the bigger engine. The "less powerful" 454-cubic-inch engine in 1970 was the LS-5, with 500 pound-feet of torque at 3,400 rpm and a modest power rating at 390 bhp at 4,800 rpm. It had a hydraulic-lifter cam, 10¼ to one compression ratio, and a single four-barrel carburetor; the triple-carb manifold was among the missing this year. The LS-5 was offered with both four-speed boxes and the Turbo Hydra-Matic.

As for the LS-7, it became a legendary engine — legendary in the sense that its specs were published, it was written up in the major auto magazines, and it never went on sale. Its output was cited as either 460 or 465 bhp at 5,200 rpm with aluminum heads and a solid-lifter camshaft. It was paired in the option listings with a new Chevrolet twin-disc clutch ten inches in diameter, along with the M-22 "rock crusher" transmission.

In December, 1969 the first LS-7 Corvette was driven from Los Angeles to Detroit by Paul Van Valkenburgh, who found that

with a full fuel tank, two aboard and a full kit of luggage it would turn the standing quarter-mile in 13.8 seconds and reach 108 mph at the end of the quarter. "Never have we tested a car that had such a secure speed potential," he wrote in *Sports Car Graphic*. "This car gives the impression that it could do *anything* you demanded." What did it ride and sound like? "Like taxiing a DC3 at full throttle up and down a freshly plowed runway."

These remained unique impressions of the highest-horsepower Corvette ever officially catalogued, because the LS-7 never made it to the marketplace. It ran afoul of GM's internal discouragement of cars with excessively high horsepower (even though Ed Cole *had* become president of General Motors, its policies hadn't changed that much) and also Chevrolet's campaign to weed out costly options that were clogging its assembly lines. This was known as the "de-pro" program, short for de-proliferation. The LS-7 was "de-proed" into instant oblivion.

Before the Corvette men could rear back and relaunch the LS-7 in 1971, Ed Cole placed an insurmountable obstacle in their path. He decreed early in 1970 that all 1971 GM cars would be able to run on fuel with a Research Octane number no higher than 91 (it had taken 103-octane fuel to satisfy the L88). This, he calculated, was low enough for the fuel companies to begin marketing the lead-free regular gasoline that Cole was certain would be needed to avoid fouling the catalytic reactors that he

In 1970 Daytona 24-Hour Owens-Corning cars were first (Thompson, No. 7) and third (DeLorenzo, No. 6) in GT Class. Greder (No. 2) entered Le Mans in

envisioned as reducing the emissions of future auto engines. This meant that the Corvette engines had to drop back to the levels of compression ratio of 1955 and 1956. Later in 1970 Cole also initiated a move to quote the net or as-installed horsepower figures for GM engines, as well as the usual gross figures, which don't show the losses from the generator, fan, air cleaner, mufflers, and heating of intake air and the inlet manifold.

After Cole's fiat Chevrolet engineers had only weeks rather than months to adjust all their engines, including those for the Corvette. With crash programs like this to cope with, it wasn't surprising that the changes the engineers made to the 1971 model — other than those in the engine room — were restricted to lily-gilding gestures like a fuel filler door that was easier to open and an automatic transmission selector quadrant that was illuminated at night.

On the Mark IV engines the compression ratio reductions were made by changing the shapes of the piston crowns, so it was relatively easy for an owner to bump the compression higher again with an appropriate set of special pistons. The LS-5 was carried over with flat-topped pistons that dropped its compression ratio to 8½ to one and its power to 365 bhp at 4,800 rpm under the gross rating, or 285 bhp net, at the flywheel.

Aluminum heads returned to the lineup on an engine that was offered for street use, the spiritual successor to the L88 and the short-lived LS-7: the LS-6. Its pistons retained modest domes for a 9.0 to one compression ratio, which helped hold the horsepower at the high level of 425 bhp gross, 325 bhp net, at 5,600 rpm. It was a costly engine at $1,220.70 over the base price; only 0.9 percent of the 1971 Corvette buyers chose it. "Maybe for street engine I make mistake," Duntov reflected then; "aluminum heads are expensive and that weight doesn't matter on the street." But it was the right kind of engine to lead the Corvette lineup, and that's what counted the most.

The base small-block engine had dished piston crowns to reduce the compression ratio to 8½ to one. Its output was down ten percent to 270 bhp gross at 4,800 rpm, 210 bhp net at 4,400. This was the only hydraulic-lifter small-block engine in the line. The high-performance 350 bhp hydraulic-cam engine that had been offered in the Corvette since 1965, first in 327-cubic-inch form and later as a 350 engine, had fallen afoul of the relentless probers for redundant proliferation. It was either this engine or the LT-1, they decreed, and Duntov, Pike and company decided they'd rather keep the high-winding solid-lifter engine they'd fought so hard to get. The LT-1 for '71 had a 9.0 to one compression ratio with flat-topped pistons, and was rated at 330 gross bhp and 275 net horses, at 5,600 rpm.

The panorama of 1971 Corvettes was placed on display by *Car and Driver*, which tested one example of each of the four engines

Trailing Ferrari, Greder/Beaumont '71 Le Mans challenge failed after thirteen hours. In Belgium, tuner Vic Heylen fitted fuel injection to a '71 Corvette.

offered. These were the statistical results:

1971 Corvette Acceleration Tabulation				
Engine option	L-48	LT-1	LS-5	LS-6
Nominal power	270 bhp	330 bhp	365 bhp	425 bhp
Transmission	Turbo Hydra-Matic	close-ratio 4-speed	Turbo Hydra-Matic	close-ratio 4-speed
Final drive ratio	3.08:1	3.70:1	3.08:1	3.36:1
Curb weight	3460 lbs.	3370 lbs.	3675 lbs.	3478 lbs.
0-60 mph	7.1 secs.	6.0 secs.	5.7 secs.	5.3 secs.
0-80 mph	12.3 secs.	9.7 secs.	9.3 secs.	8.5 secs.
0-100 mph	19.8 secs.	14.5 secs.	14.1 secs.	12.7 secs.
Standing ¼ mile	15.6 secs.	14.6 secs.	14.2 secs.	13.8 secs.
Terminal ¼ mile speed	90 mph	101 mph	100 mph	105 mph
Maximum speed	132 mph	137 mph	141 mph	152 mph

Extraordinary was the ability of the LS-5, which was burdened with all power, luxury, and convenience options and air conditioning to the total tune of $7,255.85. Its magnificent performance was achieved simply by pressing down the right foot while suspending one's doubts about the acceleration ability of heavy automatic-transmission sports cars. And the *C/D* editors validated its top speed by *cruising* at 140 mph across the Nevada desert roads.

Corvette production volumes were now at more moderate levels, with 17,316 cars made in the short 1970 model year and 21,801 cars in the 1971 model year, about the same as in 1963. This allowed the more than 500 men and women working each shift in the St. Louis plant to devote more time to the creation of a trouble-free car. The opportunity for high motivation was there, to a far greater degree than in the auto industry's many plants producing faceless utility cars with numbing monotony. Said the plant's production supervisor, Vince Shanks, "When you ask a guy where he works in St. Louis, he'll tell you 'Corvette' rather than 'Chevrolet.' Every Corvette he sees on the road is one he's worked on. That's quite an incentive."

During construction the Corvette bodies were passed through a four-minute water spray with an inspector inside, looking for leaks in no less than seventy different locations. After completion each car was driven about two miles over a bumpy, potholed road made even meaner with angled strips of macadam four inches high, designed to bring out body creaks and rattles. Then the car was driven into a special "shake shed" where it was racked on an

Low-compression engines and aluminum-head LS-6 option appeared in '71

electrically jiggled platform that felt from inside the car as if it were being driven over railroad ties, each wheel at a different speed. By such measures did perfectionist John DeLorean seek to overcome the appalling reputation for poor quality the Corvette had gained in 1968 and 1969.

Also offered in 1971 were the two special racing packages, the ZR-1 with the small-block engine and the ZR-2 with the Mark IV. These were shrewdly designed through the prohibition of radios and heaters to bar their use on the street, not as a result of some warped GM anti-racing morality but rather because Zora Duntov knew from bitter experience that some street Corvette buyers just checked the hottest-sounding items on the order blank without finding out what they really were. When Chevy said these ZR packages with their rock-hard ride, screaming gearboxes, and unshrouded radiators were for "off-road" use, they meant *racing*, and *only* racing.

One loss to both ZR combinations in 1971 was the cold-air hood, an item of special benefit to this sports car with its very compact and crowded engine room. Then in 1972 the ZR-2 vanished from the scene with the eradication of the aluminum-headed LS-6 from the Chevrolet engine lineup. Only three engines were listed for the Corvette in 1972, the smallest selection since 1956. Those that remained were carry-over engines from 1971, now with even more conservative net power ratings. The base engine became the 200 bhp ZQ-3. Ratings of the LT-1

In 1972 engine choices were cut to three by Chevy's deproliferation effort.

and LS-5 became 255 and 270 bhp respectively.

The unkindest cut of all was Chevrolet's failure to complete emissions certification of the Mark IV LS-5 in time to clear it for sale in California, where limits on oxides of nitrogen had been imposed that didn't apply in the other forty-nine states. The problem was not that the LS-5 couldn't pass the tests; it was that Chevrolet lacked the manpower to certify every engine/car combination it wanted to, and the LS-5 arbitrarily — in view of its relatively small production volume — was dropped from the test series. Such considerations as the role of California as a pacesetter in automotive styles and as the second-largest customer among the states (behind Michigan) for Corvettes carried little weight.

Other than these relatively retrograde engine realignments the main novelty in the 1972 Corvette was the exchange of the light-monitoring system for a horn-honking burglar alarm, made standard equipment on the new model. Earning the respect and grudging admiration of the nation's professional car thieves, the Corvette's alarm was turned on and off by a lock at the rear of the car. Opening either the hood or the doors when the alarm was switched on sounded the car's horn and kept it blaring until it was silenced with the owner's key in the special lock.

Trying '72 Corvettes with all three engines, *Motor Trend* found that the car's precious bodily fluids were still flowing freely. "In full song," they wrote of their favorite model, "the LT-1 screams

past those lifeless people ensconced in their movable living rooms laughably referred to as cars. It is an experience that does not soon pass from one's memory." Racer Tony DeLorenzo test-drove the cars too and commented, "You can't get a better overall performance car. I'd be hard-pressed to find a better car, for the money, than the 'Vette. It's just an incredible automobile."

DeLorenzo had gone on from his Corvette-racing days to the more ambitious world of Trans-Am competition, but he and his Owens-Corning teammates had left their imprint on the record book. In 1969 one of the red and white cars placed fourteenth overall and fourth in the GT category at Sebring, driven by Dick Lang and Gib Hufstader. Later that year Lang and DeLorenzo teamed up in the six-hour race at Watkins Glen to win the top GT placing and finish seventh overall.

In 1970 the Owens-Corning cars, based in Troy, Michigan, continued to focus on the long-distance American events so successfully that they won the GT category in both the Florida contests. In doing so, Jerry Thompson and John Mahler were sixth overall in the Daytona twenty-four-hour and DeLorenzo and Lang were tenth overall in the Sebring Twelve-hour, setting a new Grand Touring distance record in that race. At Daytona in 1971, DeLorenzo and Mahler were joined by Don Yenko in a historic drive that took them to another GT win and a magnificent fourth place in the overall race ranking.

There had been nothing modest or unspectacular about the victories scored by the team headed by Tony DeLorenzo and Jerry Thompson and heavily publicized by Owens-Corning. Their calculated flamboyance had incited a healthy desire on the part of several other racers to beat the hell out of DeLorenzo and Thompson, an urge whose satisfaction began with the purchase of one or more ZR-2 Corvettes. Most strongly motivated in this direction was another racer based in Troy, Michigan, John Greenwood.

Specializing in outstanding engine preparation, Greenwood emblazoned his cars with a striking stars-and-stripes motif and set sail after the pacesetters. John won the Central Division Championship in 1970 and went on to win the Class A Production National honors that year and in 1971. Partnered by entertainer Dick Smothers, Greenwood placed seventh overall at Sebring in '71 and continued the tradition of a Corvette GT win. With Bob Johnson, Greenwood was GT winner and fifth overall at Watkins Glen in 1971.

The 1972 season became as much a battle between makers of radial tires as a contest between Corvettes. This fast and heavy sports car had always been very demanding of its tires, and both

George Barris designed and built a small series of these Fino-Vettes under an agreement with Florida-based champion offshore boat racer Bobby Rautbord

B. F. Goodrich and Goodyear decided to take advantage of that fact to show Detroit that radial-ply tires were ready now for more extensive application, under even the toughest conditions. Goodyear was the leader in this race-within-races on the basis of outstanding performances by Dave Heinz and Bob Johnson in winning the GT category at both Daytona and Sebring, in 1972. They were eighth overall at Daytona and a stunning fourth, the best in history by a Corvette, at Sebring in what was billed as the last-ever race over the original airport course that had been the scene of so much Corvette drama since 1956.

The publicity given radial-ply tires by the Corvettes in racing paid off with much wider use of radials on 1973-model cars, including the Chevy sports car. The bias-ply wide-ovals used before were replaced by GR70 x 15 radial tires with steel belts as standard equipment. These were most helpful in improving two aspects of the Corvette that had been criticized: its harsh ride and its dicy behaviour on wet roads. Tests showed that the belted radials reduced the car's stopping distance from 60 mph by six percent on wet pavement. They also gave longer tire life while complying with Zora Duntov's criterion that the Corvette's original-equipment tires should be entirely safe at the highest speeds the stock model can reach. Not all car makers in America impose that requirement.

Aluminum wheels made a welcome return to the Corvette with the 1973 model. They were of bolt-on design, patterned directly after the wheels fitted to the experimental XP-882 mid-engined

car (see Chapter 18) first shown in 1970. They had the same handsome deep-dish section, and eight cooling vents instead of the ten vents on the experimental car's wheels. With an eight-inch rim width, the same as the standard steel wheels, the optional cast aluminum parts reduced the unsprung weight at each wheel by eight pounds, giving a useful cut of forty pounds in the weight of the complete car.

Some manufacturing cost was taken out of the 1973 Corvette by doing away with the removable rear window in the coupé and eliminating the vacuum-operated door covering the windshield wipers. New molds for the front fenders were made incorporating a simple recessed air vent on each side and dropping the separate cast vent grilles. A new longer hood panel shrouded the parked wiper blades and brought back to all Corvettes a feature that had been a racing-only option before: a cowl-induction system supplying cool air to the carburetor. This gave a practical boost in performance that didn't show up in the conservative ratings of net horsepower. The air supply was controlled, according to engine operating conditions, by a solenoid-operated valve built into the hood.

In 1973, for the first time since 1956, the standard Corvette range included no engines with mechanical-lifter camshafts. The LT-1 fell by the wayside in favor of an optional hydraulic-cam small-block engine rated at 245 net bhp. The net rating for the base V-8 was reduced to 190 bhp, while the Mark IV engine saw a slight increase in its net rating to 275 bhp with the substitution

Most extensive changes since 1968 came in the 1973 model, with its body-color nose piece, complemented by the new rear end of the 'Vette for 1974.

of an LS-4 option for the previous LS-5. One of Chevy's aids to racers, the M-22 "rock crusher" transmission, was missing from the 1973 option list. Standard equipment under the hoods of all the new Corvettes was a separate reservoir for capturing coolant that escaped from the radiator, holding it for return to the system when the engine cooled.

It was a tribute to the Corvette's staying power and its unique value to Chevrolet that it was continued into 1973 in spite of the extensive engineering and tooling cost that was incurred in bringing it in line with the latest safety standards. Inside its doors the heavy fluted steel beams were installed that General Motors had pioneered in production to reduce the chance of injury from a side impact. Extending from hinges to lock plate inside the doors, the beams tied together the body's steel "birdcage."

The most important changes in the new body since it was introduced in 1968 included a structurally novel nose for the Corvette to allow it to strike a barrier head-first at five miles an hour without damage to any of the car's lighting or safety equipment. Painted to match the color of the car, the front bumper consisted of a urethane plastic pad on a steel armature. Its main support was at the center, from a massive transverse tube bolted to the car's frame. Between the tube and the bumper there were two Omark bolts, special steel bolts which absorb energy when a forming die — pushed back by the bumper — is forced along their length. This superior front-end protection was gained at a cost of thirty-five additional pounds.

The urethane nose was chosen over the alternative, an uglier arrangement using a heavier, more boldly protruding version of the earlier bumper mounted on energy absorbers. So well did the Omark-bolt front end work at the mandatory impact speed that the Chevy engineers decided to try it, as a matter of interest, at two miles an hour faster: seven miles an hour. They mounted a pre-production car on the test rig and sent it rolling into the barrier. "The result was disastrous," said Zora. Before their stunned eyes the Corvette body shattered, all but falling apart. They gained some consolation from the car's relatively good performance in the far more severe 30 mph barrier test.

Zora Arkus-Duntov personally spurred another important change in the Corvette body for '73. He asked his engineers—chassis man Walt Zetye and body man Bob Vogelei—to do something to reduce the amount of shaking and rattling in the body over bumps. This was especially important with the new radial tires, which passed different vibration frequencies through from the road to the frame. They decided to install rubber body mounts between the body and the frame in place of the "hard" mounts that had been used since 1968. To preserve the Corvette's traditional solid feel, special mounts were developed with a steel insert that kept high lateral stiffness in the body/frame connection while the rubber moved more freely vertically to soak up noise and vibration that would otherwise be transmitted to the car's interior. Their attention to detail was such that the mounts were tailored differently to suit the characteristics of the coupe and convertible bodies.

Additional barriers to NVH (noise, vibration and harshness) were

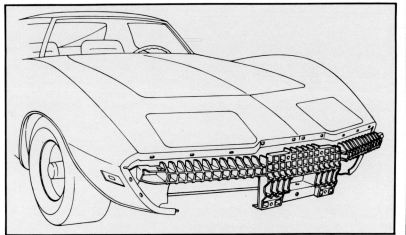
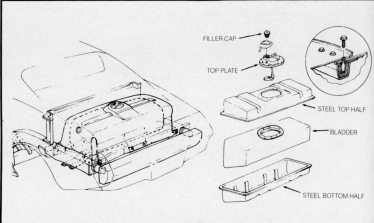

Engineering advances in the 1975 Corvette included the new cellular plastic front bumper, left, and a safer steel-enclosed rubber bladder fuel tank.

posed by pounds more insulation in the 1973 body. Most of the inner panels were sprayed with an asphalt compound that made it harder for them to transmit sound. A new blanket inside the hood and insulation of the steering column retained more of the disturbance within the engine room. Throughout the cockpit, heavier mats in the dash, console and rear quarters and thicker (up from ¼ to ⅜ inch) insulation under the carpeting made the Corvette a nicer place to live as well as visit.

As sometimes happens, the craftsmen in St. Louis fell short of perfection in their installation of this NVH package in the first run of the new-model cars, one of which was tested by *Motor Trend*. That magazine's Eric Dahlquist said nevertheless that "the new car was light-years ahead of the 'Vettes we tested last June in terms of road noise (or its absence) and ride comfort," adding that "a lot of the old fiberglass body squeaks and groans had been filtered out of the cockpit, along with some of the bone-rattling ride on rough surfaces."

Testers of the '73 model found that the new tires contributed to better cornering on wet roads and to pleasing handling on dry pavement—but at lower maximum speeds than the old crossply tires allowed. *Road & Track* reported that "our skidpad figures [maximum lateral acceleration of 0.726 g.] show that its absolute cornering power has been reduced to just above average. Zora Arkus-Duntov confirms this and adds—with some regret—that on his skidpad it has dropped from 0.85 g. to just about what our own tests showed. Braking distances are also adversely affected; they have increased from average to not-quite-average."

Though most of these factory-owned test cars had the aluminum bolt-on wheels, Chevrolet's Joe Pike states categorically that no

Corvette left the St. Louis plant with those California-made wheels installed as a regular production option. Only about a third of the several thousand wheels made came up to Chevrolet standards in appearance and dimensional accuracy, a rate of acceptance too low to make their use economical. Some sets of wheels were released to Chevy's service parts sales channels, however, and some of the good ones found their way out of GM Design Staff to special friends of the Corvette.

Most of the car magazines concentrated, understandably, on the more potent engines in the '73 stable. This was the performance recorded by *Car and Driver* on three new coupes:

1973 Corvette Acceleration Tabulation			
Engine option	L-82	LS-4	LS-4
SAE net power	245 bhp	275 bhp	275 bhp
Transmission	close-ratio 4-speed	close-ratio 4-speed	Turbo Hydra-Matic
Final drive ratio	3.70:1	3.55:1	3.08:1
Curb weight	3540 lbs.	3585 lbs.	3742 lbs.
0-60 mph	6.7 secs.	6.4 secs.	6.4 secs.
0-80 mph	10.8 secs.	10.0 secs.	10.0 secs.
0-100 mph	17.1 secs.	17.0 secs.	16.0 secs.
Standing ¼ mile	15.1 secs.	14.6 secs.	14.7 secs.
Terminal ¼ mile speed	95.4 mph	95.7 mph	97.2 mph

As in the same magazine's test of the 1971 models one of the most impressive results was the way the big LS-4 V-8 performed with the automatic transmission: super-quick, and with a lot more noise, too, in the cockpit from the new cool-air inlet in the cowl.

One magazine, *Cars*, tested the base 190-bhp engine as well as the "bigger" eights in the Corvette catalogue, and reached a surprising conclusion: *"Our choice for the all around best performer,"* italicized *Cars, "must go to the base 350 L-48 engine.* It's really a beautiful combination. The L-48 delivers all the acceleration you'll ever need on the road in a steady, forceful manner although it doesn't pin you to the seat as does the 454. In addition, the L-48 is quiet, runs cool, idles smoothly and can cruise at 100 all day if you commute in Nevada." They found that it accelerated to 60 in a respectable 6.8 seconds with the Turbo Hydra-Matic and averaged a happy 14 mpg on the highway.

The great tradition of Corvettes at Sebring stayed alive in '73 thanks to the intervention of a new sanctioning group, IMSA (International Motor Sports Association), at the Florida circuit and the willingness of Corvette racer John Greenwood to back the running of the twelve-hour event financially. With Ron Grable and Mike Brockman, Greenwood drove his Chevy to third overall, thereby duplicating the Corvette finish that Heinz and McClure had recorded at Daytona a month earlier. Both were the best-ever Corvette placings in these races.

In 1973 Corvettes set new records in the salesrooms too. An output of 30,465 units made this the first twelve-month model year (1969 was a "long" year) in Corvette history to top the 30,000 mark. If they'd built more they could have sold them: Chevrolet had to send back to its dealers 8,200 orders for Corvettes that it couldn't fill! What accounted for this sudden strengthening of demand for a car that was only subtly changed since 1968? Chief Corvette salesman Joe Pike traced it back to the introduction of the 1971 model.

When the '71 models came out, Pike theorized, with their lower compression ratios and reduced power, Corvette owners saw little reason to trade their cars in on the new ones. This caused a softening of demand, which meant there were unsold Corvettes around which could be displayed in showrooms, something that rarely happened before, and dealers who'd never been able to coax a Corvette out of Chevrolet were now able to get them. Thus the car was seen and then accepted by a new kind of customer who just liked the way it looked and bought it with an automatic transmission and all the power and luxury options.

Then, the Pike reasoning continued, the true blue Corvette enthusiasts came back into the market in 1973. Their cars were two years older now, and they liked the sneaky look of the new body-color front end, so they bought Corvettes, betraying their presence among the purchasers by the higher proportion of four-speed cars they ordered—Corvette buyers still had a choice of a four-speed or

automatic at no difference in price. They joined together with the new class of "luxury" buyers to bump the car's sales to the high '73 level and to an even more rapid rate in 1974.

A new general manager, F. James McDonald, had taken charge of Chevrolet on October 1, 1972. He was a manufacturing specialist who had worked in that field for a year at Chevy before spending almost three years as the head of Pontiac as preparation for his move to the top post at Chevrolet. Known as a quick study, McDonald lost little time in sizing up the Corvette situation and approved a boost in production from eight to nine cars an hour in 1974. This was a useful increase but not so great that it would lead to the quality problems that plagued the St. Louis builders in 1968. Corvette production rose to 33,869 for calendar 1974 and a spectacular 37,502 for the 1974 model year.

Corvettes were sellouts again in 1974 in spite of a $367 price increase. The convertible went up from $5,399 in 1973 to $5,766, in its base price, and the coupe rose from $5,635 to $6,002. In '74 (as it had been in '73) the Corvette was elected "Best All-Around Car" in the annual poll of its readers conducted by *Car and Driver*. This was the ninth time in eleven years it had been picked for this honor, holding a clear margin ahead of the Datsun 240/260Z in both 1973 and 1974.

This strong demand and adoring approval were supported by only the slightest product changes in 1974. The engine lineup was the same, though the smallest gained five horses and the biggest lost five. They were cooled better at low speeds and/or high temperatures by a new radiator with louvered fins, and air-conditioned cars with the LS-4 454-cubic-inch engine had fan and water pump improvements to keep them cooler in city traffic.

The main change on the 1974 Corvette was oddly controversial at first: its completely new body-color rear end. This replaced the squared-off tail introduced in '68 with a trim, tapering urethane plastic cone with a built-in license plate holder and four recesses for the familiar round lights. Inside it was a box-section aluminum impact bar mounted on two slider brackets, each containing an energy-absorbing Omark bolt. This qualified the Corvette to pass the Federal 5 mph barrier impact test at the rear as well as at the front. (It was exempted that year from the new pendulum impact standards that most cars had to meet.)

"Many owners are going to feel some reservations about this new look," said *Corvette News*, of all people, about the new rear end. "We did too, at first." This was apparently their way of anticipating possible criticism of the design, which was all but nonexistent. In fact, this newest design from Henry Haga's studio was beautiful, a solid hit. Apart from the carping of *Road & Track* that "The aerodynamic result is zero lift at the rear at high speeds, compared to a few pounds of downforce for the previous design," most people liked the looks of the '74 model. Said *Car and Driver*, "we think the front and rear together produce a 'molded' shape that speaks of function instead of decor."

Strictly functional was the release of a Gymkhana suspension option, RPO FE7, for a modest seven dollars extra in 1974. This was similar to the F41 heavy-duty suspension that was offered on a more limited basis in 1973, usually as part of the RPO ZO7 package that also included heavy-duty brakes. RPO ZO7 was still catalogued in 1974 as an "Off-Road" option, the familiar Chevy euphemism for its racing equipment, but the Gymkhana springing could be ordered on any new street Corvette. It included a stiffer front anti-roll bar, up from 7/8 to 15/16 inch in diameter, and front and rear springs about eighty percent stiffer. Missing were the shocks with stronger settings that were part of the F41 suspension option. Chevrolet cautioned that the Gymkhana option was fine for an owner who would compete in autocrosses and gymkhanas extensively but was too bouncy for the buyer who would use his Corvette only on the street.

Both the Gymkhana suspension and the ZO7 option (the latter with roll bar diameters of 1 1/8 inch front, 7/16 inch rear) were carried over to the 1975 model year. The rear leaf spring went from nine to ten leaves without a change in the basic stiffness; adding a leaf adapted the Corvette better to Chevrolet's system of maintaining the car's trim height, important to both looks and bumper performance, by using a computer to pick springs to suit the weights and placements of the options on each individual car.

Speaking of bumpers, the sprouting of small black-colored impact pads on both front and rear of the '75 Corvette provided the main identifiers of the new model and betrayed further changes in the bumper system. To pass both barrier and pendulum-impact tests the nose was changed to an all-plastic design with a body-color skin over an interior made of a honeycomb of plastic cells that looked like a huge ice-cube tray. These cells would "give" to absorb impact, then push the bumper face back to its original form. The Omark bolts were eliminated at the front and also at the rear, where they were replaced by Delco's hydraulic Enersorbers.

After ten happy years as a member of the Corvette power family, the great Mark IV engine was dropped from the lineup in 1975. It might have been otherwise. The proximate cause was the big 454's failure to pass the 50,000-mile durability test of emissions with GM's new catalytic converters. Two converters had been fitted, one in each exhaust system to keep back-pressure low, but by the 25,000-mile mark their ability to turn CO and HC into CO_2 and H_2O was fatally impaired by phosphorous contamination in a manner that was obscure at the time. With insufficient time and money for a retest, the decision was made to scrub the big V-8 altogether.

Emissions test troubles with a dual exhaust also delayed the '75

The '75 model could be spotted by the two black pads on the bumpers.

debut in California of the L-82 engine option. This made a tardy appearance with the same exhaust system as the base L-48: a single catalytic converter under the passenger seat, from which two pipes branched out to the separate rear mufflers. Fitted to both 350-cubic-inch eights was GM's new High-Energy Ignition, with magnetic triggering and a coil giving spark voltages up to thirty-five percent higher. It was a direct descendant of the transistorized ignition that GM's Delco had pioneered on earlier Corvettes. Net power ratings took another licking, falling to 165 bhp for the L-48 and 205 bhp for the L-82. A sign of the times was the addition of an optional economy 2.73 to one axle ratio to the range.

Unleaded fuel was specified for the 1975 model and was poured into a new fuel tank. This was a heavy rubber bladder, like those used in race cars, encased in a ribbed steel housing. The whole assembly was mounted under a "hat" in the rear floor that sealed it off from the interior of the car. Though this had the immediate purpose of meeting Federal fuel tank impact rules, its secondary value was that it all but barred the chance of severe fires inside the Corvette of a kind that had been caused, some suits against Chevrolet alleged, by the post-1963 placement of the tank virtually within the passenger compartment.

Emissions equipment, inflation and the need to make a profit on the hot-selling Corvette conspired to bump the '75 prices even higher. The base figures rose to $6,537 for the convertible and $6,797 for the coupe, and options bore new high price tags too: power brakes $55, power steering $129, AM/FM stereo radio $284 and air conditioning $490. The 1975 coupes tested by *Motor Trend* and *Car and Driver* bore sticker prices of $8,227 and $8,352 respectively. Both were fitted with

Sleeker than ever with its new hood, the '76 offered aluminum wheels.

the economy axle ratios but the *C/D* test still returned good figures: 0-60 mph in 7.7 seconds, with the base engine, a standing quarter-mile in 16.1 seconds and a timed top speed of 129 mph.

While one organization, the Federal government, was forcing Corvette power and performance down, others, those of IMSA and the SCCA, were liberalizing their rules to keep the Corvettes competitive in the GT racing events that had seized the interest of American road racing fans and entrants. In 1973 Chevrolet had won the SCCA's Trans-Am Championship thanks to John Greenwood's Corvette victory at Edmonton, which clinched a Chevy win over Porsche. In 1974 Greenwood built a spectacular new car with deep fender flares (available to other racers too) to allow extra-wide racing tires. With it he was fastest qualifier and winner in the last IMSA Camel GT race of 1974, a 250-mile event at Daytona. Formidable in both looks and performance, the 1975-model Greenwood Corvette racer was pure estate-bottled vintage essence of the spirit of the sports car from St. Louis. Unfortunately it was not so good at finishing as it was at qualifying.

In December of 1974 the McDonald era at Chevrolet ended and the Lund era began. Robert D. Lund, a salesman's salesman, moved across town from the general managership of Cadillac to the same job at Chevrolet, which he knew well from a former stint as sales manager. Another personnel change of even greater significance to Corvette lovers was the retirement, on January 1, 1975, of Zora Arkus-Duntov after twenty-one years and seven months with GM and Chevrolet. Though it had seemed that it would not, indeed could not, ever happen, the close association with the Corvette over most of those years that had capped Zora's remarkable career was finally at an end. Arkus-

Duntov's successor as chief Corvette engineer was David R. McLellan, who had understudied Zora as his assistant and who had a strong vehicle development background at both Chevrolet and the GM Proving Ground staff. No one had to describe to McLellan the dimensions of the shoes into which he had stepped.

As so often happens in the auto industry, Lund and McLellan were assigned the job of introducing a new model—the 1976 Corvette—that had been created chiefly by their predecessors. It was a model year whose main significance was negative: the elimination of the convertible model, the pure open car that had symbolized "Corvette" since 1953. This move simply recognized the increasingly overwhelming demand for the stiffer, snugger, dryer and very handsome coupe body.

Apart from a new rear nameplate and five new colors, the '76 Corvettes were little changed externally. The front bumper system was altered further, and the car's trim height was raised at both front and rear by a quarter-inch. Visible at last on cars in showrooms and on the street were the aluminum wheels that had first been promised as options in 1973. This time they were made by Kelsey-Hayes in a factory in Mexico, and offered in sets of four, with a steel spare wheel, to keep the cost of the option down.

For 1976 the L-48 was again the base engine. The optional automatic paired with it became the CBC 350, which offered better control response, especially on downshifts. The tough, high-winding L-82 was optional in all fifty states from the start of the model year. Its automatic choice remained the Turbo Hydra-Matic but with new tailoring of the torque converter to move the car quicker off the line. Both eights benefitted from a new forced-air induction system using a duct over the radiator instead of the noisy inlet at the rear of the hood.

By refining rather than radically changing its Corvette for 1976, Chevrolet kept a sensationally popular show on the road. The Corvette booked fine sales successes in the mid-Seventies in the face of a worldwide depression in the auto market that threw some of the greatest sports car marques on the rocks. It did so with only shrewd and subtle changes to a two-seater whose dramatic and sexy good looks still have few rivals.

That is not to say that Chevrolet lacked ideas for even better Corvettes. You'll see some of those ideas in the chapters just ahead. But it did mean that Chevy had trouble convincing GM management that a new Corvette was needed. When GM's board chairman was shown a mid-engined prototype at the Milford Proving Ground in June of 1972 he stopped all discussion with: "What do you want a new car for? You're selling all you can make right now!" Undeniably true, that was then and remained the ultimate tribute of the hard-bitten businessman to the charisma and the quality of the most popular Corvette in history, the 'Vette for the Seventies.

Chapter 18

MID-ENGINE XP-MACHINES

Those who maintain that competition to build a better product is dead or dying in the American automobile industry would do well to scan the recent history of the two-seater sports car in the U.S. It has been a lively fencing match between Ford and Chevrolet at auto races, in motor shows, and behind the vinyl curtains that shroud the intrigues in Bloomfield Hills and Grosse Pointe that are so vital to the lives of the Motor City magnates. It is a match that has not yet been concluded, for neither Chevy nor Ford has yet made a total commitment to the kind of car the fencing is all about: an American-made mid-engined sports car.

Nineteen sixty-seven set a high water mark for participation by Ford and Chevrolet in international sports car racing. Ford did it openly, with the Mark IV (no relation to Chevrolet's engine) coupé that won at Sebring and Le Mans, a creation of Ford and its outside contractor in Dearborn, Kar Kraft. Chevrolet took part covertly through Chaparral Cars of Midland, Texas, with the winged white Chaparral 2F, designed and constructed with substantial backing by Chevy's Research and Development Department under Frank Winchell and his successor, Jim Musser. Of the two 427-cubic-inch cars the Chaparral was the more advanced, with its rear-mounted radiators and semi-automatic transmission, and by a small margin the faster, but the Ford was the better-tested and hence the more reliable in the races that counted.

It was an open secret in Detroit that the Ford Division was eager to get into production, somehow, with a modern two-seater sports car to compete with the Corvette in the market and to capitalize on the publicity earned by two successive victories at Le Mans. It had designed such a car in parallel with its racing Mark IV and had shown it, as the Mach 2, during 1967. Ford had also announced plans to manufacture a small series of a Mark III version of its famous GT40 sports-racing car, for use on the road. Both projects represented major threats to the Corvette in its class, aesthetically as well as commercially.

After seeing the simple, straightforward Ford Mach 2, in May

of 1967, Frank Winchell of Chevrolet assigned Larry Nies of his staff to lay out a similarly uncomplicated mid-engined Corvette prototype, a car that Chevy could have up its sleeve if it heard that the Mach 2 was going into production. From its Styling Staff designation it became known as the XP-880. Winchell and Nies carried over to this car some of the components of the rear-engined experimental coupé that had posed such a challenge to the handling analysts (see Chapter 16). Like that car, the XP-880 used a spot-welded steel backbone frame.

The central frame backbone was made one foot high and half a foot wide to accommodate a twenty-gallon fuel-containing bladder. Forked at the rear to embrace the engine and connect to the rear suspension members, the frame weighed 180 pounds. Its deflection characteristics were studied in advance by means of a scale model of the frame in plastic which could be tested and analyzed just like the full-size frame but much more easily and cheaply. It helped validate the achievement of the stiffness target of 3,600 pound-feet per degree over the one-hundred-inch wheelbase, and located the points on the frame which were least subject to movement while the car was running, and hence were best for the placement of the body mounts.

The combination of the backbone frame down the center of the cockpit with thick doors, containing safety beams guarding against side impacts, made the seating space of the XP-880 very narrow and snug. Frank Winchell favored this layout because it held the driver firmly in place and allowed him to concentrate on controlling the car instead of holding himself in position. Others found it too confining and perspiration-inducing on warm days; it was a controversial feature of this car and its rear-engined predecessor.

Cockpit heat from the upward-ducted front radiator had been one of the main problems with the rear-engined car. But the R&D men didn't like to deflect the air downward either, because that tended to lift the front end of the car. They resolved this dilemma by putting the radiator in the tail of the car, in a location

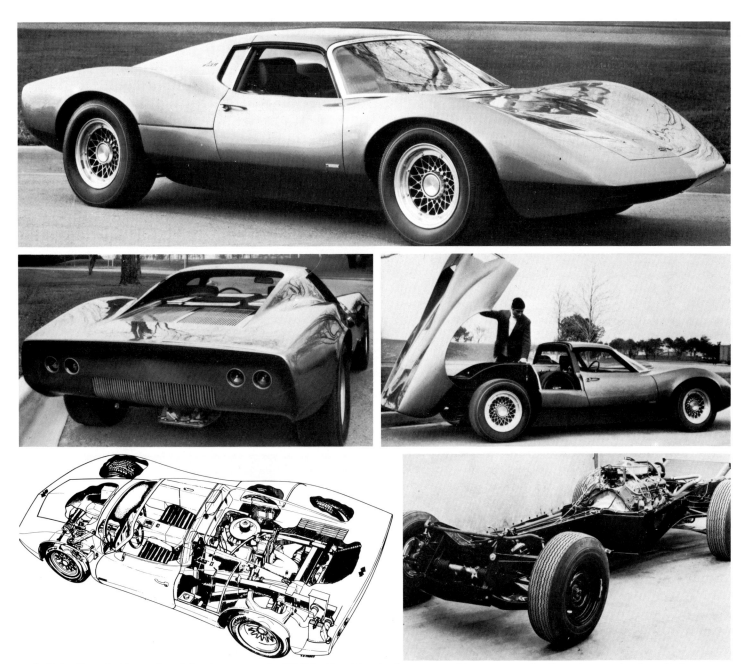

Built by Chevrolet Research and Development as the XP-880, this mid-engined prototype with rear-mounted radiator became the Astro II show car.

proved out by tests on a Chevy-owned Ford GT40. The air flowed downward from a grille in the rear deck through the angled radiator, sucked out the bottom by twin fans that were driven whenever the car was running.

The rear radiator simplified the plumbing connections to the engine, which was mounted with its normal front end pointed toward the rear of the chassis. Larry Nies estimated that this reversed mounting reduced the required wheelbase length by two and three-quarter inches, because the "front" of an engine is normally cluttered with a lot of pulleys, belts, and accessories that interfere with the reclining seating of a low GT coupé. On the stock 390 bhp Mark IV engine used in the XP-880 the ring gear and starter remained at the front, joined by a vibration damper, while the water pump was made gear-driven from the top of the cam drive gear, at what was now the rear of the block. Pulleys from the outboard side of the water pump were used to power the various accessories.

Drive to the rear wheels was through the torque converter and automatic two-speed box of a Pontiac Tempest transaxle, vintage 1963. The half-shafts to the wheels used the special sliding-type inner universal joints developed by GM's Saginaw Division for the Olds Toronado. Off-the-shelf parts were used as much as possible, such as Corvette brake calipers on Camaro discs at all four wheels and Camaro lower wishbones and knuckles at the front end. The upper suspension arms and the coil/shock units at the front were special, giving a roll center at ground level. Also custom-made for this car was the rack and pinion steering gear with its 23.6 to one ratio.

The main control member for the rear suspension was a massive boxed upper wishbone at each side. Below it were a transverse leaf spring and lateral bracing rods much like those of the stock Corvette. Final placement of the inner pivots of the lateral rods set the rear-wheel camber and established the rear roll center height at two and three-quarter inches above the ground. Consistent understeer was obtained in handling tests, with a three-quarter-inch anti-roll bar in front and F70 x 15 tires on eight-inch rims. Maximum cornering grip of 1.0 g. was measured with wider-section tires on the same rims, H70 in front and L70 in the rear, to match the car's 40/60 front/rear weight distribution.

Overall weight of the XP-880 was about one hundred pounds over the target figure at 3,300 pounds. That still left it 200 pounds lighter than a production Corvette with the same engine, which it roughly matched in its overall dimensions. Front and rear track were sixty inches, length was 181 inches and width

five inches greater than the stock model at seventy-four inches. The shape of its fiberglass body was soft and unsurprising, its strictly experimental nature underlined by an absence of headlights. Space in the car's "hips" was used for the deflated spare tire on the right side and for extra luggage accommodation on the left.

During February, 1968 the XP-880 was completed and test running was begun in Michigan. It had covered about 1,000 miles in various evaluations by mid-March, when GM officials realized they had nothing of substance with which to counter the likely appearance of the Ford Mach 2 at the New York Show. Bill Mitchell and Pete Estes decided to spruce up the XP-880 with a metallic blue paint job and put it on the Chevrolet stand in New York as the Astro II. Thus the public saw this car when it was literally fresh from the molds, early in April of 1968.

The XP-880/Astro II was a valid proposal for a future mid-engined Corvette except for the one element of the design that had halted every similar effort in the past: the transaxle. It used an automatic transaxle that was no longer in production, too weak to take the torque a high-performance version of the Mark IV Chevy could deliver, and not well suited to a sports car with only two ratio choices. A design had been prepared for a transaxle version of the new Turbo Hydra-Matic 350, with three speeds, but not even a sample of this existed. And there was still no suitable manual-shift transaxle on the shelves at Chevrolet.

Obviously the Astro II, like its rear-engined predecessor,

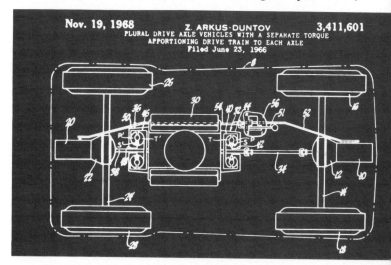

Drive train of CERV II used separate front and rear torque converters.

represented a threat to Zora Arkus-Duntov's traditional right to determine the fundamental future design direction of the Corvette. This internal competition was just as vital in spurring the development of new ideas as the external challenge from Ford. While the XP-880 was still being tested, in the early spring of 1968, Duntov and his designers started working on their alternate choice for a mid-engined sports car, the XP-882. They built their candidate around their solution to the all-important transaxle dilemma.

Just as the XP-720 that became the production Sting Ray had a CERV I to look to for suspension inspiration, so also did the XP-882 have a predecessor in the CERV II that had actually been built and tested by Duntov in 1964. It was conceived during the summer of 1963 as a possible Chevrolet response to Ford's escalating interest in long-distance racing. Ford had negotiated openly that year to buy Ferrari, and after failing in this had hired the British Lola car company to help it build the car that became the GT40, racing for the first time in Europe in 1964.

CERV II represented Chevy's proposed direct opposition to the Ford GT40. The initial plan, set forth late in 1963, called for a prototype plus six racing cars, three for race entries and three as spares. They were to be suitable both for long-distance events like Sebring and Le Mans and also for the top professional sports car races in the United States like those at Riverside and Laguna Seca. None of these events posed limits on the engine sizes of prototypes, so the CERV II was built around an all-aluminum

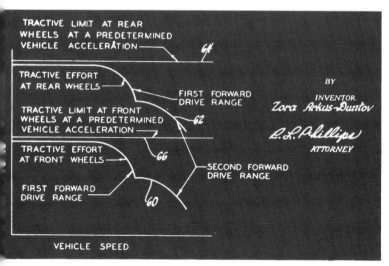

CERV II converters were tailored to match drive effort to road traction.

377-cubic-inch engine like the ones used in the Grand Sport Corvettes at the end of 1963. In fact the engines and other components in those GS racers were being tested at Nassau to determine their suitability for the CERV II.

The power unit installed in the one and only CERV II ever completed was fed fuel by Hilborn constant-flow injection instead of the Weber carburetors used in the Bahamas. This allowed methanol fuel to be used to simulate the output of the engine that was being developed in parallel specifically for the car, a completely special aluminum V-8 with gear-driven single overhead cams operating two valves per cylinder through rocker arms. Also 377 cubic inches in displacement, it was built and tested to produce well over 500 horsepower but was never installed in any car.

CERV II, thanks to Duntov's close relationship with Firestone, was able to use the most advanced racing tires that were then available. Zora was the first engineer outside Firestone to be able to test the new wider low-profile tires it was developing late in 1963 for the 1964 Indy race. He found them highly adhesive to the road and very forgiving of driver error. Duntov chose the 9.50 x 15 size for all four wheels, on rims 8.5 inches wide made up of magnesium by Kelsey-Hayes with knock-off hubs, with the long-distance races in view.

All four wheels and tires were identical in size because Duntov had decided to equip the CERV II with four-wheel drive. In 1963 the first great wave of enthusiasm for four-wheel-driven racing cars was still half a dozen years in the future. Zora elected to use it because his calculations showed that it could provide a higher cornering speed as well as much-improved acceleration with a very powerful engine, more than offsetting the weight handicap of 125 pounds that the drive to the front wheels would add.

Early in the sixties the Chevrolet R&D department had been doing the experimental work with torque converter transmissions in racing cars that led directly to the Chevy-built unit used in the Chaparrals from 1964 onward. Considering this torque converter approach, which was less efficient than the power-shifted automatic he had designed for the earlier CERV II study of 1962, but was far simpler and lighter, Zora saw he could use it for his new car, which would have more than enough power for its planned 1,900-pound design weight. And he would drive the rear wheels through one torque converter and the front wheels, from the front of the engine, through another one. It was a completely new and hence patentable principle.

For detailed torque converter design Duntov turned to GM's central Engineering Staff. He gave them the basic parameters of the car that was then known as the GS-3, later as the GS-10. Its static weight distribution was to be 53.5 percent rearward, for example, and its center of gravity fourteen inches above the ground. Zora also asked for a combination of converters that would take advantage of weight transfer to pump more torque to the car's rear wheels when it was accelerating hard than when it was moving at high speed. The assignment was carried out to perfection by Raymond Michnay of Engineering Staff.

At the back of the engine, driving the rear wheels, an eleven-inch Powerglide torque converter was used, modified so it didn't approach a "locked-up" or nearly one-to-one drive ratio until an input speed of 4,500 rpm. Then for the front wheels there was a ten-inch converter from a Corvair Powerglide, placed ahead of the front-wheel centerline just as it was ahead of the Corvair's rear wheels, rotated in the same sense by the doubly universal-jointed shaft running forward from the front end of the crankshaft. The front converter approached lockup at 4,100 rpm.

Performance calculations showed that with a low final drive ratio the CERV II would accelerate from zero to 60 mph in 2.8 seconds and reach a top speed of 115 mph. With a higher ratio, the maximum would go up to 183 mph and the time to reach sixty would be much longer — about four seconds. Deciding to have the best of both worlds, Duntov equipped both axles of CERV II with compact two-speed gearboxes like those used in the Chaparrals through 1965. Controlled by a single cockpit lever, they gave a direct drive and a 1.5 to one reduction. With the 3.55 to one axle ratio this gave speeds of 107 mph in low and 160 in high, at 6,500 rpm, taking into account the three percent slippage in the converters above 6,000 rpm. The drive to the wheels was through shafts with inner universal joints that gave lateral freedom of shaft movement. Ventilated disc brakes with modified Girling calipers were placed at the wheels.

The suspension design for CERV II was startling in its simplicity. "The front roll center height is about 3½ inches," said Duntov. "That's a standard number with me. At the rear it is about 3 inches above the ground." The trailing radius rods locating the rear hub carriers were angled to give a mild anti-squat effect at the back. On a four-wheel-drive car there's also a tendency for the front to lift up under the direct influence of drive forces, and there are the means at hand to do something about it. An anti-lift effect was built into the front suspension by inclining the axis of the lower wishbone pivots upward toward the rear at an angle of eight degrees to the horizontal.

CERV II's rear hub carriers were machined steel, and those at the front cast nodular iron with forged-steel steering arms. The

Special all-aluminum 377 CID engine intended for CERV II in late 1963 had clever adjustments for gear cam drive and valve rockers.

outer ball-joint locations at the front were angled to give a steering axis that intersected with the ground three inches inboard of the tire patch. Concentric coil springs and adjustable Armstrong shock absorbers were fitted at all four wheels. Their placement at the front provided an object lesson in the packing of a lot of machinery in a small space. Ahead of the front suspension was the Saginaw rack and pinion steering gear.

Fabricated steel arches carrying the front suspension components were welded to the monocoque frame. Made of 0.025-inch sheet steel, the frame began at the footwell, extended back around the fuel cells at the sides — where it was stiffened by glued-on aluminum braces — and ended at the transverse firewall behind the seats. From there to the rear the engine was the major frame member, a design technique that has since become common but was then extremely rare and adventurous. The engine was attached to the firewall at the front and to a two-and-one-half-inch transverse tube at the back, above the torque converter, this being braced also by two one-inch tubes at each side of the engine.

Initial tests in torsion showed that the complete frame structure was below par with a stiffness of 2,000 pound-feet per degree. The curve of frame deflection in torsion had a sharp break through the engine area, and measurements of the engine's cylinder bores showed they were being distorted detectably by

Underground stylists Lapine and Shinoda developed a body shape full-size in clay for Zora Duntov's four-wheel-drive CERV II competition car.

the application of torsion to the frame. With the addition of a four-legged tubular brace above the engine the stiffness jumped to the entirely satisfactory level of 5,000 pound-feet per degree.

Driving positions at the time CERV II was created were sinking lower and lower to reduce the frontal areas of the power-poor Formula 1 Grand Prix cars. Duntov decided not to cater to this trend, since his car was designed to do its job at relatively low speeds, through better acceleration and cornering, and would have a plethora of peak power with which to generate any required maximum speed. Using a more upright seating position allowed Zora to keep the car short, with a ninety-inch wheelbase and 157-inch overall length. Front and rear tracks were set at fifty three and a half inches, and overall width at sixty-six inches.

Around CERV II's upward-ducted front radiator and built-in roll-over bar a bold body shape was styled in the underground studio by Larry Shinoda and Tony Lapine. For the German-born Lapine this was one of the last major projects before he returned to Europe, to Opel, before becoming director of styling for Porsche. Their low-nosed roadster shape executed in fiberglass worked very well. It required only a spoiler at the rear called a "cow's tongue" by Duntov to be entirely stable at the 200 mph it reached on the Milford five-mile track with a high final drive ratio and the 377-cubic-inch engine.

CERV II first rolled on its four driven wheels in March, 1964.

It did not show to best advantage in its early tests at Jim Hall's "Rattlesnake Raceway" at Midland, Texas, in comparison with the rear-wheel-drive GS-2 (forerunner of the Chaparral 2C) built by the Chevy R&D department, for several reasons. The special two-speed box for the drive to the front wheels had not been completed, and the brake discs were then of an experimental — and unsatisfactory — aluminum protected by sprayed-on facings.

During the tests at Midland the CERV II was tried by Jim Hall and Roger Penske, both finding its traction and handling very impressive. Penske in particular liked its driving position and said he was unable to detect any sensation that the engine was powering the front wheels as well as the back ones. At the limit in a turn the CERV II did require an unorthodox technique, because releasing the throttle if speed was excessive tended to cause a fast flat spin. Up to that point, however, its tires and drive system made this the only road-racing car of its era that could make full use of a very large engine and horsepower well in excess of the 500 level.

In the on-again, off-again cycle of attitudes toward racing that prevailed during the Bunkie Knudsen regime at Chevrolet, the light facing CERV II turned from green to red late in the summer of 1964. Chevy had decided that it didn't want to use that car to pose an open challenge to Ford at Le Mans. (It did so later, indirectly, with the 2D Chaparral in 1966 and the 2F in 1967.) Several years afterward, for tire tests conducted by Corvette development driver-engineer Bob Clift, CERV II was fitted with an all-aluminum ZL-1 engine of stock 427-cubic-inch capacity. It carried a single four-barrel carburetor and individual exhaust stacks, both fitted for maximum operating ease rather than ultimate performance.

This was the nature of CERV II, the remarkable experimental car that helped form much of the engineering thought that Zora Duntov and Walt Zetye invested, in 1968, in the XP-882. Though it had never taken part in a race, the CERV II was spurred into being by the pressure of competition, which thus made another contribution to the evolution of the Corvette. Their XP-882 was intended to make full use of the knowledge gained with the CERV II, transferring it to a mid-engined road car that would have the same potential for ultimate development to extraordinarily high performance that the 1963 Sting Ray had offered. But it was to begin where the Stingray, as the car of the seventies was designated, left off.

Duntov and Zetye managed to build into the XP-882 this extra margin for high performance, by making it eminently suitable for four-wheel drive, at the same time that they were solving the very

249

difficult riddle of a low-cost drive train for a mid-engined sports car. The capability for four-wheel drive was built into the chassis of the XP-882 by providing the necessary clearance for axle shafts through the front suspension members, and also angling the pivot lines of the lower front wishbones, like those of the CERV II, so they'd be able to exert an anti-lift force when the chassis was equipped with four-wheel drive. In general the suspension geometry of the XP-882 was made very much like that of the CERV II.

How could the even more exotic idea of a drive to all four tires be combined with a power train from the engine to the wheels that would be less expensive to tool for than anything that had been proposed so far? On the surface it seemed an impossible premise. Several other engineering groups at both Styling and Chevrolet had attempted to solve the transaxle dilemma using the same pieces that now drew the attention of Duntov and Zetye: the drive train of the front-wheel-drive Oldsmobile Toronado, which had been in production since 1966 and had also been used since 1967 for the Cadillac Eldorado.

The first approach had been to move the Toronado engine/drive package to the rear of the car. No matter how it was positioned, however, it placed the engine higher than it could be in a mid-engined sports car, from the standpoints of both rear vision and center-of-gravity height. There was the additional snag that the Toronado drive was available only in automatic-transmission form, so additional tooling would be needed in any case to make a manual-shift version.

In studying the Olds components and thinking about the ways they might be used, Duntov hit on an arrangement that was sufficiently novel to warrant an application in January, 1969 for a patent that was granted in May, 1971. How it works is best understood by a look at the patent drawings on page 249.

From the Olds design, Zora kept the torque converter mounted at the end of the crankshaft and the Morse Hy-Vo chain from the output end of the converter, carrying the drive to another shaft in parallel with the crankshaft. In plan view, however, he made a major change in the placement of the engine. He rotated it clockwise through 90 degrees so the crankshaft was athwart the car instead of longitudinally aligned, and the torque converter was on the left side of the package instead of at the rear.

Duntov adopted the stronger final drive gears of the big Chevy, in an aluminum housing, placed centrally between the wheels. Now he had to connect the output of the ex-Toronado transmission with the input to the differential, which he did with a pair of bevel gears and a short shaft running rearward through

a tube in the engine oil pan, below the crankshaft, to the final drive gears. The oil pan became a sturdy casting to which the differential case was firmly fixed, as was the housing for the right-angle bevel gear pair, so the two could be connected by a shaft without universal joints running in conventional ball and tapered-roller bearings.

As to the transmission itself, there were several choices. The fully automatic Turbo Hydra-Matic unit used in the Toronado and Eldorado would bolt right in. (But by the rearrangement, and the shaft through the oil pan, the engine sat much lower than it could have otherwise.) If this were used, the only parts for which new tooling would be needed were the spiral bevel gear set and case, and the oil-pan casting. Tooling cost was low but the bill for the components was high, since quite a few pieces were needed to turn the drive through 90 degrees four times. The weight was also high, adding up to 950 pounds for the complete package using the 454-cubic-inch version of the Mark IV V-8.

Duntov's patent specifically covers an unusual manual-shift adaptation of this drive line. Instead of the automatic-shifting planetary box of the Turbo Hydra-Matic, Zora placed a small-diameter multiple-disc clutch and a conventional manual gearbox between the Morse chain and the pair of bevel gears. Keeping the torque converter both to absorb impact loads in the drive and also to supply an additional torque reduction, Zora was able to give the XP-882 enough gearing with the compact Saginaw fully-synchronized three-speed transmission.

The multiple-disc clutch could either be freed with a pedal the

Four-legged tubular brace above the engine more than doubled the frame stiffness in torsion of CERV II, which used engine as part of structure.

normal way, for making gear changes, or operated automatically with a servo link to the gear lever like the Porsche Sportomatic drive. The resulting combination of a torque converter with a three-speed manual shift was unlikely to run into heavy resistance from sports car buyers, who could be made aware that it was identical in principle to the transmission used by the Chaparrals to win at the Nürburgring in 1966 and at Britain's Brands Hatch track in 1967.

This Duntov drive line was made to order for the eventual addition of four-wheel drive. From the bevel gear case another shaft could easily be added, to run forward down the center of the car to another differential at the front. Some swapping of positions of the bevel gears and the rear-wheel ring and pinion gears would be needed to get the right shaft rotation senses, but this would have been a relatively minor matter.

Since the front and rear pairs of wheels would tend to run at different speeds in corners, a differential in the bevel box would be needed to give them that freedom. In his patent Duntov also covered the idea of introducing that differential action by means of small separate fluid couplings or torque converters powering each pair of wheels, just like those of the CERV II. These four-wheel-drive ideas were very much a part of the "sales plan" for putting across the concept of the XP-882 as a future Corvette, but they weren't built into the two prototype cars that were under construction during the 1968-69 winter. These had 400-cubic-inch (4 1/8 x 3 3/4 inches) small-block V-8 engines with the Turbo Hydra-Matic transmission.

CERV II handled best at high speed (200 mph) with a "cow's tongue" spoiler protruding from the slot at the rear of the engine compartment.

The transverse placement of the engine and its close proximity to the rear axle allowed the Corvette engineers to give the XP-882 a wheelbase that was unusually short for a big mid-engined car: ninety-five and a half inches. Overall length was about the same as the first-generation Sting Ray at 174½ inches, and the height was cut to only forty-two and a half inches, an inch less than the XP-880, and ten full inches lower than the pre-1963 Corvettes. Track dimensions were set very wide at sixty-one and a half inches, bringing the car's width to seventy-five inches. Curb weight was at the 3,000-pound level, distributed 44/56 front/rear with the 400-cubic-inch engine.

Anticipating the restrictions of future safety laws, the XP-882 was conceived solely as a coupé. This allowed the former "birdcage" supporting the GRP body to be made part of the main frame structure, which was based on a welded steel platform joined to high-level boxed steel frame members at the front and rear. The fuel tank was placed low between the front wheels, with a filler cap in the center of the front deck. An oval lid next to it gave access to the brake fluid reservoirs without the need to lift the whole swing-up front body section, which also housed the space-saver spare tire.

The XP-882 placed the coolant radiator up front. It skirted the issue of ducting the air up or down by releasing it into the front wheel houses, where a vacuum usually prevails. Luggage space was to be provided in the tail of the car, to the rear of the engine, as in the Lamborghini Miura and Ferrari Dino 256 — other transverse-engined sports cars. With its tapering rear end and "boat-tailed" roof line, the straightforward shape of the XP-882 reflected the fact that it was styled at about the same time as the Mako Shark II rework that was dubbed the Manta Ray.

Concentric coil springs and shock absorbers were part of the car's suspension at all four wheels. Exceptionally handsome and new-looking cast magnesium wheels were bolted in place and pierced by ten vent slots near the rims. These gave additional cooling to the outboard disc brakes with experimental aluminum calipers. The fifteen-inch wheels were eight and nine inches wide at front and rear respectively, carrying Firestone tires of E60 and G60 section.

These were the design highlights of a very serious effort to produce a mid-engined car that would be a fit successor to the established Corvette. The two cars were completed in the spring of 1969, and testing was just beginning to get under way when the XP-882 program came — to use a Duntov-ism —"to a screeching halt."

Several influences combined to garage these promising cars.

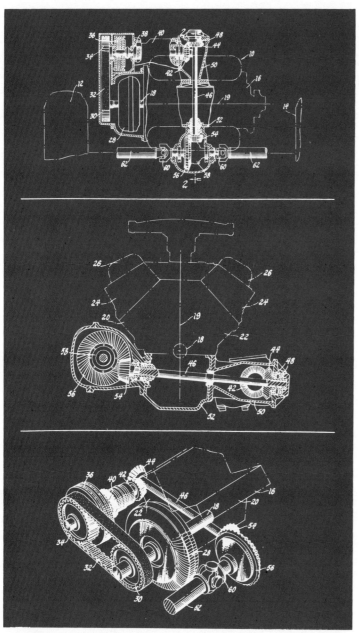

In plan view, side view and perspective, drawings in patent granted to Zora Arkus-Duntov show principle of XP-882 drive train. Shaft through engine oil pan (46) is enclosed in a tube, not exposed as shown here.

One was the protracted strike at General Motors, which raised questions about the status of many future plans. Another was the attitude of the Chevrolet sales department. It saw in the XP-882 a car which would cost substantially more than the present model and would offer no greater performance initially, no more passenger and luggage room, would be offered only as a coupé, and, for the first year or two, would be sold only with an automatic transmission. Under these conditions Joe Pike and Chevy sales couldn't be optimistic about the market outlook, even if polls of Corvette owners did indicate that they'd enthusiastically welcome a mid-engined model.

Decisive was the outlook of Chevrolet's youthful new general manager, John DeLorean. Tall, lean and good-looking, DeLorean had come from Packard to Pontiac as an engineer, and had stressed innovative product design as chief engineer and then as general manager of Pontiac. With such products as the restyled Grand Prix, built on a cheaper intermediate chassis instead of a costly low-volume full-size chassis with no loss in product appeal, DeLorean had enhanced Pontiac's profit picture by making less look like more and pocketing the difference to the good of his division and General Motors.

Now, at Chevrolet, DeLorean was being asked to be enthusiastic about a new Corvette that promised to be very tricky to tool and produce at a profitable price and volume, a car that risked not being profitable at all. This was not the kind of decision he wanted to make at the very beginning of his career at GM's biggest and most important division, in a post that was an acknowledged and proven stepping-stone to bigger and better things at General Motors.

DeLorean stopped work on the XP-882 and asked the engineers to look instead at the idea of a Corvette built on a shortened version of the new Camaro chassis that was set for introduction early in 1970. If he could build an acceptable Corvette on this low-cost basis, DeLorean reasoned, and add enough visible value in the car's styling and features to merit the cost premium the Corvette had always commanded, he'd be able to repeat at Chevrolet the triumph he had scored with the Pontiac Grand Prix. But in this he collided with an united front put up by the stylists, engineers and salesmen. None was willing to accede to such a drastic devaluation of the concept of the Corvette, i.e., to the abandonment of its independent rear suspension and four-wheel disc brakes. No positive move in this direction was made.

The *status quo* was again altered early in 1970 by the forces of competition. Word reached General Motors that Ford, after an internal battle between rival designs and factions, had decided to

Original styling of 1970 XP-882 was more successful in its high, pointed tail than its blocky front end, which housed the radiator, fuel tank, and spare.

back (and later to buy) Italy's de Tomaso in the production of a mid-engined sports car to be marketed in the U.S. by Lincoln-Mercury dealers. Also, they found, American Motors had styled another mid-engined machine that was to be made in limited numbers in Italy by Bizzarrini. This, the AMX/3, was also to be sold in the United States. Both cars were slated to make their debut at New York's International Automobile Show in the first days of April, 1970.

Attended by the world's press and featuring the products of most of the world's makers, the New York Show in these years had great aesthetic importance, if little commercial significance, to American car builders. Bill Mitchell of GM Styling was not pleased at the idea of being upstaged by other firms during this year's performance. Not long before the show, in a frank effort to get the XP-882 program in gear again, Zora Duntov took Mitchell and Chevy's chief engineer, Alex Mair, to see the completed prototypes in the inner sanctum of Chevrolet Engineering, the "design check" room, where new cars went together for the first time. Their reaction was immediate and unanimous: "Let's put it in the New York Show!"

In a tremendous rush one car was painted metallic silver and dressed for its show appearance. That its showing in New York took the industry by surprise is indicated by the comments of *Car Life*: "Nobody has secrets like Chevrolet has secrets. The day before the New York Auto Show opening, everybody knew about

Ford's Pantera, the American Motors AMX/3, the latest version of Mercedes-Benz' C-111. Official word and scuttlebutt agreed: The mid-engined Corvette was dead as Marley. Chevrolet would display its new engine, but no real show cars. And the doors opened, and lo, there was a mid-engined Corvette. It didn't even have a fancy name, simply a plain, bold label — Corvette prototype."

In *Motor Trend* Eric Dahlquist put it more dramatically: "April 2, 1970. A day that will live in infamy at Ford Motor Company. A day when Chevrolet roared out of the sun with the throttle wide-open and the wind shrieking and watched their tracers stitch into the shining sides of the new de Tomaso, sending it down in flames at the 52nd Annual New York Automobile Show. The *raison d'etre* for the de Tomaso in the first place was to dim Chevy's image, a plan frustratingly scotched before the eyes of thousands in Gotham City."

The de Tomaso was delayed more than a year in its arrival at Lincoln-Mercury dealerships, and the AMX/3 never made the move to significant production. But the impact of the confrontation in New York had been strong enough to impel Chevrolet back into the mid-engined car business. Work went ahead again on further development of the XP-882 concept. Detailed engineering was carried out on its drive train combinations. The small-block 400-cubic-inch engine was teamed with the Turbo Hydra-Matic transmission, while a new manual-shift drive was designed to suit the

454 Mark IV engine—the one that would be relied on for ultimate performance. To keep pace with tire developments the wheel rims were further widened, to nine inches in front and ten in rear. This well suited the car's weight distribution of 40/60 front/rear with the big engine and 43/57 with the smaller one.

General manager John DeLorean approved this chassis work and also authorized Bill Mitchell's stylists to give the car a completely new shape, one that John himself influenced strongly. It replaced the angular XP-882 design with more rounded coupe lines, featuring a "sugar scoop" recessed rear window, bold fender flares, a trunk compartment in the tail, NASA scoops in the front deck, and hidden headlights that swung into place around longitudinal pivot axes like those of the Opel GT. Its interior was sumptuous, with high-backed bucket seats and a deep padded cowl arching over the main instruments.

Sufficiently changed to warrant a new designation, XP-895, this new Corvette prototype was built as a running car by Chevrolet Engineering in 1971. The non-stressed outer skin of its integral steel structure was made largely of steel in this first sample, whose shape was not very faithful, in detail, to that of the clay model at GM Design Staff. Thus it was heavier than John DeLorean had hoped: about 3,500 pounds, little lighter than the production Corvette.

DeLorean was looking for added lightness when he encountered a top executive of the Reynolds Metals Company of Richmond, Virginia, the firm that had put the aluminum in the Vega engine block. "Would you be willing to make an all-aluminum body for a Corvette?" DeLorean asked. "It would be your project, but we'd help you as much as we can." Reynolds saw this as a chance to learn more about the real problems encountered in making an aluminum auto body/frame using forming and assembly methods similar to those employed in mass production. They agreed to give it a try.

On March 13, 1972 Reynolds started making a duplicate XP-895 body of aluminum. For all but a few of its parts (such as bumpers) they used their 2036-T4 alloy, which contains some copper and magnesium and which was specifically developed to be suited for use in auto bodies. Their choice of a single alloy for most of the body was made with a view toward the future recycling of aluminum bodies, aluminum being much more valuable than steel in scrap form. The fewer the alloys in a body, the higher its worth becomes as metal scrap.

The actual construction of the aluminum XP-895 was done at Creative Engineering in Detroit, a firm experienced in the building of prototypes. The steel-bodied car was just being finished there, so some temporary tools and jigs that could be used to make the aluminum counterpart were already handy. Parts were formed with dies of wood, some with plastic or metal inserts, and some of Kirksite, a metal alloy,

chiefly zinc, which can be easily cast to make stamping dies that will form as many as several hundred similar parts before they're worn out. (Remember that Chevy's plan was originally to make the '53 Corvette of steel using Kirksite dies?) In all almost 150 tons of Kirksite was used for dies during the making of the steel and aluminum XP-895 bodies.

Reynolds used normal automotive spot-welding and joining techniques as much as possible, discovering that the best bond was a combination of a spot weld with an epoxy adhesive. On June 21, 1972 they deemed the body complete and turned it over to Chevrolet Engineering for static tests and evaluation. Analyzed part by part in comparison with the steel body, it weighed 38.9 percent less—quite a substantial reduction. It amounted to a difference of some 450 pounds between the steel body/frame, which scaled about 1,150 pounds, and the 700-pound aluminum equivalent.

Reynolds expected the project to end with the delivery and analysis of the body, but it didn't quite work out that way. To the surprise of the Virginians, the Chevy men used their body to build a running car. They

In 1972 Chevrolet and Reynolds Metals Company jointly completed the XP-895, which saved 500 pounds with its all-aluminum integral frame and body.

pulled the running gear and drive train out of the steel frame and installed it in the aluminum XP-895; everything fit perfectly because they were identical. Even the interior trim was zipped out of one car and zipped into the other one. Both bodies were painted silver, so the two versions of the XP-895 can't be told apart in photos.

When the aluminum edition was built up there was, for some obscure reason, a further reduction in weight of fifty pounds. Instead of a 3,500-pound steel Corvette prototype, Chevrolet now had a much more lively aluminum car scaling only 3,000 pounds. It represented, as Reynolds said, "an important milestone in the application of aluminum in auto-body construction," even though it hadn't solved all the problems that would be raised by the making of such a body in high volume. It was a pioneer in the application of the aluminum alloy forming and joining techniques that Detroit will use more and more in years to come to lighten its products, just as the Corvette itself pioneered the glass-reinforced plastic medium that's spread, piece by piece, to more and more mass-produced cars.

The extra cost of this construction method kept aluminum from being the material of choice in 1972 when Chevrolet calculated the price tag of building the XP-895 in Corvette-sized numbers. Any way John DeLorean's men looked at it, they found that this mid-engined coupe with its rather cramped passenger compartment had to cost more, a lot more, than the existing 'Vette. To make sure that no possible way to build it had been overlooked, DeLorean even sent an emissary to Europe to solicit bids on the body and chassis from the lower-cost factories there. He failed to return with a favorable verdict, however. Like the mid-engined prototypes before it, the XP-895 came, as Zora Duntov would put it, to a screeching halt.

This remarkable chassis, the one that first took shape under the XP-882 in 1968, was offered yet another lease on life by the ingenuity of the Arkus-Duntov crew and the enthusiasm of GM's president, Ed Cole, for a new kind of engine. The horsepower of the Wankel rotary engine would, it seemed, be just what was needed to propel a new Corvette into being.

Chapter 19

ROTARY CORVETTES

The car looked brutal, even sinister. Its shovel nose flared forward from a low coupe cab, behind which there was no body at all, just high frame rails and a tangle of tubes and brackets around an engine that didn't look like an engine at all. It sounded like one, though, its roar reaching an ear-splitting crescendo and then fading, followed by backfires and gouts of flame from the exhaust pipes, as the coupe braked to a stop off the loop at the end of the dead-straight concrete highway.

The doors opened and two men in shirtsleeves stepped out, smiling. The passenger was a slim silver-haired man wearing aviator-style sunglasses. The driver was darker-haired, bespectacled, with broad shoulders and an even broader grin. Ed Cole, president of General Motors, had just driven this car to a peak speed of 148 miles an hour on the one-mile check road at the GM Technical Center. It had still been accelerating strongly when he was forced to back off the throttle. His passenger was Zora Arkus-Duntov, whose men had built this, the first experimental Corvette with a four-rotor Wankel engine. Duntov did not mind at all that Cole, an excellent driver, had gone several miles an hour faster than he.

This was July of 1972, the summer when GM's enthusiasm for the Wankel rotary engine was at its giddy peak. A year and a half had passed since GM signed (on November 10, 1970) its historic agreement with the companies that held the patent rights to the Wankel engine. This clever engine burns fuel and air in the well-known four-stroke cycle but does so without the jerky back-and-forth reciprocating motion of the conventional piston powerplant. Around each of its near-triangular rotors there are three working chambers, in each of which some part of the four-stroke cycle is taking place as the rotor both turns and "orbits," on an eccentric shaft, within its housing. Its ingenious concept lets this happen without valves of any kind, and all their attendant trappings, since the rotor's edges are used to open and close the inlet and exhaust ports.

Known as the Wankel engine after its German inventor, Felix Wankel, this revolutionary powerplant was dubbed the GMRCE (General Motors Rotary Combustion Engine) by the executives of GM's Engineering Staff, where it was being developed to suit GM's needs in 1970 and, more intensively, in 1971. Early in 1972 the responsibility of adapting the GMRCE to production was assigned to Chevrolet, which was to work with the Hydra-Matic Division, which built the prototype GM Wankels.

Where Chevy and exotic engines were being brewed together, could the Corvette be far away? Of course not! By the summer of 1972 two Corvette prototypes were roaming the roads of Milford under Wankel power: one the four-rotor missile we met above, and the other a trim little coupe powered by a two-rotor GMRCE. The use of the Wankel in a new Corvette did not have top priority in GM's plans. That honor went to a special sporty version of the Vega that was being readied for a two-rotor engine to be built in six-figure volumes in the 1975 model year—the car that came out, minus the GMRCE, as the Monza 2+2.

The Corvette and the GM rotary met in these two cars for several reasons. One was that this glamorous sports car could serve as a display case for the new kind of engine, one that could advance its cause inside GM. Another was that plans were being made then to switch all the corporation's cars over to the GMRCE, so the Corvette would inevitably follow suit. Yet another reason was that it was beginning to look like there'd be no chance at all to introduce a new mid-engined Corvette unless it offered something extra, something like Wankel power.

Chevy general manager DeLorean had not been especially warm to the Wankel at first, in the Corvette or otherwise. He considered it a gimmicky engine that posed more problems, especially of exhaust emissions, than it solved. At first grudgingly and later with enthusiasm, DeLorean became a convert to the Wankel Corvette after it was made crystal clear that there'd be no new Corvette at all unless it had a GMRCE under its hood. Both the rotary-powered Corvette prototypes were originally built while he was the general manager of Chevrolet.

The first of these cars, the one that later became known as the Corvette 2-Rotor, wasn't originally a Corvette at all. It was known simply as the "Chevrolet GT" because GM Design Staff, which had the happy inspiration to build it, felt that it could meet several different product needs in the corporation. It was seen as a successor both to the Corvette and to the Opel GT, the little two-seater coupe whose production run in Germany was drawing to a close. With the right design,

Having in common only the use of GM rotary engines and the Corvette name, the 2-Rotor and 4-Rotor experimental cars were the auto show sensations of 1973.

Completed in 1972, the Corvette 2-Rotor had a surprisingly roomy interior. Mounts for rear coil springs and shocks are visible at sides of engine room.

thought GM chief designer Bill Mitchell, a new small sports coupe could be built in several countries and sold in many. It could be the first "world sports car."

In overall charge of this project was the chief of advanced design, Clare MacKichan, whom we first met in Chapter 2 as the stylist whose superb taste helped refine the lines of the original 1953 Corvette. Heading the Experimental Studio where the car was designed was tall and taciturn Dick Finegan, a man of exceptional creative ability, and assisting him on the engineering side was a former Opel man, Otto Soeding. Design work on it began early in 1971, or soon after GM had inked its Wankel pact, under the designation XP-987GT, for the sports car was to use, amidships, the same drive train that was being planned for the projected line of Wankel-powered front-wheel-drive Nova-sized sedans that carried the XP-987 tag at GM Engineering Staff.

"We'd played with different designs for small sports cars with the rotary engine," recalled "Mac" MacKichan, "with front-wheel drive and other layouts—on paper. But our real love was always the mid-engined car. We kept it down to the absolute minimum size that we could for two people, their luggage and the various safety requirements, because there was a feeling that the Corvette had gotten too big and heavy. We wanted to start out small—about Ferrari Dino size." The dimensions of the XP-987GT were in fact very close to those of the Dino 246GT, and its lines were such that it looked even smaller than the Dino when the two were parked side by side.

By June of 1971 Design Staff had completed a full-size fiberglass model of the "Chevrolet GT" plus what the designers called a "first-class space buck," a highly realistic full-scale showing where all its components would go. It portrayed a somewhat speculative three-

rotor GMRCE offset to the right side, feeding a large catalytic converter to its left. Backed up by a detailed engineering report and production proposal, these models were shown to GM's top management and its directors that June. So convincing and appealing was the evidence displayed that Design Staff and Chevrolet were authorized to take the XP-987GT another step forward by building a complete running car.

In Dick Finegan's studio the car's shape went through another design phase, one step closer to possible production, in the fall of 1971. In subtle ways it took on a bolder, more masculine look, with deeper, richer modeling around the wheels and the nose. The next step would normally have been to have the body built in GM Design's own shops, but for several reasons this did not happen. The task was assigned to Pininfarina in Turin, Italy instead because it seemed likely that they could do it more cheaply, and also more quickly, a point that had suddenly become important because the goal was to have the running XP-987GT ready for the next showing of future products to the GM board of directors in June of 1972.

This hurry-up schedule put extra pressure on Chevrolet Engineering, which had to provide the chassis for the running car. So tight was the timing that there was no way that Zora Arkus-Duntov's group could both design and build a unique chassis that could be delivered to Pininfarina when they wanted it. So, as you will read here for the first time, they started with an existing mid-engined sports car chassis: that of the Porsche 914!

Duntov's chief chassis man, Walt Zetye, worked straight through the year-end holidays on the preparation of the car's underpinnings. He started with the platform frame of a Porsche 914, shortening it by six and a half inches to reduce the wheelbase to the desired ninety

Deep door cuts made entry into the 2-Rotor Corvette delightfully easy.

inches. The Porsche running gear was kept at the front and rear, consisting of rack and pinion steering, MacPherson strut front suspension with torsion bar springing, and trailing arms at the rear sprung by concentric coil/shock units. The use of beautiful American Racing aluminum wheels, with seven-inch rims, and changes to the mounting points of the suspension units gave the XP-987GT a wider track than the 914: fifty-six inches at both front and rear. Behind the wheels were the German-made Ate disc brakes taken from the Porsche chassis.

Equipped with a mocked-up power unit, the chassis was air-freighted to Turin on January 14, 1972, just forty-three days after Zetye started working on it. Guided by Otto Soeding, Pininfarina erected the body, according to drawings and full-size plaster surface models, in twelve weeks—a virtuoso performance. Then it was flown back to Michigan, fitted out mechanically, and prepared for its official corporate debut in June. Though it wasn't exposed to the GM board then, the "Chevrolet GT" was shown privately to top company officials at Milford. Not until more than a year later was this coupe shown to the public, at the Frankfurt Show in September, 1973. By then its trim was changed from all silver to red with a natural leather interior; and its name was changed to Corvette 2-Rotor.

It was sublimely ironic that some European journalists jibbed at the "impracticality" of the 2-Rotor when they saw it at Frankfurt, this being their routine reaction to any American "dream car." These same critics failed to spot the pure production origins of the car's suspension and seemed oblivious to the fact that its design met fully the needs of the tough American safety and bumper standards. In fact it would have been a lovely body for the Porsche 914! At both ends there were urethane plastic bumpers backed by hat-section steel beams, connected

to Delco Enersorbers with a two and a half inch stroke, painted to blend with the color of the body. Made by GM's Guide Lamp Division, the rectangular headlights were early prototypes of the ones GM introduced on many models in 1975. Indeed, the front-end design of the 2-Rotor had much in common with that of the 1975 Chevy Monza 2+2.

Wind tunnel testing of a three-eighths-size clay model helped refine the shape of the 2-Rotor and, with the simulation of internal ducting, assured that cooling air would go where it should. Slots under the car's nose, just ahead of the chin spoiler, let air into a sealed duct to a copper cross-flow radiator, in front of which were two electric fans and a condenser for the air conditioner. Behind it a vertical bulkhead diverted the warm air to the left, right and down, and formed the front wall of the small nose compartment that housed a space-saver spare, the climate control hardware and the vacuum brake booster.

Cooling for the engine room—crucial in Wankel-powered cars—flowed in through the scoops at the sides of the 2-Rotor. Air removal from the engine's enclosure was accelerated by a small dam across its leading surface under the car, by a vestigial cooling fan on the right-hand end of the transversely-mounted engine, and by an exhaust duct from the right side of the compartment to the outlet slots in the upper surface of the rear bumper. The tunnel tests showed that these flow paths would work, that the car would be stable, and that its lowest drag coefficient was a moderate 0.396 with a frontal area of 16.04 square feet. (Porsche 914 total drag is slightly higher with an area of 17.24 square feet and 0.377 drag coefficient; multiply the two together to get an indication of the relative total aerodynamic drag.)

Space was found at the rear of the 2-Rotor for the fourteen-gallon fuel tank, which was given a triangular cross-section so it would fit between the sloping seat backs and the engine compartment. In the tail was a luggage compartment of more than eight cubic feet, sized to accept the standard dimensions of popular suitcases. The coupe's interior was the work of the Experimental Interiors Studio, headed by Ed Donaldson. It featured a panel surface that swept down and around the driver and was punctured by deep recesses for the kilometer speedometer, 9,000-rpm tach, and smaller dials. The small-diameter steering wheel tilted and telescoped; the driver's seat tilted electrically, and the pedals were manually adjustable for distance.

Lifting the insulated lid at the rear of the 2-Rotor exposed its GM rotary engine—or at least the air cleaner and accessories that were mounted in the space above it. The engine was offset about seven inches to the right of the car's centerline, making room for the transaxle, also mounted transversely, to its left. This car was equipped with a fully automatic transmission with a torque converter and three forward speeds, in an aluminum housing. Between the converter and the planetary gears a train of helical gears went down and slightly to the rear of the differential, and from there half-shafts with constant-velocity universal joints took the drive to the wheels. A design for a four-speed manual gearbox, with a coaxial mainshaft and input shaft like that of the Corvair, was also prepared to fit into this drive train.

The engine itself was dubbed the RC2-266 by GM, indicating that it had two rotors and was—by GM standards—of 266 cubic inches displacement. GM counted only two of the three chambers around each rotor because, like some of the other developers of the Wankel for automobiles, they felt that this gave a rating that was like that of a reciprocating engine of comparable power output. The actual displacement of all six working chambers in the RC2-266 was thus half again as great: 399 cubic inches or 6,538 cc, the size of each chamber being 1,090 cc.

The engine used in the 2-Rotor was a Generation I GMRCE, the type being developed by GM Engineering Staff between October, 1971 and April, 1972. Instead of the cast iron rotor housings that had been tried unsuccessfully on these engines, this one had aluminum rotor housings sandwiched between cast iron intermediate and end housings. With side inlet ports, fed by a single Rochester Quadrajet carburetor, it produced about 180 bhp at 6,100 rpm with a very strong torque curve. Had it been tuned for higher power, for example with peripheral inlet ports, it could have developed as much as 250 bhp at 7,500 rpm; the car's tachometer redline was at 8,500 rpm.

A brief ride in the 2-Rotor at the GM Tech Center showed it to be a delightfully refined car. Getting in was astonishingly easy; the big door seemed to open up the whole side of the car in such a way that you could just walk in and sit down. Though it looked small, even tiny, from outside, the 2-Rotor was satisfyingly roomy inside—just the opposite of the production Corvette. The rotary engine ran with a deep, muttering, purring sound, pleasant yet authoritative. It sounded strangely familiar and then the realization dawned. It was just like a well-balanced Corvair six!

Though its power output was modest, the 2-Rotor's equally moderate weight of 2,600 pounds gave it performance about as good as that of the production Corvette with the base engine. This was lively by the standards of most sports cars, but it did not meet the standards of Zora Arkus-Duntov, as anyone familiar with Corvette history will quickly appreciate. Zora was willing enough to adapt to the Wankel era that GM then seemed to be entering but he wanted to do it on his own terms, terms that did not include a firm ceiling on horsepower and performance. The man whose team created the immortal Mark IV engine couldn't be happy with a little two-rotor Wankel that would be hard pressed to top 200 horsepower on a good day. "It's only a Nova engine!" he would moan.

Early in 1972, with the 2-Rotor a-building in Italy, Duntov decided to make his own entry into the Wankel world. He turned to his engine-wise lieutenant, Gib Hufstader, and said, "Gib, make me a fast car." The Corvette 4-Rotor was the magnificent result. Gib chose as his foundation the original XP-882, the very same car that had startled the New York Show spectators in April, 1970. (See Chapter 18.) Since then it had served as a test mule for Chevrolet Engineering. Now Hufstader pulled out its V-8 engine and made ready to adapt *two* two-rotor GM Wankels to its unique Toronado-based drive train.

First Zora and Gib had to coax two experimental two-rotor GMRCE's away from Engineering Staff—no easy matter. They managed to get two early 1971-type engines, RC2-195 models as used experimentally

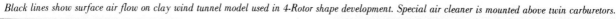

Black lines show surface air flow on clay wind tunnel model used in 4-Rotor shape development. Special air cleaner is mounted above twin carburetors.

then in the front of Peugeot 304's, mounted vertically. Gib placed them transversely in the engine bay of the XP-882, one on each side of the shaft that runs back from the bevels at the transmission output to the differential at the rear of the power pack. He connected the "back" of the right-hand engine to the "front" of the one on the left by means of a welded box of quarter-inch-thick steel plate that formed a central chassis or armature for the whole engine-transmission-axle assembly.

Inside the steel box the eccentric shafts of the two engines were joined together by an internally splined steel shaft. From a sprocket on that shaft a cogged rubber belt was driven, a belt that did many jobs. It rose up to rotate an ignition distributor developed for this engine by Delco-Remy, a special unit that turned at engine speed, instead of the usual half speed, and was powered by four coils to spark the eight plugs in all, two for each rotor. The cogged belt also drove the alternator, at the top, and a single oil pressure pump, serving both engines, at the bottom of its travel. Two vee belts at the right side or "front" of the right-hand engine turned other accessories: air conditioning compressor,

power steering pump, and the single water pump—from a Mark IV V-8!—that cooled both engines.

This was the unorthodox power unit that was propelling the XP-882, minus its rear deck, on that day in July, 1972 when Cole and Duntov gave it an airing at the Tech Center. From a standing start in March, 1972 it had taken Gib Hufstader only two months to bring this four-rotor engine to life on the dynamometer, and less than a month more to have it running in the XP-882 chassis. With 48.75 cubic inches in each chamber the complete engine would have been rated as an RC4-390 by the GM system and actually displaced a total of 585 cubic inches, or 9,586 cc, in its twelve working chambers. This made it the largest displacement Wankel engine ever installed in an automobile. Never officially measured, its output was on the order of 350 bhp at 7,000 rpm—a speed at which its exhaust note was described as an "incredible shriek."

Some of GM's stylists had a chance to drive the Wankelized XP-882 in its original crude state that summer of '72. This certainly helped

Both experimental Wankel Corvettes—the 4-Rotor is in the foreground—starred in the General Motors display at the Paris Salon of October, 1973.

Digital clock/timing readout is located at front of 4-Rotor console.

energize the interest at Design Staff that led to the decision, in January, 1973, to style and build a completely new body for the car. To be precise the design work began in January, in Henry Haga's studio under Chuck Jordan's direction, on a shape intended to be that of a future Corvette, and not until April was the design altered to suit the XP-882 chassis and the order given to build it into a runner, again with a target in view: a debut at the Paris Salon in October. Bill Mitchell established this specific goal to keep the project moving ahead as fast as possible.

"These days," said Henry Haga in 1973, "we start by drawing a datum line where the rules say the bumpers have to be, and then we design a car between them." If only it were really that easy to design a sports coupe as clean, sleek and exciting as the 4-Rotor, as it came to be named. Its profile was characterized by the steep 72-degree slope of its windshield (against 66 degrees on the 2-Rotor) and by its tapered nose and tail, breaking away from the boxy, wedged, chopped-off sports car shapes of the Sixties.

The shape is aerodynamically as good as it looks. Tests of a three-eighths-scale model in the GALCIT wind tunnel in California in April, 1973 revealed the exceptionally low drag coefficient of 0.325. The tests showed that drag was reduced by the release of warm air from the engine room through louvers just behind the rear windows, designed to be opened electrically when the ignition was switched on, and also through fixed glass louvers in the rear quarter windows. Cool air

entered the engine room through scoops at the sides; during the tunnel tests the flares of the front wheel openings were reshaped to improve the flow of air into these scoops.

All the glazing in the 4-Rotor used a new thinner, lighter safety glass. Its side windows were fixed in place, making the coupe fully dependent on the happy working of its air conditioning. Entry was by swing-up doors of an unique "bi-fold" design. To open one from the outside you first inserted your fingers in a horizontal grip slot in the body side and squeezed it to unlatch the door. Then you lifted up, swinging the door out and up in the familiar gull-wing manner. The difference was that there was a hinge just below the window that kept the lower part of the door tucked in. Its motion was controlled by a parallelogram link, and gas-filled struts helped you heft the door upward.

The 4-Rotor driver eased himself through a rather narrow opening and into a plush suede-and-leather seat. A single small toggle switch adjusted the car to him: Moved up and down it tilted the seat electrically, around a pivot at the front, and pressed forward or back it directed the pedals to the right position. The steering column could be telescoped and tilted, and when the latter occurred the smoked black instrument binnacle behind the wheel moved up and down with it.

That black binnacle came alive with glowing lights and numbers when the 4-Rotor was switched on. In it were three digital displays, the main one, using gas-discharge tubes, being the speedometer. The others had two alternate driver-selected functions apiece: fuel level and oil pressure in one display, and water temperature and battery voltage in the other. Below them there was a horizontal row of twenty-nine light-emitting diodes (LED's) that comprised a 7,000 rpm tachometer, with an LED at every 250 rpm space. As the engine revved up the LED's brightened in sequence with crisp, inertia-free response. At 6,250 rpm their color switched from green to amber, and those above were red.

Another digital display was mounted on the console in this ingenious interior, worked out by the Design Staff's Interior Studios, under Don Schwarz, and especially by Jim Orr of Chevrolet Interiors. It had multiple functions, showing the frequency to which the radio was tuned, or the time, or the date, or several different elapsed time readings that could be useful for touring or rallying. Also on the console were some warning lights, climate controls, the handbrake and transmission range selector, radio and other minor controls.

Using GRP panels on a framework of rectangular-section steel and aluminum tubes, Design Staff's own shops built and assembled this complex body and interior and could point with pride, afterward, to having done so in half a week less than it took Pininfarina to make the 2-Rotor body. That half-week was important because the all-silver car was just ready in time to be air-freighted to Paris for its debut, sharing a stand with the 2-Rotor, at the Salon in October. To say that the sight of the two beautiful rotary Corvettes together created a fine impression would be to indulge in understatement. They were among the major hits of the show.

Since Paris the Wankel Corvettes and the 4-Rotor in particular have been centerpieces for Chevy displays at many auto shows. A name change for the 4-Rotor was in prospect because plans were firm, at this writing, to convert its power train back to a reciprocating V-8. This was scheduled because the big dual-twin rotary engine had never been fully developed to run well at all speeds. While it was a bear at full power it wasn't too tractable at idle and part throttle. Not intended to cast doubt on the viability of the Wankel program at GM (though the production of Chevy's rotary was indefinitely postponed at the end of 1974), this swap to a V-8 will simply make the car more useful as a show vehicle and more realistic as the prototype of a possible future production Corvette.

The 4-Rotor was especially significant as a car to which important contributions were made by up-and-coming members of the GM groups that care about the Corvette. Walt Zetye's stamp was on its chassis (and that of the 2-Rotor) and Gib Hufstader's brand was on its unique engine. Working with Henry Haga on its exterior styling was Jerry Palmer, who took over direction of the Corvette Studio (officially Chevy III) when Haga was reassigned to Opel late in '74.

In the light of these contributions it was noteworthy that one of the many gifts received by Zora Arkus-Duntov at his retirement dinner on January 13, 1975 was a stunningly beautiful and meticulously detailed scale model of the 4-Rotor Corvette. This Design Staff creation depicted a car that was one of the most exciting ever to leave Zora's hands. It also portrayed a car that showed how extremely able the people were who had been apprentices, so to speak, in the Arkus-Duntov school of high performance, and whose responsibility it would be to bear the Corvette banner in the years to come. It spoke well for the continuation of one of the proudest traditions the American auto industry has ever known.

Novel design features of 4-Rotor included bi-fold gullwing doors, wiper pivots placed far outboard, and transparent glass engine room vent louvers.

CORVETTES IN COLOR

We wish they could be three-dimensional too, accompanied by those distinctive,
ominous sounds that have said "Corvette coming!"
for some two decades now. But, as the next best thing, herewith we present
a Corvette treasury: a portfolio of drawings of the production cars,
portraits of the historic first Corvette and its
descendant twenty years later, a collection of experimental and show cars,
and a miscellany of Corvettes as they are happiest—in action.
Dimension and sound are left to your imagination—which, come to think
of it, is something every Corvette aficionado naturally possesses in abundance.

PORTFOLIO OF
CORVETTE PRODUCTION CARS

Illustrations by Ken Rush

The First Corvette: Introduced September, 1953
In Production Through December, 1955. Units built: 4,640

1956: Units built—3,467

'56

'57

1957: Units built—6,339

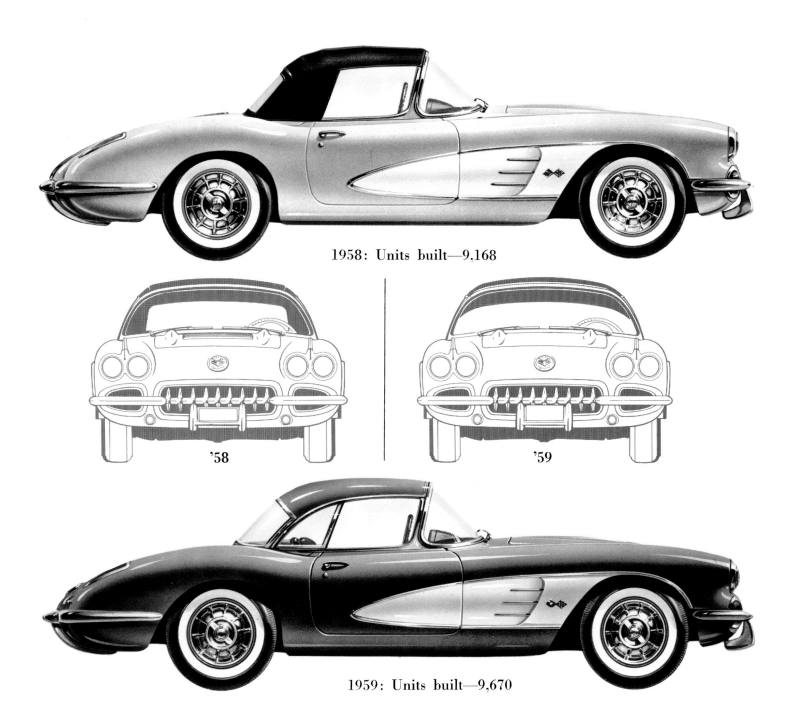

1958: Units built—9,168

'58

'59

1959: Units built—9,670

1960: Units built—10,261

'60

'61

1961: Units built—10,939

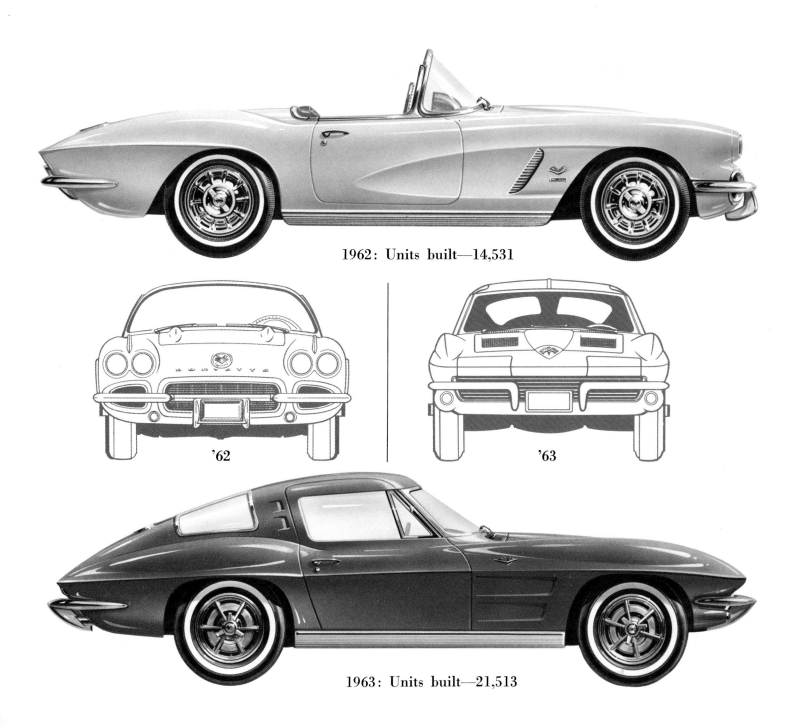

1962: Units built—14,531

'62

'63

1963: Units built—21,513

1964: Units built—22.229

'64

'65

1965: Units built—23,562

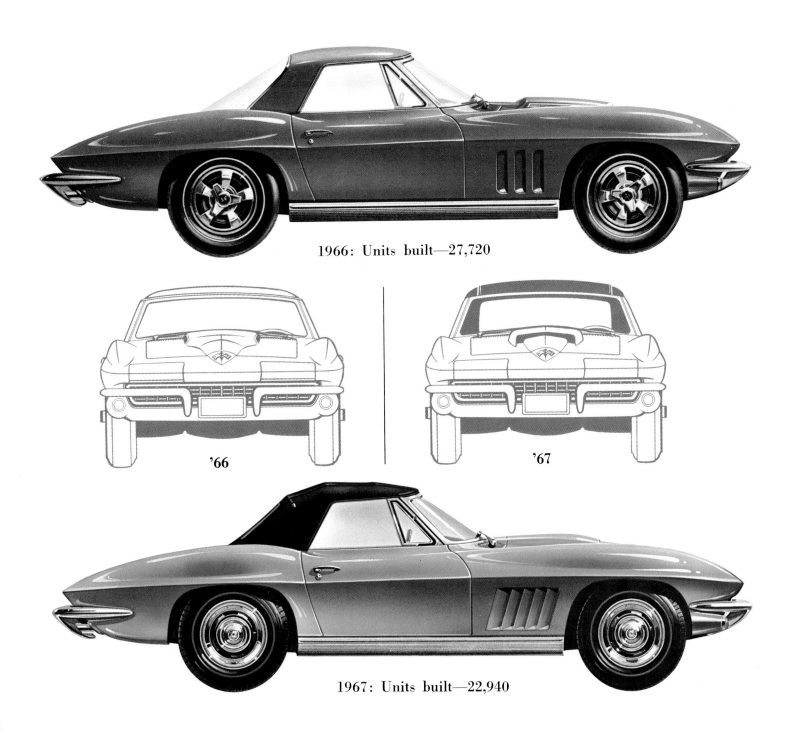

1966: Units built—27,720

'66

'67

1967: Units built—22,940

1968: Units built—28,566

'68　'69

1969: Units built—38,762

1970-71-72: Total units built—66,121

'70-71-72

'73

1973: Units built—34,464

1974: Units built—37,502

'74

'75

1975: Units built—38,465

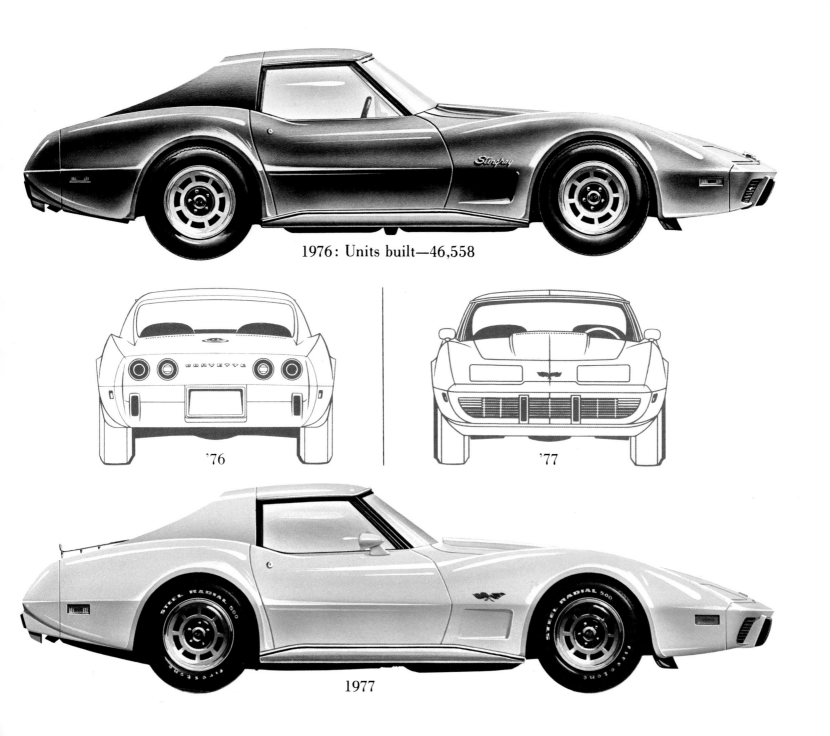

1976: Units built—46,558

'76

'77

1977

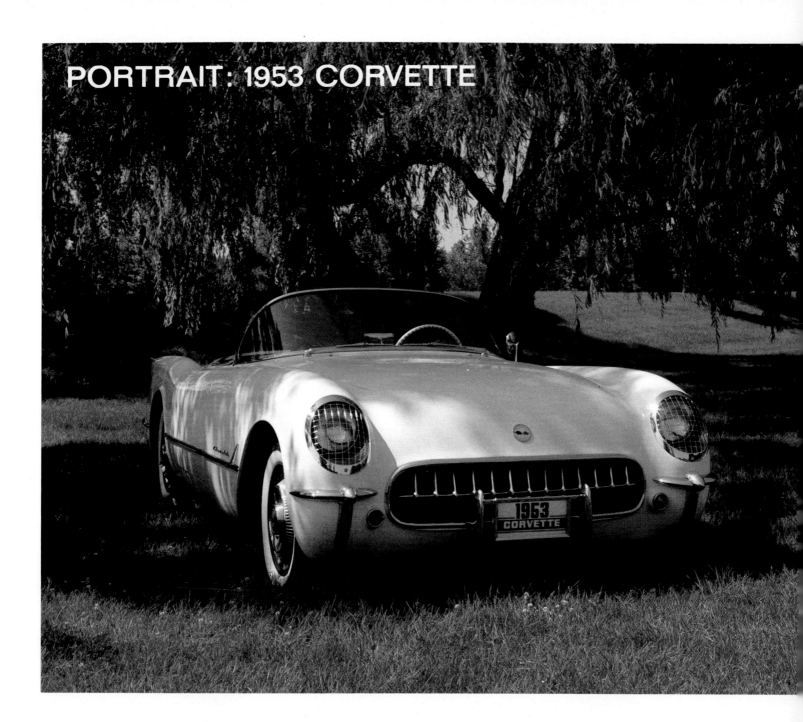

PORTRAIT: 1953 CORVETTE

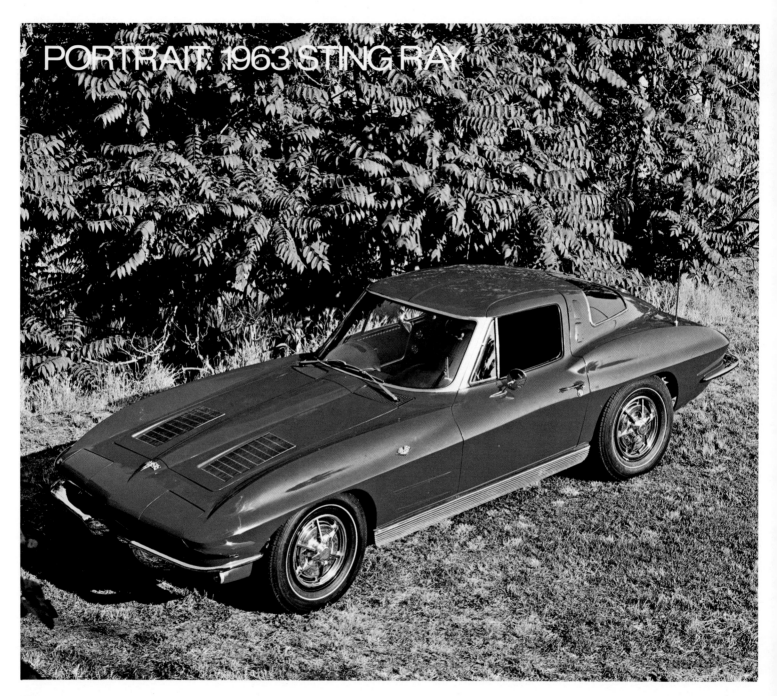

PORTRAIT: 1963 STING RAY

PORTRAIT: 25th ANNIVERSARY CORVETTE

Corvair fastback coupé (at left), Nomad station wagon and non-production detachable hardtop were 1954 Motorama stars. In 1956 (above) Harlow Curtice tries out the special car for Sweden's Prince Bertil, and crew gathers next to racing SR-2. GM stylists (opposite) show off their cars above special '56 car built for Curtice.

SR-2 of 1957 was painted like a racing plane for its February Daytona debut, driven there by Buck Baker. Trim was tamed in time for Sebring race, 195

Experimental "mule" version of 1957 Corvette SS was built secretly to test new chassis features, had carbureted engine and fiberglass body at first.

er-helmeted Piero Taruffi drove the white Corvette SS "mule" in practice at Sebring and piloted the magnesium-bodied SS in the race — for one lap.

Bill Mitchell's Stingray, the rebodied Corvette SS "mule," was driven by Dr. Richard Thompson to the SCCA's C Modified National Championship in 1960

After 1961 the Stingray became a show car, first in silver and then in its original red. It was fitted with Dunlop disc brakes and a big Mark IV engine.

As built in the summer of 1958: Bill Mitchell's XP-700.

Successor to the XP-700, the Shark was built in 1961 to foreshadow the '63 Sting Ray.

XP-700 reappeared in 1960 after extensive changes that included a longer tail, narrower bumper-grille, and double-bubble roof with a periscope.

The racing Sting Ray and XP-700 (foreground) helped inspire the design of the 1963 Corvette, seen (background) in its December, 1960 internal GM de

The late-1960 models of the '63-to-be had louvers, vents and fuel cap locations, as well as an opening rear deck, that were not cleared for production.

Four-wheel-drive CERV II (Duntov at wheel) racing prototype was built in 1964. Late in '65 the Mako Shark II appeared, shown here with the Mako Sh

Mako Shark II (Chapter 15) excited worldwide controversy with its bold combination of crisp basic forms with elaborate surface decoration and coloration.

After it had inspired the design of the 1968 Corvette, the Mako Shark II was restyled for the 1969 auto show season and newly christened the Manta R

The Manta Ray featured a deeper front spoiler, exposed exhaust pipes, and an elongated tail with pop-up lights for turn signals and braking warning.

In 1969 Styling Staff transformed a Corvette into the Aero Coupe show car with Chaparral-type wheels, a high windshield and a pop-up roof panel.

Styling details of the Aero Coupe (top) appeared on the '70 Corvette. Shown in 1968 was the blue mid-engined XP-880 Corvette, known as the Astro II.

Enigmatically named "Corvette prototype" for its April, 1970 debut in New York, the XP-882 was designed in 1968 and running in the spring of 1969.

Powered by a V-8 placed transversely between the rear wheels, the XP-882 has an unique drive train that would allow it to be four-wheel-driven.

A refined successor to the XP-882, the XP-895 mid-engined prototype was built with both aluminum (shown) and steel unit body/frames in 1972.

Conceived as a possible replacement for the Opel GT as well as the Corvette, the XP-987GT was dubbed the 2-Rotor after the design of its mid-placed Type RC2-266 GM Wankel engine.

The beautiful Corvette 4-Rotor was photographed in GM Design Staff's private viewing yard before being crated for air shipment to Paris Show.

PORTFOLIO OF CORVETTES IN COMPETITION

Seven Corvettes dominated the start of the Sebring 12-Hour Race in 1962. "Doc" Wyllie and Duncan Black finished highest in 18th place overall.

Gaston Andrey drives to 12th overall and a class first at Sebring, 1957.

1968 a D/Altered '57 model took to the drag strip at Englishtown, N. J.

Dancer, a '62 model, dances in 1968 NHRA Englishtown Springnationals.

A favorite Corvette playground is Wisconsin's Elkhart Lake: '58 June Sprints.

Late-fifties Corvettes raced nose to tail on real roads at Put-in-Bay, Ohio.

Corvettes of the same vintage race in 1962 at Virginia International Raceway.

305

Guldstrand/Thompson Grand Sport, Sebring, '66.

Johnson/Morgan Grand Sport at Sebring, '64.

Mecom-entered Grand Sports of Thompson and Hall lead at the start of the Nassau Tourist Trophy, 1963.

Jerry Thompson wins in 1968 in B Production.

A 1963 Corvette Sting Ray looms above a British Lola on one of the high banks at Florida's Daytona track.

...ly-powered: Corvette and Chaparral 2 at Bridgehampton, 1965.

...the NHRA Winternationals at Pomona, 1969: a 1965 coupé.

The Cornelius/Boo/Brown Corvette was 20th overall and 3rd in class at Daytona, 1966.

...ss B Production car brakes hard at Indianapolis Raceway in October, 1968.

Sometimes there are problems. A 1963 coupé pits at Bridgehampton.

Weaver/Thompson/DeLorenzo No. 11 Corvette, Daytona, '72.

At Le Mans, France, in 1971 the Corvette of Aubriet/Rouget/"Sylvain" retired after 15 hours

DeLorenzo/Lang: GT win and 10th overall at Sebring, '70.

Greenwood/Smothers: 1971 Sebring 1st G

French-entered Corvette in action at Belgium's Spa track.

Belgian entry in the Spa 1000-kilometer event.

Owens-Corning Corvette team in 1970.

Jerry Thompson placed 2nd and set fastest lap in '70 ARRC at Road Atlanta.

At Daytona in '70 the Greenwood/Barber/Lang trio was 10th overall, class 3rd.

After 50 laps of the 1971 Sebring 12-hour Barker/Harrington (50) retired.

DeLorenzo, Thompson won SCCA Divisional and National '69 Championships.

Dave Heinz and Bob Johnson drove No. 57 to GT victories plus 8th overall at Daytona and 4th overall, highest ever for a Corvette, at Sebring in 1972.

At Sebring in '72 the Kemp/Koveleski car later hit that sand bank.   GT winner and 6th overall at Daytona, '70.   GT winner and 6th overall at Sebring

DeLorenzo and Lang: GT winners and 7th overall at Watkins Glen in

Skat-Rinzler '72 Daytona entry for Kemp and Smith failed to finish the race.

John Greenwood/Tony Adamowicz were luckless during '72 Daytona 24-H

At Daytona in '71 DeLorenzo, Yenko and Mahler won class and placed fourth.   Jerry Thompson's '72 Daytona race ended with a blown tire after an ho

Corvettes were popular in 1974 Camel GT races, as here at Road Atlanta.

Frank Panzarella raced No. 55 Corvette at Lime Rock in April, 1975.

Alex Davidson in Daytona Camel GT race, 1973.

Ted Mathey, in '74 an SCCA Division champ.

Stingray leads Sting Ray at Road Atlanta in April, 1974.

Driving the Jim Robbins Corvette, J. Marshall Robbins (shown at Road Atlanta) ranked third behind two Porsches in the 1974 SCCA Trans-Am Championship.

DeLorenzo/Carter entry retired after 101 laps of Daytona 24-Hour, 1974.

Jim Moyer and Rick Ortman placed 17th in Mid-Ohio Camel GT, June, 1975.

In June, 1974 Don Yenko and Jerry Thompson competed in Mid-Ohio 6-Hour.

In April, 1974 Rich Hay/Bob Nagel were 21st in Road Atlanta GT race.

Camel GT contestant at Daytona, 1973 was Tony DeLorenzo.

First appearance of new-look John Greenwood racer was in Atlanta 6-Hour, April, 1974.

APPENDICES

Early in 1956 an Arlington, Virginia gentleman shopping for a station wagon happened to pass a dealer's showroom
wherein he glimpsed a spanking new Corvette. All thoughts of utilitarian transport
were quickly put behind him. He bought the Corvette, and the year following decided that fellowship
with like-minded enthusiasts might be a great deal of fun. Out of this idea and a
first meeting of but eight owners was born an organization soon to be known as the Corvette Club of America.
About the same time Chevrolet hastened to the fellowship idea as well, beginning publication in 1957
of *Corvette News*, a magazine made available without charge to owners of Chevrolet Corvettes which would serve as a
channel of communication among them, most especially those who, in ever increasing numbers, were anxious
to organize their enthusiasm into clubs. In 1958 *Corvette News* listed twenty-five such clubs in its directory;
today, nineteen years later, the number has swelled to over six hundred,
comprising a membership of more than 25,000 owners. These clubs are affiliated with either the National
Council of Corvette Clubs, Inc., whose origins date back to 1959; the Western States Corvette
Council, founded in 1966; or the more recent Canadian Council of Corvette Clubs,
founded in 1976. Moreover, Corvette enthusiasm shows no signs of waning with virtually each successive
issue of *Corvette News* welcoming yet further additions to club ranks from Kannaoplis, North Carolina,
to Traverse City, Michigan, to Vancouver, Washington. To keep on top of this perpetual flurry of activity is a
task of Joe Pike, since 1960 the indefatigable editor of *Corvette News*, under whose guidance
the magazine's circulation has grown to more than 225,000. He has made available for the asking a complete and
ever-updated directory of Corvette clubs. (Readers need only write Corvette News, 2-129 General Motors Building,
Detroit, Michigan 48202, for the latest edition.) For this service, and his
invaluable assistance in providing data for the appendices which follow, our appreciation is extended to Mr. Pike.
Owners of Corvettes from years 1953-1955 may be particularly interested in a special independent
organization: the Vintage Corvette Club of America, 2359 West Adams, Fresno, California 93706.

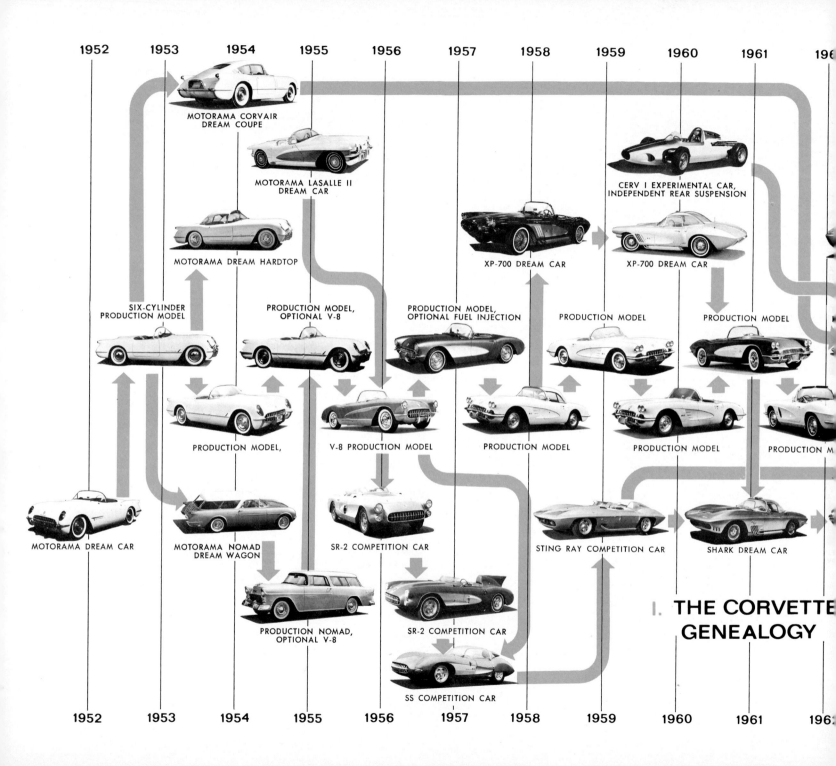

1952 1953 1954 1955 1956 1957 1958 1959 1960 1961 196

MOTORAMA CORVAIR
DREAM COUPE

MOTORAMA LASALLE II
DREAM CAR

CERV I EXPERIMENTAL CAR,
INDEPENDENT REAR SUSPENSION

MOTORAMA DREAM HARDTOP

XP-700 DREAM CAR

XP-700 DREAM CAR

SIX-CYLINDER
PRODUCTION MODEL

PRODUCTION MODEL,
OPTIONAL V-8

PRODUCTION MODEL,
OPTIONAL FUEL INJECTION

PRODUCTION MODEL

PRODUCTION MODEL

PRODUCTION MODEL,

V-8 PRODUCTION MODEL

PRODUCTION MODEL

PRODUCTION MODEL

PRODUCTION M

MOTORAMA DREAM CAR

MOTORAMA NOMAD
DREAM WAGON

SR-2 COMPETITION CAR

STING RAY COMPETITION CAR

SHARK DREAM CAR

I. THE CORVETTE
GENEALOGY

PRODUCTION NOMAD,
OPTIONAL V-8

SR-2 COMPETITION CAR

SS COMPETITION CAR

1952 1953 1954 1955 1956 1957 1958 1959 1960 1961 196

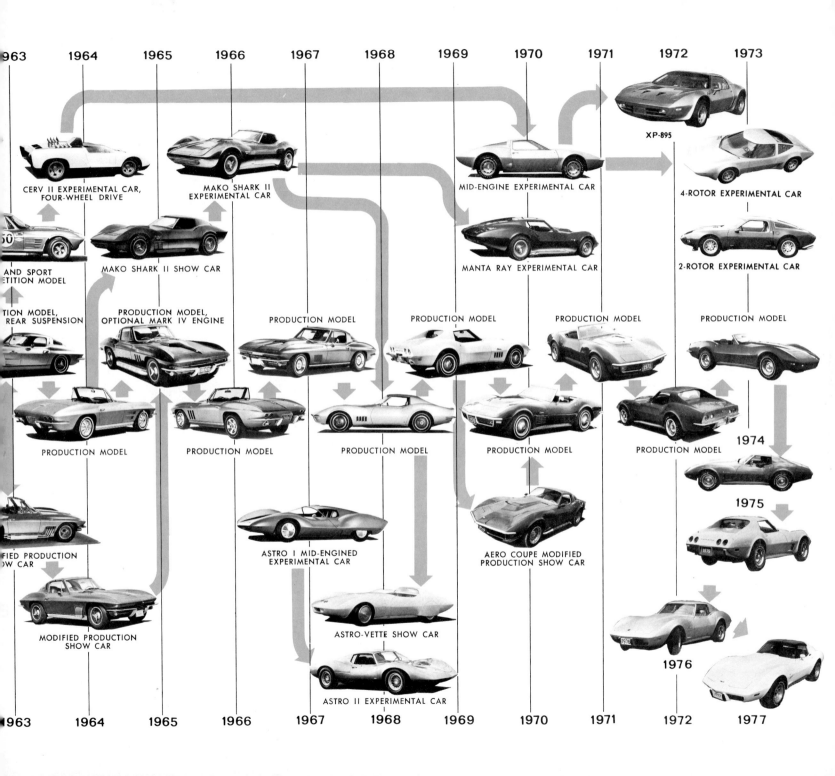

1963 1964 1965 1966 1967 1968 1969 1970 1971 1972 1973

CERV II EXPERIMENTAL CAR,
FOUR-WHEEL DRIVE

MAKO SHARK II
EXPERIMENTAL CAR

MID-ENGINE EXPERIMENTAL CAR

XP-895

4-ROTOR EXPERIMENTAL CAR

...AND SPORT
...ETITION MODEL

MAKO SHARK II SHOW CAR

MANTA RAY EXPERIMENTAL CAR

2-ROTOR EXPERIMENTAL CAR

...TION MODEL,
...REAR SUSPENSION

PRODUCTION MODEL,
OPTIONAL MARK IV ENGINE

PRODUCTION MODEL

PRODUCTION MODEL

PRODUCTION MODEL

PRODUCTION MODEL

PRODUCTION MODEL

PRODUCTION MODEL

PRODUCTION MODEL

PRODUCTION MODEL

PRODUCTION MODEL

PRODUCTION MODEL

1974

...FIED PRODUCTION
...OW CAR

ASTRO I MID-ENGINED
EXPERIMENTAL CAR

AERO COUPE MODIFIED
PRODUCTION SHOW CAR

1975

MODIFIED PRODUCTION
SHOW CAR

ASTRO-VETTE SHOW CAR

1976

ASTRO II EXPERIMENTAL CAR

1963 1964 1965 1966 1967 1968 1969 1970 1971 1972 1977

II. ENGINES

	Cubic Inches	Bore & Stroke	C.R.	Gross bhp @ rpm	Model Years Offered
SIXES	235	3⁹⁄₁₆″ X 3¹⁵⁄₁₆″	8.0	150 @ 4200	53 54
	235	3⁹⁄₁₆″ X 3¹⁵⁄₁₆″	8.0	155 @ 4200	55
SMALL BLOCK V-8'S	265	3¾″ X 3″	8.0	195 @ 5000	55
	265	3¾″ X 3″	9.25	210 @ 5200	56
	265	3¾″ X 3″	9.25	225 @ 5200	56
	283	3⅞″ X 3″	9.5	220 @ 4800	57
	283	3⅞″ X 3″	9.5	245 @ 5000	57 58 59 60 61
	283	3⅞″ X 3″	9.5†	250 @ 5000	57 58 59
	283	3⅞″ X 3″	9.5	270 @ 6000	57 58 59 60 61
	283	3⅞″ X 3″	10.5†	283 @ 6200	57
	283	3⅞″ X 3″	9.5	230 @ 4800	58 59 60 61
	283	3⅞″ X 3″	10.5†	290 @ 6200	58 59
	283	3⅞″ X 3″	11.0†	275 @ 5200	60 61
	283	3⅞″ X 3″	11.0†	315 @ 6200	60 61
	327	4″ X 3¼″	10.5	250 @ 4400	62 63 64 65
	327	4″ X 3¼″	10.5	300 @ 5000	62 63 64 65 66 67 68
	327	4″ X 3¼″	11.25	340 @ 6000	62 63
	327	4″ X 3¼″	11.25†	360 @ 6000	62 63
	327	4″ X 3¼″	11.25	365 @ 6200	64 65
	327	4″ X 3¼″	11.25†	375 @ 6200	64 65
	327	4″ X 3¼″	11.0	350 @ 5800	65 66 67 68
	350	4″ X 3¹⁵⁄₆₄″	10.25	300 @ 4800	69 70
	350	4″ X 3¹⁵⁄₆₄″	11.0	350 @ 5600	69 70
	350	4″ X 3¹⁵⁄₆₄″	11.0	370 @ 6000	70
	350	4″ X 3¹⁵⁄₆₄″	8.5	270 @ 4800	71 72
	350	4″ X 3¹⁵⁄₆₄″	9.0	330 @ 5600	71 72
	350	4″ X 3¹⁵⁄₆₄″	8.5	195 @ 4400‡	73 74
	350	4″ X 3¹⁵⁄₆₄″	9.0	250 @ 5200‡	73 74
	350	4″ X 3¹⁵⁄₆₄″	8.5	165 @ 3800 ‡	75 76 77
	350	4″ X 3¹⁵⁄₆₄″	9.0	205 @ 4800 ‡	75 76 77
MARK IV V-8'S	396	4³⁄₃₂″ X 3⁴⁹⁄₆₄″	11.0	425 @ 6400	65
	427	4¼″ X 3⁴⁹⁄₆₄″	10.25	390 @ 5400	66 67 68 69
	427	4¼″ X 3⁴⁹⁄₆₄″	11.0	425 @ 6400	66
	427	4¼″ X 3⁴⁹⁄₆₄″	10.25	400 @ 5400	67 68 69
	427	4¼″ X 3⁴⁹⁄₆₄″	11.0	435 @ 5800	67 68 69
	427	4¼″ X 3⁴⁹⁄₆₄″	12.5	430 @ 5200	69
	454	4¼″ X 4″	10.25	390 @ 4800	70
	454	4¼″ X 4″	12.25	465 @ 5200	70
	454	4¼″ X 4″	8.5	365 @ 4800	71 72
	454	4¼″ X 4″	9.0	425 @ 5600	71
	454	4¼″ X 4″	9.0	270 @ 4400‡	73 74

† fuel injected   ‡ net horsepower figure with emission controls

III. PRODUCTION AND SALES

	CALENDAR YEAR		MODEL YEAR PRODUCTION			Percent
	Sales	Production	Total	Convertible	Coupe	Coupes
1953	183	300	300	300		
1954	2,780	3,265	3,640	3,640		
1955	1,639	700	700	700		
1956	4,012	4,987	3,467	3,467		
1957	6,904	7,330	6,339	6,339		
1958	8,821	9,298	9,168	9,168		
1959	9,299	9,088	9,670	9,670		
1960	11,374	12,508	10,261	10,261		
1961	11,668	11,410	10,939	10,939		
1962	15,240	15,726	14,531	14,531		
1963	22,115	23,632	21,513	10,919	10,594	49.2
1964	19,908	19,892	22,229	13,925	8,304	37.3
1965	26,171	27,700	23,562	15,376	8,186	34.7
1966	24,754	24,939	27,720	17,762	9,958	35.9
1967	23,475	23,775	22,940	14,436	8,504	37.1
1968	29,874	32,473	28,566	18,630	9,936	34.8
1969	24,791	27,540	38,762	16,608	22,154	57.2
1970	22,776	22,586	17,316	6,648	10,668	61.6
1971	25,364	26,844	21,801	7,121	14,680	67.3
1972	26,652	27,004	27,004	6,508	20,496	75.5
1973	29,661	32,616	34,464	5,583	28,881	83.8
1974	29,750	33,869	37,502	4,629	32,873	87.6
1975			38,465		38,465	
1976			46,558		46,588	

IV. SERIAL NUMBERS

YEAR	DESIGNATION	BEGINNING	ENDING	NOTES
1953	E53F	-001001	-001300	
1954	E54S	-001001	-004640	In 1955 the V-8's
1955	E55S or VE55S	-001001	-001700	bore the VE55S
1956	E56S	-001001	-004467	designation.
1957	E57S	-100001	-106339	Beginning in 1963
1958	J58S	-100001	-109168	the digits "37"
1959	J59S	-100001	-109437	indicate the coupe,
1960	00867S	-100001	-110261	"67" the convertible,
1961	10867S	-100001	-110939	with the first
1962	20867S	-100001	-114531	entry each year
1963	30837S or 30867S	-100001	-121513	indicating the first
1964	40867S or 40837S	-100001	-122229	car off the line.
1965	194375S or 194675S	-100001	-123564	In 1972 the
1966	194676S or 194376S	-100001	-127720	designation was
1967	194677S or 194377S	-100001	-122940	revised as follows:
1968	194378S or 194678S	-400001	-428566	"1" for Chevrolet;
1969	194379S or 194679S	-700001	-738762	"Z" for Corvette;
1970	194370S or 194670S	-400001	-417316	"37" for body style;
1971	194371S or 194671S	-100001	-121801	"Y" for the 454
1972	1Z37Y2S	-400001	-427004	engine (the 350
1973	1Z37Y3S	-400001	-438464	carries the letter
1974	1Z37J4S	-400001	-437502	"J"); "2" for model
1975	1Z37J5S	-400001	-438465	year 1972; "S"
1976	1Z37L6S	-400001	-446558	for St. Louis
1977	1Z37L7S	-400001		factory manufacture.

V. COLORS BY MODEL YEAR

MODEL YEAR/COLOR	DUPONT	I/R-M*	DITZLER
1953			
Polo White	1783-H	54V91	8011
1954			
Polo White	1783-H	54V91	8011
Onyx Black	88-L	A-946	9000
Pennant Blue	1927	54V23	11238
1955			
Polo White	1783-H	54V91	8011
Onyx Black	88-L	A-946	9000
Harvest Gold	2004-H	55V71D	80739
Gypsy Red	1973-H	55V51R	70575
Aztec Copper	2414	56V84	21295
Cascade Green	2416	56V36	41973
Arctic Blue	2413	56V29	11537
Venetian Red	2415-H	56V52R	70694
Copper Met.	2187-H	55V84	50405
1956			
Polo White	1783-H	54V91	8011
Onyx Black	88-L	A-946	9000
Aztec Copper	2414	56V84	21295
Artic Blue	2413	56V29	11537
Venetian Blue	2415-H	56V52R	70694
Cascade Green	2416	56V36	41973
Shoreline Beige	1726	54V81	21054
Silver Met.	2080	56V14	31259
1957			
Polo White	1783-H	54V91	8011
Onyx Black	88-L	A-946	9000
Silver Met.	2080	56V14	31259
Venetian Red	2415-H	56V52R	70694
Aztec Copper	2414	56V84	21295
Cascade Green	2416	56V36	41973
1958			
Snowcrest White	2697-L	58V92	8160
Charcoal	2703-L	58V11	31742
Signet Red	2704-LH	58V52R	70869
Silver Blue	2696-L	58V25	11755
Regal Turquoise	2702-L	58V26	11836
Panama Yellow	2705-LH	58V74	80986
Inca Silver Met.	2436-L	56V13	31425
1959			
Snowcrest White	2697-L	58V92	8160
Tuxedo Black	88-L	A-946	9000
Crown Sapphire	2930-L	59C24	12001
Roman Red	2931-LH	59C51R	70961
Inca Silver	2436-L	56V13	31425
Classic Cream	2924-L	59V71	81092
Frost Blue	2925-L	59V21	12018
1960			
Tuxedo Black	88-L	A-946	9000
Ermine White	4024-L	A-1199	8259
Roman Red	2931-LH	A-1138R	70961
Sateen Silver	4023-L	A-1203	31928
Tasco Turquoise	4025-L	A-1211	12001
Horizon Blue	4030-L	A-1210	12018
Honduras Maroon	4034-LH	A-1221R	50568
Cascade Green	4029-L	A-1214	42693
1961			
Tuxedo Black	88-L	A-946	9000
Ermine White	4024-L	A-1199	8259
Roman Red	2931-LH	A-1138R	70961
Sateen Silver	4023-L	A-1203	31928
Honduras Maroon	4034-LH	A-1221R	50568
Jewel Blue	4143-L	A-1396	12398
Fawn Beige	4146-L	A-1397	22005
1962			
Tuxedo Black	88-L	A-946	9000
Ermine White	4024-L	A-1199	8259
Roman Red	2931-LH	A-1138R	70961
Sateen Silver	4023-L	A-1203	31928

MODEL YEAR/COLOR	DUPONT	I/R-M*	DITZLER
Honduras Maroon	4034-LH	A-1221R	50568
Fawn Beige	4146-L	A-1397	22005
Almond Beige	2964-L	A-1133	21733
1963			
Daytona Blue	4395-L	A-1539	DDL-12696
Riverside Red	2931-L	A-1138	DDL-70961
Sebring Silver	867-96417	- -	DDL-32312
1964			
Tuxedo Black	88-L	A-946	DDL-9300
Silver Blue	4250-L	A-1481	DDL-12546
Daytona Blue	4395-L	A-1539	DDL-12696
Riverside Red	2931-LH	A-1138R	DDL-70961
Saddle Tan	4392-L	A-1537	DDL-22269
Ermine White	4024-L	A-1199	DDL-8259
Satin Silver	4247-L	A-1477	DDL-32173
1965			
Tuxedo Black	88-L	A-946	DDL-9300
Ermine White	4024-L	A-1199	DDL-8259
Nassau Blue	4690-L	A-1747	DDL-3364
Glen Green	4691-L	A-1745	DDL-3366
Milano Maroon	4689-LM	A-1746M	DDL-3365
Silver Pearl	4621-L	A-1708	DDL-3314
Rally Red	4688-H	A-1744	DDL-3395
Goldwood Yellow	4530-LH	A-1612	DDL-3231
Crocus Yellow	4620-L	A-1715	DDL-3313
1966			
Tuxedo Black	88-L	A-946	DDL-9300
Ermine White	4024-L	A-1199	DDL-8259
Rally Red	4688-LH	A-1744R	DDL-7149
Nassau Blue	4690-L	A-1747	DDL-13057
Laguna Blue	4710-L	A-1826	DDL-13188
Trophy Blue	4712-L	A-1825	DDL-13199
Mosport Green	4713-L	A-1827	DDL-43535
Sunfire Yellow	4711-L	A-1828	DDL-81540
Silver Pearl	4621-L	A-1708	DDL-32449
Milano Maroon	4689-LM	A-1746M	DDL-50706
1967			
Tuxedo Black	88	A-946	9300
Ermine White	4024-L	A-1199	8259
Rally Red	4688-LH	A-1744R	71491
Marina Blue	4850-L	A-1920	13364
Lynndale Blue	4833-L	A-1912	13348
Elkhart Blue	4834-L	A-1911	13347
Goldwood Green	4835-L	A-1913	43652
Sunfire Yellow	4711-L	A-1828	81540
Silver Pearl	4621-L	A-1708	32449
Marlboro Maroon	4836-LM	A-1914F	71584
1968			
Tuxedo Black	88	A-946	9300
Polar White	4714-L	A-2005	8631
Rally Red	4688-LH	A-1744R	71491
LeMans Blue	4908-L	A-2007	13549
International Blue	4909-L	A-2008	13550
British Green	4949-L	A-2011	43795
Safari Yellow	4906-L	A-2009	81621
Silverstone Silver	4907-L	A-2000	8596
Cordovan Maroon	4915-LH	A-2006M	50775
Corvette Bronze	4910-L	A-2010	22969
1969			
Tuxedo Black	88-L	A-946	9300
Fathom Green	5013-L	A-2102	2079
Burgundy	5063-LH	A-2107M	50700
Cortez Silver	5032-L	A-2108	2059
LeMans Blue	5030-L	A-2083	2083
Hugger Orange	5021-LM	A-2111R	2084
Daytona Yellow	5026-LH	A-2119	2094
Can-Am White	5050-L	A-1802	8631
Monza Red	5027-LH	A-2120R	2089
Riverside Gold	5029-L	A-2122	2092

MODEL YEAR/COLOR	DUPONT	I/R-M*	DITZLER
1970			
Laguna Gray	5134-L	A-2258	2198
Bridgehampton Blue	5132-L	A-2263	2199
Donnybrook Green	5133-L	A-2267D	2200
Daytona Yellow	5026-LH	A-2119	2094
Ontario Orange	5128-LM	A-2274G	2182
Monza Red	5027-LH	A-2120R	2089
Marlboro Maroon	5131-LH	A-2280M	71584
1971			
Classic White	5040L	A-1802	8631
Nevada Silver	5276L	A-2438	2327
Mulsanne Blue	5327L	A-2262	2213
Bridgehampton Blue	5132L	A-2263	2199
Brands Hatch Green	5288L	A-2447	2336
Sunflower	5283L	A-2422	2338
Mille Miglia Red	5291LM	A-2460R	2349
War Bonnet Yellow	5292LM	A-2464LF	2351
Ontario Orange	5293LM	A-2469F	2357
Steel Cities Gray Firemist	5294L	A-2470D	2358
1972			
Classic White	5040L	A-1802	8631
Pewter Silver	5426L	A-2541	2629
Bryar Blue	5461L	A-2547	2434
Targa Blue	5460L	A-2544	2432
Elkhart Green	5462L	A-2551	2438
Sunflower	5283L	A-2422	2338
Mille Miglia Red	5291LM	A-2460R	2349
War Bonnet Yellow	5292L	A-2464F	2351
Ontario Orange	5293L	A-2469F	2357
Steel Cities Gray Firemist	5294L	A-2470D	2358
1973			
Classic White	5040L	A-1802	8631
Corvette Silver Met.	5563L	A-2619	2519
Corvette Med. Blue Met.	5564L	A-2621	2213
Corvette Dark Blue Met.	5565L	A-2544	2432
Corvette Blue-Green Met.	5288L	A-2447	2336
Elkhart Green	5462L	A-2551	2438
Corvette Yellow	5566L	A-2635G	2534
Corvette Yellow Met.	5567L	A-2636F	2535
Mille Miglia Red	5291LM	A-2460R	2349
Corvette Orange Met.	5568L	A-2652F	2548
1974			
Classic White	5040L	A-1802	8631
Corvette Silver Met.	5563L	A-2619	2519
Corvette Gray Aflair	42817LH	A-2698F	2630
Corvette Med. Blue Met.	5564L	A-2621	2213
Corvette Bright Yellow	5026-LH	A-2119	2094
Corvette Dk. Grn. Aflair	42816L	A-2706F	2644
Corvette Dk. Brown Met.	5483L	A-2647D	2543
Medium Red Met.	42810LM	A-2718F	2658
Mille Miglia Red	5291LM	A-2460R	2349
Corvette Orange Met.	5568LM	A-2652F	2548
1975			
White	**5040L**	A-1802	8631
Silver	**43537L**	A-2618	2518
Medium Blue	**43467L**	A-2797	2744
Dk. Steel Blue	**43466LH**	A-2800F	2747
Bright Green	**43465LH**	A-2830G	2749
Bright Yellow	**43464LH**	A-2809	2756
Med. Saddle	**43463L**	A-2815G	2762
Flame Red	**43462LM**	A-2817R	2764
Red Irid.	**42810LM**	A-2718F	2658
Red	**5291LM**	A-2460R	2349
1976			
White	5040L	A-1802	8631
Silver	43537L	A-2618	2518
Medium Blue	43467L	A-2797	2744
Bright Yellow	43464LH	A-2809	2756
Flame Red	43462LM	A-2817R	2764
Medium Red	5489LM	A-2648F	2544
Dk. Brown Met.	42804L	A-2716	2656
Mahogany Met.	44131LM	A-2931G	2864
Buckskin Met.	44180L	A-2938	2869
Dk. Green Met.	44171LH	A-2993	2877

*Inmont 1953-1962; Rinshed-Mason 1963-1975

1977: Black, Corvette Dark Blue, Corvette Light Blue Met., Corvette Orange, Corvette Dark Red, Medium Red, Silver, Corvette Tan, Classic White, Corvette Yellow

VI. BASE SPECIFICATIONS

MAJOR CORVETTE MODEL SERIES	1953 to 1955	1956 to 1957	1958 to 1962	1963 to 1967	1968 to 1973	1974 to 1977
Overall length, ins.	167.0	168.0	177.2	175.2	182.5	185.5
Overall width, ins.	72.2	70.5	72.8	69.2	69.0	69.0
Overall height, ins.	52.1	52.0	52.4	49.6	47.8	48.0
Wheelbase, ins.	102.0	102.0	102.0	98.0	98.0	98.0
Front track, ins.	57.0	57.0	57.0	56.8	58.7	58.7
Rear track, ins.	59.0	59.0	59.0	57.6	59.4	59.5
Curb weight, lbs.	2850	2880	3080	3130	3280	3530
Weight distribution, front/rear percentage	53/47	52/48	53/47	48/52	49/51	48/52

VII. EQUIPMENT BUYING TRENDS

PERCENTAGES OF CORVETTES EQUIPPED AT THE FACTORY WITH ITEMS INDICATED

Code	1961	1962	1963	1964	1965	1966	1967	1968	1969	1970	1971	1973	1974	1975	1976
I	22.6	11.6	4.3	3.2	1.7	2.0	1.9	1.1	0.6	NA	NA	NA	NA	NA	NA
II	64.1	77.9	83.5	85.7	89.7	89.3	88.0	81.2	78.4	70.5	53.9	41.2	32.9	27.1	21.4
III	13.1	10.5	12.2	11.1	8.6	8.7	10.1	17.7	21.0	29.5	46.1	58.8	67.1	26.1	21.4
IV	51.9	55.5	52.5	50.4	50.6	47.7	47.6	46.9	39.8	38.5	36.8	6.7	6.7	57.4	NA
V	NA	NA	1.3	8.9	10.3	12.7	16.5	19.8	30.6	38.5	52.7	70.8	78.4	82.8	87.6
VI	NA	NA	14.2	14.0	13.7	20.2	25.1	43.3	59.2	68.8	82.1	91.5	95.9	97.7	STD
VII	NA	NA	15.5	10.0	17.0	19.7	20.8	33.5	44.0	53.6	62.2	78.9	88.9	93.1	STD
VIII	6.4	6.8	17.4	16.6	16.2.	16.5	17.6	24.7	25.3	27.8	28.4	46.0	63.8	74.7	83.1

CODE: I = three-speed transmission; II = four-speed transmission; III = automatic transmission; IV = detachable hardtop for convertibles; V = air conditioning; VI = power steering; VII = power brakes; VIII = power windows. "NA" indicates that the equipment specified was not available from the factory.

VIII. CORVETTE RACING RECORD

SPORTS CAR CLUB OF AMERICA

National Championships

Class B Sports-Racing: J.E. Rose, 1957
Class C Sports-Racing: Richard Thompson, 1960
Class A Production: Richard Thompson, 1962; Gerald Thompson, 1969; John Greenwood, 1970, 1971; Jerry Hansen, 1972; J. Marshall Robbins, 1974; Frank Fahey, 1975; Gene Bothello, 1976
Class B Production: Richard Thompson, 1957; James Jeffords, 1958, 1959; Robert Johnson, 1960; Richard Thompson, 1961; Donald Yenko, 1962, 1963; Frank Dominianni, 1964; Allan Barker, 1969, 1970, 1971, 1972; Bill Jobe, 1973, 1974
Class C Production: Richard Thompson, 1956

SPORTS CAR CLUB OF AMERICA

Divisional Championships

Class A Production

1962: A. W. Joslin, Central; Ben Moore, Northeast; Joe Freitas, Pacific Coast; George Robertson, Southeast; Delmo Johnson, Southwest
1963: Ralph Salyer, Central; Mack Yates, Midwest; John Caley, Northeast; Bill Sherwood, Pacific Coast; George Robertson, Southeast; Jerome Moore, Southwest
1965: John Martin, Midwest
1966: Herb Caplan, Northern Pacific; Jim Hall, Southwest
1967: David Morgan, Midwest; Robert Frayar, Northeast; Rex Ramsey, Southern Pacific
1968: Tony DeLorenzo, Central; Donald Yenko, Midwest
1969: Tony DeLorenzo, Central; Donald Yenko, Midwest; Herb Caplan, Northern Pacific; H. C. Whims, Southeast; Garry Gregory, Southern Pacific
1970: John Greenwood, Central; Cliff Gottlob, Midwest; John Paul, Northeast; Herb Caplan, Northern Pacific
1971: James Greendyke, Central; Ronald Weaver, Midwest; Fred Kepler, Northeast; Herb Caplan, Northern Pacific; Bill Matzen, Southeast
1972: Peter Ritos, Central; Michael Oleyar, Northeast; Ted Mathey, Northern Pacific; Charles Kemp, Southeast; Lynn Butler, Southern Pacific
1973: Paul Jones, Central; Gary Sullivan, Midwest; Ted Mathey, Northern Pacific; Bill Matzen, Southeast

1974: Richard Thompkins, Southeast; Tim Startup, Central; Gary Sullivan, Midwest; Ted Mathey, Northern Pacific; Frank Fahey, Southern Pacific
1975: Frank Fahey, Southern Pacific; Dick Vreeland, Southeast; Tim Startup, Central
1976: Ron Weaver, Central; Frank Panzarella, Northeast; Robert Baechle, Southeast; Gene Bothello, Northern Pacific

Class B Production

1962: Ralph Salyer, Central; Paul Reinhart, Pacific Coast
1963: Brad Brooker, Midwest; Don Meline, Pacific Coast
1964: Donald Yenko, Northeast
1965: Brad Brooker, Midwest; Zoltan Petrany, Southwest
1966: Allan Barker, Central; Donald Yenko, Northeast; Frank Search, Northern Pacific
1967: Bill Petree, Central; Brad Brooker, Midwest; Robert Frayar, Northeast; Frank Search, Northern Pacific; Phil Weider, Southern Pacific
1968: Allan Barker, Central; Dick Durant, Midwest; Rick Stark, Northern Pacific
1969: Dick Durant, Midwest; Rich Sloma, Northern Pacific; Neben Evol, Southern Pacific
1970: Allan Barker, Central; W. Marvin Shoenfeld, Midwest; Tom Rizzo, Northeast; Rich Sloma, Northern Pacific
1971: Allan Barker, Central; John Orr, Northeast; Rich Sloma, Northern Pacific; Bill Jobe, Southwest
1972: Bob Johnson, Central; Allan Anderson, Northeast; Rich Sloma, Northern Pacific; Bill Jobe, Southwest
1973: Michael Manner, Central; John Orr, Northeast; Rich Sloma, Northern Pacific; Bill Jobe, Southwest
1974: Jim Sherman, Central; Andy Porterfield, Southern Pacific
1975: Gary Carlen, Northern Pacific; Howard Park, Central; Jim Barnett, Southwest; Allan Anderson, Northeast; Randy Stafford, Midwest
1976: Gary Carlen, Northern Pacific; Sylvan Cornblatt, Northeast; John Carosso, Southwest; David Preston, Midwest

BEST-PLACED PRODUCTION CORVETTE

Year/Drivers	Overall	GT	Class/Cat.
SEBRING 12 HOURS OF ENDURANCE			
1956 Crawford/Goldman	15th	1st	3500+ cc
1957 Thompson/Andrey	12th	1st	3500+ cc
1958 Doane/Rathmann	12th	1st	3500+ cc
1960 Hall/Fritts	16th	1st	3000+ cc
1961 Johnson/Morgan	11th	1st	4000+ cc
1962 Wyllie/Black	18th	5th	Class III
1963 Johnson/Morgan	16th	2nd	4000+ cc
1964 Hudson/Grant	16th	1st	5000+ cc
1965 Boo/Robertson	33rd	1st	5000+ cc
1966 Moore/Wintersteen	9th	1st	GT
1967 Yenko/Morgan	10th	1st	5000+ cc
1968 Morgan/Sharp	6th	1st	GT
1969 Lang/Hufstader	14th	4th	GT
1970 DeLorenzo/Lang	10th	1st	GT
1971 Greenwood/Smothers	7th	1st	GT
1972 Heinz/Johnson	4th	1st	GT
1973 Grable/Greenwood/ Brockman	3rd	3rd	GT
1975 Arnold/Doran	20th	14th	2000+cc
1976 Keller/Gray	18th	2nd	GT
DAYTONA CONTINENTAL			
1966 Guldstrand/Moore/ Wintersteen	12th	1st	GT
1968 Grant/Morgan	10th	1st	GT
1969 Gimondo/Trembley/ Drolet/Belperch	16th	1st	5000+ cc
1970 Thompson/Mahler	6th	1st	GT
1971 DeLorenzo/Yenko/ Mahler	4th	1st	GT
1972 Heinz/Johnson	8th	1st	GT
1973 Heinz/McClure	3rd	2nd	GT
1975 Thompson/Bach/ Yenko	19th	14th	200+cc
1976 Currin/Gottlob/ Knab	9th	1st	GT
WATKINS GLEN 6 HOURS OF ENDURANCE			
1968 Johnson/Johnson	11th	2nd	GT
1969 DeLorenzo/Lang	7th	1st	GT
1971 Greenwood/Johnson	5th	1st	GT
1972 Kepler/Orr	10th	2nd	GT
1973 Greenwood/Rutherford	9th	2nd	GT
1974 Pierce/Mills	11th	9th	TA
1975 Headley/Misuriello	9th	1st	TA
1976 Headley/Feinstein	12th	2nd	TA

OTHER NOTEWORTHY PERFORMANCES. Daytona Flying Mile Speed Trials: 1955, Zora Arkus-Duntov, 150.583 mph
24 Hours of Le Mans: 1960, Fitch/Grossman, 8th overall, 5th GT class ● 3 Hours of Riverside: 1962, Doug Hooper, 1st overall
Bonneville National Speed Trials: 1967, Bob Hirsch, 192.879 mph ● 1000 Kilometers of Spa-Francorchamps: 1969, Tuerlinckx/Stalpaert, 23rd overall, 4th GT class

BIBLIOGRAPHY

Arkus-Duntov, Zora; Brown, Arnold R.; and Shaw, Arthur R.; *High Caliper Braking*. SAE Paper, Detroit, Michigan, January 11-15, 1965.
Full details on design and development of four-wheel disc brakes for the Corvette.

Arkus-Duntov, Zora, *Sports Car Development*. SAE Mid-Michigan Section Meeting, Lansing, Michigan, September 28, 1953.
General views of the author on the history and purpose of the sports car.

Arkus-Duntov, Zora; Hansen, Kai H.; and Jakust, Carl C., *The 1963 Corvette*. SAE Paper 611B, Detroit, Michigan, January 14-18, 1963.
General concept and detail engineering of the extensively changed Corvette of 1963.

Bowler, Michael,"Corvette—15 Years Later." *Motor*, July 22,1967, pp. 13-16.
General history of the Corvette.

Cumberford, Bob, "The $1.5 Million Sportscar." *Sportscar Quarterly*, Petersen Publishing Co., Fall, 1958, pp. 6-13.
Detailed and informed behind-the-scenes story of the creation of the 1957 Corvette SS.

Dolza, John; Kehoe, E. A.; Stoltman, Donald; and Arkus-Duntov, Zora, *The General Motors Fuel Injection System*. SAE Paper 16, Detroit, Michigan, January 14-18, 1957.
Evolution and application of Rochester injection introduced on the Corvette.

Fitch, John, with Nolan, William F.; *Adventure on Wheels*. New York, G. P. Putnam's Sons, 1959.
Uniquely close and informed observations on Corvette entries at Sebring in 1956 and 1957.

Girdler, Allan, "Wildest Corvette Test Yet." *Car Life*, July, 1969, pp. 45-60.
Most complete road test ever conducted on virtually all models and drive trains of one Corvette model year.

Ludvigsen, Karl, *Corvette News 15th Anniversary Issue*. Chevrolet Motor Division, Detroit, Michigan, April-May, 1972.
Issue entirely devoted to Corvette history, including press comments and customized cars.

Ludvigsen, Karl E., *Guide to Corvette Speed*. New York, Sports Car Press, 1969.
Chiefly stresses general Corvette maintenance and chassis preparation for racing of both early and late models.

McKibben, Jon, "Corvette Chronology." *Car Life*, November, 1967, pp. 27-31.
General history of the Corvette.

O'Brien, Robert, "The American Sports Car Comes of Age." *Esquire*, November, 1961, p. 140.
Very good background on origin and philosophy of the Corvette.

Olley, Maurice, *The Evolution of a Sports Car . . . The Chevrolet Corvette*. SAE Detroit Section Meeting, Detroit, Michigan, October 5, 1953.
Description by the designer of the way the original Corvette chassis was created.

Passon, P. J., *The Corvette Story*. SAE Paper 377A, 1961 SAE Summer Meeting.
Special coverage of body manufacture and assembly of the Corvette.

Premo, E. J., *The Corvette Plastic Body*, SAE Paper 212, Detroit, Michigan, January 11-15, 1954.
Body design of first Corvette and review of research and development leading to the decision to produce it in GRP.

Ritch, OCee, *Chevrolet Performance Handbook*. Los Angeles, Petersen Publishing Co., 1963.
Well-informed chapter on Corvette preparation for racing.

Road & Track, Corvette road tests. June, 1954; July, 1955; July, 1956; August, 1957; January, 1959; January, 1961; October, 1962; March, 1964; December, 1964; August, 1965; February, 1967; January, 1968; March, 1969; June, 1969; September, 1970.
Reprints of road test reports as originally appeared in issues cited.

Schofield, Miles, and others, *The Complete Chevrolet Book*. Los Angeles, Petersen Publishing Co., 1970.
Includes chapter on the history of the Corvette.

Shattuck, Dennis, *Corvette*. Long Beach, California, Parkhurst Publishing Co., 1968.
Very informative paperback devoted to the Corvette, including illuminating interviews by Gene Booth with designers.

Taruffi, Piero, *Works Driver*. London, Temple Press Books, 1964.
Offers Taruffi's view of Corvette SS racing at Sebring in 1957.

Thompson, Dick, and Tanner, Hans, *New Corvette Guide*. New York, Sports Car Press, 1958, revised 1965.
Particularly valuable for its account of early racing development by driver-author Dick Thompson.

Tuthill, William R., *Speed on Sand*. Daytona Beach, The Museum of Speed, 1969.
Records speed records set by Corvettes at Daytona Beach.

Van Valkenburgh, Paul, *Chevrolet = Racing . . . ?* Newfoundland, New Jersey, Walter R. Haessner and Associates, 1972.
Illuminates behind-the-scenes role of Chevrolet in racing, including the relationship with Chaparral.

INDEX

INDEX OF ILLUSTRATIONS

NOTE: Numbers in boldface refer to color illustrations

PHOTO CREDITS

Corvette advertisements interspersed throughout the text reprinted courtesy of Campbell-Ewald Company • 11 above; 12; 14 right; 15; 41 above; 49; 64 left; 66 right; 79 right; 82 above; 93 below; 97; 119 above right; 183; 211 above; 216; 217 left; 220 left; 225 above left, center, below left and right; 232 below left; 250; 251; 257-63; 290 above left; 300, 301, 307 center left; 310 above right and center right (Car No. 14): Karl Ludvigsen • 11 below left: Courtesy of the Long Island Automotive Museum • 14 left: Courtesy of Richard M. Langworth • 35 right; 67; 99 above right; 192; 238: George Barris • 46; 47 below; 82 below: Ernest Weil • 69 below: Courtesy of Ed Wayne • 100-01; 234 right; 235 left; 309 above right: Jesse L. Alexander • 103 below right: Pierre Perrin • 103 above; 104-07: Courtesy of William Mitchell • 127: Gordon Chittenden • 159: Courtesy of Carrozzeria Pininfarina • 174: Courtesy of Zora Arkus-Duntov • 177; 178 above and center; 179; 180 below left; 181 below left: Bernard Cahier • 230; 231: Photos Conrath • 276-77: Warren Fitzgerald • 278-79: 1963 Stingray owned by Paul Webb, photographed by Rick Lenz • 280-81: Courtesy of Rick Lenz • 305 center left and right, below left; 306 above and center left, below right; 307 above left and right, below right: Stan Rosenthall/Mobility Systems • 308 above and center left; 309 above left and below; 310 above left and center, center left, below left and right: Barry M. Tenin • 308 below left and center; 309 above right: J.J. Mollitt • 308 center right; 309 center left: Pete Biro • 308 below right; 309 center right: William E. Hazard, Jr. • 310 center right (Car No. 48); 311 above left and right (Car Nos. 71 and 55), center left (Car No. 20) and middle, and below; 312, all photographs on the page: Bill Oursler • 311 center right: Bob Bodnar